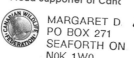
SCOTTISH CUSTOMS

SCOTTISH CUSTOMS

FROM THE CRADLE
TO THE GRAVE

MARGARET BENNETT

Birlinn

This new edition published in 2004 by
Birlinn Limited
West Newington House
10 Newington Road
Edinburgh EH9 1QS

www.birlinn.co.uk

Reprinted 2007, 2009

First published in 1992 by Polygon, Edinburgh

Copyright © Margaret Bennett 1992, 2004

ISBN 978 1 84158 293 1

British Library Cataloguing-in-Publication Data
A catalogue record for this book is available from the British Library

Typeset by Textype, Cambridge
Printed and bound by CPI Antony Rowe, Chippenham

In memory of H.H. and H.H.

Dedicated with appreciation, esteem and affection

Contents

Preface to the Second Edition
and Acknowledgements

Change is an inevitable fact of life, difficult or impossible to predict, yet, with
hindsight, often becoming the focus of attention and discussion. Changes and
trends may be food and drink to the statistician; they are grist to the mill to the
folklorist listening to the constant turning of the wheels of tradition. In 1992, as
I reflected upon the mass of material from which I made the selection for the
first edition of *Scottish Customs*, I suggested that, 'Despite the fact that custom
is rapidly becoming etiquette in today's terms, Scotland still has an enormous
range of traditional customs.' In the twenty-first century many of these very
customs are rapidly being reinvented and marketed as big business.

Within the past decade, arguably the greatest change to have taken place
in Scotland is the advent of the Scottish Parliament. In preparing this
second edition I have been conscious of the fact that the earliest excerpts
quoted in the first edition were from a time when Scotland still had its own
parliament. A substantial amount of the material for the new edition is from
the era of the new parliament. Whether this fact has much effect on changes
in Scottish customs that have taken place in the meantime is a matter for
debate. What is certain, however, is that customs can be greatly affected by
new legislation. For example, the Marriage (Scotland) Act 2002 allows civil
marriages to take place outside the registry office, which, in the past, had
been the only place where they could legally be held. As a result, the choice
seems limitless – weddings have been held in castles, supermarkets, football
grounds, underwater in 'Deep Sea World' and in other previously off-limit
settings. 'Approved venues' are ones which have obtained a general licence
to hold wedding ceremonies; in Edinburgh alone they include the Zoological
Gardens, the Royal College of Physicians, the Royal Botanic Garden, the
Usher Hall and the Edinburgh Business School. We might wonder if, in this
modern world where the British working week is significantly longer than in
most other countries, the new Marriage (Scotland) Act offers a convenient
way of fitting in life's social activities.

Ever aware of the changing nature of tradition, folklorists are fond of
discussing the influences that bring about changes. Some, which have

existed over countless centuries, suddenly disappear; others seem to come back in a new guise; and most have variants all over the world among peoples of differing races and religions. While amassing his remarkable nineteenth-century Gaelic collection, *Carmina Gadelica*, Alexander Carmichael found that some of the reciters insisted on telling him how or why particular traditions were fading. In 1870, for example, while he was visiting the Isle of Barra, Catherine MacNeill told him:

> Is iomadh dòigh neònach a bha measg nan seann daoine; ach thòisich coigrich air tighinn a steach dhan dùthaich, agus thòisich iad air magadh air luchd na dùthcha, agus mar sin leigeadh cleachdannan ceanalta na dùthcha uidh air n-uidh air chùl, agus cuid air chall. Cha mhòr feadhainn a sheasaidh ri magadh feadhainn is fear ionnsachadh na iad fhèin. Cha mhòr idir.

Translation

> There were many curious customs among the old people; but strangers began to come into the country, and they began to mock the people of the country, and the beautiful customs of the country were allowed bit by bit to drop, and some of them to be lost. There are not many people who would stand to be made fun of by people of more learning than themselves – not many at all.[1]

Nevertheless, only a few generations later, Gaels themselves were opting to speak English in the home, thus denying their own children a linguistic birthright.[2] Since language is the vehicle that carries tradition from one generation to the next, when Scots or Gaelic become replaced by Britain's universal language, changes are to be expected.

Regardless of how subtle such changes may be, there are usually significant reasons for why they take place. In this anthology I have generally refrained from interweaving speculative explanations for customs described by individual tradition-bearers or writers. Some have given their own ideas on why they do this or that – even if the reason is simply 'We've always done it this way,' or 'My mother always did it this way.' Meanwhile, I have enjoyed many discussions that have arisen from the first edition, not only among readers who have written or e-mailed, but also among audiences who have invited me to speak about the subject. (I have included a selection of contributions from those who have generously sent them.)

---

[1] A. Carmichael, *Carmina Gadelica*, vol III, p. 8–9. See also Part I, Baptism, where Catherine MacNeill gives an example of these traditions.
[2] The situation among Gaels in the New World echoes the old. To cite one of many examples, a man whose Lewis-born family refused to speak Gaelic to their children said: 'Well, that was a mistake; a bad one too. . .' M. Bennett, *Oatmeal and the Catechism: Scottish Gaelic Settlers in Quebec*, p. 284.

I continue to invite comments, corrections, contradictions, variations, new information, as there has invariably been a marvellous response. Several items added to this edition have been chosen, or sought out, in response to inquiries I have received, or indications of omissions. Some simply aroused my curiosity, such as marriage lintels, silent witnesses to an ancient custom. And, since I have encountered nobody (so far) who could tell me more than any passer-by can read, I have simply included photographs, which speak for themselves. Past experience has shown, however, that certain old customs have been given a new lease of life by readers who 'just liked the idea'. Perhaps that in itself is a testimony to the basic human need to be rooted in tradition, and to retain customs that light up our lives. I will keep my eyes peeled for the first sighting of a lintel carved with two sets of initials in the year 20♥04.

From time to time I try to encourage students of folklore to examine their own customs, record their families and communities, discuss the significance of their traditions and ultimately try to make sense of them in our modern world. In this context, my occasional university, college and summer-school classes have regularly wrestled with an observation from the American folklorist Alan Dundes: 'Folklore as a mirror of culture provides unique raw material for those eager to gain a better understanding of themselves and others.' (*Interpreting Folklore*, p. viii, 1980). Were I to include my own ideas, therefore, I might risk depriving readers, young and old, of the pleasure of enjoying their own opinions and answering questions that arise.

Nearly thirty years ago, as a postgraduate student in the Folklore Department at Memorial University of Newfoundland, I shared with my peers the pleasure of trawling library shelves to find a few gems from the past that might serve to add sparkle to our fledgling ideas. 'Why do customs change?' was the question asked. 'The shriek of the engine has sounded the death-note of many once popular festivals,' proposed one student, eliciting a restrained smile from the professor. 'Ditchfield,' he interjected, adding the title, date and place of publication. Nobody dared ask, 'Page number?' though we suspected he probably knew that too. In this new century we might suggest that the click of a mouse has done infinitely more to alter traditional customs than any single influence in the past; the old tutor would probably nod agreement.

Herbert Halpert (1915–2000), still widely regarded as the world's foremost bibliophile of British folklore, was that class professor. For many of us who became folklorists, he became our friend, continuing to inspire and teach long after we had left the classroom. As years went by, his wisdom somehow took on even more significance than when we first listened to him, and his 'Why don't your record that?' became imprinted in our minds.

In one of many invited lectures, Halpert explained to the general public:

> The study of folklore is a serious attempt to record fully and carefully all
> aspects of a people's culture: to describe accurately what is said and done.
> What is equally important but more difficult, the folklorist attempts to learn
> why. What is its meaning to the people who do and say these things?
>
> . . . The folklorist is interested in people's beliefs and practices, and in their
> expressive culture: the imaginative richness of language and its various uses in
> sayings and proverbs, riddles, rhymes, song texts, folk plays, and the
> multifarious varieties of folk narrative . . .
>
> I should stress to you, however, that folklorists are quite aware that a culture
> is never static but always changing. But for the folklorist to study changes in
> culture, he needs to have a full knowledge of the past to serve as a base-line
> against which to monitor such changes.

One of my aims has been to make available Scotland's rich store of
traditional customs, to keep that 'base-line' strong, while aspiring to observe
and record changes. In so doing, it is hoped that anyone interested in
culture and tradition may draw from this ever-deepening well.

On receiving his copy of the first edition in 1992, Professor Halpert
enthusiastically wrote to me, delighted, he said, that some of his students
actually listened to him. Attached to the letter, however, was a list of
corrections to the bibliography – dates of reprints, second editions, along with a
few rare specimens I had missed. (To the best of my ability, they have all been
updated in this edition.) And finally, a request for his own library – perhaps I
could track down some books that had hitherto escaped his attention.

As fieldwork has been an on-going activity, I have also been more than
fortunate to share discussions with Scotland's foremost twentieth-century
folklorist, Hamish Henderson (1919–2002). Internationally recognised as a
poet, song-maker, soldier, scholar and political activist, he was at the heart
of collecting and preserving folklore throughout Scotland. He was also my
colleague, friend, neighbour and kindred spirit for many years. It may be
more than some twist of fate to find that Henderson and Halpert, two 'old
soldiers' who recorded wartime traditions in the midst of conflict, also
enjoyed fifty years of friendship and fellowship. I owe an enormous debt of
gratitude to both of them for sharing their profound knowledge and
understanding of traditional culture. Rather than lament their passing, I
would like to celebrate their lives by dedicating this edition to two inspiring
leaders in the field of folklore scholarship. Finally, to their wives, who
enriched my experience, Letty and Kätzel, I accord my love and
appreciation for warm-hearted friendships I continue to enjoy.

Acknowledgements

In preparing a collection such as this I have incurred a huge debt of gratitude to many individuals, families and groups who have so willingly contributed both information and assistance in gathering the material. First and foremost, my sincere thanks goes to all those who permitted me to record their treasury of memories and to everyone who gave permission to print transcripts and/or photographs. Thanks also go to those who wrote to me after reading the first edition – some of their remarks appear in this edition. While all the names are listed in the Table of Contents and within the text, I would like accord my personal and warmest appreciation to each and every one of them. It would no exaggeration to say that warm friendships have grown out of the many visits I have had the pleasure of making while on the quest for information.

I am also grateful to all who lent or gave photos, especially my father, George Bennett, and Ian MacKenzie, photographer and at the School of Scottish Studies, who assisted with archive photos. Thanks also to Chris Higham for permission to choose material from his transcription of the remarkable recordings he made with my friend and former colleague, the late Dr Alan Bruford. Finally, to Marie Salton, whose late husband Bill helped considerably with my original tape transcriptions, my heartfelt thanks. Not only did she patiently proofread various stages of manuscript but she also encouraged me, often with notes in her inimitably witty style. I value her friendship beyond words.

Margaret Bennett, Edinburgh, 2004

Introduction

Folklore-customs and beliefs were no idle play, but
earnest attempts to safeguard vital human interests.*

At every stage of life from birth until death there are innumerable customs
which have been handed down from generation to generation. We take most
of them for granted, and very often it is not until there is a sudden or
dramatic breach of established custom that we actually recognise their
importance. If, for example, a bride and her bridesmaids all appeared
dressed in black at a wedding in any Scottish village or town, there would be
more than a few raised eyebrows. Such a wedding party might, however, 'get
away with it' in one of our cities at the marriage of two members of the
modern 'Gothic cult', for it would be in keeping with that particular group's
accepted style.

Nowadays, established 'businesses' take over many of the responsibilities
and decisions that are concerned with life and death. To cite three basic
examples: the highly trained staff at maternity hospitals deliver most babies,
and the 'Hurry-hurry! Boil-the-water' routine is mainly a feature of old
movies; wedding preparations and ceremonies are usually performed as
prescribed by an elaborate range of 'brides' magazines', which not only
inform the participants about general etiquette but also threaten to
standardise the whole procedure from John o' Groats (or indeed Baltasound
in Unst) to Land's End; and top-hatted undertakers not only remove the
body of the newly-deceased from a house but also relieve the bereaved of all
duties attached to the disposal of it.

Despite the fact that custom is rapidly becoming etiquette in today's
terms, Scotland still has an enormous range of traditional customs which
have survived for countless generations and are still flourishing. Certain
customs appear to have been adapted over the years; others seem to have
disappeared, then at a later date resurfaced stronger than ever; while others

---

* Reidar Th. Christiansen, 'The Dead and the Living', *Studio Norvegica*, No. 2,
1946, p. 4.

may bear only faint resemblance to their colourful past. Nevertheless, in this fast-changing world it is still possible to examine our nation's customs, to consider the direction in which we are going and to reflect on where we have been. I hope this book will make a start on all three.

We are fortunate that many writers from the past have recorded for us, often in meticulous detail, the way of life as they observed and experienced it. Several centuries of travellers, clergymen, dominies, soldiers and 'ordinary folk' have spontaneously contributed to this rich heritage, leaving us descriptions of an extensive range of Scottish traditions. One of the more notable Scottish collectors of the nineteenth century was the Revd Walter Gregor, who carefully preserved in print the many facets of customs he observed in the North-east. Two of his books, long considered 'old friends' by local people, have also come to be regarded by folklorists all over the world as the major, reliable and standard reference works on the folklore of that area: *An Echo of the Olden Time*, published in 1874 (reprinted 1973), and *Notes on the Folk-Lore of the North-East*, which covers much of the same material (often word for word) but with a considerable number of additional chapters, published in London for the Folk-Lore Society in 1881. To date, however, the latter is long since out of print.

The Revd James Napier was another minister who made an admirable contribution to the study and documentation of customs and beliefs from his local parish in the Glasgow area. His book *Folk Lore: or, Superstitious Beliefs in the West of Scotland, within this Century,* published by Alex Gardner of Paisley in 1879 (reprinted by E.P. Publishing in 1973), combines his own theories on various aspects of life with descriptions of customs and beliefs he actually observed. From his writing it is clear that he sometimes struggled to reconcile opposing aspects of tradition, such as when he confidently explained away belief in death-warnings as 'superstitious nonsense', then immediately gave his own testimony of warnings which were actually *known* to precede death. Even so, the reader can easily separate Napier's ministerial moralising from his invaluable observations of the customs of his locality.

Many nineteenth-century writers were encouraged and inspired by the work of the Folk-Lore Society (founded in 1879) to preserve a record of traditions extant in their own localities. From this era, Scotland can boast of a fine treasury of writings on a very wide range of subjects. The reader will encounter several of these writers in this book, as some of those that deal with the cycle of life are quoted in the text, referred to in the notes, and a wide selection is included in the bibliography at the end.

Considering the fact that the nineteenth-century writers did such a fine job, why then, in the closing decade of the twentieth century, write yet another book on the very same subject? My initial motivation stemmed from the growing popularity of the study of Custom and Belief at the University of Edinburgh, and the resulting problem of large numbers of students having to share single copies of rare books. After only one year's use, the two copies of Gregor and Napier needed to be rebound, thus the old proverb, 'necessity is the mother of invention', suggested a practical solution. I began, then, to put together this anthology of writings in order to make the older material more readily accessible, and at the same time took the opportunity to follow the subject through the twentieth century – a pursuit that often took me out of the library and into other people's kitchens. Spoiled for choice on both counts, the contents of this book attempt to offer a balance between older texts and previously unpublished transcriptions from up-to-date recordings on the same range of subjects.

For reasons already mentioned, the core of the anthology is based on selected readings from Gregor and Napier. I make no apology for relying on these two stalwarts; instead, I give them full credit. Although one of my original aims was to give samples from 'a the airts and pairts' (for Scotland is an intricate mosaic of cultural variations) I regret that it has proved impossible to do justice to this at present. While I have extended the regional spread far outside the neighbourhoods of these two ministers, there are areas of Scotland which are less well represented than I would like. This is partly due to copyright rules which prohibit the reprinting of some of the more recent writings, partly because I did most of my fieldwork recording during weekends and 'free time', but mostly because I quickly realised that to achieve such detailed coverage would require an encyclopaedia and another ten years' work. Meanwhile, however, I have tried to maintain a balance between rural and urban traditions, and I hope the reader will observe that there are many more customs and beliefs which unite humanity than threaten to divide it.

No sooner have we concluded that Scotland is a small nation of many regional variations than we are faced with a rather paradoxical concept: the universality of customs throughout the nation. The reader will recognize many aspects of tradition which are replicated from one area to another, sometimes with slight variations, and at other times virtually identical to a custom already encountered in an entirely different region. It is not due to some careless repetition on the part of the editor that these themes recur and even echo throughout many pages; they are deliberately included to highlight the universal aspect of customs and beliefs.

The present selection also aims to prove that the intricate web of tradition which, through time, has held together the fabric of Scottish life is still strong enough to weave a fine tapestry of yesterday, today and even tomorrow. Many of the delicate threads in it appear to have become threadbare, but just as they are pronounced 'worn out' by the writers of one generation, they turn up again, some as colourful as ever, others in a slightly muted shade – and a few downright psychedelic. The span of time is a crucial aspect of this phenomenon, and while some readers may consider it more desirable to have the items arranged in chronological fashion (from 1549 to 2004), I have chosen not to do this; in exploring the wide range of material across several centuries I found the startling juxtaposition of ancient and modern to be far more exciting, as it emphasises the indomitable strength of tradition that prevails throughout Scotland.

Although this collection was initially created with students in mind, I would regard it as a failure if it did not automatically have a much wider appeal. My final choice is intended for the enjoyment of ordinary folk, 'fae courtiers tae cottars', who share life's common experiences from birth to death. And to the student who created havoc and irritation among his fellow labourers by keeping Gregor's *Notes on the Folk-Lore of the North-East* at home for three weeks 'because my father wouldn't let me take it back till he finished it' I can now confess that I was quietly reassured by that 'second opinion' from the man 'who couldnae put it down'. This collection is not intended to replace the old writers, but to guide the readers to further exploration if they so desire. The notes and bibliography at the end should help complete the picture for the most inquiring readers.

The book is divided into three sections: *Childbirth and Infancy; Love, Courtship and Marriage*; and *Death and Burial*. Each one begins with a short introduction which also contains a selection of Scottish sayings or proverbs about these stages of life. Proverbs, as Lord Bacon once said, reflect the 'genius, wit and spirit of a nation'; they are, in the words of Lord John Russell, 'the wisdom of many and the wit of one'; and, as Henderson suggested in the preface to his own collection, 'the domestic habits of a people are best known by their proverbs' – just three of the reasons why I have included so many of them.

Notes on the Editing of Texts and Transcriptions

All the passages selected are headed by the name of the writer or speaker, with the date of writing or recording. A full citation of the text or tape is in the notes, along with any additional information that adds to the reader's understanding. Where it has not been possible to publish complete transcriptions of tape recordings I should like to have included (but for practical reasons could not do so) there are brief summaries and tape references in the notes. Words in Scots are explained in the glossary.

As far as possible all texts remain true to the original. Very few of the spellings have been changed, and where there is some doubt I have included both, with my suggested update in square brackets. For the sake of brevity, some of the text has been cut, and I have indicated this by the use of ellipses.

In the tape transcriptions I have tried to be as faithful as possible to the speakers, retaining individual style and syntax, though ever aware that the printed page gives only a pale image of the speaker. A few, though by no means all, the 'uhms' and 'ehs' have been omitted; where there was excessive repetition of detail some of this has also been cut; and where speech irrelevant to our subject occurred, this has also been omitted, as I believe that the reader may not have the same interest as I had in interjections such as 'Do you take milk in your tea?' All such omissions are indicated by . . . in the written versions. Occasionally there are some transcriptions which need a little clarification, not because the original speaker was unclear but usually because I had been given part of the information some time beforehand (so it seemed obvious at the time of recording), or because the speaker was gesticulating silently, such as when I was told that 'it reached right down to here' [indicating ankles]. My additions for all these instances are added in square brackets, which I hope will not intrude too much into the printed versions. On a few occasions I have omitted the names of people and places and indicated these with a long dash. Generally speaking such omissions to not detract from the information given but have been presented in this form either because I was unable to obtain permission to use a name from the individual concerned or because I considered the material to be of a sensitive nature.

PART I
Childbirth and Infancy

Childbirth and Infancy

> There's something very special about seeing a mother
> with a new baby; the expression on her face, and just the
> joy that a new life brings. . .[1]

'Children are the poor man's wealth' is an old saying known internationally which attempts to make the time-worn connection between socio-economic status and family size. It is, however, cold comfort to families who struggle against poverty. Young people getting married today can console themselves that modern contraception gives them a choice which was not available in the past, yet couples who have scarcely announced their engagement are invariably asked when folk can expect the first new arrival to the family. 'There's nae sport whaur there's neither auld folk nor bairns' was echoed in various forms throughout Scotland, occasionally heard at weddings, though more often applied to households in which there were no children:

> Taigh gun chù, gun chat, gun leanabh beag,
> Taigh gun ghean, gun ghaire.
> [A house without a dog, a cat, or a little child,
> Is a house without joy or laughter.]

And as soon as news reached the community that a child was expected, then in good auld-fashioned Scottish tradition there was always (whether you wanted it or not) plenty of advice: 'Naething is got without pains but an ill name.'

Nevertheless, from the onset of her confinement a young mother was offered continuous support and understanding from her elders; the concept of community care existed long before our modern Social Work Department or National Health Service. Not only was there the local midwife to attend to all her physical needs but she was also surrounded by the constant attention of female family and friends. Naturally she would experience an enormous change in her entire lifestyle: 'Altruim do leanabh am bliadhna is

---

[1] This short excerpt is from a tape of Scottish midwife Florence Clow recalling her experiences as a midwife in Scotland and in Tonga. She was recorded in Dumfries on 6 January 1985 by Margaret Bennett [hereafter cited as MB]. SA1985/130.

dean do ghnìomh an ath bhliadhna.' [Nurse your child this year and do your business next year.] This was said as advice to young mothers who needed to get used to the idea of putting the care of a baby before all other domestic or personal concerns. The importance of upbringing was emphasised time and time again in numerous oft-quoted proverbs which emphasised that youth is the time for training. 'Train up a child in the way he should go: and when he is old, he will not depart from it.' (Proverbs 22, v. 6). In Scots it is expressed in the axiom, 'Between three and thirteen, Thraw the woodie when it's green,' and in Gaelic as 'Am fear nach do dh'ionnsaich aig a' ghlùin, Cha'n ionnsaich e ris an uileinn.' [He who has not learned at the knee, Will not learn at the elbow.]

Parents were continually exhorted to pay attention to the fact that 'Bairns speak in the field what they hear by the fireside,' and the old idea of 'spare the rod and spoil the child' was stated in the Scots proverb: 'Gie a bairn his will and whelp his fill, and neither will do weel.' Similar advice was given in 'Is e anacladh na h-òige a nì 'n duine' [Careful attention in youth builds the man], and 'rule youth weel and age will rule itsel.'

In moments of despair, however, we can always remember that 'bachelors' wives and maidens' bairns are aye weel bred', and in time-honoured fashion just try to do the best we can, remembering that we may have some control over the upbringing of a child but precious little over the birth. For expectant mothers childbirth was anticipated as a perilous journey. Folk prayed for survival, took every precaution known and rejoiced at every safe delivery.

The Mother and Child in Days Gone By

Belle Stewart and her daughter Sheila MacGregor
Blairgowrie, 1992

BS I wis born in a wee bow tent on the bank of the River Tay on the 18th of July, 1906, so I'm no a chicken o yesterday's hatchin. . . born in a wee bow tent, no doctors, no nurses, nobody, just my aunt, my mother's sister; that was all that was there with her. And my father wis fishin the Tay at that time, and he got one o the biggest pearls that ever was known up to this day out of the Tay that mornin. . . Well, when my father got that pearl that mornin he had to walk up to Dunkeld for to sell it to the jeweller.[2] And if he had that pearl the day he could a got a couple o

---

[2] Sheila notes that the travelling people often sold their pearls to a chemist since chemists used the same weights for measurement as jewellers.

hundred pound for it. An he got either eight or ten pound, I think. I don't reckon he got all that, but anyway, that was a lot of money in his time. And he jist came back to the camp, and I suppose they would hae a dram, but they would celebrate me in some way, you know, the way travellers do, or tinkers to put it polite – my father was a great tinsmith, he was that; he was really counted [among skilled craftsmen], but I never knew him because he died when I was seven months old. . .

MB *When he brought the pearl back to your mother she must have been overjoyed. And [harking back to when you told me this story several years ago] wasn't there something he said when he got word of his new baby daughter?*

SM There wasn't a thing to eat in the camp, or even a drop of tea for the new mother, so when he got the money for the pearl he went to the shop to get food for everyone. And he said to the shopkeeper, 'That's two pearls I got the day!' You know, the one he got in the Tay, and his new wee baby.

BS Well, you see, there was other lasses [born] before me, but I was the only one that was spared, you know. And of course, the De'il is aye good to his own, ye ken!

But unfortunately [seven months later] he had a cold come over him. . . so I never had the pleasure [of getting to know my father], and at that time, no traveller woman to my knowledge, at least the MacGregor clans and the Stewarts, would ever take another man to father the bairns she had to her first man, oh no.[3]

Revd Walter Gregor
North-east, 1874

A mother . . . the holiest thing in life.

On the occasion of a birth there were present a few of the mother's female friends in the neighbourhood, besides the midwife. But it was not every woman that was permitted to attend. A woman with child was not allowed to be in the room; and if two women with child happened to be living in the same house when the one felt the pains of labour, they took a straw, or a stalk of grass, or some such thing, and broke it, each repeating the words, 'Ye tak yours, an I tak mine.' Neither could a woman giving suck seat herself on the edge of the bed of the lying-in woman, from the belief that such an action stopped the flow of the milk of the lying-in woman. If a woman in this condition did do so unwittingly, and the milk ceased, the lying-in mother whose milk had departed had to get secretly the child of her who had been the cause of the disappearance of the milk, and, with the aid of a friend, to pass it

---

[3] Belle Stewart and her daughter Sheila MacGregor were recorded by MB in Blairgowrie on 19 March, 1992. Sheila has since written her memoirs of life as a traveller.

under and over her apron to bring back her milk. While the woman was in labour all locks in the house were undone. One who might enter the house during labour spoke to the woman, and wished God speed to the birth. If the labour was difficult, the first who chanced to enter gave her something, as a little water to moisten the mouth, and there were those whose giving was reputed as of great virtue in easing and hastening the birth. A doctor was called only in cases of danger.

When the child was born there was a feast, called the *merry meht,* part of which was the indispensable cheese, or *cryin kebback.* In some districts a *cryin bannock,* made of oatmeal, milk and sugar, and baked in a frying-pan, was served up. Each one present carried off a piece of the cheese to be distributed among friends, and everyone who came to see the mother and baby also took away a piece for the same purpose.

The belief in fairies was universal, and their power was specially dreaded in the case of women in childbed and of unbaptised infants. These beings were believed to have a great liking for human milk, and to be constantly on the watch for opportunities to gratify their liking, which could be done only by carrying off *unsained* or unchurched mothers. There have been mothers carried into their subterranean palaces and been soon reduced to mere shadows of their former selves, and when they could no longer supply the delicious drink they have been permitted to return to their homes on condition of giving the best mare under milk to take their place. The husbands have then fulfilled the condition, and the mare has disappeared, and after a time returned so lean and weak as to be scarcely able to support her own weight. Nor did they show less anxiety to get possession of infants. Every seven years they had to pay 'the teind to hell', and this they endeavoured to do by a human being rather than by one of themselves.

> There came a wind out of the north,
> A sharp wind and a snell,
> And a dead sleep came over me,
> And frae my horse I fell;
> The Queen of Fairies she was there,
> And took me to hersel.
>
> And never would I tire, Janet,
> In fairy-land to dwell,
> But aye, at every seven years
> They pay the teind to hell;
> And though the Queen mak's much o' me,
> I fear 'twill be mysel.

Sometimes they succeeded in carrying one off, and sometimes in substituting one of their own. Sometimes their attempt has been foiled in the very moment of being accomplished, and the infant snatched from them as it was passing through the *dog-hole*.

On the birth of the child, the mother and offspring were *sained*, a ceremony which was done in the following manner: A fir-candle was lighted and carried three times round the bed, if it was in a position to allow of this being done, and if this could not be done, it was whirled three times round their heads; a Bible and bread and cheese, or a Bible and a biscuit, were placed under the pillow, and the words were repeated, 'May the Almichty debar a' ill fae this umman, an be aboot ir, an bliss ir an ir bairn.' When the biscuit or the bread and cheese had served their purpose, they were distributed among the unmarried friends and acquaintances, to be placed under their pillows to evoke dreams.

Among some of the fishing population a fir-candle or a basket containing bread and cheese was placed on the bed to keep the fairies at a distance. A pair of trousers hung at the foot of the bed had the same effect.

Strict watch was kept over both mother and child till the mother was churched and the child was baptised, and in the doing of both all convenient speed was used. For, besides exposure to the danger of being carried off by the fairies, the mother was under great restrictions till churched. She was not allowed to do any kind of work, at least any kind of work more than the most simple and necessary. Neither was she permitted to enter a neighbour's house, and had she attempted to do so, some would have gone the length of offering a stout resistance, for the reason that, if there chanced to be in the house a woman great with child, travail would prove difficult with her.

The Kirk of Scotland has no special service for the churching of women, and churching was simply attending the ordinary service. The mother put on her very best attire, and contrived if possible, however poor, to have a piece of new dress; and generally a larger contribution was given for the poor. On her journey home a neighbour by the wayside took her in, and set before her both food and drink. If the distance from the church and the state of the mother's health delayed the churching too long, she betook herself to the ruins or to the site of some old chapel that chanced to be near, and on that hallowed ground returned thanks to God for His goodness. The site of the chapel of St Bridget, with its little churchyard and a few nameless stones, near Tomintoul, was the resort of many a mother. And under the dome of Heaven, with the hills for temple walls, and the green grass for a carpet, above the long, long forgotten dead, in a temple not made with hands,

Kneeling there,

Down in the dreadful dust that once was man,

Dust . . . that once was living hearts,

did she pour forth her heart for two human lives. Despite all superstition, it was a grand sight. Such mothers have made Scotland what it is.[4]

Christina [Ciorstaigh] Docherty
Kingussie, 1992

MB *Your mother talked of the churching of women?*

CD Yes, she always thought it was very heathen[5] for people not to be churched after they had a baby. In her time [up to the 1930s] everyone had to have a churching ceremony, the first visit to church after the baby was born.

MB *Did she herself do that?*

CD I think probably the answer would be 'Yes'.

MB *Now, she was from Barra and came to Badenoch as a young woman. In her family what was the procedure?*

CD Well, the mother and baby went to the church and in her day they were met at the church door by a priest who sort of handed the mother a lighted candle. That was a Christian follow-on from the Jewish law of purification, really.[6] So the lighted candle sort of signified the purifying of the person. And they were blessed with holy water and there was a psalm said and various prayers said, and the mother was led into the church by the priest, holding the priest's stole. And there was various prayers and things, but as they went into the church he said 'Enter into the Kingdom of God,' and he took the mother down to the church altar where the mother and baby were again blessed and various prayers and intercessions said, and thanksgiving for the life of the mother being spared and the child being born. . .

It was her first real outing, [and it] would be to the church. She would maybe

---

[4] All excerpts from the Revd Walter Gregor are published in both of his books, *An Echo of the Olden Time from the North of Scotland*, Edinburgh, Glasgow and Peterhead, 1874 [hereafter cited as *Echo*], and *Notes on the Folk-Lore of the North-East of Scotland*, PFLS, London, 1881 [hereafter cited as *Notes*]. Both page references are given thus: *Echo*, pp. 84–89, and *Notes*, pp. 4–6.

[5] In her essay 'Rites of Passage as a Meeting Place', *The Good People: New Fairylore Essays* [hereafter cited as *The Good People*] pp. 215–223, Ann Helene Bolstad Skejelbred notes that in Norwegian tradition, where the churching of women was standard procedure until the 1930s, 'the woman in confinement is characterized as heathen', which 'means un-Christian', as her status was that of one who was outside the church. Similarly, in parts of Scotland the same word was used.

[6] See *Genesis*, chapter 3, verse 16.

meet up with friends afterwards. It would be an occasion, definitely an occasion . . . it was special to her, wasn't it? Everything's very ordinary now. . .[7]

Alexander Polson
Caithness, 1907

The day of birth, if not also the hour, is significant. As to the day, the following rhyme – a variation of one well known all over Scotland – is by some believed to afford a clue to the child's future:

> Sunday's child is full of grace,
> Monday's child is full in the face,
> Tuesday's child is solemn and sad,
> Wednesday's child is merry and glad,
> Thursday's child is inclined to thieving,
> Friday's child is free in giving,
> Saturday's child works hard for his living.

No very particular account is taken of the hour, however, except that it is believed that a child born at midnight will grow up to be 'uncanny' – a notion which may have in later life given some unfortunates the character of wizard or witch. Occasionally a child is born with a thin membrane – a caul – over its head, and this is regarded as a specially good sign. A child so fortunate can never be drowned; and besides, there is no fear of the fairies effecting an exchange in such a case.[8]

Meigle SWRI
Perthshire, 1932

The people of Meigle . . . were of the belief, too, that the 'fairy men' would steal their new-born babes and their maidens and carry them off to their caverns or underground houses in the Sidlaw Hills. Perhaps there may have been a reason for this belief. It may have come from the days of the Picts, when they invaded the land and took away many of their women and young folk with them. Great care was taken of newborn babies, and many very foolish stories were in circulation, how to avoid the fairies and try and keep them at bay.[9]

---

[7] Ciorstaigh Docherty was recorded in her home at Torcroy, near Kingussie, on 16 March 1992, by MB.

[8] Alexander Polson's essay 'The Folklore of Caithness' in *The County of Caithness*, edited by John Horne, [hereafter cited as 'Folklore'] pp. 91–92.

[9] Meigle SWRI, *Our Meigle Book*, pp. 143–144.

Revd James Napier
Renfewshire, 1879

When writing of fairies I noticed a practice common in some localities of
placing in the bed where lay an expectant mother, a piece of cold iron to scare
the fairies, and prevent them from spiriting away mother and child to elfland.
An instance of this spiriting away at the time of child-bearing is said to have
occurred in Arran within these fifty years. It is given by a correspondent in
Long Ago:

> There was a woman near Pladda, newly delivered, who was carried away, and
> on a certain night her wraith stood before her husband telling him that the
> yearly riding was at hand, and that she, with all the rout, should ride by his
> house at such an hour, on such a night; that he must await her coming, and
> throw over her wedding gown, and so she should be rescued from her tyrants.
> With that she vanished. And the time came, with the jingling of bridles and the
> tramping of horses outside the cottage; but this man, feeble-hearted, had
> summoned his neighbours to bear him company, who held him, and would not
> suffer him to go out. So there arose a bitter cry and a great clamour, and then all
> was still; but in the morning, roof and wall were dashed with blood, and the
> sorrowful wife was no more seen upon earth. This . . . is not a tale from an old
> ballad, it is the narrative of what was told not fifty years ago.

Immediately after birth, the newly-born child was bathed in salted water, and
made to taste of it three times. This, by some, was considered a specific
against the influence of the evil eye; but doctors differ, and so among other
people and in other localities different specifics were employed. I quote the
following from Ross's *Helenore*:

> Gryte was the care and tut'ry that was ha'en,
> Baith night and day about the bonny weeane:
> The jizzen-bed, wi rantry leaves was sain'd,
> And sic like things as the auld grannies kend;
> Jean's paps wi saut and water washen clean,
> Reed that her milk gat wrang, fan it was green;
> Neist the first hippen to the green was flung,
> And there at seelfu words, baith said and sung:
> A clear brunt coal wi the het tangs was ta'en,
> Frae out the ingle-mids fu clear and clean,
> And throu' the cosey-belly letten fa,
> For fear the weeane should be ta'en awa'.

Before baptism the child was more liable to be influenced by the evil eye than after that ceremony had been performed, consequently before that rite had been administered the greatest precautions were taken, the baby during this time being kept as much as possible in the room in which it was born, and only when absolutely necessary, carried out of it, and then under the careful guardianship of a relative, or of the mid-wife, who was professionally skilled in all the requisites of safety. Baptism was therefore administered as early as possible after birth. Another reason for the speedy administration of this rite was that, should the baby die before being baptised, its future was not doubtful. Often on calm nights, those who had ears to hear heard the wailing of the spirits of unchristened bairns among the trees and dells. I have known of an instance in which the baby was born on a Saturday, and carried two miles to church next day, rather than risk a week's delay. It was rare for working people to bring the minister to the house. Another superstitious notion in connection with baptism was that until that rite was performed, it was unlucky to name the child by any name. When, before the child had been christened, anyone asked the name of the baby, the answer generally was, 'It has not been out yet.'

When a child was taken from its mother and carried outside the bedroom for the first time after its birth, it was lucky to take it up stairs, and unlucky to take it down stairs. If there were no stairs in the house, the person who carried it generally ascended three steps of a ladder or temporary erection, and this, it was supposed, would bring prosperity to the child.

A child born with a caul – a thin membrane covering the head of some children at birth – would, if spared, prove a notable person. The carrying of a caul on board ship was believed to prevent shipwreck, and masters of vessels paid a high price for them. I have seen an advertisement for such in a local paper.

When baby was being carried to church to be baptised, it was of importance that the woman appointed to post should be known to be lucky. Then she took with her a parcel of bread and cheese, which she gave to the first person she met. This represented a gift from the baby – a very ancient custom. Again, it was of importance that the person who received this gift should be lucky – should have lucky marks upon their person. Forecasts were made from such facts as the following concerning the recipient of the gift: Was this person male or female, deformed, disfigured, etc. If the party accepted the gift willingly, tasted it, and returned a few steps with the baptism party, this was a good sign; if they asked to look at the baby, and blessed it, this was still more favourable: but should this person refuse the gift, nor taste it, nor turn back, this was tantamount to wishing evil to the child, and should any serious calamity befall the child, even years after, it was connected with this circumstance, and the party who had refused the baptismal gift was blamed for the evil which had befallen the child. It was also a common belief that if, as was frequently the case, there were several babies, male and female, awaiting baptism together, and the males were baptised before the females, all was well; but if, by mistake, a female should be christened before a male, the characters of the pair would be reversed – the female would grow up with a masculine character, and would have a beard, whereas the male would display a feminine disposition and be beardless. I have known where such a mistake has produced real anxiety and regret in the minds of the parents. We have seen that it was not until after baptism that the child was allowed out of the room in which it was born, except under the skilful guardianship of a relative or the midwife; but, further than this, it was not considered safe or proper to carry it into any neighbour's house until the mother took it herself, and this it was unlucky even for her to do until she had been to church. Indeed, few mothers would enter any house until they had been to the house of God. After this had been accomplished, however, she visited with the baby freely. In visiting any house with baby for the first time, it was incumbent on the person whom they were visiting to put a little salt or sugar into baby's mouth, and wish it well: the omission of this was regarded as a very unlucky omen for the baby. Here we may note the survival of a very ancient symbolic practice in this gift of salt. Salt was symbolical of favour or good will, and covenants of friendship in very early times were ratified with this gift; sugar, as in this instance, is no doubt a modern substitute of salt. Among Jews, Greeks, and Romans, as well as among less civilised nations, salt was used in their sacrifices as emblematic of fidelity, and for some reason or other it also came to be regarded as a charm against evil fascinations. By Roman Catholics in the middle ages salt was used to protect children from evil influences before they had received the sacrament of baptism. This practice is referred to in many of the old ballads and romances. In a ballad called *The King's Daughter*, a child is born, but in circumstances which do not admit of the rite of baptism being administered. The mother privately puts the baby into a casket, and, like the mother of Moses, sends it afloat, and as a protection places beside it a quantity of salt and candles. The words of the ballad are:

> The bairnie she swyl'd in linen so fine,
> In a gilded casket she laid it syne,
> Mickle saut and light she laid therein
> Cause yet in God's house it had'na been.

Let us return to the mother and child whom we left visiting at a friend's house, and receiving the covenant of friendship. It was unsafe to be lavish in praise of the child's beauty, for although such commendation would naturally be gratifying to the mother, it would at the same time increase her fears, for the *well faured* ran the greatest risk from evil influences, and of being carried off by the fairies. There was also the superadded danger of the mother setting her affections too much upon her child and forgetting God, who then in jealousy and mercy would remove it from her. This latter was a very widespread superstition among religiously-minded people, even among those who, from their education, ought to have known better. I well remember the case of a young mother – a tender loving woman, who, quite in keeping with her excitable affectionate nature, was passionately fond of her baby, her first-born. But baby sickened and died, and the poor mother, borne down with grief, wept bitterly, like Rachel refusing to be comforted. In the depth of her affliction she was visited by both her pastor and elder. They admonished her to turn her mind from the selfish sorrow in which she was indulging, and thank God for His kindly dealing toward her, in that He had removed from her the cause of sin on her part. She had been guilty, they said, of loving the baby too much, and God, who was a jealous God, would not suffer His people to set their affections on any object in a greater degree than on Himself; and therefore, He, in his mercy toward her, had removed from her the object of her idolatry. The poor woman in her agony could only sob out, 'Surely it was no sin to love my own child that God gave me.' The more correct term for such a theological concept would not be superstition, but blasphemy.

Another danger from which children required to be shielded was the baneful influence of the *evil eye*. Malicious people were believed to possess the power of doing harm by merely looking upon those whom they wished to injure. This belief is very ancient. From Professor Conington's *Satires of A. Persius Flaccus*, I extract the following notice of it:

Look here – a grandmother or a superstitious aunt has taken baby from his cradle, and is charming his forehead and his slavering lips against mischief by the joint action of her middle finger and her purifying spittle; for she knows right well how to check the evil eye . . .

The Romans used to hang red coral round the necks of their children to save them from falling-sickness, sorcery, charms, and poison. In this country coral beads were hung round the necks of babies, and are still used in country districts to protect them from an evil eye. Coral bells are used at present. The practice was originated by the Roman Catholics to frighten away evil spirits.

I have quite a vivid remembrance of being myself believed to be the unhappy victim of an evil eye. I had taken what was called a *dwining*, which baffled all ordinary experience; and, therefore, it was surmised that I had got 'a blink of an ill e'e'. To remove this evil influence, I was subjected to the following operation, which was prescribed and superintended by a neighbour 'skilly' in such matters: A sixpence was borrowed from a neighbour, a good fire was kept burning in the grate, the door was locked, and I was placed upon a chair in front of the fire. The operator, an old woman, took a tablespoon and filled it with water. With the sixpence she then lifted as much salt as it could carry, and both were put into the water in the spoon. The water was then stirred with the forefinger till the salt was dissolved. Then the soles of my feet and the palms of my hands were bathed with this solution thrice, and after these bathings I was made to taste the solution three times. The operator then drew her wet forefinger across my brow – called *scoring aboon the breath*. The remaining contents of the spoon she then cast right over the fire, into the hinder part of the fire, saying as she did so, 'Guid preserve frae a' skaith.' These were the first words permitted to be spoken during the operation. I was then put in bed, and, in attestation of the efficacy of the charm, recovered. To my knowledge this operation has been performed within these forty years, and probably in many outlying country places it is still practised. The origin of this superstition is probably to be found in ancient fire worship. The great blazing fire was evidently an important element in the transaction; nor was this a solitary instance in which regard was paid to fire. I remember being taught that it was unlucky to spit into the fire, some evil being likely shortly after to befall those who did so. Crumbs left upon the table after a meal were carefully gathered and put into the fire. The cuttings from the nails and hair were also put into the fire. These freaks certainly look like survivals of fire worship.

The influence of those possessing the evil eye was not confined to children, but might affect adults, and also goods and cattle. But for the bane there was provided the antidote. One effective method of checking the evil influence was by *scoring aboon the breath*. In my case, as I was the victim, *scoring* with a wet finger was sufficient; but the suspected possessor of the evil eye was more roughly treated, *scoring* in this case being effected with some sharp instrument so as to draw blood. I have never seen this done, but some fifty years ago an instance occurred in my native village. A child belonging to a poor woman in this village was taken ill and had convulsive fits, which were thought to be due to the influence of the evil eye. An old woman in the neighbourhood, whose temper was not of the sweetest, was suspected. She was first of all invited to come and see the child in the hope that sympathy might change the influence she was supposed to be exerting; but as the old woman appeared quite callous to the sufferings of the child, the mother, as the old woman was leaving the house, scratched her with her nails across the brow, and drew blood. This circumstance raised quite a sensation in the village. Whether the child recovered after this operation I do not remember. Many other instances of the existence of this superstitious practice in Scotland within the present century might be presented, but I content myself with quoting one which was related in a letter to the *Glasgow Weekly Herald,* under the signature F.A.:

> I knew of one case of the kind in Wigtownshire, in the south of Scotland, about the year 1825, as near as I can mind. I knew all parties very well. A farmer had some cattle which died, and there was an old woman living about a mile from the farm who was counted no very canny. She was heard to say that there would be mair o' them wad gang the same way. So one day, soon after, as the old woman was passing the farmhouse, one of the sons took hold of her and got her head under his arm, and cut her across the forehead. By the way, the proper thing to be cut with is a nail out of a horse-shoe. He was prosecuted and got imprisonment for it.

This style of antidote against the influence of an evil eye was common in England within the century, as the following, which is also taken from a letter which appeared in the same journal, seems to show:

> Drawing blood from above the mouth of the person suspected is the favourite antidote in the neighbourhood of Burnley; and in the district of Craven, a few miles within the borders of Yorkshire, a person who was ill-disposed towards his neighbours is believed to have slain a pear-tree which grew opposite his house by directing towards it 'the first morning glances' of his evil eye. Spitting three times in the person's face; turning a live coal on the fire; and exclaiming, 'The Lord be with us,' are other means of averting its influence.

We must not, however, pursue this digression further, but return to our proper subject. It was not necessary that the person possessed of the evil eye, and desirous of inflicting evil upon a child, should see the child. All that was necessary was that the person with the evil eye should get possession of something which had belonged to the child, such as a fragment of clothing, a toy, hair, or nail parings. I may note here that it was not considered lucky to pare the nails of a child under one year old, and when the operation was performed the mother was careful to collect every scrap of the cutting, and burn them. It was considered a great offence for any person, other than the mother or near relation, in whom every confidence could be placed, to cut a baby's nails; if some forward officious person should do this, and baby afterwards be taken ill, this would give rise to grave suspicions of evil influence being at work. The same remarks apply to the cutting of a baby's hair. I have seen the door locked during hair-cutting, and the floor swept afterwards, and the sweepings burned, less perchance any hairs might remain, and be picked up by an enemy. Dr Livingstone, in his book on the Zambezi, mentions the existence of a similar practice among some African tribes. 'They carefully collect and afterwards burn or bury the hair, lest any of it fall into the hands of a witch.' Mr Munter mentions that the same practice is common amongst the Patagonians, and the practice extends to adults. He says that after bathing, which they do every morning, 'the men's hair is dressed by their wives, daughters, or sweethearts, who take the greatest care to burn the hairs that may be brushed out, as they fully believe that spells may be wrought by evil-intentioned persons who can obtain a piece of their hair. From the same idea, after cutting their nails the parings are carefully committed to the flames.'

Besides this danger – this blighting influence of the evil eye which environed the years of childhood – there was also this other danger, already mentioned, that of being spirited away by fairies. The danger from this source was greater when the baby was pretty, and what fond mother did not consider her baby pretty? Early in the century, a labourer's wife living a few miles west of Glasgow became the mother of a very pretty baby. All who saw it were charmed with its beauty, and it was as good as it was bonnie. The neighbours often urged on the mother the necessity of carefulness, and advised her to adopt such methods as were, to their minds, well-attested safeguards for the preservation of children from fairy influence and an evil eye. She was instructed never to leave the child without placing it near an open Bible. One unhappy day the mother went out for a short time, leaving the baby in its cradle, but she forgot or neglected to place the open Bible near the child as directed. When she returned baby was crying, and could by no means be quieted, and the mother observed several blue marks upon its person, as if it had been pinched. From that day it became a perfect plague; no amount of food or drink would satisfy it, and yet withal it became lean. The *girn*, my informant said, was never out its face, and it *yammered* on night and day. One day an old highland woman having seen the child, and inspected it carefully, affirmed that it was a fairy child. She went the length of offering to put the matter to the test, and this is how she tested it. She put the poker in the fire, and hung a pot over the fire wherein were put certain ingredients, an incantation being said as each new ingredient was stirred into the pot. The child was quiet during these operations, and watched like a grown person all that was being done, even rising upon its elbow to look. When the operations were completed, the old woman took the poker out of the fire, and carrying it red hot over to the cradle, was about to burn the sign of the cross on the baby's brow, when the child sprung suddenly up, knocked the old woman down and disappeared up the *lum* filling the house with smoke, and leaving behind it a strong smell of brimstone. When the smoke cleared away, the true baby was found in the cradle sleeping as if it never had been taken away. Another case was related to me as having occurred in the same neighbourhood, but in this instance the theft was not discovered until after the death of the child. The surreptitious or false baby, having apparently died, was buried; but suspicion having been raised, the grave was opened and the coffin examined, when there was found in it, not a corpse, but a wooden figure. The late Mr Rust, in his *Druidism Exhumed*, states that this superstition is common in the North of Scotland, and adds that it is also believed that if the theft be discovered before the apparent death of the changeling, there are means whereby the fairies may be propitiated and induced to restore the real baby. One of these methods is the following: The parents or friends of the stolen baby must take the fairy child to some known haunt of the fairies, generally some spot where peculiar *soughing* sounds are heard, where there are remains of some ancient cairn or stone circle, or some green mound or shady dell, and lay the child down there, repeating certain incantations. They must also place beside it a quantity of bread, butter, milk, cheese, eggs, and flesh of fowl, then retire to a distance and wait for an hour or two, or until after midnight. If on going back to where the child was laid they find that the offerings have disappeared, it is held as evidence that the fairies have been satisfied, and that the human child is returned. The baby is then carried home, and great rejoicing made. Mr Rust states that he knew a woman who, when a baby, had been stolen away, but was returned by this means.[10]

James Thomson
Aberlour, 1887

The writer has heard his maternal grandmother tell how she narrowly escaped the fate . . . It was in the memorable '45 that she first saw the light, in a lonely Highland cottage. Her father being 'oot wi the Prince', the mother was left alone with her child, when one night she awoke in time to clutch the feet of my respected grandmother as she was being carried out of bed by the fairies, who fled up the lum with an impish laugh, disappointed of their prey. After that night, when my great-grandmother had an infant by her side she never went to sleep without having a Bible below her head.[11]

---

[10] Revd James Napier, *Folk Lore: or, Superstitious Beliefs in the West of Scotland within this Century* [Hereafter cited as *Folk Lore*], 1879, pp. 29–42.

John Firth
Orkney, 1920

Not one or two, but sometimes as many as half a dozen women were called to the house on an occasion of this kind to keep away the 'peerie-folk' – those unearthly visitants who were particularly busy when a new arrival came. For several nights the neighbours by turns rocked the cradle all night, and watched so that the baby was not stolen away. If, through any defect, either physical or mental, the child did not fulfil the promise of its infancy, the parents had no hesitation in saying that the fairies had taken away their child, and for it had substituted a weakling. To ensure a child's good-luck its first drink had to be taken off silver, and though the humble Orcadian peasant would have preferred a silver cup or the proverbial silver spoon, he was not in his poverty to be baffled in his efforts to secure his child's prosperity; so he placed a silver coin in the ram's horn spoon, which, as a charm, acted, no doubt, as effectually as either of the former. But sometimes chill penury denied the household even the silver coin, in which circumstance it had to be borrowed from a less impecunious neighbour. A man well known in business in this locality, and who died only a few years ago, stated that he had often been called upon to lend a shilling for this purpose.

. . . To ward off evil during her time of indisposition, the mother kept beside her, in the bed, a Bible and a knife, the peerie folk being equally as afraid of cold steel as of the Scriptures. We are aware of this custom being observed even so recently as the year 1887. An old lady well acquainted with the superstitious practices of former times, when paying a congratulatory visit, was quick to notice the end of a large Bible protruding from underneath the mattress. When relating the circumstance to some friends she jocularly remarked that she was sure the *gullie* (a large knife used for butchering pigs and cutting cabbages, and hence called the butching-gullie or kail-gullie) was not far off. Her astonished listeners asked for an explanation, and urged that the woman must have had the Bible there for reading; but such could not have been the case, for the bed occupied by the young mother and her child was of the long-doored, shut-in type, in whose dark enclosure it was impossible for the keenest vision to discern even large type. It is remarkable how enlightened people, even within the last generation, believed in, and feared, the malicious tricks of the fairies on the occasions of births and deaths, though long since they had ceased to believe in their interference in the ordinary affairs of life.[12]

---

[11] James Thomson, *Recollections of a Speyside Parish Fifty Years Ago*, p. 60.

. . . After a birth all the neighbours on visiting terms were expected to call and offer their congratulations, and the more intimate acquaintances were specially invited to the blide-maet (blithe-meat) or joy-feast. Scones and ale or more ardent spirits were offered to the guests, who gave their best toasts, and duly expressed their admiration of the child, discreetly prefacing their compliments by a brief ejaculatory prayer, such as, 'Guid save hid', or 'Safe be hid'. It was very unwise audibly to admire or praise a child without this safeguard, for should any untoward circumstance befall it, people were not slow to say that the little one had been *fore-spoken*. If the ejaculation happened to be omitted, some interested person would seek to counteract the evil influence by hastily adding, 'Oh, spake o' hid wi' a guid tongue.' 'Too good to live' was an old adage in which a great number of people had a strong belief. Any child of a particularly quiet and docile nature was spoken of as being ready for the grave; and if a child that exhibited an unusually affectionate disposition or great precocity died in early life, one often heard such remarks as, 'We might hae kent hid wad be taen, for it was sic a fainfu' ting,' or, 'Hid was ower weel seen hid wad never kame (comb) a grey head, for it was as witty (knowing or intelligent) as a' auld body. Ay, hid was truly a faey bairn.'[13]

Dr Harry P. Taylor
Shetland, 1948

I will relate a rather amusing argument I had with . . . a shrewd old woman, perhaps better described as a 'hard old case'. She had a rich vocabulary, a fluent tongue, and could use it. One day . . . shortly after District Nurses were appointed in this parish, I suggested that my patient should call in the new nurse, a charming young lady, who would give the old lady helpful advice. The old woman snorted – 'What do I want wi' yer nurses, they are nae use to me' . . . I continued to talk about the Nurses, and said what a help they were to women having babies. 'Weel, doctor, I am no gan to hae any mair bairns noo, I've had thirteen and never a doctor or any o' yer new

---

[12] The writer, a native Orcadian, may have been expressing his own wishful thinking here. Not only in Orkney but virtually all over Scotland there are widespread beliefs in the influence of the fairies. Several hundred recordings from oral tradition (made between 1952 and 1992) would not uphold Firth's notion that belief in the fairies had ceased to exist in the 1920s. As recently as March 1992 (and not too far from Edinburgh) I heard several stories of encounters with fairies.

[13] John Firth, *Reminiscences of an Orkney Parish*, [hereafter cited as *Orkney*] pp. 74–77; several passages are omitted. Firth suggests that during this 'all female' occasion which was (and still is) surrounded by a host of dangers, all the women involved (mother and midwives alike) were usually 'the worse of drink', capable only of 'incompetent obstetrics'.

fangled nurses – only auld — frae — and she browt a testament and a razor wi her, and I had me bairn wi nae fuss.' I was rather taken aback and said, 'What on earth did the woman do with the razor and testament?' 'Weel, she pat the razor under the pillow to keep awa the trows trows, and read me a chapter frae the testament noo and again to keep me spirits up.'[14]

Changelings

The idea that fairies stole children and left changelings in their place may seem inconceivable in the 1990s. Within this century, however, such beliefs have been widespread, not only in Scotland, but in many parts of the world.[15] Numerous reports exist of babies stolen by the fairies and another child left in its place, and within living memory there are several reports from virtually all over Scotland of people who actually saw and spent time in the company of a changeling. The following is only one of many that have been documented.

Dòmnhull Mac —,[16]
1968

Naidheachd an t-sìbhrigh . . . Chuala mise seann duine seo ga innse – bhith ga fhaicinn. Tha 'n duine seo marbh o chionn . . . Bha e 'na sheann duine, bhiodh e còrr math is ceithir fichead bliadhna sin ann a' 1913: Iain C—. Agus bha e cluinntinn naidheachd an t-sìbhrigh 's thuirt e ris fhéin a' latha seo 's e shuas am Port — no shuas an dùthaich, 'Théid mi ga fhaicinn.'

S o bha e faicinn an t-sìbhrigh 's bha e fantail ann an taigh dùreach ann an gualainn na beinne, os cionn Port —.

Bha sìbhreach 'na laighe 's bha e 'g aimhreachd air. 'S chaidh Iain a null 's chunnaig e a' sìbhreach. Bha Iain ag radha gu robh leaba fada – gu robh e aon de tràighean a dh'fhaid. Dh' fhoighneachd Iain dhe 'Dé mar a tha thu, Sheumais?' 'Se Seumas a bh'air. Cha robh staigh ach a' chailleach.

'Miau-au-au!' bheireadh a' sìbhreach, 'Mach am baile, Seumas. Miau-au-au!' Sin na bha Iain a' faotainn as. Tha cuimhneam e bhith 'g innse na naidheachd.

Agus mar a bha 'sìbhreach aca, an ùine bha e aca, *phrosper* iad gu fiadhaich. Bha iad

---

[14] Dr Harry Pearson Taylor, *A Shetland Parish Doctor*, pp. 92–93. The book is based on his forty years of experience as a general practitioner in the Shetlands.

[15] *The Good People,* edited by Peter Narváez, 1991, is a collection of essays by sixteen international scholars from several disciplines. This comprehensive study has extensive notes and references which offer scope for further research.

[16] Because this is a relatively sensitive subject, I have decided not to include the surname or place of origin of the informant.

a' faotainn prìs mhór 's cha robh iad a' call beathach. Bha iad gu math dheth. Ach nuair a bhàsaich a' sìbhreach – a chaochail a' sìbhreach, chaill iad na bh'aca. Bhàsaich na beothaichean agus a chuile nì a bh'aca uair a dh'fhalbh a' sìbhreach . . . Bha e fichead bliadhna, corr is fichead bliadhna – fichead bliadhna bha a leotha-san – 'n aois a bha e nuair a chaochail e. . .

. . . Bha na seann daoine dèanamh a-mach gun tug na sìbhrichean leotha 'm pàisde. Bha iad a-mach a' buain 's dh'fhàg iad am pàisde ann an creathall. Agus nuair a thill iad a thogail a' phàisde, thuirt a' chailleach, 'Chan e seo, chan e seo – chan e tha seo againn idir.' Thug iad leotha dhachaidh.

'S ann a sin nuair a thug iad leotha dhachaidh e bha daoine 's mnathan a' faicinn nach e bh'ann idir. Bha iad a' dèanamh dheth . . . gun do dh'fhàg iad a' fear seo 's gun tug iad leotha am pàisde a-staigh don bheinn.

Bha e leotha sin 's thog iad e gus a robh e còrr is fichead bliadhna agus chaochail a' sìbhreach 's chaill iad na bh'aca.

Sin agad naidheachd sìbhreach a chuala mise 'san àite seo: Sìbhreach na —; Seumas a bh'air: Seumas na —. Ach bha . . . naidheachd ud aig a chuile duine san àm, Seumas Sìbhreach na —.

Well, a nis, bha 'n duine seo 'na dhuine òg san àm ud . . . Cha robh ann ach duine òg nuair a chunnaig e 'sìbhreach – ann a' 1913 a chaochail am bodach ach chunnaig e 'sìbhreach; bha e ga fhaicinn ach cha robh e ach 'na dhuine òg 'san àm. Tha mi cinnteach gu bheil a' sìbhreach marbh . . . còrr math agus ceud bliadhna, co-dhiùbh, dhiùbh, dhiùbh.

Cha b'aithne dhomhsa móran am Port — ann. Cha b'aithne dhomh móran dhaoine shuas a sin ann, ach chan eil gin aca sin beò. Tha iad marbh . . . O cha robh iad airson a ghrà gur e sìbhreach a bh'ann. Ach cha do choisich a' sìbhreach riamh; cha robh e ach 'sa leabaidh 'na laighe. Ach cha robh math dhuit a ghrà gun e sìbhreach a bh'ann.

Màthair a thuirt ris a' bhoirionnach òg a bha seo am bu leithe am pàisde. 'Chan e seo e. Chan e seo e. Chan e seo Seumas idir,' ars ise. ''Se Seumas eile th'air fhàgail a seo. Chaidh a chall . . . Chaill sibh a-mach e,' thuirt i.

Bha sin a chuile duine dol a dh'fhaicinn an t-sìbhrigh . . . Sin agad a' naidheachd a chuala mise man t-sìbhreach.

Translation

The story about the Fairy . . . I heard an old man here telling it – that he had seen him. This man is long dead. He would have been well over eighty then, in 1913: Iain C —. And he had been hearing talk about the Fairy and this day when he was up in Port — he said to himself 'I'll go and see him.'

And he went to see the Fairy, and the Fairy lived in a house on the shoulder of the hill, above Port —.

The Fairy was lying in bed and he was looking at him. And Iain went over and saw him. Iain said it was a long bed – it was about six feet long. Iain asked him 'How are you, James?' He was called James. There was no-one else in but the old woman.

'Miau-au-au!' the Fairy would say, 'Out of here [out of town], James. Miau-au-au!' That's all Iain could get out of him. I remember him telling the story.

And while they had the Fairy with them – all the time he was with them – they prospered tremendously. They were getting high prices [for their animals] and they never lost a beast. They were well off. But when the Fairy died they lost all they had. The beasts died and everything, when the Fairy went. He was over twenty years old – he was with them for twenty years before he died . . .

The old folk were making out that the fairies had taken the child away. They were out harvesting and they left the child in a cradle. And when they came back to pick the child up, the old woman said 'This is not, this is not, this isn't him at all!' They took him home.

It was then, after they took him home, that men and women saw that it wasn't him [their own child] at all. They were making out . . . that they had left this one, and that they had taken the child away into the hill.

[The changeling] was with them then, and they reared him till he was over twenty years of age, and the Fairy died, and they lost everything they had.

That was a fairy story I heard in this place: The Fairy of —; James he was called . . . James of —. But everyone at that time knew that story, James the Fairy of —.

Well now, this man [who told me the story] was just a young man at that time . . . he was just a young man when he saw the Fairy. It was in 1913 that the old man died, but he saw the Fairy; he went to see him . . . I'm sure the fairy died, oh, well over a hundred years ago at the very, very least.

I don't know many people in Port — at all. I don't know folk up there, but none of these folk are alive. They are all dead. Oh, they didn't want it said that he was a fairy. But the Fairy never walked; he just lay there in bed. But you daren't say he was a fairy.

It was her mother who said to this young woman who had the child 'This isn't him! This isn't him! This is not James at all,' she said. 'This is another James who has been left here. He was lost! You lost him out there,' she said.

Then everyone was going to see the fairy . . . That's the story I heard about the fairy.[17]

---

[17] I am grateful to Joan MacKenzie at the School of Scottish Studies for drawing my attention to this tape recording made in 1968 by D.A. MacDonald, A.J. Bruford and I.A. Fraser, and to Donald Archie MacDonald for transcribing and translating it. SA1968/90.

In almost all the eighteenth- and early nineteenth-century books surveyed for this collection, there are references to beliefs associated with changelings. In his book *Northern Mythology*, Benjamin Thorpe confirms the widespread existence throughout northern Europe of similar beliefs, noting also that 'the Scotch too had their changelings, though they appear to have been of a far more social character than those of Scandinavia.'[18] Many of these beliefs are reflected in Gaelic songs (usually lullabies) and some of the older Scots songs and ballads.

In his *Letters on Demonology and Witchcraft*, Sir Walter Scott also gives an account of a woman in East Lothian who was said to have been taken by the fairies during the birth of her fourth baby. Her husband buried the corpse (said by the neighbours to have been a substitute), and bitterly lamented his loss. A year later when he planned to remarry, his wife appeared by his bed to tell him that he could regain her from her unwilling captivity by the fairies. She appeared a second, then a third night, and this time convinced him of her reality by taking up the infant during whose birth she had 'died' and giving it suck; 'she spilled a drop or two of her milk on the poor man's bedclothes, as if to assure him.' Thoroughly perplexed, he sought advice from his minister, who advised him to marry a new bride immediately so as to be rid of such visitations.[19]

Regardless of the host of writers who have recorded their own views or those of others, we may consider the most serious food for thought on the subject of changelings comes from one of the great names in European church history, Martin Luther.

Dr Martin Luther
Germany, 1541

Changelings *[Wechselbalge]* and Kielkropfs, Satan lays in the place of the genuine children, that people may be tormented with them. He often carries off young maidens into the water, has intercourse with them, and keeps them with him until they have been delivered, then lays such children in cradles, takes the genuine children out, and carries them away. But such changelings, it is said, do not live more than eighteen or twenty years. Eight years ago there was a changeling in Dessau, which I, Dr Martin Luther, have both seen and

[18] Benjamin Thorpe, *Northern Mythology, comprising the Principal Popular Traditions and Superstitions of Scandinavia, North Germany, and the Netherlands*, vol. ii, pp. 174–176. See also Robert Chambers, Popular Rhymes of Scotland, p 55.
[19] Sir Walter Scott, *Letters on Demonology and Witchcraft*, pp. 162–6.

touched: it was twelve years old, and had all its senses, so that people thought it was a proper child; but that mattered little, for it only ate, and that as much as any four ploughmen or thrashers, and when any one touched it, it screamed; when things in the house went wrong, so that any damage took place, it laughed and was merry; but if things went well it cried. Thereupon I said to the Prince of Anhalt, 'If I were prince or ruler here I would have this child thrown into the water, into the Moldau, that flows by Dessau, and would run the risk of being a homicide.' But the Elector of Saxony, who was then at Dessau, and the Prince of Anhalt, would not follow my advice. I then said: 'They ought to cause a paternoster to be said in the church, that God would take the devil away from them.' This was done daily at Dessau, and the said changeling died two years after.[20]

One might wonder if the church could possibly have turned a blind eye to the sort of belief that seems to have been perpetuated over the centuries. Or was it in those days, even in those not-so-far-off days, the only possible explanation that could be put forward for the existence of children with genetic abnormalities or metabolic disorders?[21]

Protection and Prevention

Martin Martin
Western Isles, *c.* 1695

There was an ancient custom in the island of Lewis to make a fiery circle about the houses, corn, cattle, &c., belonging to each particular family: a man carried fire in his right hand, and went round, and it was called *dessil* [deiseal] . . .

There is another way of the dessil, or carrying fire round about women before they are churched after child-bearing; and it is used likewise about

---

[20] Reprinted in Thorpe, *Northern Mythology*, vol. ii, pp. xxi–xxii. It should be noted, however, that regardless of how harsh Martin Luther's words on the subject of changelings may seem, a perusal of his *Letters* and written records from his *Table Talk* show that this recommendation is somewhat uncharacteristic of his otherwise compassionate attitude to the wide range of issues he discusses. See bibliography, Bainton, Lawson, Luther, Smith, and especially Tappert's *Luther: Letters of Spiritual Counsel*.

[21] For a comprehensive discussion on the medical aspects of abnormalities which are suggested as explanations for changeling children, see Narváez's section 'Physical Disorders: Changelings and the Blast' in *The Good People*, pp. 225–97 (including photographs).

children until they be christened: both [of] which are performed in the morning and at night. This is only practised now by some of the ancient midwives:[22] I inquired their reason for this custom, which I told them was altogether unlawful; this disobliged them mightily, insomuch that they would give me no satisfaction. But others, that were of a more agreeable temper, told me the fire-round was an effectual means to preserve both the mother and the infant from the power of evil spirits, who are ready at such times to do mischief, and sometimes carry away the infant; and when they get them once in their possession, return them poor meagre skeletons: and these infants are said to have voracious appetites, constantly craving for meat. In this case it was usual with those who believed that their children were thus taken away, to dig a grave in the fields upon quarter day, and there to lay the skeleton till next morning; at which time the parents went to the place, where they doubted not to find their own child instead of this skeleton.[23]

Revd Walter Gregor
North-east, 1874

When the child was born, if it was a boy it was wrapped in a woman's shirt, and if it was a girl it was wrapped in a man's. If the operation was reversed the luckless victim of such an untoward act never entered into the joys of married life.

In washing the new-born infant great care was used not to let the water touch the palms of the hands, and this care was continued for a considerable length of time, under the belief that to wash the palms of the hands washed away the luck of this world's goods. By some a live coal was thrown into the water in which the new-born infant was washed. By others it was carefully poured under the foundation of the dwelling-house, to prevent it from coming in contact with fire, and thus to preserve in coming years the child from the harm of burning. When dressed it was turned three times heels over head in the nurse's arms, and blessed, and then shaken three times with the head downward. These ceremonies kept the fairies at a distance from the infant, and prevented it from being frightened when suddenly awaked from sleep, as well as from growing in a knot. The same ceremonies were gone through every time the child was dressed. When it was laid down from the

---

[22] In 1953 Calum MacLean recorded the Revd Norman MacDonald in Glenelg, Skye, describing a birth custom where the women carried the newborn infant round the fire (in the middle of the floor) to receive a blessing and bring good luck. SA1953/23, text and translation printed in *Tocher*, 38, p. 53,1983.
[23] Martin Martin, *A Description of the Western Isles of Scotland, circa 1695*, Edinburgh, 1716 [hereafter cited as *Description*, 1934 edition], pp. 116–18.

arms, as to bed, the words, 'God be with you,' or 'God bless you,' were repeated.

To guard the child from being *forespoken*, it was passed three times through the petticoat or chemise the mother wore at the time of the accouchment. It was not deemed proper to bestow a very great deal of praise on a child; and one doing so would have been interrupted by some such words as 'Gueed sake, haud yir tung, or ye'll forespyke the bairn.' Such a notion of forespeaking by bestowing excessive praise was not limited to infants, but extended to full-grown people, to domestic animals, and to crops. If the child was sickly, and there was a suspicion that it had been forespoken, recourse was had to the well-approven modes of discovering the truth or untruth of the suspicion.

Here are two modes: A new shilling, after being put three times round the *crook*, was placed on the bottom of a wooden cap. The cap was filled with water, which was immediately poured off. If the shilling came off with the water, the child had not been forespoken. Three stones – one round, to represent the head, another as near the shape of the body as possible, and a third as like the legs as could be found – were selected from a south-running stream, that formed the boundary between *twa lairds' laan*, heated red hot, and thrown into a vessel containing a little water. A new shilling was laid on the bottom of a wooden cap, and this water was poured over it. It was then decanted, and if the shilling stuck to the bottom of the cap, the sickness was brought on by forespeaking. The water used in the ceremony was administered as a medicine.

To turn off the *evil eye*, and to preserve the child from the power of the fairies, a small brooch, of the shape of a heart, was worn on one of the petticoats, usually behind.

There were those who had the reputation of having the power of showing to the parents or relatives the face of the one who had been guilty of casting ill upon the child. If ill had been cast upon the child it was cured by taking its own first shirt, or the petticoat the mother wore before confinement, or the linen she wore at the time of delivery, and passing it through it three times, and then three times round the *crook*.

If the child became cross and began to *dwine*, fears immediately arose that it might be a 'fairy changeling,' and the trial by fire was put into operation. The hearth was piled with peat, and when the fire was at its strength the suspected changeling was placed in front of it near as possible not to be scorched, or it was suspended in a basket over the fire. If it was a 'changeling child' it made its escape by the *lum*, throwing back words of scorn as it disappeared.

One mode of bringing back the true child was the following. A new *scull* was taken and hung over the fire from a piece of a branch of a hazel tree, and into this basket the suspected changeling was laid. Careful watch was kept till it screamed. If it screamed it was a changeling, and it was held fast to prevent its escape. When an opportunity occurred, it was carried to a place where four roads met, and a dead body was carried over it. The true child was restored.

On the first symptoms of the child's cutting teeth, a *teethin bannock* was made. It was baked of oatmeal and butter or cream, sometimes with the addition of a ring, in presence of a few neighbours, and without a single word being spoken by the one baking it. When prepared, it was given to the child to play with till it was broken. A small piece was then put into the child's mouth, if it had not done so of its own accord. Each one present carried away a small portion. Such a bannock was supposed to ease the troubles of teething. It went also by the name of *teethin plaster*.

When once a child was weaned, suck was not on any account again given. Thieving propensities would have been the result of such an action. Neither was it lawful to cut its nails with knife or scissors. That, too, begot a thieving disposition. Biting off was the only mode adopted.

If a child spoke before it walked, it turned out a liar.

When a child entered a house something was given it. Its hand was crossed with money, or a piece of bread was put into its hand. If this was not done, hunger was left in the house. It was sometimes a custom to put a little meal into the child's mouth the first time it was carried out and taken into a neighbour's house.

The cradle was an object of much care. A child was never put into a new cradle. A live cock or hen was first placed in it; and the first-born was never put into a new cradle, but into an old one, borrowed. In sending the cradle it was not sent empty. In some districts, if it was borrowed for a girl's use, a live cock was tied into it, and if for a boy's, a live hen. In other districts it was filled with potatoes, a bag of meal, or such like, respect being commonly had to the state of the borrower. It was not allowed to touch the ground till it was placed on the floor of the house in which it was to be used.[24]

---

[24] W. Gregor, *Echo*, pp. 90–95, and *Notes*, pp. 7–10.

Alexander Laing
Newburgh, Fife, 1876

It is still considered unlucky by many to use a new cradle for a newborn infant. Old cradles are, therefore, in special request and are constantly borrowed to avoid the mysterious peril of using a new one.[25]

Alexander Stewart
Dunfermline, 1886

It was also believed to be uncanny to weigh an infant before it was a year old, or to let the moon shine on its face whilst it was asleep. It was also very desirable to cut an infant's nails for the first time over an open Bible.[26]

Alexander Polson
Caithness, 1907

Nowadays 'science is measurement,' but some Caithness matrons continue to object to have their babies measured or weighed, as being unlucky . . . When the first tooth is 'cast' it is carefully rolled up in paper and hidden in the hole of a mouse – a common Scottish practice. Sometimes salt accompanies the tooth.

As the child gets older, it is by no means advisable to cut its hair when the moon is on the wane, if 'a good head of hair' is desired, as such a proceeding seriously checks its growth.[27]

Elizabeth Stewart
Mintlaw, 1988

MB *Did you have any sayings about the care of little ones?*

ES Oh yes. You didn't cut the child's nails until it was a year old.

MB *Then how would you pare the baby's nails?*

ES You'd take them off with your teeth.[28]

---

[25] Alexander Laing, *Lindores Abbey and its Burgh of Newburgh: Their History and Annals*, pp. 383–4.

[26] Alexander Stewart, *Reminiscences of Dunfermline: Old Customs and Superstitions*, p. 42.

[27] Alexander Polson, 'Folklore', pp. 93–4.

[28] Elizabeth Stewart of Mintlaw was recorded at the School of Scottish Studies on 19 May 1988 while she was guest at one of MB's lectures. At the mention of this custom a large number of the students nodded and murmured agreement, indicating that this is still widespread in Scotland today. SA1988/25.

Practical Midwifery and Care of the Newborn

J.J. Vernon and J. McNairn
Hawick, 1911

The children born in Hawick in the olden times were, with few exceptions, ushered into the world with the aid of the howdie or midwife; for the practice of midwifery was, unless in very special cases, almost confined to women. Qualified physicians and surgeons were rather scarce; like Roderick Random, they were expected to do little more than 'bleed and give a clyster, spread a plaster, and prepare a potion'. Fashion and habit are not easily changed, and therefore medical practitioners in the days of our grandparents continued to eke out their livelihood in a way that would be considered beneath the dignity of the modern physician. In country towns like Hawick a medical man, on taking a house, would change a room entering from the street into a small shop, dignify it by the title 'Medical Hall', and proceed to supply to all and sundry tea, spices, herbs, medicine, leeches, etc. The following announcements in the newspapers illustrate the usual practice of those days:

> Surgeon's Hall, Edinburgh, April 1st, 1800. – In the presence of the Royal College of Surgeons, appeared Mr Walter Turnbull, from Hawick, and being examined in his Skill in Anatomy, Surgery, and Pharmacy, was found fully qualified to practice in these Arts. Extracted by
>
> William Balderstone, Clerk.

> Dr Turnbull respectfully informs the Inhabitants of Hawick and its Vicinity, that he has entered upon the exercise of his Profession as Physician and Man-Wife; where he will always have a supply of genuine Medicines.

> N.B. Apprentices Wanted.
> Acidulated Aeriated Waters.
> Alkaline Aeriated Mephitic Water, 5/6 per doz. half pints.

Not much is known of the career of this gentleman, but it was of him that a worthy old lady in Hawick testified: 'I understand that Dr Turnbull is not only very clever, but he can afford comfort to the soul as well as the body.' When the birth of a child was expected, the necessary preparations included the purchasing of a whole cheese. This was indispensable, no matter what the circumstances of the family might be – it was imperative that the cheese be whole, and that it be cut for the first time on the joyous occasion. It was the prerogative of the howdie to do this. In addition to the cheese, it was usual to provide a currant or spice loaf and a bottle of whisky, for every visitor during the first two or three weeks after the event was expected to partake of all three; refusal to do so would entail bad luck on the child. A curious belief prevailed among local midwives in those days with regard to the washing of new-born infants. In doing this, the greatest possible care was exercised not to let the water touch the palms of the hands, and this care was continued for a considerable period, in the belief that to wash the palms of the hands washed away all good luck from the child. Others, again, were in the habit of throwing a live coal into the water in which the new-born infant was to be washed.[29]

Margaret Ann Clouston
Orkney, 1985

Margaret Ann Clouston was born in Orkney in 1880. She spent her entire life on these islands, and in old age could clearly recall more than a century of memories. The day after her hundred and fifth birthday she talked of the many years when she was the local midwife, called upon by countless families to deliver new babies.

MC You go whar they asked them to go . . . travelled by gig and carriage; someone took me . . . snow and storms, but I had to get there, and it was fine. Some days when I wid be called there, it would tak so long . . . [And there were] box-bed, and bed-doors – slid them along, closed in the middle. You're in pitch darkness then . . . Jist paraffin oil lamps, and rushes stickin oot o them . . . Cruisie oil – you wid nivver understand it! You peel the ooter skin off [the rushes]. And bed sacks wi chaff in them; they wir right cosy and warm tae lie in; oh nice and fine. [You'd keep the chaff] aboot half a year, then you burnt it.

   Peat fire, they built up like that. There wir a [? length] in the chimney and they hung the pot tae that; they boil the water, then we washed wir hands.

MB *Did you give anything to the mother to take if she was in pain?*

MC She wid be in plenty o pain – just suffer it oot.

MB *What sort of care did you give the mother?*

MC We jist stayed wi her until she was oot o most o her pain – until the baby got a sook of her tits.

MB *When the baby was born did the midwife cut the cord?*

MC Oh yes, get the scissors and clip it across.

MB *Did you have to boil up the scissors?*

MC I suppose we nivver paid attention, just the kitchen scissors and that was all.

---

[29] J.J. Vernon and J. McNairn. *Pictures from the Past of Auld Hawick*, 1911, pp. 89–91.

MB *How did you measure the cord?*

MC [Demonstrates: she indicated by using her fingers and pointing that the length was from the tip of the middle finger to the knuckle where it joins the hand.]

MB *What did you do with the afterbirth?*

MC Buried it . . . I wid dae it mesel, dig a hole in the garden and pit it in. It would just waste away.

MB *Did some of the mothers have difficulty nursing the baby?*

MC Oh they had lots of difficulties – and they always had it, and pain.

MB *If the baby wouldn't suck what would you do?*

MC Nothing – you could get one of the other bairns to sook.

MB *To relieve the mother? So she wouldn't have so much pressure on the breast?*

MC And they would have to sook and spit it oot – I've done it mesel.

MB *Sometimes the new baby doesn't want milk. Did you ever give it water?*

MC Oh you could.

MB *How would you feed it?*

MC Put it in a teaspoon – and be careful in case it chokes.

MB *Usually how long would the new baby take to be sucking normally?*

MC It maybe tak a week.

MB *Meanwhile did you care for the mother?*

MC You always had to care for the mother and the bairn.

MB *What would you do if the mother got a tear during the birth?*

MC Noo they stitch it up but they didna stitch in them days. We just left hir tae heal up – and it healed up tae.

MB *Was there any special care for that kind of misfortune?*

MC Nothing. Nothing till the doctors came . . . from Sooth. They wir trained when they came.

MB *Would they stay at the hospital in Kirkwall?*

MC Yes.

MB *And you would call him after the baby was born?*

MC Yes. Look at the mother, and look at the bairn. See everything was right.

MB *Do you remember anything special the doctor used to do?*

MC Nothing special . . . Whit could they dae?

MB *Did they give any medicine?*

MC No. They couldna give medicine either.

MB *Did they make any special lotion or bathing for the new mother? Like – if she had a tear, would they recommend washing in a special way?*

MC They couldna dae that in that days for there wir nothing in the hooses tae dae it wi.

MB *No bathrooms? Where did the baby sleep?*

MC In the mither's bosom.

MB *To begin with?*

MC Yes.

MB *Did they have a cradle as well?*

MC Oh yes.

MB *What kind?*

MC Rockin back an fore – wooden. They put the baby in the cradle and tied it roon so it couldna rise up. They hed no more sense, so tie it doon.

MB *When the baby was small did they ever put a special binding around the baby's middle?*

MC Oh yes.

MB *What did they do?*

MC They kept thir body straight, it wis for keeping him warm tae, jist flannel or anything.

MB *Was it a long piece?*

MC No – whit would go roon a baby wisna much.

MB *How would they fasten it?*

MC Safety pins.

MB *Did they have special treatment for the cord – the navel?*

MC They hed tae burn cloots for the cord. They burnt it in the fire . . . And they take the piece of stuff that wis left, that wisna burnt, and take the piece o stuff that wis hauded taegither and pit it on the bairns naveel.

MB *Like, it was burnt cloth they put on the navel?*

MC Yes. That's whit they done.

MB *Then they put the binding on top of that?*

MC Yes.

MB *Did they change that every day or did they leave it till it fell off?*

MC That kept it dry. I learned it off them [the doctors] – I did it then.

MB *How long would you do that?*

MC Mebbe aboot three weeks . . . until it was just, nae need for more, it was grown up [healed] and firm, and dry.

MB *And fell off?*

MC Yes.

MB *What did you do with the piece that fell off?*

MC Oh we jist buried it – we chiefly buried it, outside.

MB *Now who would do that?*

MC Sometimes the midwife. Well they hed tae dae that, it wis common to dae that . . . It wis done that way for tae keep safety in the hoose, tae hinder a rat or anything tae be in the hoose.

MB *Did the mother lie on just an ordinary chaff mattress?*

MC Aye, on a chaff mattress.

MB *Did they ever have to burn the mattress after the birth of the baby?*

MC Oh yes. And get a new one.

MB *How long did the new mother stay in bed after her baby was born?*

MC Sometimes a fortnight, and then it cam tae be less and less, and noo it jist cam tae be aboot a day.

MB *Did you stay with her all fourteen days?*

MC No you couldna dae that, ye had other folk tae go tae.

MB *How long would you stay?*

MC Mebbe aboot a day.

MB *And who would look after the mother on the other days?*

MC Jist somebody that wis experienced – jist a friend or anybody that was experienced . . . the husband he'd tae dae the work – oh he did that![30]

Meigle SWRI
Perthshire, 1932

Births were times of celebrations. The proceedings were stage-managed by the local handywoman or 'skillybuddy,' who, on her arrival, was treated to a stiff glass of whisky to fortify her. Soon as baby was born he was plunged into a basin of cold water, not by way of a bath, but to avert evil. Likewise, in the days of the peat fire, he was passed through the peat reek to avert 'the evil eye'.[31]

Dolly Wallace
Harris, 1985

MB *Can you remember anything in particular [concerning a new baby] that they were very careful about?*

DW The evil eye more than anything else – the 'droch shuil'. If somebody, that was suspected of having anything to do with the supernatural, praised a child, said what a bonny child it was, the parents disagreed with her (or him).

MB *They were afraid of people who were too complimentary to a new child?*

DW Yes! That was one thing that I do remember.

MB *Did anyone ever express a fear of any other supernatural beings, over a new child?*

DW They protected their child with all sorts of things. There was always a silver sixpence handy. Against anything really, there was always a silver sixpence in the cradle.

MB *And what about even earlier than that? Mother's confinement bed – there would not always have been a doctor at hand?*

---

[30] Mrs Margaret Ann Clouston, aged 105, was recorded in Kirkwall, Orkney, on 24 May 1985 by MB, accompanied by ethnology student Gail Chrisie. SA1985/145.
[31] *Our Meigle Book* was compiled by the women of the Meigle branch of the Scottish Women's Rural Institute as part of a national competition in 1931; p. 129.

DW No, a midwife – 'bean ghlùine'.

MB *Yes. And she would have learnt this from . . . ?*

DW Oh, probably handed down from mother to daughter . . . I can't remember the last one that was there. But she was a Mrs MacKillop.

MB *And everyone called on her?*

DW Yes! In fact I think it would have been her that would have delivered my mother.

MB *Did she stay for a few days?*

DW Oh no! She just came and delivered the child and went away again. But somebody would come and look after the mother – a sister or maybe a mother or an aunt or something would come and look after the mother for her ten days in bed.

MB *And then did the fathers have any acknowledged part in all this?*

DW Nothing at all! They were just very much in the background. They were kept well out of the road. Mostly they weren't even there. They'd be away at sea or at their fishing or crofting or somewhere.[32]

Captain Edward Burt, a soldier stationed in Inverness
Letter 'to a gentleman in London', 1726

The moment a child is born, in these northern parts, it is immerged in cold water, be the season of the year ever so rigorous.

When I seemed, at first, a little shocked at the mention of this strange extreme, the good women told me, the midwives would not forego that practice, if my wife, though a stranger, had a child born in this country.[33]

Dr David Clow
Glasgow, 1985

DC If one takes the history of resuscitation of babies we realise that babies were sometimes slow in crying and that some of them would come on with stimuli – a smack or a prod – and so grew up the traditional spanking of all babies when they are born. It's in all the text-books from way back. In spite of the fact that [*in a few extreme cases*]some were hit with such enthusiasm that they had broken backs and were left paralysed. Then the next great advance in getting babies to breathe, in modern medicine, was the realisation that cold helped the babies to breathe. They

---

[32] Dolly Wallace (née MacKenzie) was born and brought up on the Isle of Harris. She was recorded by MB at her home in Glendale on 23 July, 1985. SA1985/156.
[33] Captain Edward Burt, *Letters from a Gentleman in the North of Scotland to his Friend in London . . . begun in 1726* [hereafter cited as *Letters*], Vol. I, 1754, p. 209. The practice was still current in Scotland well into the second half of the twentieth century. There are numerous recordings from oral tradition, e.g. Calum MacLean's recording SA1953/23, printed in *Tocher*, 38, p. 52.

are normally in a warm environment. So they were put into cold water on delivery. Unfortunately some were put in head first. Then someone else had the brilliant idea that when they got far too cold this would stop them breathing, which is very true. So they put them alternately into cold and hot water, which added scalding to the list of hazards in the treatment of resuscitation. Whereas now I think we're a bit more logical, having looked at the things which work, for getting babies to breathe, we find we use what works and steer clear of those which go to extreme.[34]

Dr Harry P. Taylor
Shetland, 1948

In the early days of my professional career in Yell, forty-five years ago, when an illegitimate child was to be born, the doctor was supposed to insist on the mother divulging the name of the father of the child whose advent was about to take place. I will give one rather amusing case I had to deal with. It was mid-winter with deep snow, and not having any means of conveyance in those days I had to walk a distance of nine miles carrying my bag of tools on my back. I knew nothing about the case until I was summoned by telegram in orthodox fashion to 'come on at once . . . childbirth'. As often happened, and being a first case *(primipara)*, it was a false alarm, but the actual event not being very far off I decided to hang around until I was really needed, rather than wade home through deep snow, only to be called back again at a moment's notice, so I sent a telegram to my wife that I would be delayed indefinitely. I resigned myself to spend the time as best I could, which generally resolved itself into visiting neighbouring houses and yarning with the folk. One old lady, a humorous and witty body, who lived alone, was my hostess for a cup of tea and a chat, or shall I say a gossip. It was not very long ere she asked me 'if the lass had telt you the name o' the fayther.' I replied, No she hadn't and not being any business of mine I didn't intend to ask her, all I wanted was to get the job over and get away home. 'Ah, but my dear man, it's yer duty to fin oot, and the lass must tell you or the 'med woman' (midwife) afore ye pit a hand upon her.' The old lady then whispered to me 'Ah ken wha it was, bit ye manna tell — (the girl's name) it was me 'at telt you.' She went and took a Shetland Almanac out of her kist, looked up a page where she had put a mark on a certain date and pointing to it said 'That's the night — was wi' her. Ye'll ken him, — frae —.' It so happened that the date was very strong presumptive evidence that the old lady might be right.[35]

---

[34] Dr David Clow, Consultant Paediatrician at Creswell Maternity Hospital, was recorded in Dumfries on 6 January 1985 by MB. This is a part of his discussion on the subject of childbirth and infancy. SA1985/130.
[35] Harry P. Taylor, *A Shetland Parish Doctor*, pp. 100–01.

Iain Nicolson
Uig, Skye, 1988

Iain Nicolson was born in a thatched house in Seadar, Uig, Isle of Skye on 30 October 1903. Known locally as 'An Sgiobair' [the Skipper], he has had a lifelong interest in oral tradition and has composed many Gaelic songs. Although Gaelic is the daily language of his household, on this occasion he chose to speak in English as he 'had visitors in'.

IN It was Murchadh 'n Mhàrtainn's mother who was my midwife, the 'bean ghlùine'. Her and 'Bean Fleidsear', they was the two favourites. [The cattle that shared the dwelling] were no harm to us at all, going outside their own door. They were handy enough in the wintertime, [especially at milking time]. It wasn't the milk of the cow that our children was getting. They were from the breast, every one of them. We had eight of family and everyone of it was the mother's breast we got. But today it's the bottle everywhere. I don't say it's anything better . . . and didn't do the mothers any harm either. My mother was eighty-seven when she died and she was as strong as a bullock. [In those days if a mother couldn't feed her own child for one reason or another] the next door neighbour would come and breast feed for that baby.[36]

Martin Martin
Western Isles, *c.* 1695

[On Skye] I have observed several [of the children] walk alone before they were ten months old; they are bathed all over every morning and evening, some in cold, some in warm water; but the latter is most commonly used, and they wear nothing strait about them. The mother generally suckles the child failing of which a nurse is provided, for they seldom bring up any by hand: they give new-born infants fresh butter to take away the miconium, and this they do for several days; they taste neither sugar, nor cinnamon, nor have they any daily allowance of sack bestowed on them, as the custom is elsewhere, nor is the nurse allowed to taste ale.[37] . . . The abstemiousness of the mothers is no small advantage to the children: they are a very prolific people.[38]

---

[36] Iain Nicolson was recorded at Cuidreach by Earlish, Isle of Skye, 9 December 1988 by Thomas A. McKean and MB.

[37] The twentieth-century discovery of foetal alcohol syndrome prompted advice to pregnant women and nursing mothers to abstain from alcohol; Martin Martin, traveller, teacher, and medical physician from Skye, noted this practice existing in tradition long before formal medicine made the 'discovery'.

[38] Martin Martin, *Description*, pp. 194–5.

The limpet is parboiled with a very little quantity of water, the broth is drunk to increase milk in nurses, and likewise when the milk proves astringent to the infants. The broth of the black periwinkle is used in the same cases . . .

I had an account of a poor woman who was a native of the isle of Jura, and by the troubles in King Charles the First's reign was almost reduced to a starving condition; so that she lost her milk quite, by which her infant had nothing proper for its sustenance: upon this she boiled some of the tender fat of the limpets, and gave it to her infant, to whom it became so agreeable that it had no other food for several months together; and yet there was not a child in Jura, or any of the adjacent isles, wholesomer than this poor infant, which was exposed to so great a strait.[39]

Nan Courtney
Glasgow, 1991

NC It was only youth that saved ye: I often say we didnae know we were deprived . . . There were families born in poverty, in single ends with seven or eight living in them; Ah mind when my neighbour's last baby was born [in a single end] . . .

MB *Who delivered her baby?*

NC . . . Her mother, because that's what she did – she went out delivering babies . . . And it was very very seldom they could afford to bring in a doctor. It was only in the final stage, if there was any difficulty or else if [the mothers] were attendin the Rotten Row [Maternity Hospital] at that time they could mebbe call out a doctor . . . And the doctors came and delivered the babies, if it was a difficult case . . .

MB *Did they have any special name for these women who delivered babies?*

NC Well, they used to be called 'howdies'. A howdie – that wis a handy woman, that wis the Scotch term for handiness. They possibly attended funerals, dressed dead people, attended tae people if they wir ill. They wir first on the list tae be called out. An mebbe they worked along wi a doctor, instead o' a trained nurse.

MB *Were they paid by the people who called them out?*

NC They wir paid by the people who called them out. You hired this help-woman tae come and help ye, ye know, tae deliver the baby, and only if there wis any complications wis a doctor called in. But there wis still lots o babies born in the Maternity, Glasgow Maternity, you know . . . A set fee? Oh it would jist mebbe be about a pound, if it wis that, ye know.

---

[39] Ibid. pp. 145–6.

MB *What if a person couldn't pay?*

NC Well, it wis jist too bad. They jist mebbe paid them in kind. She would go anyway, as a rule.

MB *That's what Granny Bennett did, isn't it?*

NC That's right, she wis a howdie.

MB *Did she use the word?*

NC I don't remember her using it, but Jimmy [Nan's husband] he used to refer to them as 'rabbit catchers'!

MB *. . . You were saying that she worked along with doctors.*

NC Yes. She worked along wi Doctor Anderson . . . from Dumbarton Road in Knightswood – Yoker. She went out with him tae cases . . . She would sit with the mother, and if the labour wisnae imminent she would just be on call, you know. It was jist a case o . . . There wisnae so much telephones then, but she wid mebbe go up an doon regular, or mebbe stay if there wis a lot o difficulty she'd mebbe stay a' day.

MB *Oh . . . she used to say 'Oh I've delivered lots of babies myself.' Was it the case that if there were no complications this howdie woman would just go on and –*

NC And deliver them . . . Quite expert!

MB *[When she used to tell this to us as children] we didn't pay a lot of attention, but I realize now that she really did see life at the front line.*

NC That's right. She went out nursin people that wis ill, made their food, cleaned their houses, and attended tae them, did any dressins – that sorta thing.

MB *In her capacity as a howdie, a midwife, would she go back then, day after day till the mother was on her feet again?*

NC Yes. She would go back every day, bath the baby, attend tae it, see tae its washin an mebbe if there were other children see that they got their meals, an that sorta thing, you know.

MB *Really important to the family.*

NC Oh aye, yer granny worked wi Doctor Anderson, eh, then of course Doctor Anderson wis one o the main doctors in Blawarthill Hospital, an she worked on different cases wi him, yes.

MB *So she might have two or three of these women to go to on the one day, then?*

NC She could be . . . [Now in later years, say in the late 30s and 1940s] there wis nurses that wis trained midwives, and ye engaged them. My two boys wis born in nursing homes. That wis [early 1940s]. The doctor wis really quite happy if ye engaged to go into a nursin home, and he came to the nursin home and delivered the baby . . . When you felt your pains wir startin, ye went tae the nursin home an the doctor came in an delivered the babies. . . . Well mines wis in Balshagray . . . and it wis very good . . . it was a mother and daughter. The daughter wis a fully trained Sister and the Mother wis the Matron. But she had jist been a midwife, and they had set up this nursing home and it was really very nice, the other sister wis the cook – she did the cookin, ye know.

MB *How long did you stay in?*

NC Well we were in practically a fortnight at that particular time . . . You were booked for two weeks, mebbe a day or two earlier just before the fortnight wis up.

MB *Nowadays they make you get out of your bed the minute you've given birth – what was it like then?*

NC That's true. Well, they always advised ye, you know, they kept you in bed, and that was a rest, and you were attended tae, ye know yer meals wis brought tae ye. And you were washed and sponged an if ye were stitched, well ye had stitches taken out. But ma own paternal grandmother, my father's mother, had seventeen of a family. Now I've heard her repeat this story time an time again . . . Well, my Granny Pollock came from Ayrshire and she had some o her family in Glasgow. Well, the custom was that your neighbours always looked in on ye. And my grandfather was going out tae his work in the early hours of the mornin, an the neighbour met him and asked him how Mrs Pollock was; and he told her, whatever she had, whether it wis a boy or a girl. Well a few hours later the neighbour went ower wi a bowl o gruel, across the landin tae ma grandmother. My grandmother opened the door, and the neighbour dropped the bowl o gruel on the stairheid, she got such a shock! But my grandmother swore that she never lay a day in bed wi one, and she lived tae well intae her eighties, and she had seventeen o' a family! . . . Because even then it wis a custom for ye tae lie in bed for a day or mebbe aboot a week, ye mebbe wouldn't get as long [as a forthnight] at that particular time; but she opened the door!

MB *Was that also a custom, giving someone –*

NC Yes. Well ah think it wis jist, mebbe it would be gruel or porridge . . . oh it would be hot. . . . Or it could be pease brose . . . A neighbour comin in, just tae give a wee meal, usually there would be other children to be attended to, and [the neighbour] would mebbe put them oot tae school. That wis the custom then, the neighbours a' sort o rallied roon an that.

MB *There was a wonderful neighbourliness then?*

NC Oh yes, there was. Ah mean, everybody wis closer![40]

---

[40] Nan Courtney, aged 78, Glasgow, was recorded on 7 July 1991 by MB.

George Penny
Perth, 1836

When the inlying approached, a notice was sent to all the gossips, requesting them to repair forthwith, and give their presence at the birth. The house, of course, was very soon crowded to excess, so that in addition to the pangs of labour, the poor woman had to endure the noise and heat occasioned by such an assemblage. The child brought to light in health, was rolled up in bandages, as tight as a post, with the arms fastened down by the sides as carefully as if they were to be pinioned there for life. This accomplished, preparations were next made for *the merry meat*. A large pot was put on the fire, with plenty of butter, flour, bread, ale, and sugar, from which a strong pudding was made and served up to the company. Then the pot was filled with ale, brandy, and sugar, with the addition of a small quantity of bread, and the beverage thus formed, termed *hot pint*, was served about, until the whole, both men and women, were tolerably elevated.[41]

Margaret Wilson
Lilliesleaf, 1990

MW This knock came tae the window of the wee house . . . so my mother said 'Who's there?' . . . 'It's me, it's Mrs Scott,' she says, 'Peggy's no very well. Do you think you could come?' So ma mother said 'Yes, I'll come.' So she got up an put on her clothes and went away down. It was three or four houses further down. So she went down, and ma mother said 'Will it be the baby?'

'Oh no,' she says, 'oh no, it's no time fer the baby, it'll no be that. But,' she says 'she's no well. I dinna ken whether I should give her the doctor or not.' So ma mother went up stair to Peggy – Peggy an I went tae school together actually . . . Anyway . . . ma mother sorta kept an eye on the time, an she was having these pains an ma mother said 'I'm sure it's the baby.'

'Oh, no,' she says, 'the baby's no due.' Well, ma mother says . . . 'I think you ought to phone for the doctor because I'm sure it's the baby.' An [Peggy's] mother, although she'd brought up five of a family she wis quite in a flap about this . . . So she phoned the doctor, an ma mother stayed up wi Peggy until the doctor came, an of course, ma mother knew the doctor, so he said tae her 'Do you think you could stay an give me a han?' So ma mother said 'Yes, I would.'

So, ehm, he said he would need plenty a hot water an he'd need this an that and the next thing, see. So ma mother was doing this running up an down the stairs –

---

[41] George Penny, *Traditions of Perth*, pp 28–9.

an ma mother wisnae used wi a stair! I think the next day her legs ached because she wisnae used wi these stairs! An Peggy's mother never wint up the stair at all, 'Oh, I couldnae,' she says . . . 'oh no,' she says, 'no, I couldnae, no, no, no, no.' An every time ma mother . . . come down for somethin she's fair lookin, you know, 'Eh, is , is there, eh, anythin, eh, can I – ?'

I cannae remember her weight now, but ma mother wrote tae me (as I say, I wish I never burnt letters), she was so tiny, she wis premature . . . and she wis pit intae this, just intae a little clothes basket, cotton wool, heaps of cotton wool round her and everything [to] keep her warm . . . It's unbelievable now they're in ventilators and all the rest of it if they're premature.[42]

Wilma Forret
Kirkcaldy, 1992

MB *How did the mothers use to treat the umbilical cord?*

WF What they did was they put a penny, an old penny, in a piece of linen, and they put the penny over the belly-button and tied the piece of linen firmly round the baby's middle and stitched it on.

MB *How did they manage that with a tiny baby?*

WF Well, you just slipped your fingers under the bandage and so you were stitching it on to your own hand . . . They kept it there – they took it off to clean it – but anyway they kept it on, and this was so that you wouldn't have a protruding belly-button when the cord fell off; it would be a nice, tidy, neat one.

I thought everybody all over the country did this; that was what was done with a new baby. But in those days [1920s and '30s] they wore the barricots and binders . . . A barracot, you know, like a long petticoat, with a double [fabric] back, and you embroidered the back. It was the herringbone stitch, I remember; like a wee liberty bodice, you know, the same principle as a liberty bodice, and it wrapped over in the front – it was a wrap-over.[43]

---

[42] Margaret Wilson (1919–91) of Lilliesleaf in the Borders was recorded by Scottish Ethnology student Susan Huntly who was, at the time, preparing a dissertation on Mrs Wilson's family traditions. SA1990/18.
[43] Wilma Forret told me about this when I visited Kirkcaldy as a guest lecturer on 19 March 1992. Recorded by MB.

Care of the Mother, Then and Now

Ina Mason
Liberton Mains Farm, Midlothian, 1986

Ina Mason was born in 1918 and wrote her reminiscences in a notebook for her grandchildren.

My mother had another baby, Mary, and I remember going out for the cabbages and cutting them up to look for another baby as I had been told that's where they came from. Nowadays they know at two years old where babies come from. I think the old way was the best as nothing is a surprise now. That was 11th February and I was five in the May. Mary was a poor wee soul and bothered with twitches and fits. I often think now it was because mother was so down in body and mind with all the worry she had. . . . [When Mary was a year old, mother had twins, Em and John, then a year later she] . . . had twins when we were at Whitekirk New Mains. [They were called] Margaret and Robert. Em and John were two, I was eight, and Mary three. What a handful she must have had, and a husband who thought his meals should be on the table when he came in. Mother was very ill three days after they were born and we were all separated. I went to an Aunt and Uncle at East Linton . . . I yearned for my mother; I asked Auntie if mother was dead and she held me close on her knee and explained how ill mother had been but was getting better and as soon as she was able I would get home, but it was to be a long time as the hospital kept mother for six months. I often wonder what would have happened if it had been now.

Mother got no help from anyone when she got home although we worked as much as we could. She once kept Em off the school for a day to help her as she was feeling unwell and the 'whipper in' [school attendance officer] came to see why Em was not at school and when mother told him she was not well, he said 'Too bad but she goes back to school.' He wanted to take her then but mother's neighbour who was a great character and did not worry about anyone, said she would knock him off his bike if he took Em away, so he left but mother had to send Em to school in the afternoon. You did not get away with much in those days.[44]

---

[44] This excerpt is from an unpublished notebook titled 'My Life', written in 1986 by the late Ina Mason who compiled it for her family. I am grateful to her granddaughter-in-law, Chloe Deas, who brought it to the School of Scottish Studies in 1990.

Dr David Clow
Dumfries, 1985

DC What I have noticed, working in Cresswell Maternity here for the last ten years, is the revolution that has taken place in the care of pregnant mothers – a revolution not dictated by the medical profession but by the patients. When I first came [from Glasgow to Dumfries], down there was the standard oil-bath enema; the preparation of the complete shave of the genital area; the accent on cleanliness being next to godliness. So that these sterile objects, called pregnant women, were suitably batched, processed and delivered, with a lack of touch, perhaps of humanity, occurring in certain areas, I will certainly concede. As you see, I will defend what is defensible but not what is indefensible. With the advent of militant, vocal, intelligent mothers talking about the inanities of hospital, it's all changed. Husbands, who were seen on sufferance, are now expected to come and are actually welcomed. It's very good. It means there's always someone with the mother. Because, except for when husbands go to the toilet, they are in constant attendance, unlike nurses who are liable to be called away to manage other patients. I welcome the father being there at delivery – if he can take the process. If he can't, he's much better leaving it to those who can. Mothers are no longer shaved. All the talk of how it was essential for preventing infection disappeared when someone did a controlled trial. After some fifty or sixty years of shaving every pregnant mother, leaving them with a horrible itch as the hair grows in.

But all this has changed due to popular pressure – for the better, I am quite convinced. What worries me is that some of those who sensed what was wrong with hospitals then said 'Let's abandon hospitals.' I remain unrepentant: for the safety of the baby, women should be delivered in hospital, but there is no reason why hospitals shouldn't be human, and that they shouldn't be for the benefit of the patients and not run for the benefit of staff. But, of course, the best solution would be in fact to run your hospital so that the patient's interests and the staff's interests are identical.[45]

Hanselling the Baby

Margaret Wilson
Lilliesleaf, 1990

MW The first time [my mother saw a new baby], oh now that was something my mother didn't like to do, was to look at a new baby an not be able to have

---

[45] Dr David Clow, Dumfries, was recorded on 6 January 1985 by MB. SA1985/130.

some[thing], a coin, or something. An they used to all just lay them onto the baby's pillow. The mam would lift them after, you know; but they used to just lay them onto the pillow. Or if it's some'dy you knew well, you possibly knitted a little something or bought a little gift. But a lot of people, although they didny have a gift, it was a coin, a silver coin that they would give them . . . They thought it was unlucky to look at a child and not give them something.[46]

Betsy Whyte
Montrose, 1988

BW [Traveller women] didnae believe in keepin things about them at all. And especially if a lassie was expectin they would not allow that lassie tae keep anythin for the bairn. No even a pram. Nothing. She would be told to wait until the bairn had arrived and then she would soon get plenty for it. And if they saw a lassie or a woman take oot the baby clothes an wash them a few weeks afore the time there would be mutterins aboot the wisdom o such preparations. They thought it was really stupid.

MB *When the baby really did arrive did you have the custom of giving it silver, or giving it a gift?*

BW Oh they gave it gifts. It was always silver as you say. Money. A hansel. They hanselled the baby. Well, they would open the wee fingers and put a silver coin in. And if he kept a tight hold on it they would say 'Oh, he goin tae be a grippie one this. He's no goin tae let go o anything.' They would give as much as they could afford – a sixpence, a shilling or a half-crown.[47] The more you gave, the more luck to the giver. And if it was twins ye had tae give whatever ye had in your pockets.

MB *And was this generally done without the mother having anything to do with it? Was it just between the person giving and the baby?*

BW Just between the person and the baby. It wasn't the same if you gave it tae the mother. You had tae put it in the baby's hand. Open the wee hand and then warn the mother tae remove it. Oh aye, they could hold it tight; the younger they are, the better the grip they have. Even at a few days auld they have a strong grip.[48]

---

[46] Margaret Wilson was recorded in Lilliesleaf by Susan Huntly. SA1990/18.
[47] 2½ pence, 5 pence, and 12½ pence in today's coinage.
[48] Betsy Whyte was recorded at the School of Scottish Studies while guest at a lecture given by MB on 28 April 1988. SA1988/24.

Maureen Jelks
Dundee, 1992

MB *Maureen, when you were a wee girl can you remember your Mum doing anything special when she saw a new baby?*

MJ I don't think so, except maybe puttin a bit o silver in the pram, that wis aboot the only thing . . . It was just for good luck, an everybody did that; it was usually a sixpence or a silver thrupenny . . .

MB *When your Mum gave a baby silver did you wonder why?*

MJ No, I just took it that that was the natural thing to do. The funny thing is that I don't do it masel. I did years and years ago, but ehm, I suppose livin down in England for years you get out o the way of it, and then when you come back [you find you've gotten out of the way of the old customs]. But some people still do that, in Forfar as well they put a bit o silver in the pram, and in Dundee they still keep it up.[49]

Charles Hunter
Oban, 1994

I still have my own cheap, very thin, silver christening bowl from a Church of Scotland service in India conducted in 1928 by an army minister (Revd Lachlan MacEdward).

My wife reminded me that one of her father's neighbours in Glasgow (a very well-educated and much travelled professional man) placed a half-crown into the hand of our six week old son, in 1956, when we returned to the UK from Tripoli, Libya, where he was born.[50]

Ian R. MacIntosh
Sydney, Nova Scotia, 2003

Your mention of the silver given to babies was especially resonant for me as I still have a 50 cent piece that one of my grandmothers (Mary Belle MacIntosh of Dundee, Cape Breton, born Mary Ross in St George's Channel, Cape Breton in 1894) gave me 'for luck' when I was an infant in 1954.[51]

---

[49] Maureen Jelks is from Dundee and now resides in Kirriemuir. In 1957, at the age of 15, she left Dundee to live in England, then returned fifteen years later. She has retained a strong interest in Scottish tradition, and has been involved in traditional singing for over ten years. She was recorded at the School of Scottish Studies by MB on 2 April 1992. SA1992/02.

[50] From a letter sent to me, 22 November 1994, after Mr Hunter had attended an evening talk in Oban.

[51] E-mail, October 2003 after a series of folklore lectures I presented as part of Cape Breton's Celtic Colours Festival. As this note affirms, the custom of giving a piece of silver was also retained in the New World.

Maeve MacKinnon
Glasgow, 2001

My mother told me that shortly after my brother was born, 1986, she was at the shops pushing his pram. She had met several people, mostly mothers, whilst going round the shops and it wasn't until she had gone home that she came across eight or nine coins hidden in the hood of the pram! People had probably slipped the coins in without her noticing.[52]

Wetting the Baby's Head

Ardella Hurd
Dunkeld and Texas, 2002

MB *Ardella, you happen to be on a tour of Scotland when you got this wonderful news. Tell me about it.*

AH On the twelfth of May I called my son in Texas, because I was to be given a number eight grandchild. He and his wife gloriously had an eight-pound, thirteen-ounce little boy they named Connor Thomas, born on the tenth of May, which would have been the eleventh of May in Scotland. But I didn't find out until the twelfth of May, which in the States is Mother's Day – that makes it even more special. And so when I got the news, for the evening meal I bought two pleasantly tasting wines to share with everybody on the tour – it was called 'wetting the baby's head.' I had not heard that custom before.

MB *So how did you first hear about that?*

AH I'm not sure who told me that at the dinner. I think it was ah – Margaret Bennett [who did an after-dinner talk for the tour]. Yes, it was . . . And the next morning, before breakfast, I went out to find a shop that would make me real coffee, [*Laughs*] and it was directly across from the hotel. And when I asked the man if it was real coffee he made, and he showed me his beans! And I looked out the door and here comes Ed Miller, and Fran, and Bill Millhouse, on the tour with us, and I said 'Come in, come in, I'm having real coffee!' And one of them mentioned to the baker that I was a grandmother for the eighth time, and that we had wetted the baby's head the night before at dinner. And he said, 'Well then we shall just do it again this morning!' This is seven-thirty on Monday morning. And he slipped off in the back-shop and brought out glasses – one each for he and his wife, and one, two, three, four for us, standing there. He wanted each of us to have a little bit of

---

[52] From Maeve's essay, written while a student in my folklore class at the Royal Scottish Academy of Music and Drama.

Drambuie to wet the baby's head on this glorious Monday morning at seven-thirty. And so that's what we did – we had Drambuie and real good coffee . . . And the other really, really delightful thing was, he said, 'How much did this baby weigh?'

And I said 'eight pounds and thirteen ounces.'

And he said 'a good salmon even for the river Tay!' And I asked him to put that down on his card and he did – and his name: Ken Steven. And his wife's name was Madeline. And when I go back to Dunkeld I will surely look them up.

MB *So, your baby is well and truly celebrated.*

AH Yes. Very much so. And when I get back to Texas I will go and see that my son knows this story and that it is recorded, so that when the lad becomes old enough he too can be told – a good salmon, even for the river Tay, at eight pounds and thirteen ounces![53]

Joe McAtamney
Glasgow, 2004

MB *Joe, tell me what it means to wet the baby's head – when would that happen?*

JM Well, usually what happened is, when the baby's born and the father gets the news that the baby's arrived, he usually phones up his brothers an friends and they usually go out that night and they a' have a big booze-up. A celebration of the new arrival, commonly known in Glasgow as 'wettin the wean's heid'.

MB *Have you done that recently?*

JM About six months ago, a pal Martin Docherty had a wee girl, and we went out to the Scotia Bar.

MB *That's a singing pub – any songs?*

JM Not particularly. It was mainly just a chat, a blether about everything else. You usually just gave a toast to the man and his new child an then after that the boys reverted to talking about their normal subjects – football, whatever, whatever, whatever. But the celebration o' goin out to wet the wean's heid, och, it's quite a regular custom in Glasgow – most people I know have always done it.[54]

Elma Stanage
Falkirk, 2004

MB *What does 'wetting the baby's head' mean?*

ES You christen the bairn, have the baptism in the church, then you go back to the house and you fill the whisky glasses and you have a right good swallie.

---

[53] Ardella Hurd was recorded in Dunkeld by MB, May 2002.
[54] Recorded in Glasgow by MB, 10 April 2004.

MB *How do folk use the saying?*

ES Well there'd be the family, and the people who had been at the christening, and they'd say, 'Are you all comin back to wet the baby's head?' And there would be the christening cake and it would be cut up and served at the same time. And there was the wee cuppie tea, but in the main I think it was the whisky.

MB *Did the women take whisky?*

ES I think some of the older ones would rather have that than the wee cuppie tea [*laughs*].[55]

Baptism, Christening and Choosing a Name

Sir Donald Monro
High Dean of the Isles, 1549

The inhabitants [of Hirta, i.e. St Kilda] are simple poor people, scarce learnit in aney religion, but M'Cloyd of Herray, his stewart, or he quhom he deputs in sic office, sailes anes in the zear ther at midsummer, with some chaplaine to baptize bairnes ther, and if they want a chaplaine, they baptize ther bairns themselves.[56]

Catherine MacNeill
Breubhaig, Isle of Barra, *c.* 1870

Chuala mise an rann seo aig seann chailleachan bho chionn fada an t-saoghail. Dar a bheirte leanabh chuireadh a' bhean-ghlùin trì braona beaga burn air clàr-ung an leanabain, an aimn Athar, an ainm Mhic, and ainm Spiorad, agus theireadh i mar seo i:

> Braon beag an Athar /Dha do bhathais bhig, a luaidh.
> Braon beag a' Mhic /Dha do bhathais bhig, a luaidh.
> Braon beag an Spioraid /Dha do bhathais bhig, a luaidh.
> Dha do chomhnadh o'n a siodh, /Dha do dhionadh o'n a sluagh;
> Dha do chomhnadh o'n a frid, /Dha do dhionadh o'n a fuath;
> Dha do thasgadh dha na Tri, /Dha do dhionadh, dha do chuairt;
> Dha do ghleidheadh dha na Tri, /Dha do lionadh le na buaidh;
> Braon beag nan Tri /Dha do liobhadh le na buaidh.

---

[55] Elma, who now lives in Fife, was recorded by MB, April 2004.
[56] Sir Donald Monro, *Description of The Western Isles, 1549*, 2nd edn, 1884, p. 50.

Translation

I heard this rune from the old women in the long ago of the world. When a child was born, the midwife would put three small drops of water upon the forehead of the little one in the name of the Father, in the name of the Son, in the name of the Spirit, and she would say in this wise:

> The little drop of the Father / On thy forehead, beloved one.
> The little drop of the Son / On thy forehead, beloved one
> The little drop of the Spirit / On thy forehead, beloved one.
> To aid thee from the fays, / To guard thee from the host;
> To aid thee from the gnome / To shield thee from the spectre;
> To keep thee for the throne, / To shield thee, to surround thee;
> To save thee for the Three, / To fill thee with the graces;
> The little drop of the Three / To lave thee with the graces.

Then the midwife would give the child to a nurse to wash it, and the nurse would put a small palmfull of water on the poor little infant, and she would sing the sweetest music that ever ear heard on earth, and she would say in this wise:

> A wavelet for thy form, / A wavelet for thy voice, / A wavelet for thy sweet speech.
> A wavelet for thy luck, / A wavelet for thy good, / A wavelet for thy health;
> A wavelet for thy throat, / A wavelet for thy pluck, / A wavelet for thy graciousness;/
> Nine waves for thy graciousness.

That rune would be on the nurse's tongue till she was finished of bathing the little infant.[57]

Revd John Lane Buchanan
Western Isles, 1782

Their baptisms are accompanied with ceremonies that are innocent and useful, for cementing the peace of the country, more especially among themselves. Baptism is administered either in public or in private – just as it suits the conveniency of themselves and their minister. After this the parents present the child to some neighbour, and call him *gosti*, [*goisdidh*] or god-father; and after kissing and blessing the child, the *gosti* delivers the infant to the mother, and ever afterwards looks upon himself as bound not only to be careful of that infant, but also very much attached to the parents. They call one another *gosties* during life. This name becomes more familiar to them than their own Christian names.

---

[57] A. Carmichael, *Carmina Gadelica*, vol. 3, 1940, pp. 6–9. (The last three paragraphs are in English only.)

Nay, if they had formerly been at variance, by this simple union they become reconciled to one another. They never come to the minister, without a bottle of spirits, and are commonly merry on the occasion.[58]

Revd Walter Gregor
North-east, 1874

Baptism was administered as early as circumstances would permit, and for various reasons. Without this sacrament the child was peculiarly exposed to the danger of being carried off or changed by the fairies. It could not be taken out of the house, at least to any great distance, or into a neighbour's, till it was baptised. It could not be called by its name till after it was baptised. It was unlawful to pronounce the name, and no one would have dared to ask it. At baptism the name was commonly written on a slip of paper, which was handed to the minister. Death might come and take away the young one, and if not baptised its name could not be written in the 'Book of Life,' and Heaven was closed against it. Many a mother has been made unhappy by the death of her baby without baptism; and, if the child fell ill, there was no delay in sending for the minister to administer the holy rite, even although at a late hour at night. It was a common belief that in such cases the minister either 'killed or cured'. There was an undefinable sort of awe about unbaptised infants, as well as an idea of uncanniness in having them without baptism in the house.

The system of registration has in a great measure put an end to this anxiety for having the child early baptised.

'Oh, Sir,' said the wife of a working man to the minister, on asking him to baptise her child along with others, whose mothers were present, 'this registration's the warst thing the queentry ever saw; it sud be deen awa wi athegeethir.'

'Why?' asked the minister in astonishment at the woman's words and earnestness of manner.

'It'll pit oot kirsnin athegeethir. Ye see the craitirs gets thir names, an we just think that aneuch, an we're in nae hurry sendin for you.' Baptism was administered sometimes in private and sometimes in public. The child was dressed in white, and wore a fine cap. It was commonly the sick-nurse that carried in the infant, handed it to the father, and received it from him after baptism. On the conclusion of the rite in private, bread and cheese, with

---

[58] Revd John Lane Buchanan, *Travels in the Western Hebrides, 1782–90,* [hereafter cited as *Travels*] pp. 168–9.

whisky, were set before the guests. It would have been regarded as an utter want of respect, and unlucky, not to have partaken of the bread and cheese, and not to have put the glass with whisky to the lips. In doing so, there were repeated the words – 'Wissin the company's gueede health, an grace an growan to the bairn.' Sometimes, instead of the latter phrase, were substituted the words, 'Fattenin an battenin te the bairn'. A feast usually followed.

Each guest gave a small gift in money to the child, and the sum so given was the nurse's fee.

The child must sleep in its baptismal dress.

In sprinkling the water, all care had to be used to keep it from entering the eyes, as it was believed that the least drop of it entering the eyes opened them to the seeing of ghosts in the journey of life.

When the water fell upon the child, unless it cried it was augured that it would be short-lived, and it is said that, if it did not cry, the woman who received it from the father handled it roughly, or even pinched it, to make it utter the desired cry.

The water of baptism was carefully kept for a time – at least eight days – and then reverentially poured below the foundation of the dwelling-house; or it was drunk, under the belief that it strengthened the memory. Alongside the basin with the water needed for the rite, some placed bread and a Bible.

If the child was taken to a neighbour's house at a distance, or to church to be baptised, the woman who carried the child carried also some bread and cheese, and another of the party was provided with a bottle of whisky and a *dram glass*. The person first met received bread and cheese and a *dram*, and usually turned, and walked a short distance. If it was a woman that was first met, she carried the baby as far as she went. One of the cloths indispensable to a baby was also carried, and cast away by the road.

If a boy and a girl were to be baptised together, the greatest care was taken to have the parents so placed that the minister must baptise the girl first. If there was the least suspicion of the minister reversing the order, great uneasiness was manifested, and if he did proceed to baptise the boy first, the girl was put forward, and when baptised first a gleam of satisfaction lighted up the faces of the girl's friends. This procedure was followed under the belief that, if the boy was baptised before the girl, he left his beard in the water, and the girl got it.

If it happened that a girl was brought to church to be baptised, and returned without baptism, she died unmarried.

In returning home a neighbour by the wayside took the party in, and prepared a dish called in Gaelic *fuarag*. It was made of oatmeal and cream, or of oatmeal and whisky. Each of the party received a spoonful, and a small portion was put into the child's mouth.[59]

Alexander MacDonald
Inverness-shire, 1914

Among the most important events in the life of the country homestead are, of course, birth and baptism, and in this respect our district was no exception. But child-bearing, even among the olden time Highlanders, had its risks and troubles; and those would seem to have been not only the more or less usual physical ones, but also such as were believed to be of a nature somewhat beyond. The nurse, *a' bhean-ghluine*, was always present – the doctor is a very modern innovation in the capacity of midwife – and she rendered the best aid possible. Generally her skill was two-fold: she certainly was not ignorant of midwifery – she had to have been a mother herself; and she knew a lot about the various rites which had to be practised by way of counteracting the influence and interference of the thousand and one spirit powers that had always to be guarded against. In far back times charms and spells, with their appropriate incantations, were much in vogue at births, by way of warding off mishaps, but later, herbs were more resorted to, which showed a significant advance.

Partly from the fear of uncanny possibilities, and also, no doubt – in later times – from the influence of preaching against the neglect of baptism, and the fear of the awful consequences in the event of death without receiving the benefit of that sacrament, the people attached much importance to the rite. Most persons, especially Roman Catholics, were careful that their children should be baptised within eight days of birth. Generally speaking this was observed with a degree of attention which went to show that considerable importance attached to it. All things considered, then, the baptism of a child was frequently an event in the countryside. The hoary-headed spectre, superstition, played its part in connection with the function in many ways. If a word of the baptismal service was lost – not distinctly spoken by the minister – the child would grow up to be a somnambulist; if a girl and boy were being baptised at the same time, and that the respective names were by mistake transposed, the former would have a man's beard, and the latter a woman's bare face. These were, of course, dreadful considerations, and great precautions were taken to ensure that there would be no hitch. And there was also a wicked influence believed to be abroad, known as *An Droch Shuil* ('The

---

[59] W. Gregor, *Echo*, pp. 96–100, and *Notes*, pp. 11–13.

evil eye'), which was thought to have a particular predilection for exercising its powers on infants; and no doubt it was by way of presenting its ravages that the very old charm called 'The Bathing Blessing' was at one time commonly resorted to in many places. As the child was being bathed the following lines were repeated:

> Boiseag air t'aois,
> 's boiseag air t'fhas,
> 's air do chuid a ghabhail ort;
> 's a chuid nach fhasadh anns an oidhche dhiot,
> Gu 'm fasadh anns an latha dhiot:
> Tri baslaichean na Trianaid Naoimh,
> Ga d' dhion 's ga d' shabhaladh
> Bho bheum sul,
> 's bho chraos fharmad nam peacach.

which, translated, means:

> A palmful of water for your years,
> A palmful of water for your growth,
> And for your taking of your food;
> And may the part of you which grows not during the night
> Grow during the day:
> Three palmfuls of the Holy Trinity,
> To protect and guard you
> From the effects of the Evil Eye,
> And from the jealous lust of sinners.[60]

Meigle SWRI
Perthshire, 1932

Up until recently, children on the Kinloch estate were not considered properly baptised unless with water from the Lady's Well.[61]

---

[60] Alexander MacDonald, *Song and Story from Loch Ness-side*, pp. 13–41.
[61] Meigle SWRI, *Our Meigle Book*, p. 130.

Sandy Stanage
Carnbee, Fife, 2004

MB *Does this well have a name?*

SS It's just the Carnbee Christening Well.

MB *And how would it feature in the life of the community?*

SS When there's a christening, the minister stops at the well on his way to the church, scoops out fresh running water from it, and carries it to the church to put in the christening font. So all the babies are baptized from this water.[62]

Gladys and Charles Simpson
Keith, 1985

The Simpsons both grew up in the town of Keith in Banffshire. Although they left there more than forty years ago to live in Skye, they both have clear recollections of many aspects of the customs that characterised the way of life in Banffshire in the 1920s.

MB *Did they have christenings [in Keith]?*

GS Oh indeed they had christenings.

CS Mostly christenings were at home. In the house.

MB *Was there cake? Or ever the top layer of a wedding cake?*

CS I just can't remember about that at all. That's strange now. You remember about the deaths but not the christenings!

GS We had a christening robe in the family which I think I still have, that all the babies were christened in – a special lacy robe.

MB *When somebody had a new baby was it a tradition to give the baby a gift?*

GS Oh yes! Of money! Silver!

MB *And was it into the baby's hand?*

GS Yes, into the baby's hand. And if the baby gripped it he would be all right. But if he let it go he would be a spendthrift. In fact I still do give every baby in the village – usually a 50 pence piece now. And I was very surprised, and rather hurt, that one mother refused to take it. But she wasn't a [local] girl. She came from [the South] actually.

MB *Yes, she probably thought this was the right thing to do.*

GS Well, I said it was for luck. We just used to say it was a penny for luck.

CS She would think maybe you needed the 50 pence yourself!

GS But if you met a woman with a new baby, even in the street, even if you only knew her slightly, you always put at least half-a-crown in the baby's hand.[63]

[62] Sandy grew up in Glasgow and moved to Fife. Recorded by MB.

[63] Mr and Mrs Charles Simpson from Keith, Banffshire, were recorded by MB in their home in Armadale, Skye, on 5 May 1985. SA1985/141.

Ishbel Morris
Aberfeldy, 1990

IM Granny McDougal, who lived further up the road, and Granny Irvine, the minute
that a baby was imminent, and heaven knows, I was the last of my family, but
apparently, when the stoor got up, they flew about, kettles of water, pans of water,
sheets, towels, everything, and the baby was delivered with no fuss at all, and it was
carried triumphant – even if it arrived through the night – the brothers and sisters
were disturbed. 'Look what we've got for you now!' Whether they were pleased or
not might be debatable! But there was great pride if a baby was safely delivered,
washed, sorted out. My sister's last recollection – I was the youngest of my family
– but she said that she was poked into wakefulness, about two a.m. and this thing
was presented to her. 'Here's a wee sister for you! That's what you wanted.' She
had two brothers already. And she said I was in a black shawl, and she thought 'If
that's all I'm going to get, I would as soon do without!'

NM *And when it came to the christening, would they have it in the church, or in the house?*

IM In these days, it was preferable in the house, because we didn't make a great ***thing***
about it, it was done properly and reverently in the house, and the minister came,
and there was one crystal bowl, tucked aside for that sort of occasion.[64]

Mrs Janet Faulds
Fionnphort, Isle of Mull, 1994

MM *You had a lovely story of your father bringing the minister over [from Iona to
Fionnphort] to christen the Livingstones . . . What was that again?*

JF He christened them in their bed.

MM *Was there a new baby?*

JF No, none of them had ever been christened. The whole nine were there . . . and [four
or five of the youngest ones] were put in the one bed so as they could be christened –
every one of them at once. The [ones in bed] were sound asleep, [in a wee row].

MM *And you were a wee girl . . . ?*

JF I was a wee girl and was allowed– my mother was a midwife and was at every one
of their births. And when my father [Coll Maclean, the ferryman] brought the
minister over – it was sort of in the early evening and we were allowed in. I
remember him sprinkling the water over them and he did the service as though he
was in a church! Oh, it was lovely – it's great memories.[65]

---

[64] Ishbel Morris, aged *c.* 70, Aberfeldy, was recorded by Neil MacGregor on 5
November 1990.
[65] Janet Faulds, born 1904, was recorded by Mairi MacArthur in Fionnphort on 29
April 1994. Words in square brackets are from a later interview.

Queen Victoria
Balmoral, 1868

A Highland 'Kristnin' (Christening)
Sunday, October 24.

At a quarter to four I drove, with Louise, Beatrice and Lady Ely, to John Thomson the wood forester's house for the christening of their child, three weeks old. Here, in their little sitting-room, in front of the window, stood a table covered with a white cloth, on which was placed a basin with water, a bible, and a paper with the certificate of the child's birth.

We stood on one side, and John Thomson in his Highland dress next the minister, who was opposite me at the head of the table. Barbara, his wife, stood next to him, with the baby in her arms, and then the old Thomsons and their unmarried daughter, the Donald Stewarts, Grants, and Victoria, Morgan and sister, and Brown.

Dr Taylor (who wore his gown) then began with an address and prayer, giving thanks 'for a living mother and a living child', after which followed another prayer; he then read a few passages from Scripture, after which came the usual questions which he addressed to the father, and to which he bowed assent. Then the minister told him – 'Present your child for baptism.' After this the father took the child and held it while the minister baptized it, sprinkling it with water, but not making the sign of the cross, saying first to those present: 'The child's name is Victoria' and then to the child:

> Victoria, I baptize thee in the name of the Father, and of the Son, and of the Holy Ghost, One God blessed for ever – Amen.
>
> The Lord bless thee and keep thee! The Lord make His face to shine upon thee and be gracious unto thee! The Lord lift up His countenance upon thee and give thee peace!

The service was concluded with another short prayer and the usual blessing. I thought it most appropriate, touching, and impressive. I gave my present (a silver mug) to the father, kissed the little baby, and then we all drank to its health and that of its mother in whisky, which was handed round with cakes. It was all so nicely done, so simply, and yet with such dignity.[66]

---

[66] Queen Victoria, *More Leaves from the Journal of A Life in the Highlands from 1862 to 1882*, pp. *77–8*. Queen Victoria described 'A Second Christening, 1868', held on Monday 1 November, where the baby was named Albert. She noted similarities and differences between the two christenings. Likewise, at the christening of my god-daughter in Bishopbriggs in 2004, the congregation sang 'The Lord bless thee and keep thee'. My gift to her was a silver bracelet, engraved *Mia 12-09-04.*

John Firth
Orkney, 1920

To be invited to a *cirsening,* as it was termed [in Orkney], was esteemed a high honour. The women dearly loved the gossip, and though the fare was plain and homely, consisting of scones, bread, cheese and ale, there was plenty of it; and if their minds were more affected by the glass of whisky with which the feast was rounded off than by the solemnity of the preceding ceremony, who, that recognizes the gloom and austerity of their daily life, shall dare condemn them?

To have been 'bapteezed oot o' ae water' was looked upon as a permanent bond of friendship; but in the event of a male and female being presented at the same time, the minds of the parents were sorely exercised as to the order of arrangement before the minister, so that the male child should be baptized before the female; for, if it should happen otherwise, fears were entertained that the girl, on reaching womanhood, would be afflicted with a full flowing whisker, while the other would remain beardless to the end of his days.[67]

Thomas Pennant
Traveller, 1776

After baptism, the first meat that the company tastes is *crowdie*[68], a mixture of meal and water, or meal and ale thoroughly mixed. Of this every person takes three spoonfuls.

The mother never sets about any work till she has been *kirked.* In the church of Scotland there is no ceremony on the occasion: but the woman, attended by some of her neighbours, goes into the church sometimes in service time, but oftener when it is empty; goes out again, surrounds it, refreshes herself at some public house, and then returns home. Before this ceremony she is looked on as unclean, never is permitted to eat with the family; nor will any one eat of the victuals she has dressed.

It has happened that, after baptism, the father has placed a basket, filled with bread and cheese, on the pot-hook that impended over the fire in the middle of the room, which the company sit around; and the child is thrice handed across the fire, with the design to frustrate all attempts of evil spirits,

---

[67] John Firth, *Orkney,* p. 78.
[68] *Crowdie* is not, as Pennant says, 'a mixture of meal and water'; it is akin to cottage cheese, made by letting sour milk stand in a warm place till it separates into curds and whey. The curds are strained, thus producing crowdie, which is sometimes mixed with cream or simply eaten on oatcakes or scones.

or evil eyes. This originally seems to have been designed as a purification, and
of idolatrous origin, as the *Israelites* made their children pass through the fire
to *Moloch*. The word used for charms in general is *Eolas* or *Knowledge*, a proof
of the high repute they were once held in. Other charms were styled *Paiders*, a
word taken from the *Pater noster*. A necklace is called *Padreuchain*, because on
turning every bead they used one of these *Paiders*. Other charms again are
called *Toisgeuls*, from the use of particular verses of the Gospel.[69]

J.J. Vernon and J. McNairn
Hawick, 1911

[In Hawick] when a christening was about to take place, it was all-important,
before setting out for the church, to cut a bit of cheese and a piece of cake,
wrap them in paper, place them on the breast of the infant, and give them to
the first person met on the way – or, rather, if the infant was a boy, to the first
female; if a girl, to the first male . . . When baptism was administered in
private, a numerous company of relatives and friends were invited to be
present at the ceremony, and bread, cheese, and whisky were supplied, of
which all were expected to partake. Each guest gave a small sum of money to
the child, and the sum so given was termed the howdie-fee or nurse's
perquisite.[70]

The Town Council
Aberdeen, 1624

Feb. 18. – The Town Council of Aberdeen had occasion to consider an abuse
which had lately crept into their burgh, in the form of 'costly banqueting at
the baptism of bairns,' and the 'convocating of great numbers of people
thereto.' It is mentioned that on these occasions there were 'all sorts of
succours [sugars], confections, spiceries, and dessert, brought from foreign
parts, beside great superfluity of venison, and wild meat of all sorts . . . and
withal, extraordinary drinking and scolling [health-drinking] . . . to the
slander of the town, in sic a calamitous time, when God is visiting the whole
land with dearth and famine, and many poor anes [are] dying and starving at
dykes and under stairs for cauld and hunger.'

The Council ordained that hereafter no person of whatever degree should
have 'mair than four gossips and four cummers at the maist' at their

---

[69] Thomas Pennant, *Tour*, vol. ii, pp. 45–6.
[70] J.J. Vernon and J. McNairn, *Pictures from the Past of Auld Hawick*, 1911, pp. 91–3.

baptisms, that not more than six women be invited 'to convoy the bairn to and frae the kirk,' and that twelve should be the utmost amount of company present 'at the dinner, supper, or afternoon's drink.' All extravagances at table were at the same time strictly forbidden.[71]

Margaret Bennett
Diary entry, 2003

Dec. 28, 2003. The Sunday after Christmas, not only the last Sunday of the year, but also the last christening of 2003 in St Michael and All Saints' Church. The nativity scene, with the baby Jesus in the crib, Mary and Joseph beside him and the shepherds looking on, take on a special meaning for this occasion. Everyone received a candle along with the day's order of service intimating a baptism. No names are included – simply 'The priest addresses the parents and grandparents.' We find out that Paula is from Edinburgh and Will is from Hamilton; they had been married here, the bride's church.

When the priest ends his sermon, the baptism begins with the singing of 'Away in a manger'. The parents, godparents and baby move to the front of the church, the 'house-lights' fade and Father Kevin leads the group down the aisle, to the back of the church where they gather round the baptismal font. During the singing, the congregation light their candles and turn to watch. More than a hundred little candles have an amazingly special effect in the church and on all the faces watching the baby being handed over to Father Kevin. Solemn vows are said around this tiny person with the long name: William Peter Hamilton Frame. He makes not a sound as the baptismal water wets his head, and finally the priest holds a candle for him, saying 'Receive this light, Peter. This is to show that you have passed from darkness into light. Shine as a light in the world to the glory of God the Father . . .' The newly welcomed baby is carried round the church, so we can not only see him but may also appreciate the importance of tradition to his family – he is dressed in the christening robe that first belonged to his maternal great-great-grandfather and his shawl is a beautiful embroidered cashmere heirloom from his father's family.

In the church porch where the congregation usually gather for a cup of tea after the service, everyone is offered glass of champagne and a piece of christening cake to celebrate. And finally, a tray of christening favours is handed round – I'd never seen this at a christening before: sugared almonds

---

[71] Robert Chambers, *Domestic Annals of Scotland*, 1885 edn, pp. 224–225, quoted from David Calderwood, *History of the Kirk of Scotland*, 1842. [The square brackets are Chambers'.]

in a dainty little package adorned with nursery-type picture and tied with a little ribbon. I ask where are they from. France, I'm told. But that's not as far away as the home of the christening party, as Paula and Will moved to California last year. Even though baby Peter was born in San Francisco on August 20, it was important for them to come home to have him christened. The men wore kilts, including the godfather, who happens to be Californian – he's delighted and honoured to be part of the celebration. They will all fly back to California reassured that little Peter belongs to this old Edinburgh church and that his roots are firmly planted in Scotland.

Rose MacDonald
Glasgow, 2004

RM Oh, well the christening robe, there were various kinds, you know – some were handsome and others were not so handsome. I think it all depended on how much the people could spend. In recent years I think I've only seen two in our church [in Ibrox] . . . And shawls – I've only seen about two babies come in wi' these. And it brings back memories of sewing them. [laughs]

I'm going back a long time, now, you know – well over sixty years. And it was really the awfully well off people that got those christening shawls. This shop that I worked in, it was all mohair and things like that they sold, but there was only about a dozen shawls brought in at any time. They were done in Paisley Mill and brought to where our place was. One of the van men would bring them to save us time, because in those days you had to work hard. It was that fine cashmere – it was absolutely beautiful! And there was only two of us who made the shawls. This woven cashmere came to us in the raw state – oh, it was beautiful. Very, very delicate to handle. And first of all we'd to put a hem on it, by machine, round the whole thing. We did that first and then we got the fringes, and they were absolutely beautiful. They were about 12 inches long, you know, and it was like loops, you know – in gorgeous silk. It was like silk cord, and they came, not in balls, or anything like that, because the fringes were too long – they came on a board, and they'd hang on the board. But they were very difficult to sew on. Once you got the hemming done, that was it ready for the fringe. It took us a long time, but we didn't get a lot of them to do, because it wasn't at that time, you know, it was better off people that had these shawls.

MB *What colour were they?*

RM Oh, the faintest cream was the base, but the fringes were white – gleaming, absolutely gleaming. And I must say they always complimented us. Oh, they were lovely, and when we finished, all the girls that worked up the stair came down to see these lovely shawls.

MB *When it came to the christening, then, the shawl would be the big show-piece?*

RM Oh, yes, it was lovely. And everybody'd be like this [craning their necks] to see this baby! It's happy memories for me.[72]

Nan Courtney
Glasgow, 1991

MB *Can you tell me about christenings in your day?*

NC It used to be the custom they'd have long long robes, and there was cashmere shawls – had to be the best cashmere shawl! . . . usually they were handed down fae one generation to another (or you borrowed one), but the cashmere shawl was really the creme! . . . They were bundles o [Ayrshire] lace, and then they had capes on the babies too. And petticoats! Oh, the work that was involved in dressin a baby at that particular time was unbelievable, you know! They had fancy capes, made into sorta, I think it wis a sorta [white] flannel wi braid round them, you know, and then this cashmere shawl . . . it wis the custom round about Glasgow an that, the cashmere was really the thing . . . An then of course they had woollen shawls too, but the big long cashmere, woven, wi a lot o embroidery on it, an big silk fringes . . . always white, embroidery too . . . An wee bonnets for boys, an the girls wore wee bonnets too, but a boy's bonnet wis round with sorta, what we called 'lappit' . . . it wis ribbon a' round the inside, fashionable, an swan's down. Ah always remember ma cousin in America, when her son was born, she sent over for a 'right boy's bonnet', and it had tae come out o Cromars's on Crown Street, an it wis sent over tae America – it wis a right boy's bonnet, you know, wi the swan's down an the right shape.

MB *And did the girls not have swan's down?*

NC Oh yes! It was . . . a hood shape. The boys' were round, you know – they come right round the crown but the girls' wis the hood shape, you know the bonnet shape wi the thingmy, you know, an the veil; it had tae huv a veil . . . oh it wis really quite an event, you know, the christenin!

MB *Was there a tradition of godmothers[73] or godfathers?*

NC Oh yes, there wis godmothers.

MB *How would you choose a godmother?*

NC Well usually the custom in – I don't know about any of the rest o the places but usually in Glasgow it wis whoever was your bridesmaid, you know, an ah wis this girl's particular bridesmaid, you know, an [when her baby was christened] we'd to go over to this church [in Bridgeton].

---

[72] Rose (b. 1911) was recorded by MB for her project and exhibition 'See When You Look Back', featured in Ibrox Library, March to April 2004.

[73] In the Church of Scotland the term 'godmother' is not generally used. The female friend who carries the baby into church is generally referred to as the 'supporter'.

MB *Was there usually a godfather too?*

NC Not always.

MB *Did the godmother have any duties afterwards?*

NC Well, you always, eh, had a very special corner in your heart, an you always kept in touch, till such time as you move out their kenning athegither, you know.

MB *And when the baby was christened did folk use to make a christening piece?*

NC It was an old Scottish custom; well it wis still carried on in Glasgow – when a baby was taken out to be christened the custom was ye made up what was called a 'christening piece'. Now the christening pieces that I remember was made up of Abernethy biscuits, thick with butter, and spread with carvey, and it was put in a poke and a piece of silver, sometimes a half-crown, sometimes a sixpence, it all depended on what the people could afford. And you had to accept that piece – it was called a lucky piece, christening piece. You had to eat it, or the baby would not have been lucky. It was for the luck, and it was jist an old Scottish custom.

MB *Did you never get one?*

NC No, but I had taken my friend's baby. I was her bridesmaid and we made up the piece on our way out to have the baby christened. And that was during the depression in Glasgow in the early 'thirties. And we had to take the baby over tae a church in Bridgeton. And the minister, ye just gave him five shillings. But on the way out we met a wee girl and we gave her the christening piece. And it was supposed to be lucky for the one who received the christening piece as well as the baby.[74]

John MacLeod of Dalquhurn
Renton, Dunbartonshire, 1859

Old customs and superstitious beliefs, similar to those of other countries, prevailed here, such as reading cups, forecasts from dreams, and spaeing fortunes . . . At birth, there was the danger of being carried away by fairies or being injured by the influence of an evil eye; and many charms were used as a protection and preventative, particularly before baptism. The woman who carried the child to church to be baptised must be a lucky person. She carried with her a parcel of bread and cheese to be given to the first person she met, as a gift from the baby. Forecasts were made of the future of the child from the character of the person who received the gift.[75]

---

[74] Nan Courtney was recorded by MB on 7 July 1991.
[75] From a lecture to the Renton Literary Association, *c.* 1859, quoted by Revd John Kennedy in his introductory 'Memoir' of Dr Alexander Cameron; *Reliquiae Celticae*, p. lxxxi.

Hugh Hagan and Howard Mitchell
Port Glasgow and Lennoxtown respectively, 1991

HH Christening pieces? Well, I remember as a boy getting christening pieces. Well, ye gathered aboot cos ye knew yer mother wid send ye oot, somebody wis goin tae get their wean christened and ye would go out, ye knew there'd be a christening piece gonnae go. And when the family came oot they wid gie it tae the first boy or wee lassie that they seen, depending on what sex the wean wis. If the wean wis a wee lassie they gied it tae the first boy, and if the wean wis a wee boy they gied it tae the first lassie they met on the street. And you got this poke wi a christening piece in it.

MB *What was it?*

HH Aye well, it was always a piece o some description, whether it'd be butter or jam or whatever'd be on it.

MB *White bread?*

HH Aye. Normally, aye – just whitever they had in the hoose. I don't suppose it would matter, just whitever they had, make up a piece o somethin. That, and mebbe a biscuit or somethin, in a wee poke, you know.

MB *Did you know what it was about?*

HH When we wir weans? Not really! Jist somebody giein ye a piece and a biscuit in a poke and that wis good enough! [*Laughs*] That wis it! Ye weren't particularly interested in whit it wis all aboot ye know. But later on in life, like roon aboot noo, like, when my sisters hud weans, they done the same thing, and ye remember it from then, and it wis quite an important thing tae dae, like – they thought it wis quite important tae get a christenin piece. But they nivver handed it oot [in the same way] because the weans never run aboot the streets they way they did when we were young. So they would jist, when they came oot the chapel eftir the christening, they wid gie it tae the first wean cos the christening wid usually be after a mass, you know, so there would always be a load o people about anyway. Then they wid jist gie it tae some wean comin oot the chippie, you know . . . Twenty year ago . . . Fae when I remembered them as a wee boy? Aye, mid-sixties. I was born in '59, so it'd be mid-sixties – '66, '67 – just aboot the time when Celtic won the European cup, you know! [*Laughs*] Just thought Ah'd get that on tape you know!

HM I hope this is going to be edited!

MB [*To Mitch*] *You had the same thing?*

HM Yes, although I never went looking for it – I was a complete innocent! I wasn't one of these town boys, you know! I was in the country, aye, Lennoxtown. It'd be about 1961, '62; I'd be six or seven. I jist remember comin home from school at dinner time one day and bein sort of summoned fae the garden gate. 'C'm 'ere!' And they jist handed me this, wrapped up in a [table] napkin and said 'That's eh . . . our daughter's jist been christened – There ye are!' And I wis totally flabbergasted. But it wis two digestive biscuits wi butter and a half a crown wrapped up in the paper napkin.

MB *Did somebody explain to you at the time?*

HM Well, my mother explained a wee bit, but not very much. And it's the only time I've ever seen it or heard of it. It's probably more a Catholic thing?

HH I couldn't tell ye! I know it's done regularly. It's very common tae be done amongst Catholics, you know, but I wouldn't know whether it's more a Catholic thing or no. It wis very, very common, I remember quite a lot when I wis a wean. I don't remember getting quite a lot, but I remember getting wan or two, ye know, up the street.[76]

Audrey Fletcher
East Kilbride, 2003

We originally come from Bridgeton, Glasgow, and now living in East Kilbride, although still travelling to Bridgeton St Francis-in-the East Church of Scotland every Sunday. The custom of the christening piece seems to have been handed down from generation to generation and the last time our family did it, to my knowledge, is when my own daughter was christened in 1992. The only difference to what you say is that we gave it on the way to church and not necessarily to the first child . . . The baby was carried to and from the church by a supporter (godmother), and the baby's mother prepares the piece. As to the wrapping, I believe I wrapped mine in tin foil.[77]

May Anderson and Nan Millar
Ibrox, Glasgow, 2004

MA Christening piece. Well, it's two Abernethy biscuits wi a piece of silver in between. An' if it's a wee baby girl you give it to the first boy you meet, or the first man, and vice versa; if it's a wee boy you give it to the first lady.

MB *And who prepares it?*

MA The baby's mother.

MB *Is that the same with you, Nan?*

NM Aye, two Abernethy biscuits The silver is in between the biscuits.

MA Put butter on it and then put in the money and go like that [like a sandwich].

NM And if they knew there was a christening, a baby goin to be christened [in days gone by], they would a' try to get first, you know. An' whoever was first got it. Because it was a two-shillin piece – to get that was for luck.

---

[76] Hugh Hagan and Howard Mitchell were recorded by MB in Edinburgh, 6 February 1991.

[77] Sent in an e-mail, November 2003.

MB *Would they eat the biscuit as well?*

NM I don't know if they ate the biscuit but I think they jist wanted a two shillin piece in thae days! That was a lot of money then, you know.

MA I don't think they do it now, though. I never see it now.[78]

John Firth
Orkney, 1920

It was not customary then, as now, to have the child's name written on a slip of paper ready to be handed to the officiating clergyman . . . The naming of an infant caused much cogitation on the part of the parents. Every well-cared-for child must needs be provided with a name-father and name-mother, after whom or by whom it received its name. It was the duty of the name-mother to carry the child into church; and, though the name-father and name-mother did not assume the part of sponsors, they were expected to take a special interest in their name-child; and it was hoped by the parents that their little one might inherit at least the virtues and graces, if not anything of monetary value, from its name-parents. The name of the new baby was guarded with great secrecy. For that to become public before baptism was regarded as detrimental to the child's best interests, and anyone making enquiry regarding the name was looked upon with disfavour. In connection with this an amusing dialogue took place between the first official registrar of the then united parishes of Firth and Stenness and a man who came to record the birth of his child. The man willingly and unhesitatingly gave all particulars necessary for filling up the schedule except the child's name, and that, he affirmed, he would not disclose to any man but the minister. The registrar explained over and over again why the name must be given, but the man remained obdurate, asserting that the name could not be revealed till it had been announced at baptism. 'Well,' said the registrar at last, 'it will cost you a day's journey back here, and I shall fine you a shilling besides.' The man turned round and for a few minutes gazed through the window in profound meditation. Then suddenly wheeling round, he burst out, 'Bi me saul! I'll risk hid' and in hesitating voice he mentioned his daughter's name.

Prior to the passing of the Registration Act, 1855, the only record of births was the list of baptisms kept by the minister, and very often when changes came in the ministry those records were lost. It was, however, customary to have a list of all the names of a family, with their dates of birth, written out in

---

[78] Nan and May were recorded by MB.

the big Family Bible, and if this were omitted there was seldom any other means by which ages could be ascertained. In passing, it may be mentioned that in the absence of any other available data the Family Bible is frequently used by the Pension Officer when determining whether or not the applicant has reached the age to qualify him or her for an Old Age Pension.[79]

Alexander Polson
Caithness, 1907

It is considered especially unlucky that [a child] should be baptized in another year than that in which it was born – hence the great number of baptisms annually taking place during the last weeks of December. Then, whatever arrangements parents may make between themselves as to what the little one's name is to be, they take care not to let an outsider call it anything but 'Baby' until it has been christened. Even at the ceremony, many prefer not to speak its name; and for that purpose they hand the acting clergyman a slip on which the name is written, so that it may first be spoken by his lips.[80]

Scotland has a wealth of anecdotes about choosing children's names.

George Penny
Perth, 1836

The baptism always took place in church; the minister seldom inquired the name till he was about to confer it. On one occasion, a Highlandman had determined to call his child after Prince Ferdinand, a great warrior at the time. When asked for the name, he had either forgot it, or mispronounced it; for the clergyman, thinking he meant to name his child after some of his Gaelic ancestors, christened it 'Fartin Andrew', by which mortifying appellation the young hero was ever after distinguished. To avoid mistakes of this nature, one clergyman never named the children he baptized. The plan of handing up the name written on a slip of paper obviated this difficulty; although in one instance it was productive of a somewhat ridiculous mistake. On the occasion of getting any new article of dress, it was customary for the drouthy cronies to exact a certain donum – on the payment of which the owner was exempt from further annoyance: the article was then said to be *sealed*. An individual who had mustered an addition to his wardrobe, in order

---

[79] John Firth, *Orkney*, pp. 78–80.
[80] Alexander Polson, 'Folklore', p. 92.

to improve his personal appearance at his child's christening, when the minister asked the name, he in mistake handed up a document certifying that his new coat had been duly *sealed* the previous evening. On another occasion, a man presented a merchant's account instead of the child's name. The clergyman, being an eccentric character, read aloud the first item, 'Twa ells and a half o' plaiding!' exclaiming 'Wha ever heard o' such a name for a bairn?'[81]

Bill Salton
Edinburgh, 1992

BS My former minister, the Very Revd Dr Bill Johnston, had a fund of stories about the Kirk and its characters.

One that I remember particularly clearly concerned the man who brought his infant daughter for christening, and when asked what name she was to be given was heard to mutter something like 'Spindoana'.

'Spindoana,' said the minister, 'that's a strange name.'

'Her name's Spindoana' said the man with unusual vehemence. Whereupon the minister picked up the infant, put his fingers in the font and, making the sign of the cross on her head, pronounced the words 'I name this child Spindoana.'

'Naw, naw,' said the man, 'her name's no Spindoana! It's *pinned oan 'er,*' and pointed to the place where a small piece of paper with writing on it was pinned to the child's shawl.[82]

Sir Walter Scott
Abbotsford, *c.* 1830

It is said . . . that a gallant baron, having returned from the Holy Land to his castle of Drummelzier, found his fair lady nursing a healthy child, whose birth did not by any means correspond to the date of his departure. Such an occurrence, to the credit of the dames of the Crusaders be it spoken, was so rare, that it required a miraculous solution. The lady, therefore, was believed, when she averred confidently that the Spirit of the Tweed had issued from the river while she was walking upon its bank, and compelled her to submit to his embraces; and the name of Tweedie was bestowed upon the child, who afterwards became Baron of Drummelzier, the chief of a powerful clan.[83]

---

[81] George Penny, *Traditions of Perth*, p. 29.
[82] Bill Salton, who has been an invaluable helper and friend during the preparation of this manuscript, told me this anecdote one day when he was proof-reading a part of the text. Recorded at the School of Scottish Studies, March 1992.

Dolly Wallace
Harris, 1985

MB *Were there any traditions about keeping a piece of the [wedding] cake for the first christening?*

DW . . . Yes. The top layer of the wedding cake.

MB *Did they have any set time of baptism or christening?*

DW No. It was usually oh, three, six months – by the minister, and more often than not in the home.

MB *Any traditions in naming?*

DW Yes! The first son – the father gets to name him – or the first daughter. They were usually called after one of his parents. The second child, whatever it is, is after the wife's parents. And then after that they can go – they usually took turn about. It would be an aunt or an uncle.

MB *Would they keep family names?*

DW Oh yes! Very much so.

MB *Now, a lot of double-barrelled names occur on the islands. Was this a tradition in your family as well?*

DW No!

MB *Your own name for example, Dolina, obviously after . . .*

DW Oh, Donald, after my grandfather.

MB *So was that your maternal or your paternal grandfather?*

DW Maternal.

MB *Yes. So he was Donald, and you were Dolina. Now where did you come in the family then?*

DW I'm the only one. It's my mother's father I was called after.

MB *Do you have a second name?*

DW No, no! There was only one double name in our family when one of my uncles was named Donald Alex.

MB *Any particular reason?*

DW No. Well, my grandmother had eight. So there was no need to have double names. But I do know lots of families that have two or three Johns in various forms. There would be an Iain, a John and a John Norman – in the one family. That was quite common.

MB *Because they were each after a different John?*

DW Yes! There would maybe be her father, his father and an uncle. Or a grandfather or something.

MB *And did people sometimes take offence if this tradition wasn't acknowledged?*

DW Oh yes! Very much so!

---

[83] Walter Scott, Notes to 'The Lay of the Last Minstrel', Note XII, in J. Logie Robertson, *The Poetical Works of Sir Walter Scott, with . . . Notes*, p. 59.

MB *Yes, there's been a fair shift away from this now. For example, you get Kims, and Tracys, and Cindys. How do the old people look upon this?*

DW With horror, I would imagine!

MB *Really? Are they quite amazed?*

DW Yes. When Eddie was born – his isn't a family name – he was called after a surgeon who saved my life when I was ten. He's got the Edward. And a cousin of my grandmother's gave my mother such a dressing-down. Not me. He didn't meet me, luckily. He met my mother and gave her such a dressing-down for letting me even think about breaking the family tradition. She could have called him after her uncle who was killed in the war. There was nothing wrong with Farquhar's name!

MB *Yes, I can see how that might have caused a stir at the time.*

DW Yes it did. Very much of a stir.

MB *So you called Morag after . . . ?*

DW My mother. She's Morag MacDonald MacKenzie.

MB *So that pleased everybody?*

DW Oh yes! That pleased everybody. They were quite happy with that.

MB *What about Colin?*

DW Colin's Colin George. Colin's just a name Jim and I liked, and George is after Jim's father.

MB *So, again that's in keeping with family tradition?*

DW Yes![84]

Duncan 'Major' Morrison
Stornoway, Isle of Lewis, 1996

MB *Everybody knows you as Duncan 'Major' Morrison. Where does the name 'Major' come from?*

DM Major Matheson who owned the island. And I'm called after him because when he heard that his employee, the castle joiner, was expecting a baby [he said] 'If it's a boy, you must call him after me.' So I'm Duncan Matheson Morrison . . . The 'little Major'. [laughs] . . . That's how I got the Major. So to this day [everybody calls me Major, and even] the convenor of the island has addressed me as 'Dear Major Morrison' when he offered me the Freedom of the City, in Stornoway . . . The Western Isles.

MB *What relation was this Matheson to Sir James Matheson who originally bought the island in 1844?*

DM A grand-nephew . . . they were owners of the castle [in my parents' time] . . . I started playing the piano at four when Mrs Matheson said 'Duncan, you must

---

[84] Recorded by MB, 23 July 1985. SA1985/156.

come and practise on the grand piano in the ballroom of the castle' [laughs] . . .

MB *And where did your family live?*

DM Here . . . in the seminary, I was born over in that corner.

MB *My word, we're in the very room! 74 Keith Street . . . The Seminary?*

DM You see this was a school . . . The big room was one of the schoolrooms . . . It had four teachers . . . the school stopped in 1905. And they came to live here then when the headmistress left.

MB *So you spent ninety years in this house –*

DM The headmistress lived in this flat and it was very grand . . . When my mother came here, it had gas. It had a loo. It had running water. That was almost unheard of in Stornoway, in those days, when they came in eighteen-something. [And years before I was born, 1906] they were staying in the castle . . .

My older brother was twenty and living in London at the time [of my birth] and he went round all the Highland servants that he knew, all the Lewis girls that were servants, and they all said, 'Our day off is on Wednesday, we'll go to a shop.' A big shop had newly opened – Selfridges. And I was beautifully dressed with a cap and a fur – they all put their [contributions together], pooled their savings then, to buy something for me.

MB *So even then you were a celebrity?*

DM Even my pram was [special]. They had finished having a family in the castle and I had the pram with a coat of arms on it. Oh I was lucky. All those older brothers and sisters, oh, they spoiled me but I loved it![85]

West Highland Free Press
Isle of Skye, 6 June, 2003

Father welcomes about-turn over ban on using Gaelic name

The Lochalsh father who was told that he could not register the birth of his daughter in Gaelic claimed a victory for the language this week after the General Register Office for Scotland reversed its decision . . . Austin Boyle, from Erbusaig near Kyle, had been told initially by officials at GRO Scotland that he could not register his daughter, Aoiffe NicBhaoille, in Gaelic, as it was a foreign language. A spokesman for the Scottish Executive said at the time that index entries had to be identifiable to non-Gaelic speakers.

However, earlier this week Mr Boyle received a letter from GRO Scotland saying: 'I am pleased to tell you that there is no legal obstacle to registering in

---

[85] A celebrated pianist and composer who toured the world accompanying the famous Scottish tenor Father Sidney MacEwan, Duncan was recorded by MB just after his ninetieth birthday.

the form you requested, and that the Registrar General has agreed that the registration should proceed accordingly.'

After hearing the news, Mr Boyle told the *Free Press*: 'The thing is to stress the importance of the Gaelic issue. I'm happy I've got what I want, but the wider issue is more important.' . . . The newly appointed Gaelic Minister, former Highland Council convener Peter Peacock, said: 'Gaelic is a living language and part of Scotland's diverse culture. I am pleased that this misunderstanding has been quickly cleared up and that Mr Boyle and others are now free to register their children's names in Gaelic, as only seems right and proper.'[86]

Rocking the Cradle and Keeping Amused

Peigi Stewart and her brother Murdo Stewart
Uig, Skye, 1985

PB I was born [in 1919] in Glenconon . . . All the babies were born at home at that time . . . I was called Peigi Iain Phàdruig.[87]

MB *What kind of house did your parents have at that time?*

PS Well, I was born in the old thatched house . . . When my next sister was born [in 1921] she was born in the existing family home, [a traditional croft house] . . . When I was little they used to have a wooden cradle on a rocker and my mother could sit with her foot on the rocker if the baby cried and just rock it, and she would be sitting doing her knitting (or whatever) at the same time, with her foot on the rocker.

MB *Did she sing to the little ones?*

MS Yes, when they were small, [in the] cradle – there were no prams in them days.

MB *Who made the cradle?*

MS Oh, some joiner or other in the village.

MB *Did your father take any part of this aspect of child care?*

PS Oh yes, my father was really very good with children. He used to sit us on his knee and sing to us . . . the knee used to be going, and we really used to be shoogled up and down . . . you know singing [dandling songs][88] . . .

---

[86] The issue, which was also reported on BBC Scotland, attracted many letters to the press. Several drew attention to the many nationalities that have encountered no opposition whatsoever to the registration in Scotland of children's names in languages not 'identifiable to non-Gaelic speakers'– i.e. not the English versions of names chosen.
[87] Although her family name was Stewart, according to the local custom in Gaelic-speaking areas, Peigi was known locally by her patronym, which gives her own Christian name followed by that of her father and grandfather. Thus her name literally means 'Peigi [daughter of] John [son of] Peter'. Such a naming system allows individuals to be instantly recognizable in a community where several families may have the same surnames.

MB *Did he have rhymes?*

PS Oh yes, . . . [such as this rhyme for the naming the fingers. It is usually said to a small child sitting on your knee. The adult would hold the little hand while simultaneously reciting and touching the tip of each finger in turn.]

> Ordag, sgalbag,
> Gille fada
> Mac an Aba
> 'S ciste bheag an airgid.[89]

Oh, he had such a lot of patience, my father. Yes, he used to play games . . . Oh, he was always showing us how to tie knots. Of course, you know why . . . he was an old seaman. He had a fishing boat at that time and he would show us how to tie the different knots . . .

MB *Did he have names for them . . . like 'round turn and two half hitches'?*

PS Well, he certainly wouldn't call them that . . . he had Gaelic [terms] for all those.

MB *Did he have any other funny little rhymes?*

PS Oh yes, lots, if only I could remember them. Certainly he had lots of stories of things that actually happened . . . funny stories . . . Well I remember him telling the Gilleasbuig Aotrom stories . . .[90]

Elizabeth Stewart
Mintlaw, 1988

MB *Would you always rock the baby to sleep?*

ES Oh aye! The travelling people were very, very loving to their children.

MB *Did you sing lullabies?*

ES Hmm mm. [Demonstrating: You'd hold the baby in your arms and sing and rock back and forth.]

MB *Were the songs special lullabies or just any songs?*

ES Sometimes it wid be funny songs. It didna need tae be something connected wi the child. I've got two grandchildren, I got them last year, and I'd nurse them and sing songs

---

[88] On the tape recording she gives a sung example of vocables.

[89] *Translation:* Thumb, little splinter [index finger] / the long fellow / MacNab / and the little chest of silver (or money). There are many versions in both Gaelic and Scots; see R.C. MacLagan, *Games and Diversions of Argyllshire* and R. Chambers, *Popular Rhymes of Scotland*, p. 20, for older versions, and also N. and W. Montgomerie, *Sandy Candy*, p. 66.

[90] Gilleasbuig Aotrom [light-headed Archie] was an eccentric local character, about whom many 'wise fool' stories were told. He was said to have lived in the late eighteenth century. Skye writer William MacKenzie devotes a short section to him in *Iochdar Trotternish*. On this tape Peigi retold one of the stories in Gaelic and also in English. She was recorded at the School of Scottish Studies while visiting the Honours class, and was recorded by MB. SA1986/79.

like 'Hishie ba, fa kens fa's yer faither' and ma daughter says 'Mum! That's terrible!' But she liked it.

MB *Would you like to sing it?*

ES Yes, certainly. [Sings]

> Oh hishie ba, fur Ah'm yer ma
> Hishie ba ma bairn o;
> It's hishie ba, fur Ah'm yer ma
> But Guid kens fa's yer faither o.[91]

> When I was a maid o sweet sixteen
> In beauty all a-bloomin o
> It's little, little did I think
> That at seventeen I'd be greetin o.

> Oh hishie ba, fur Ah'm her ma . . .

and so on.[92]

Alexander Polson
Caithness, 1907

There are two rather strangely opposed beliefs regarding rocking an empty cradle. Some believe that 'If you rock the cradle empty/Then you shall have babies plenty', while others hold the exactly opposite belief – that rocking the empty cradle thoughtlessly, as one may sometimes do, is an omen of the child's death. How both came to be held by people in the same county is somewhat puzzling. It is not fortunate to have a kitten in the house while the infant is being nursed, for cats are believed to suck its breath away – or, maybe, to smother it.[93]

Dolly Wallace
Harris, 1985

MB *With small children, were there any songs that you associated with children? And stories?*

DW Oh yes! All the lullabies were sung for the children in those days. They wouldn't sleep without that. They were rocked in the cradle and somebody sang for them.

---

[91] There are several versions of this song, all with the theme of the young girl left to hold the baby and to regret not paying attention to her mother's warnings. One variant of the chorus has the last line 'But Guid kens whaur's yer daddie o', giving an entirely different meaning to the song.

[92] Elizabeth Stewart was recorded at the School of Scottish Studies. SA1988/25.

[93] Alexander Polson, 'Folklore', p. 93.

MB *My own grandmother was the same. She wondered how could a baby go to sleep without being rocked and being sung to. What about stories? I know you told stories to your own children. Were stories told to you?*

DW Very much so.

MB *What kind?*

DW Well, my grandfather was marvellous really because he had all the old islands stories. Well, they were always connected with fairies and ghosts.

MB *At what stage in your life then would you pick up the ghost stories?*

DW Oh, from the time I was five or six. All the old men used to come to ceilidh in our house to see my grandfather.

MB *And did you listen there?*

DW Oh, very much so. My cousin Willie and I used to hide in a corner and hope my mother would ignore us and forget about us. [We were scarcely seen] and we weren't heard. We wouldn't dare be heard. And we lived for these stories, which meant that we were terrified to go out in the dark. Absolutely scared stiff. The two houses were side by side, and if I was going from one to the other somebody had to stand in the door till I got there. Or if Willie was coming from one to the other somebody had to stand in the third door till he got to us.

MB *Did you have electricity then?*

DW No! Oil lamps.

MB *Can you remember any of your favourite stories or one that really took your fancy in those days? Maybe you'd like to tell one?*

DW Yes, I can. Can I say it in Gaelic?

MB *Oh yes, certainly.*

DW [Bha naidheachd] ann ma dheodhainn fear a bha 'dol dhachaidh far an Tairbeart dha na Baigh. Agus nuair sin bhiodh iad a' dol gu airigh as t-samhradh leis a' chrodh – na h-ighnean oga. Agus thachair e air an airigh a bha seo. Agus o, dithis nighean cho breagha 's a chunnaic e riamh 's cha do dh'aithnich e iad. Agus, o abair thusa gun tug iad dha bainne 's gu robh iad a' bruidhinn ris, 's chan innseadh iad dha c'ait as a' robh iad, no co a bh'annta.

Agus chaidh e dhachaidh an ceann treis 's dh'innis e 'staigh ca' robh e. 'S thuirt a mhathair ris, 'Chaneil airigh a' sin.'

'O,' as esain, 'bha mi as an airigh.' 'S dh'innis e dhith cia mar a bha na h-ighnean, 's cha robh i 'tuigsinn co bh'ann. 'S chaidh e fhein agus a nabaidh air ais lairne mhaireach, 's cha robh airigh ann.

MB *Có as a thàinig an sgeula seo?*

DW Well, 's e mo sheanair a bha dha'n innse dhomsa. Agus feumaidh gun do . . . gun cuala esain o athair iad . . . dìreach tighinn a-nuas, beul aithris.

MB *Agus bha iad a bruidhinn mar seo, ri taobh an teine anns an taigh agadsa . . . dìreach gach oidhche, neo uaireannan?*

DW Bha, bha . . . Bhiodh trì oidhche ' s an t-seachduin. 'S bha aon bhodach ann a bhiodh a' tighinn a-staigh le lainntir – Fionnlagh Uilleam. Agus an uair sin, 's e taigh tughaidh a bh'againn. Thigeadh e 'staigh air an dorus, is bhiodh an dorus againn duinte – dorus a' rum. Neiste, bhiodh solus a' lainntir a' deàrrsadh fo'n dorus, 's bhiodh Fionnlagh 'na sheaseamh ag eisdeachd co bha 'staigh. 's cha robh e 'tuigsinn gu robh solus a' lainntir a' dearrsadh, is fios aig a h-uile duine bha 'staigh gu robh e 'g éisdeachd a-muigh!

Translation

DW There was one about a man who was going home from Tarbert to the Bay. And at that time they used to go to the sheiling in the summer with the cattle – the young girls. And he came to this certain sheiling, and oh, two girls as beautiful as he had ever seen [were there] and he didn't know them. And to be sure they gave him milk, and they were speaking to him. And they wouldn't tell him where they were from, or who they were.

And he went home after a while, and he told those at home where he had been. And his mother said to him, 'There is no sheiling there.'

'Oh,' he said, 'I was at the sheiling.' And he told her all about the girls, and she couldn't understand who it was [he was speaking about]. And he and his neighbour went back the next day and there was no sheiling there.

MB . . . *Where did this story come from?*

DW It was my grandfather who told them to me, and he heard them from their father . . . just passed down, [from] oral tradition.

MB *And they used to talk like this by the fireside in your house . . . every night or [just] sometimes?*

DW Yes, yes, it would be three nights a week. And there was one old man who used to carry a lantern – Finlay son of William. And at that time we had a thatched house. He would come in the main door and our [inside] door would be closed – the room door. Now, the light of his lantern would be shining under the door, and Finlay would stand and listen to hear who was inside. And he didn't realize that the people inside [could all see the beam of his lantern light shining under the door, and they] all knew that he was listening outside![94]

[94] This Gaelic story told by Dolly Wallace is only one of many she told during my visit. I am most grateful to Joan MacKenzie for the transcription and to Peigi Bennett for the translation. SA1985/156.

Sandra Miller
Orkney, 2004

MB *Sandra, where are your people from?*

SM My folk are from Orkney, my father's side came from Stromness, the town in the West Mainland, but my mother's folk are from Orphir, one of the parishes in the West Mainland.

MB *Roughly when were your grandparents born?*

SM My maternal grandparents were both born in 1891.

MB *Can you tell me a little bit about how your grandfather used to keep you amused as children?*

SM Coming from farming folk both my mother and father worked on the farm. When there was a lot of work on, like the harvest and peat cutting, Grandad was always on hand to keep an eye on me. He showed me games and thing to make, like Chukkie Stones, Soldiers and how to make a Rashie Rattle.

Chukkie Stones involved me looking for small enough stones to play with. Once I had found them, the object of the game was to take one in your hand and throw it up in the air and catch it on the back of your hand. This you then repeated with two, three and so on. If you missed one you had to start all over again!

Soldiers are played by two people with the plantain plant. You collect a few plantain flowers – its head is like a soldier's furry hat. Then the object of the game is to try and knock the head off your opponent's 'soldier' using your own.

MB *We played that too, in the Hebrides. You'd stand opposite your opponent, both holding your 'soldiers' by the stem. If it was your turn to go, your opponent would hold out theirs, and you'd briefly place your soldier over the other one, sort of neck on neck. That was only so you could draw back to take a sharp swipe on that exact position, so you could chop off his head! But we didn't have any rashie rattles that I know of.*

SM The Rashie Rattle is made using four very long rashes [rushes or reeds], one short one and a small stone. My part was always to go and find the required items and then to learn how to make one. It's like a corn dolly, the same idea, only you put a small stone in it before it's closed at the top.

MB *And it has its own woven handle too. It's a pretty ingenious rattle!*

SM I suspect, thinking about it, the main objective was always finding the right things . . . the smallest stone, the longest rash and so on. This is what occupied the time, not the actual game, I do remember the first stone or whatever was never just right. It had to be a bit smaller or a bit bigger. This could go on for ages!

MB *Endless amusement for a child. Ingenious – and blessedly free from 'buy-me-this, that or the other'.*[95]

---

[95] Sandra sent two rashie rattles to MB as part of her project for the University of the Highlands (Orkney College) degree in Cultural Studies. The dialogue was via e-mail.

Pat Christie
Shetland, 2001

I thought I would send you this version of the traditional nursery rhyme 'Baa, Baa Black Sheep':

> Baa, baa moorit yow,
> Haes doo ony oo?
> Yis sir, yis sir,
> Tree secs foo.

> Wan fur da maister,
> Wan fur da dame,
> Wan fur da peerie boy,
> Dat bydes doon da Lanes.

My father used to sing this to us when we were little. He used to sing all sorts while combing my sister's and my hair in front of the peat fire, after our bath on Sunday nights. It was a tin bath and I remember one side of the bath was roasting hot from the fire and the other side was cold. My mother and grandmother boiled the water for the bath on the stove in winter, and on a peat fire outside in summer. Sometimes we were allowed to bath outside in the summer as a treat but it had to be fine weather. The order we bathed in was youngest to oldest. The elders after we had gone to bed. This is only 35 to 40 years ago . . . I sing it to myself sometimes even now, and I sang it to my own children and now my grandchildren.[96]

Fosterage and Adoption

William MacKay
Inverness-shire, 1914

Fosterage was common to the Celts of Scotland, Ireland and Wales. By it the child of one person was adopted by another person, who gave him bed and board and sometimes education, and treated him in every respect as his own child. Sometimes men exchanged children. The custom probably originated in the troubles of the olden times, the constant danger to life and property, and the consequent desire to form alliances for mutual protection, not only by marriages and bonds of manrent, but also by fosterage of children.

---

[96] E-mailed by Pat, who is from Aith, Cunningsburgh, December 2001.

Numerous instances are recorded of extraordinary love and fidelity between foster parents and foster brothers – the best known in literature being that told by Sir Walter Scott in *The Fair Maid of Perth*, where Torquil and all his sons sacrificed their lives for his foster child, Eachin MacIan.

The contract of fosterage was commonly by word of mouth, but it was sometimes committed to writing. The first specimen I shall submit is a contract entered into in 1580 between Duncan Campbell of Glenurquhay (the laird of Breadalbane) and his 'native servant' – that is, his slave – Gillecreist Makdonchy Duff Vc Nokerd (Christopher son of Black Duncan son of the Mechanic) and his wife Catherine Neyn Donill Vekconchy (Catherine daughter of Donald son of Duncan), by which these two humble persons bound themselves

to take in fostering Duncan Campbell, son to the said Duncane, to be sustained by them in meat and drink and nourishment till he be sent to the school with the advice of friends, and to sustain him at the schools with reasonable support, the said father and foster father giving between them of makhelve guddis in donation to the said bairn at Beltane thereafter the value of two hundred merks of ky, and two horses or two mares worth forty merks; these goods with their increase to pertain to the said bairn as his own chance bears him to, but their milk to pertain to the said foster father and mother so long as they sustain the said bairn and until he be sent to the schools, except so much of the said milk as will pay the mails of pasture lands for the said cattle . . . and in case the said bairn shall die before he be sent to the schools, his father shall send another of his children, lass or lad, to be fostered in his stead, who shall succeed to the first bairn's goods; and the said foster father and mother being bound to leave at their decease a bairn's part of gear to their said foster son or to the bairn that enters on his place, as much as they shall leave to their own children.

There is extant a contract of fosterage written in Gaelic between Macleod of Macleod and John, son of the son of Kenneth, dated 1614:

Ag so an tachd agus an cengal ar affuil Macleod ag tabhairt a mhac, iodhon Tormoid, d'eoin mac mic Cainnigh, agus ase so an tachd ar affuil se aig Eoin iodhon an leanamh . . . This is the condition and agreement on which Macleod is giving his son, namely, Norman, to John the son of the son of Kenneth, and this is the condition on which he [the child] is with John, namely if so be that John die first the child to be with his wife until she get another husband for herself, but the guardianship of the child to belong to Angus, son of the son of Kenneth, so long as she is without a husband.

. . . The foster father puts the following stock in possession of the foster child

– seven mares; these and their increase to be kept by Macleod for the foster child.[97]

Betsy Whyte
Montrose, 1975

[The travellers] were awfy fond o bairns. There wis lots o bairns that the tinkers brought up that didnae belang tae themselves – hundreds an hundreds. Even gentry's bairns they brought up, because long ago it used tae be an awfy shame for any [unmarried] lassie tae hae a bairn, ye ken. Oh, it wis a terrible thing, an there wis nothin they could dae tae prevent it in those days. So if there wis tinkers in the vicinity they usually got the bairn. But that bairn wis as well done tae as far as love an that wis concerned. The bairn wis well done tae. They brought the bairns up well, an they nivver went back tae the folk for tae ask money nor nothin aff them, nae matter how rich they were.[98]

Bill Innes
South Uist, 1998

BI   I was born in the village of Kinlochleven . . . My father was a foreman in the local aluminium factory . . . We moved about seven miles away, to a fairly lonely corner of Glencoe, a bit out of the village . . . Then my father took ill and died in 1940 when I was seven . . . My mother was left to look after two children in an isolated part of Glencoe on a widow's pension of 10 shillings a week . . .

MB   *That's fifty pence nowadays!*

BI   Life was very, very tough for my mother . . . and eventually she was taken to hospital . . . there was no children's home in Argyllshire at the time.

MB   *So what happened to you?*

BI   We were parked in Oban in an old people's home.

MB   *A little boy of seven and a little boy of –*

BI   Three and a half.

MB   *In a home for the elderly?*

BI   Yeah.

MB   *Can you remember it?*

BI   Oh yes, yes, it was a bit like a hospital. This was wartime and a lot of the able-bodied nurses and so on were required in other places. But we had, for example,

---

[97] William Mackay, 'Life in the Highlands in the Olden Times', *TGSI*, 1914.
[98] Betsy Whyte was recorded by Linda Williamson and Alan Bruford. SA1975/51.

nurses called VADs who used to wear red crosses on their uniform. But I have to say that in fact people were very kind to us there. It was obviously quite novel for the nurses to have two little boys to look after, but we were left pretty much to our own devices. And one of the things the old people in the home used to do, (a) for occupational therapy, but (b) to make a few pence, was they used to assemble blocks of firewood. They would chop up old strippings from trees, and so on, into sticks for firewood, and bundle them up with string. There was a little machine, which compressed all the sticks together so you could put a string round and sell these bundles, and we were allowed to help with that. And what is more, the great piles of wood strippings made fantastic playgrounds for kids. Of course, things like toys were not available.

MB *How long did you stay in the old folks' home?*

BI It was about six or seven months. Now Oban at the time had a very large island population and in particular some of the people that worked in the old people's home had island connections. And one of the priests in the Oban Cathedral was from the island of South Uist. He was later to become quite famous as 'Father Rocket' because he resisted the rocket-range eventually sited in South Uist. But at the time he was plain Father John Morrison, and he announced from the pulpit one day, there were two little boys in the old folks home – was there any family in the islands that would consider taking them? Originally they were going to split us up, but having lost both parents, we depended very much on each other – they couldn't really separate us. Eventually, there were two sisters working in Oban hotels there, from a family in South Uist, and they said – well, they thought their mother would take these two little boys.

It has to be said that there was quite a custom of sending children from orphanages, particularly from Glasgow, to the islands, where their fates could vary enormously. Some of them were educationally subnormal, and many of them became effectively slave labour out there. But it was a convenient way for Glasgow to get rid of its unwanted children. Some of them were extremely well treated. Our case was slightly different – we hadn't actually come from the homes in Glasgow. So we were taken to South Uist by a lady named Mary Bowie.

MB *So it was announced to you that you were to be leaving the old people's home?*

BI I don't remember too much about that. I think by that stage we just – [pause] – you know, it was a terrible wrench losing my mother, because she was the only security we had. But I think that having been in the home for six or seven months we just thought – we had to go with the flow, I suppose, is the modern expression.

MB *Do you remember being on the boat to Uist?*

BI It was quite an adventure in those days, in wartime, because the Outer Hebrides in those days played quite a strategic part in the war in that they were the closest airfields to the Atlantic. And so there were quite a lot of service personnel shuttling back and forth to the islands, as the result of which, there were considerable security precautions. Before you could even travel you had so show identity cards to get on the boat . . . Oban Bay itself was full of flying boats, which were used for Coastal Command patrols. And the ship, of course, instead of having its peacetime livery of red and black funnels and white paint was all painted grey. Anyway, we set off on the little *Lochearn*, which was all of 542 tonnes and cruised flat out at nearly nine knots.

The sail out to South Uist took most of the day because the boat had to call in at Tobermory, Kilchoan, Coll, Tiree and out across the Minch to Barra and eventually to Lochboisdale. One of the very vivid memories I have was that this little boat was armed – it had two machine guns. Halfway across the Minch – we came across a mine bobbing on the surface. Mines are tethered beneath the surface, but this one had obviously come free and the crew spotted it on the surface. They tried to sink it with their machine gun. So we actually saw this machine gun in action. Now for two little boys, this was fantastic!

Eventually we arrived at Lochboisdale and it was a completely different world . . . in those days, at least forty to fifty years behind the rest of the country . . . And Mary Bowie got a little car, a little Austin Ruby, to take us nine miles to Howbeg, which was where we were going to end up. No buses in those days.

MB *Had Mary told you anything about the home you were going to, about the family?*

BI No, she hadn't . . . We had never seen thatched houses of the type they had on the islands. People talk about 'black houses'. I am not sure that is the correct description . . . I've got a feeling that 'black houses' are a misinterpretation of the Gaelic word 'taigh-tughaidh', which is a thatched house. But anyway, we saw these houses as we were going along, and to our absolute horror, this car stopped outside one of them . . . a low stone wall with a thatched roof above it, two chimneys, one on either side. The house would have two and a half rooms effectively – the kitchen/living area at one end and a bedroom at the other end . . . No electric light, of course; no running water; no toilet facilities; no bathrooms; no modern conveniences of any kind . . . And not the least alarming feature of this was that everyone was speaking in a foreign language . . . Gaelic was their natural language – some of them hardly spoke any English at all . . . The other thing that terrified us was this house was so dark inside because it was now very late in a summer's evening and it was still relatively light outside but the house inside was very dark. So we just sat on the bench and burst into tears, the pair of us.

But, we had in fact fallen on our feet . . . Old Mrs Bowie had brought up a family of ten in that little house. And everybody said that she was even kinder to us than she had been to her own family. She was pure gold as far as we were concerned. Before long, we called her Granny.

MB *So obviously that first traumatic introduction to the house, to the family, was soon* *behind you . . . Where did you sleep that first night?*

BI Well, there were about three beds crushed into this tiny bedroom at one end of the house. We were allowed to share the small bed, and the young Mary Bowie had one bed and the other son, her youngest brother, called Pàdraig, had the other bed.

MB *And where did the parents sleep?*

BI Well, the parents slept in the small bedroom, the *clòsaid* . . . The old man, Donald Bowie, was a typical islander of the time, wearing a sort of guernsey and dark, thick woollen trousers. Smoking a pipe, which most men did, and wearing one of these bonnets – you see them in old pictures, not a flat cap, but sort of raised cap . . . he didn't speak any English at all . . . But it helped that Mary Bowie who brought us was now staying with the family for the summer to do the work, the croft work for the summer. So, she was there, and then Pàdraig, who was only about nineteen, but of course in our eyes, an adult . . . He was very friendly, very helpful.

MB *So you soon settled in. I understand the old man didn't last too long –*

BI No he didn't . . . cancer . . . he died a few months later and we had really never gotten to know him because we had to pick up Gaelic . . . But we did so relatively quickly, although it took us some years to be able to pass for natives.

MB *You went to the local school?*

BI The little local two-room school was one and a half miles away – you had to walk of course . . . Now, you could escape from this school at the age of eleven if you passed the Bursary . . . to go to the local secondary school. But some didn't pass the Bursary and had to stay till fourteen, the legal leaving age. Others weren't even allowed to sit the Bursary because their parents needed them on the croft. And that indeed should have been our fate because this family, who were very poor, had taken on these two little kids – the plus side for them should have been that we'd have grown up and worked the croft.

MB *Do you remember working on the land even at seven?*

BI Oh yes, everybody had to help . . . Well, our primary job was to herd cattle. There were few fences in those days . . . So the cattle were herded. When you weren't at school, you spent the morning with the cattle out on the croft . . . After the milking they were released out to the care of the herdsman till about lunchtime when they were taken out to moor grazing where they could be left to roam about in open land, there was no arable land nearby.

MB *Did you like herding?*

BI Well, of course it was an incredibly boring thing to do. You had to find some way of passing the time. You could read, if possible, although you couldn't get too involved in a book otherwise cattle had a delight in finding illegal places to eat. I used to pass a lot of the time by making up stories in my head about various adventures. I had a miniature race of people that I used to make up stories about . . . But it kept me out of, kept the mind up . . .

MB *Seems a bit more profitable than what I used to do – I'd make daisy chains!*

BI Oh, I probably did that as well, in the summer, yes.

MB *I love the smell of herding cattle – the grass and the meadows and the clovers – such a fresh smell.*

BI I had a friend who was a couple of years older than me who lived in the next house, which is about a quarter of a mile away, and he and I would leave each other messages under stones. We had secret stones that we could leave each other messages under, and that was very exciting: to go out and find the stone, turn it over and there was a new message in there. Simple amusements . . .

MB *You very quickly adapted to your childhood in South Uist.*

BI It is probably true in retrospect, but I think we went through some very traumatic times, particularly later on when we had to go to the mainland to school and so on.

MB *When you left this wee two-room school? I take it there were only two teachers?*

BI That's right . . . well, we used slates . . . and slate pencils . . . pen and ink, made out of ink powder, and the old steel nib pens, which you had to dip in ink-wells on the desks . . . and quite a lot of serious education was done at these little schools. Then, at the age of eleven we sat what was to later become the 11-plus. You could sit for the Bursary to enable you to go to the higher grade school – and I passed . . . And although Daliburgh is only nine miles away, nobody owned cars in those days, except for the priest or the doctor, or the landlord. There was no public transport, so I had to go and live in Daliburgh for the term. You couldn't even get home for weekends.

MB *So another wrench at the age of eleven?*

BI Yeah, and Daliburgh school took the first three years of secondary education . . . a corrugated iron shed with three classrooms, one for each year . . . But I can't complain about the education that I had . . . Then the final three years of secondary education boarding in Fort William . . . You thought the term would never end . . . By then Uist was home . . . Old Mrs Bowie was once asked, 'What good is it going to do you that he is getting all this education?' And she said, 'Well, it might do some good for somebody.' What an incredibly philosophical view to take when you have no money at all . . . The income of the croft was probably something like £150 a year, yet they allowed me to become a totally non-productive member of the family . . . gone for most of the year at school, and they had to provide me with clothes and pocket money and things like that. But they did it, and I have to be eternally grateful.[99]

---

[99] Bill Innes was recorded by MB, July 1998.

Ethel MacCallum
Tiree, 2000

EM I remember being in Cullin, in Banffshire – the couple I stayed with were very kind to me . . . And I left there about five years old. [Then] I was in Glasgow, I would reckon for about six months – in an orphanage . . . And it was bombed . . . I have memories of all the noise and getting us into an air raid shelter . . . I was frightened of that [and for a long time afterwards] I was terrified of loud noises. We were taken back to the home but it wasn't suitable for us to stay in, so, bit by bit, the children were moved. We were told that we were going to Tiree – they never told us where Tiree was nor nothing. I think it was terrible how they treated the children – couldn't they just have sat down and said 'We're going to take you to this nice place'? No! 'They're goin to Tiree,' and we were put on the train.

MB *Were you accompanied?*

EM Yes. There was a crowd of children and Nurse MacDonald, who was nice to us really, she was there with us – wi' tea and the soggy sandwiches! [laughs] I remember the commotion of going on the train because there wasn't just us, there was other children going to other islands. I could have been goin to Barra for all I knew. I don't remember an awful lot apart from getting on the boat. It was a wild day!

MB *Had you ever been in a boat before?*

EM No! And I can remember being on the *Hebrides*. And I remember the big stove in the middle of the floor, on the deck, and – the hard decks an the hard floors 'n the hard seats. An it was blowin an I was cold. And you had nobody. I was six.

MB *Were you adequately clad?*

EM Yes. I think that's one thing about the Glasgow Corporation, I think we were well enough clothed. And I had a little case, an a Bible, and a savings bank book. A wee case with whatever was in it – I suppose it was my clothes. But we were a sad little band when we got to Tiree, because it was a terrible day. It was wet and cold and we were all frightened and all these people talking – a language that – well it was the same on the boat. That was quite frightening for, you know, they weren't speaking English. All the crew had Gaelic in those days.

MB *That was the first time you heard Gaelic?*

EM Yes!

MB *Did anyone explain to you?*

EM No! [laughs] Well I suppose I thought I was in a foreign land or something, a foreign ship. It was quite frightening . . . the only one that was speaking English was this Nurse MacDonald, but seemingly she was full of Gaelic as well!

MB *And when you got to Tiree, what happened?*

EM Well, we got there and got off the boat and it was a terrible, terrible wild day and they were all there with their yellow oilskins and their sou-westers, and helped us. They were very kind to us, right enough. Lifted us off the gangway, y'know, we were just tiny little things. And we walked up this big long pier – the Tiree pier was not as long as it is now, but quite long in those days. We walked up the pier, and, there, lo and behold, was a Glasgow taxi! [laughs] I couldn't believe it! There were other cars there, but I was put in the Glasgow taxi, an then they distributed you throughout the island, wherever they had names, you know, of people that were looking for children, who'd like to foster kiddies. And the nurse had the addresses – she knew where she was going, right enough.

MB *So people had actually indicated an interest?*

EM Yes. They must've done.

MB *Was it clear at the time that you were going to be there literally for life, or that you'd be fostered just a short time, for the duration of the war?*

EM I think a lot of them were there for the war, and yet an awful lot of them never went back, they were there till they'd leave school. There were quite a number of people there for just the duration of the war and then they went back to their parents.

MB *And so had people volunteered to care for these children?*

EM Yes, they must've done, I think they got paid for it from the Glasgow Corporation. They also got their clothes given, they never had to buy any clothes for them. They didn't get much – the recompense they got was very little. I suppose it fed the children.

MB *And how was it decided who would take you in?*

EM Well, I'm not terribly sure about that because Kate and Hugh I went to had a boy who had died while he was a young man in his twenties – John. So they wanted a boy for the croft to replace John. And I arrived on the scene, and I became the boy for the croft, but they were happy enough with that.

MB *Was that the first house you stopped at?*

EM No. They went round all these houses and folk came out and had a look at you, and walked away. But I'm not very sure how that worked, I've never really found out . . . maybe every three months there would be so many children come to Tiree. There possibly was this wee lassie there, who looked like a waif, you know . . . I was last in the taxi.

MB *Did you feel as if nobody was going to choose you?*

EM Yes, I felt terrible! But, I mean, I really think it was meant to be, because this lady came to the taxi, and she'd such a lovely kind face. I'll never forget it. There was a light in her face – she was such a very good Christian lady. There was something about her, and she took me by the hand and [said] 'Coiseach comhla ruimsa' – [come along with me] . . . And I went into this house and it was a huge, big house, like a palace, a great big house. Not just an ordinary Tiree house, but 'twas a big, big, Tiree stone house.

MB *What village?*

EM Ruaig. We went into the house and the first thing I did – trip over the cat! There was *cats!* And they had a range . . . with the chrome on it! Down in the skullery they had the black stove, but this was in the – anns a' *chidsean* – [in the kitchen] they had a lovely big range and – with all this chrome on it, and a great big long stool . . . An all these cats were sitting on it – but there was this stray thing wandering about, and a dog! Great big collie dog – tail was wagging and . . . It was warm and it was welcoming, and then she said, 'Would you like a glass of milk and a pancake?' I'd seen milk before, but I never knew what a pancake was! Oh, I enjoyed it!

They had the post office, so she didn't have a lot of time – the mails were coming in by the time I was – delivered like the letters! So I was left with all these animals, and I was given a book and she had to go and attend to her duties there. And he was out on the croft. But Hugh came in, a great, big tall man and – in fact he wasn't that tall, but I thought he was a big man in those days, course he looked tall. He'd a cap on, an old 'geansaidh' [Guernsey] and the heavy tweed trousers, and the big boots – and he came in an [said]: 'Now you've to be a good girl!'

I asked them, once or twice, seemingly, 'Will I get to stay? Can't I stay here?' and they didn't want to say, 'Well yes, you can stay,' because the Nurse MacDonald might come back and say 'Oh well, I've organised such and such for this little girl and you can't keep her.' So they didn't say anything till she came back and they said to her that they didn't want me to be taken away – and I wanted to stay, so I was left. I must've been awful good for a fortnight!

I've often thought after, as a grown-up with my own children, I've got a granddaughter now, it must've been difficult. A couple with no family of their own, possibly in their fifties – they never had any children, and they ended up with this little scrap of a thing.

MB *And what do you call them?*

EM Aunt Kate and Uncle Hugh.

MB *And what was their other name?*

EM Lamont. We were very lucky, Aunt Kate and Uncle Hugh had a bathroom. Bha taigh mòr breagha aca! A beautiful house! And the bone of contention was the hot water tank! [laughs] It was in the kitchen, and, when it was put in, a big copper tank, she wanted it covered up – to put doors on it. 'No, no, no!' He thought it was such a great show-piece and he said he would keep it clean. He never cleaned it once, this great big copper boiler in the kitchen! But it gave off a lot of heat. They'd a porch downstairs and a bathroom upstairs . . . Three bedrooms upstairs, it was a beautiful house. Aunt Kate was very house proud and taught me to be the same.

MB *Did you help in the house?*

EM Yes, I swept the floor and washed and dried the dishes. I'd my jobs too. When I came home from school I knew that she was busy in the office and he was in the croft. When I got old enough I was running after cows and calves and they used to laugh, I'd be away on the bicycle – 'Am faca tu na laoigh? [Have you seen the calves?] People used to leave the gate open, and of course, the calves got out, and when they got away they were gone! I helped in the house and I helped in the croft.

MB *Were they still making butter and milk and all?*

EM Yes, yes. That's where I learned to sing! She used to make [butter] – she had a barrel churn. And there was this dairy – oh, great acoustics in it, you know! And there I was myself, churning the butter and singing all them songs! I often think that's where I got such a good strong voice.

I went to school in Ruaig, and it was just across the way. I was very fortunate because they were very kind to me . . . I grew up as their own daughter really. Because I am now hearing that there were families who were not so lucky . . . Aunt Kate had all these brothers and sisters, and Uncle Hugh had all these brothers and sisters – from day one y'know – An té bheag [the little one] . . . They made a fuss of me and when – I often think of it – there was never a Christmas but there was always something in the parcel home from Glasgow from Auntie Flora or Auntie Nancy, or Uncle Donald. Uncle Hugh's brother was Dr Donald Lamont of Blair Atholl. Do you know, the prose writings of Dr Donald Lamont? I remember him too . . . And nothing spoken in the house but Gaelic . . . They reckoned by maybe about two years I was fluent, I could chat away, quite the thing. Now there was a lot of other children on the island did not get the chance to learn Gaelic . . . I can always remember the first week I was there I was playing in the kitchen wi' the dog and cats and the games and things, people would come to the house with toys and things for me – that *their* children had. Dolls and things like that. They were busy in the post office, anyway, these people were coming in for their pension, and they would say to Aunt Kate, 'Show us your *cailleag bheag! Tha i laghach!*'[100]

Maryann Hollingan, aged 88
Newcraighall, East Lothian, 1995

MH I came off a strong Catholic family and was born and brought up in Newcraighall miners' rows. Mum and Dad were married a good few years before I arrived – eight or nine maybe, but they still hadn't any children. A woman in the village adopted a baby through a column in the local paper. Under the heading, 'miscellaneous', she'd answered an advert for a child. My mum and dad thought that they would do a similar thing. A couple in Nicolson Street in Edinburgh were advertising. So off they went into the town to meet the mother of the child, which hadn't yet been born. A deal was struck and they returned.[101]

[100] [Show us your little girl! She's lovely!] Ethel MacCallum was recorded on 15 December 2000 at her home in Invereray, Argyll, by MB along with Rosie Morton, who transcribed the tape as part of her dissertation at the Royal Scottish Academy of Music and Drama.
[101] Mrs Holligan (1912–2002) was recorded in her home in Portobello by Alan Bruford and Chris Higham, who transcribed the tapes.

PART II
Love, Courtship and Marriage

Love, Courtship and Marriage

From an early age children play games that reflect love, courtship and marriage. On a summer's day many a daisy was (and still is) plucked to find out if 'he loves me – he loves me not – he loves me . . . !' And many an hour has been spent jumping over and through skipping ropes choosing partners, or counting buttons to find out who to marry: 'Tinker, tailor, soldier, sailor . . .' While girls have tended to play a huge range of such games, boys seem to have been more selective about the games to join – some say there could be a lot of excitement in 'Kiss-Cuddle-Torture', especially if they chose torture: 'It's far better than huvin tae kiss a girl ye dinna want!' The old saying 'Nipping and scarting is Scotch folks' wooing' has more than a grain of truth in it.

Marriage was the social norm, the expectation of every family until the closing years of the twentieth century. Even for the most cautious individual it was generally considered the best option for life – 'Marriage has many pains, but celibacy has no pleasures', as Samuel Johnson put it. If an unmarried son or daughter was thought to be 'getting on in years', the concern about whom to marry became more urgent with the passing of time, and, as expected, there is plenty of proverbial advice for every stage of courtship. 'Wha may woo without cost?' and 'A fair maid tocherless will get mair wooers than husbands' give cautionary advice with a hint of irony, while 'Better half hanged than ill married' bluntly states a sentiment often expressed. The social implications of marriage are dealt with in 'Marry aboon your match and get a maister' and 'Better marry ower the midden than ower the muir' [Better marry among those you know than among strangers]. If a couple married very young or if they were considered to marry late in life, they might hear 'Is minig a bha 'm pòsadh luath 'na phòsadh truagh, 's am pòsadh mall 'na phòsadh dall.' [An early marriage was often a poor marriage and a late marriage was often a blind marriage.] For those who find the business of choosing a life-partner very much of a dilemma there is 'Dà nì ro dhuilich an taghadh, bean agus claidheamh' [Two things very difficult to choose, a wife and a sword] and 'Choose thy wife amang the virtuous, and thy friend amang the wise.'

Folk have always had plenty to say in response to love-matching: 'Sùilean goibhre an cinn bhan gu taghadh fhear' [Women have goats' eyes in their heads for choosing men], and of course the well-worn (and less sarcastic) 'Better to have loved and lost than never to have loved at all.' The important place of love in a marriage can be considered from several viewpoints: 'Love is as warm amang cottars as courtiers'; 'Love and a cough cannot be hid.' Unfortunately, for unrequited love there is little consolation: 'Nae herb will cure love.'

Scots law (1999) recognises two kinds of marriage: religious, performed by a celebrant authorised under the Marriage (Scotland) Act 1977, and civil, solemnised by an authorised registrar. Both require publication of notice (a safeguard against bigamy) and two witnesses. Couples must be over sixteen, not related in any way that prevents marriage, not of the same sex, and must be capable of understanding the ceremony.[1] A third type, irregular marriage, is recognised by custom and repute of co-habitation (though not by government bodies such as the Department of Social Security or by certain legal bodies), and dates back to 'handfasting', common all over Scotland till the eighteenth century.

Once the decision to marry has been made, a couple can expect to hear plenty of advice on every aspect of the wedding day: 'Marry in May and you'll rue the day' discourages wedding plans for that month. As she dresses for the wedding ceremony the bride is still told that she should have 'Something old, something new, something borrowed, something blue'. And for the bridesmaid who makes sure she does her duty in adhering to tradition, yet a third party cautions her to beware 'Three times a bridesmaid, never a bride!' Yet the prevailing tone of the wedding guests is one of goodwill, concisely expressed in Scots by 'Lang may yer lum reek,' or more elaborately in Gaelic:

Saoghal fada, sona dhuit,
Do choluinn fallain, slan,
Do bhoth gun bhoinne snighe ann,
Do chiste-mhine làn.

[May you have a long, happy life, A sound and healthy body, a cottage which does not leak, and a meal-chest which is always full.][2]

In more recent years, many such greetings have arrived in the form of

---

[1] For an up-to-date summary, see 'Marriage in Scotland' (Leaflet RM1), issued by the General Register Office at New Register House, Edinburgh, and available from all registration offices.

[2] My mother gave me a variant of this saying, which she sometimes sends as a telegram to friends or family who are getting married:
A h-uile latha sona dhuit
'S gun latha idir dona dhuit.
[May every day be happy for you, And no day at all bad for you.] Telephone conversation, March 1992.

telegrams read out at the wedding feast by the best man, and often causing much hilarity among the guests.

In Scotland there are very few couples unfamiliar with the saying 'When poverty comes in the door love flies oot the windae.' Young men were frequently reminded that the best possible goal to aim for is a good balance between love and hard work: 'Marry for love and work for siller.' Couples are still reminded that 'not everything will be a bed of roses', which re-echoes the sentiment of an old Gaelic saying: 'Tha am pòsadh coltach ri seillean – tha mil ann 's tha gath ann' [Marriage is like a bee – it contains both honey and a sting].

Until the second half of the twentieth century, the very mention of divorce could shock most families. So seriously was it viewed that most divorces were reported in national newspapers, often including details of the court proceedings, no matter how embarrassing, tragic or scandalous to a family or community. The Bible provided the main sources of reference, such as conditions for divorce spelled out in Deuteronomy 24, or New Testament citations such as Matthew 19; 3–11. But there is very little mention of it in Scottish tradition, apart from the context of one pre-Christian site in Orkney. For most people, however, there was simply no question of divorce in days gone by. The finality of marriage was a serious business: 'Ye hae tied a knot wi' your tongue you winna loose wi' your teeth.' All the more reason, then, to make sure you marry the right person in the first place!

Twenty-first-century statisticians report a remarkable drop in the number of marriages in Scotland – 29,826 in 2003, compared to over 41,000 in 1951. At the same time, there is a corresponding rise in cohabitation. The average age of marriage has also increased by seven years since 1981, according to a Scottish Executive report (2004), which gives the average age as 32.3 for women and 34.8 for men. Nevertheless, the 'marriage business' in Scotland has never known such a boom, indeed explosion, as that enjoyed in the current decade. Suddenly, self-styled 'wedding consultants' will, for a fee, advise bridal couples how to have a so-called traditional Scottish wedding, costing an average of £11,000 in 1999 and over £16,000 in 2004. Undoubtedly the 'Madonna effect' (as the wedding of the year 2000 is now remembered) boosted global publicity for romantic weddings in Scottish castles. An ancient building with a backdrop of glorious scenery, tartan, bagpipes and whisky may represent the few threads of Scottish tradition woven through whims and fads of the day. The wedding business may put money into the economy while creating a few well-lined pockets, but may also contribute to the erosion of time-honoured Scottish tradition. There is more than a risk that, similar to what Catherine MacNeill in Barra described over a century ago, the collective pressures of marriage consultancies, wedding shows, and hard-sell media will diminish basic confidence in customs solely dependent upon Scottish traditional knowledge and not upon bank loans to pay for borrowed fashions.

A Reflection of Former Times

Thomas Pennant
Traveller, 1776

Matrimony is avoided in the month of January, which is called in the *Erse* the *cold month*; but, what is more singular, the ceremony is avoided even in the enlivening month of May. Perhaps they might have caught this superstition from the Romans, who had the same dread of entering into the nuptial state at that season; for the amorous Ovid informs us:

> Nec vidux taedis eadem, nec virginis apra
> Tempora, quae nupsit no diuturna fuit.
> Hac quoque die causa, si te proverbia tangunt,
> Mense malas Maio nubere vulgus ait.
>
> *Fasti*, V. 485.

> No tapers then shall burn, for never bride,
> Wed in ill season, long her bliss enjoy'd.
> If you are fond of proverbs, always say,
> No lass proves thrifty who is wed in May.[3]

Revd James Napier
Renfrewshire, 1879

A very important event in a man's [person's] life is marriage, and naturally, therefore, to this event there attached a multitude of superstitious notions and practices, many of which, indeed, do still exist. The time when marriage took place was of considerable importance. One very prevalent superstition, common alike to all classes in the community, and whose force is not yet spent, was the belief that it was unlucky to marry in the month of May. The aversion to marrying in May finds expression in the very ancient and well-known proverb, 'Marry in May, rue for aye,' and thousands still avoid

---

[3] Thomas Pennant, *Tour*, vol. II, pp. 44–5.

marrying in this month who can render no more solid reason for their aversion than the authority of this old proverb. But in former times there were reasons given, varying, however, in different localities. Some of the reasons given were the following: That parties so marrying would be childless, or, if they had children, that the firstborn would be an idiot, or have some physical deformity; or that the married couple would not lead a happy life, and would soon tire of each other's society. The origin of this superstition is to be found in ancient religious beliefs and practices . . . We find that among the Romans this national festival was held during the month of May, and during its continuance all other forms of worship were suspended, and the temples shut; and further, for any couple to contract marriage during this season was held to be a daring of the Fates, which few were found hardy enough to venture. Ovid says:

> Pause while we keep these rites, ye widowed dames,
> The marriage time a purer season claims;
> Pause, ye fond mothers, braid not yet her hair,
> Nor the ripe virgin for her lord prepare.
> 0, light not, Hymen, now your joyous fires,
> Another torch nor yours the tomb requires!
> Close all the temples on these mourning days,
> And dim each altar's spicy, steaming blaze;
> For now around us roams a spectred brood,
> Craving and keen, and snuffing mortal food:
> They feast and revel, nor depart again,
> Till to the month but ten days more remain.

Superstitions of this sort linger much longer in the country than in towns, and the larger the town the more speedily do they die out; but, judging from the statistics of late years, this superstition has still a firm hold of the inhabitants of Glasgow, the second city of the Empire. During the year 1874 the marriages in May were only 204, against 703 in June; but as the removal term[4] occurs at the end of May, that must materially affect the relations, in this respect, between May and June, and accounts, in part, for the great excess of marriages in June. But if the average of the eleven months, excluding May, be taken, then during that year there was a monthly average of 441, against 204 in May – being rather more than double. For the ten years preceding 1874, the average of the eleven months was 388, against 203 in

---

[4] The 'term day' in May was Whitsun, a fixed day when rents were due, and farm labourers usually moved to work on another farm.

May.[5] As if to compensate for the restraint put upon the people in May, *Juno*, the wife of Jupiter, after whom June was named, and whose influence was paramount during that month, took special guardianship over births and marriages; hence June was a lucky month to be born in and get married in, and thus June is known as the marrying month. Here, again, our registers show that the number of marriages are in June nearly double the average of the other months, excluding May and June. The average during the ten years is, for the ten months, 375 per month, whilst the average for June is 598. It may be noticed in passing that, in Glasgow, January and July stand as high as June, owing, doubtless, to the holidays which occur during these two months making marriage at those times more convenient for the working classes.

There were many marriage observances of a religious or superstitious character practised in ancient Rome which were quite common among us within this century, especially in the country districts, but which now are either extinct or fast dying out. When a Roman girl was betrothed, she received from her intended a engagement ring which she wore as evidence of her betrothal. When betrothed she laid aside her girlish or maiden dress – some parts of which were offered as a sacrifice to the household gods – and she was then clothed in the dress of a wife, and secluded from her former companions, and put under training for her new duties. When the time drew near for the consummation of the ceremony, it became an important consideration to fix upon a lucky day and hour for the knot to be tied. With this object astrologers, soothsayers, and others of that class were consulted, who, by certain divination ascertained the most auspicious time for the union to take place. When the day arrived every occurrence was watched for omens. A crow or turtle dove appearing near was a good omen: for these birds symbolised conjugal fidelity. The ceremony was begun by sacrificing a sheep to Juno, the fleece being spread upon two chairs on which the bride and bridegroom sat: then a prayer was said over them. The young wife, carrying a distaff and spindle filled with wool, was conducted to her house, a cake, baked by the vestal virgins, being carried before her. The threshold of the house was disenchanted by charms, and by anointing it with certain unctuous perfumes; but as it was considered unlucky for the new-made wife to tread upon the threshold on first entering her house, she was lifted over it and seated

---

[5] An up-to-date look at marriage statistics in Scotland reveals that May is still not favoured as a month in which to marry. Looking at more than a century of records produced by the Scottish Records Office, there is not one year which offers an exception to this: taking the months April, May, and June in every decade from 1810 to 1990, there is a marked down-swing from April to May, and then a dramatic up-swing in June of each decade. This clearly testifies to the fact that Scottish people still regard May weddings with suspicion.

upon a piece of wool, a symbol of domestic industry. The keys of the house were then put into her hand, and the cake was divided among the guests. The first work of the young wife was to spin new garments for her husband. It will be seen that many of these practices were mixed up with superstitious notions, many of which were prevalent in this country sixty years ago, and some of which still remain in country districts. Sixty years ago when a young woman became a bride, she in a great measure secluded herself from society, and mixed but little even with her companions, and on no account would she show herself at church until after her marriage, as that was considered very unlucky. The evening before the marriage her presents and outfit were conveyed to her future home under the superintendence of the best maid (bridesmaid), who carried with her a certain domestic utensil filled with salt, which was the first article of the bride's furnishing taken into the house. A portion of the salt was sprinkled over the floor as a protection against an evil eye. The house being set in order, the best maid returned to the bride's house, where a company of the bride's companions were met, and then occurred the ceremony of washing the bride's feet. This was generally the occasion of much mirth. And this was in all probability a survival of an old Scandinavian custom under which the Norse bride was conducted by her maiden friends to undergo a bath, called the bride's bath, a sort of religious purification. On the marriage day, every trifling circumstance, which would have passed without notice at other times was noted and scanned for omens of good or evil. If the morning was clear and shining, this betokened a happy cheerful life; if dull and raining, the contrary result might be anticipated. I have known the following incidents cause grave concern about the future prospects of the young couple: A clot of soot coming down the chimney and spoiling the breakfast; the bride accidentally breaking a dish; a bird sitting on the window sill chirping for some time; the bird in the cage dying that morning; a dog howling, and the postman forgetting to deliver a letter to the bride until he was a good way off, and had to return. Some of these were defined for good, but most of them were evil omens.[6]

Revd Robert D. Higham
Tiree and Berwick 1999

With regard to the belief that evil spirits lurk at doorways, I have looked up four biblical references that may be of interest.
1 Samuel 5: 4–5. '*And when they arose early on the morrow morning, behold, Dagon was fallen upon his face to the ground before the ark of the Lord; and the*

---

[6] Revd James Napier, *Folk Lore*, pp. 43–7.

head of Dagon and both the palms of his hands were cut off upon the threshold; only the stump of Dagon was left to him. Therefore neither the priests of Dagon, nor any that come into Dagon's house, tread on the threshold of Dagon in Ashdod unto this day.' There, the image of the Philistine god, Dagon, had fallen across the threshold of its own temple. The threshold was regarded as the boundary between the profane and the sacred, so, thereafter, the priests of Dagon did not step on the threshold; it had become sacred.

Zephaniah 1:9 refers to the superstition of not treading on the threshold of pagan temples: *'In the same day also will I punish all those that leap on the threshold, which fill their masters' houses with violence and deceit.'* Whether or not this dates from the occurrence at the Dagon temple at Ashdod, which would have been around 1000 BC, cannot be verified. Zephaniah is reckoned to have prophesied circa 640–630 BC.

Trust in Yahweh would allay superstitious fears about doorways and evil sprits that were thought to lie in wait. Such trust is encouraged in Psalm 121:7–8. *'The Lord shall preserve thee from all evil: he shall preserve thy soul. The Lord shall preserve thy going out and thy coming in from this time forth, and even forever more.'* But I wonder if protection against possible influence of evil spirits may be preserved superstitiously, though unintentionally, by those who instituted the practices in the mezuzin on the doorways of Jewish households and in the receptacles for holy water in R.C. churches . . .

In Genesis 4:7 is the Lord's admonition to Cain: *'But if you do not do what is right, sin is crouching at your door; it desires to have you, but you must master it.'*

As you know, there is unending academic controversy over the dating of the Pentateuch. For myself I have sufficient faith, and it is backed by the opinion of many academic commentators, that Moses and his contemporaries collected the ancient historical traditions in the late fifteenth century BC.

This concept of 'sin crouching at the door' is reflected in the ancient Babylonian belief that demons crouched at doors of buildings to threaten the occupants. Abraham, having originally come from Ur of the Chaldees, which was in the lower Euphrates / Tigris valleys, the area of ancient Babylonia, could have brought this tradition with him. The Hebrew word for 'lie in wait' is very similar to the word for demon in Akkadian, the ancient language of Mesopotamia.

Thus the source of this superstition has been pushed back, not just to the date of its recording in the 15th century BC, but to tradition's origins in the early dawn of human history.[7]

---

[7] Letter to MB, 22 June, 1999 after I visited Tiree where Revd Mr Higham was minister in Tiree Parish Church (1995–2002). He retired to Berwick.

Carrying the bride over the threshold is now generally regarded as an attractive image for inclusion in the wedding album. In the chosen doorway, the groom may be reminded to hold the pose for the perfect photograph. Seldom, if ever, is his attention drawn to the fact that, traditionally, he carried his wife across it as a public gesture of his commitment to protect her from all harm.

Divination[8]

Revd Walter Gregor
North-east, 1874

> Your vessels, and your spells, provide,
> Your charms, and everything beside.

Means were frequently taken to find out who was to be the husband or wife. There were various modes of doing this. Some of the incantations could be gone through only on Hallowe'en. Here are two that could be performed at any time.

The first time one slept in a strange bed a ring was put on the finger, one of the shoes was placed below the bed, the bed was entered backwards. The future husband or wife was seen in a dream.

The maid who was desirous of seeing who was to be her husband had to read the third verse of the seventeenth chapter of the Book of Job[9] after supper, wash the supper dishes, and go to bed without the utterance of a single word, placing below her pillow the Bible, with a pin stuck through the verse she had read. The future husband was seen in a dream.

The first time the note of the cuckoo was heard the hearer turned round three times on the left heel against the sun, searched in the hollow made by the heel, and in it a hair of the colour of the hair of the future husband or wife was found.

To find out whether the lover would remain true and become the husband, three stalks of the *carl-doddie*, or Ribwort (*Plantago lanceolata*), were taken when in bloom. They were stripped of their blossom and laid in the left shoe, which was placed under the pillow. If the lover was to become the husband, the three stalks were again in full bloom by morning. If the lover was to prove untrue, the stalks remained without blossom.

---

[8] Revd W. Gregor sub-titled this section 'Into the Future', chapter 18 of *Echo*. 'Divination' is the general term which refers to methods employed by people who deliberately tried to find out what the future held.
[9] 'Lay down now, put me in a surety with thee; who is he that will strike hands with me?'

Of those that were performed on Hallowe'en the following were most common:

Pulling the Castoc: You went to the kail-yard, and with eyes blindfolded, pulled the first stock of cabbage or greens touched. According to the quantity of earth that remained attached to the root and according to the form of the stock, whether well or ill shapen, were augured the amount of worldly means and the comeliness of the future husband or wife. It was placed inside the door, and the baptism name of the young man or young woman who entered first after it was placed, was to be the baptismal name of the husband or wife, according as it was a young woman or a young man that had pulled and placed the castoc.

Sowing Lint-seed: When the shades of evening were falling, the maiden had to steal out quietly with a handful of lint-seed, and walk across the ridges of a field, sowing the seed, and repeating the words:

> Lint-seed I saw ye,
> Lint-seed I saw ye;
> Lat him it's to be my lad
> Come aifter me and pu' me.

On looking over the left shoulder she saw the apparition of him who was to be her mate crossing the ridges, as it were, in the act of pulling flax.

Fathoming a Rick: This incantation was performed by measuring or fathoming with the arms round a stack of oats or barley three times, against the sun. In going round the third time the apparition of the future husband or wife was clasped when the arms were stretched out for the last time.

Win'ing the Blue-clue: In this incantation the person had to go secretly and in the gloaming to the kiln, carrying a clue of blue worsted thread. This clue was cast into the *Kiln-logie*. The end of the thread, however, was retained, and the performer unrolled the clue, forming a new one. Towards the end it was held tight. It was then demanded who held the thread. A voice answered, giving the name of the future husband or wife.

Winnowing Corn: Go the barn secretly. Open both doors, as if preparing the winnow corn. Take a sieve or a *waicht*, and three times go through the form of winnowing corn. The apparition of the future husband entered by the one door to the windward, passed through the barn, and made his exit by the other door.

Washing the Sleeve of the Shirt: The maiden went to a south-running stream, or to a ford where the dead and the living crossed, and washed the sleeve of her shirt. She returned home, put on a large fire, and hung the shirt in front of it. She went to bed, and from it kept a careful watch. The apparition of him who was to be her partner in life came and turned the wet sleeve.

Roasting Peas: A live coal was taken, and two peas (nuts were not always to be had) were placed upon it, the one to represent the *lad*, and the other the *lass*. If the two rested on the coal and burned together, the young man and young woman (represented by the two peas) would become man and wife, and from the length of time the peas burned, and the brightness of the flame, the length and happiness of the married life were augured. If one of the peas started off from the other, there would be no marriage, and through the fault of the one whom the pea that started off represented.

Eating an Apple in Front of a Looking-glass: This incantation had to be done in secret, like most of the others. An apple was taken and sliced off in front of a looking-glass. Each piece before being eaten was stuck on the point of the knife, and held over the left shoulder of the performer, who kept looking into the glass, and combing the hair. The spectre of the man who was to be her husband appeared behind her, stretching forth his hand to lay hold of the piece.

By Three Caps or Wooden Basins: Three wooden basins were placed in a line on the hearth. One was filled with pure, another with dirty water, and the third was left empty. The performer was blindfolded, and a wand or stick was put into her hand. She was led up to the caps, when she pointed towards one of them. This was done three times, the position of the caps being changed each time. 'The best of three' decided her fate; that is, choosing the same cap twice. The choice of the cap with the pure water indicated an honourable marriage; the choice of that with the dirty water betokened marriage, but in dishonour. If the choice fell on the empty cap, a single life was to be the lot.

As for the number of the family, it was divined in the following fashion: The inquirer into the future went to the stackyard, took a position beside a stack of oats, with the back turned towards it, and from over the head pulled a stalk of oats. The number of grains on the stalk represented the number of the family. If the stalk drawn from the stack by a female wanted the *tap-puckle*, or top grain, she went to the marriage bed deflowered.

To gain love there were various methods. The roots of the orchis[10] were dug up. (The old root is exhausted, and when cast into water, floats – this is hatred. The new root is heavy, and sinks when thrown into water – this is

---

[10] Many varieties of orchis (wild orchid) grow in Scotland. Throughout Europe the roots of the plant have an ancient history of having aphrodisiac properties [see Geoffrey Grigson, *The Englishman's Flora*, 1975, pp. 460–5]. The wild orchid is now a protected species in the British Isles.

love, because nothing sinks deeper than love.) The root – love – was dried, ground, and secretly administered as a potion. Strong love was the result.

Two lozenges were taken, covered with perspiration and stuck together, and given in this form to the one whose love was sought. The eating of them excited strong affection.

There was another method talked of, but it was of such a nature that it must be passed over in silence.[11]

Unluckily for all these charms, the love gained by them was dissipated by *Jouissance du mariage*, and the hatred of the one on whom the charm had been wrought became as strong as the love had been.[12]

When a live coal tumbles from the fire on the hearth towards one who is unmarried, it is regarded as a token that marriage is at hand. Hence the saying 'Fire bodes a marriage'.

When a young woman's apron-string or garter unloosed itself, she was at that time the subject of her lover's thought.

If a woman is forsaken by her lover, she has but to write out the 109th Psalm, send a copy of it to him, and he will never thrive.

When a young man and a young woman were seen in company, those boys who had manners not very refined used to cry:

> Lad and lass
> Wi' the fite cockade,
> Mairrit in the coal-hole
> An' kirkit i' the barn.

The lore about colours was embodied in these words:

> Blue
> 'S love true,
> Green
> 'S love deen,
> Yellow
> 'S forsaken[13]

---

[11] In his book *Ozark Magic and Folklore*, Vance Randolph records several love potions from the Ozark Mountains of Southern Appalachia (settled by Scotch-Irish in the eighteenth and nineteenth centuries) which might echo the indelicate nature of the Revd Gregor's reference. For example, 'every mountain girl knows that if she puts a drop of her menstrual fluid into a man's liquor he is certain to fall madly in love with her.' See Randolph, *op. cit.*, pp. 166–70.

[12] W. Gregor, *Echo*, pp. 101–7, and *Notes*, pp. 83–7.

[13] W. Gregor, *Notes*, p. 87.

Margaret Wilson
Lilliesleaf, 1990

MW When I was [young], right silly, I used to do these things with friends, girls together. I must have been about sixteen. The girl I worked beside she used a Bible; this Bible was opened at a certain place and a big door key was put in, and string tied round. You each put a finger below the key and you said letters. It was supposed to move at a certain letter; it moved, but I don't know whether the other person was helping it move or not!

If you got a bit of bride's cake you put it below your pillow and you were supposed to dream of who you were going to marry. Then you had another thing with a candle and a mirror, you were to see an image in the mirror.

There used to be a cook down at — Estate, she did fortune – telling with cards and we all used to descend down there and say 'Come on, tell our fortune,' and think it most marvellous! Just ordinary cards, she would tell you to cut them into three heaps or whatever, and then she used to count certain cards and lay them out. She had all their meanings; different cards meant something.[14]

Alexander Polson
Caithness, 1907

A Caithness lass may have but few means of 'charming' the young man on whom she has set her heart, but naturally she is somewhat anxious to know (as early as possible) all she can of her future partner; and she does not lightly miss any chance of ascertaining his form, features, character, and means. If she wishes to calculate the years that she is still to remain single, she may get to know by counting the cuckoo notes when she first hears them in spring. Another method is to pluck a full-blown dandelion – the number of puffs required to blow off the seeds indicates the number of unmarried years yet ahead. The dandelion, it may be remarked, is an omen-plant of diverse possibilities. Then, on Hallowe'en, she has only to go to the cabbage-plot after dark, bend down and pull the stock on which her hands fall; and she may know her husband's form by the length and development of the stalk and leaves, and his wealth by the amount of earth which clings to the root. There may have been sowing of hempseed and an addressing of the loved one to come and harrow, but this belief is quite gone:

> Hempseed I sow, hempseed I hoe,
> And he that is my true love,
> Come after me and mow.

---

[14] Margaret Wilson was recorded in Lilliesleaf by Susan Huntly. SA1990/18.

The three plates – one empty, the other two containing clean and dirty water respectively – to which each single person is led blindfolded and asked to choose (by putting the fingers in either of the plates) no spouse, a single lover, or a widow or widower – this is still in vogue.

Dreams in this connection are regarded as of much importance – and some on the same night eat a salt herring, expecting that in their dreams they will see their loved one approach them with a drink. To dream of a 'likely' sweetheart by means of a piece of bridescake under the pillow is also considered a good thing.[15]

Courtship and Bundling

Revd John Lane Buchanan
Western Isles, 1782

The common, as well as better sort of people, court sweet-hearts at nights, over all this country. The unlocked doors yield those lovers but too easy access to their favourites. The natural consequences of their encounters often occasion squabbles in kirk courts, in which the minister and elders take cognizance of the fornication committed in the parish.

This severity, however, is not often productive of the amendment pretended to be designed. I say *pretended*, for in many instances they who are least shrewdly suspected of lewdness, as well as intemperance themselves, are the severest and most curious and prying inquisitors into the failings of others.

In the part of the country we are describing, however, this frailty still prevails . . . the bastard is as much esteemed as the lawfully begotten child.

The woman, if she is pregnant by a gentleman, is by no means looked down upon, but is provided in a husband with greater eclat than without forming such a connection. Instead of being despised, numberless instances can be produced, where pregnant women have been disputed for, and even fought for, by the different suitors.[16]

---

[15] Alexander Polson, 'Folklore', pp. 95–6.
[16] Revd John Lane Buchanan, *Travels*, pp. 109–11.

Martin Martin
Western Isles, *c.* 1695

[In St. Kilda] it is ordinary with a fowler, after he has got his purchase of fowls, to pluck the fattest, and carry it home to his wife as a mark of his affection; and this is called the rock-fowl.

The bachelors do in like manner carry this rock-fowl to their sweethearts, and it is the greatest present they can make, considering the danger they run in acquiring it.

The richest man in the isle has not above eight cows, eighty sheep, and two or three horses. If a native here have but a few cattle he will marry a woman, though she have no other portion from her friends but a pound of horse hair to make a gin to catch fowls.[17]

Scottish National Dictionary
Isle of Lewis, 1933

Amongst the people of the black houses, there is a curious custom in courtship, and, like all primitive sex customs, it is based on economic conditions. The time for making love is during the long winter nights when the young men are at home. On that bleak windswept coast it would be difficult for two people to make love out of doors. So the young man goes to the girl's house. Again, with one living-room where the family are sitting, it is difficult to make love. The girl goes into the sleeping-room. There is no fire there, nor any light, because the burning of tallow candles and oil is a consideration to people who are poor. So, for warmth, the girl goes to bed. Once in bed, both her legs are inserted into one large stocking, which her mother ties above her knees. Then the young man goes into the sleeping-room, and lies beside her. It is called 'the bundling'.[18]

Arthur Edmondston
Shetland, 1809

When a courtship is somewhat advanced, the lover pays a visit to his mistress on Saturday night, and generally remains a day or two in the house. This is considered as an open avowal of his intentions, and it is occasionally repeated

---

[17] Martin Martin, *Description*, p. 295.
[18] As a definition of building, The Scottish National Dictionary, vol. ii, p. 317, quotes Halliday Sutherland's book *Ashes of the Years*, p. xxii.

until the marriage ceremony gives to his arms the object of his choice. The weddings generally take place in the winter time, and as the guests come from a distance, the entertainment sometimes lasts for several days in succession.[19]

Revd Walter Gregor
North-east, 1874

> If heaven a draught of heavenly pleasure spare,
> One cordial in this melancholy vale,
> 'Tis when a youthful, loving, modest pair
> In other's arms breathe out the tender tale.

Wooing was for the most part carried on under cover of night. At a late hour the young man set out for the abode of his lady-love. By the time he arrived all the family had retired to rest. He tapped at the window. The happy maiden 'wha kens the meaning o the same' was quickly at the door, undid the bar and admitted her lover. If he could not be admitted by the door, the window was lifted, and he made his entrance by it.[20]

Murdo Murray
Ness, Isle of Lewis, 1999

Though he emigrated to Canada in the mid-1950s, memories of the community that had been home to his family for generations are bright and clear, almost as if he had never left.

MB *Can you remember anything of the furnishings in the thatched houses in Ness?*

MM The 'beingidh' . . . it's a sort of settle, made of wood and it was about six feet long and when there was a crowd in the house it would be used. And then there would be wooden chairs, and then if there were many people in the house you would bring out a wooden box and sit on it – a box, or anything at all . . . The chimneys were about three feet thick and a big open fireplace and there was a slabhraidh, a chain, hanging down and the pot, the kettle, was hanging on that . . . and the fire underneath it . . . Also, most houses had a bed in the kitchen, a box bed – really well-built beds, so they were.

MB *Did they have a curtain?*

MM Oh yes, you had all the privacy in the world.

MB *Who slept in the box bed?*

---

[19] A. Edmondston, *A View of the Ancient and Present State of the Zetland Islands*, vol. ii, p. 64.
[20] W. Gregor, *Echo*, p. 108, and *Notes*, p. 87.

MM Mostly the parents, and maybe later on the young girl in the house might sleep in that bed and her lover probably come during the evening and visit her there.

MB *Do you recall that?*

MM Not in our house! No. But I knew it happened . . . 'Caithris na h-oidhche' . . . It was all done at night and done secretly, quite different from now . . . Caithris na h-oidhche . . . I [remember] going to school and seeing young men on bicycles coming home from Caithris na h-oidhche.

MB *Do you recall any word of the girl's mother arranging her to be in a certain configuration of blankets or a sort of stocking?*

MM No, I never heard of that . . . the girls were trusted and I think the girls were intelligent enough to know how far to go . . . That's really strange, I don't know, but they were well behaved, that's all I can say. Very few pregnancies occurred before marriage, very, very few.[21] . . . It was a real fear. You had to go and get baptism – everybody had to be baptised in those days. You had to go to the kirk session . . . and this was the girl herself, on her own, which must have been quite an ordeal for her to go to the minister and all these elders to ask permission. And then she would have to make a public appearance in the church where she was told off in no uncertain terms for her evil doings.

MB *This is a girl with an illegitimate child?*

MM With an illegitimate child . . . Yes, I heard my mother talking about it . . . and I knew it was an ordeal.

MB *Was there compassion, among the other women, for example?*

MM No, I couldn't say there was any compassion for her. No, she had sinned and she deserved what she got. I think that was what kept the women, the girls, from getting pregnant [But the man], he got off Scot-free . . . No reflection on him whatsoever . . . He was following [laughs] – he was following nature I suppose! No, he was getting away with it.[22]

Handfasting

In the closing decade of the twentieth century the idea of 'living together' became a fairly common one. Certain couples who have an established relationship may set up house together, and (with or without parental consultation) will live together until such time as they decide to marry or to part. Even in the so-called liberal sixties when the phrase 'trial marriage'

---

[21] Statstics for the 1880s and 90s show that the illegitimacy rate in rural Lewis was less than 2 per cent, whereas in Banff, where the customs differed, it was seven times higher. See T.C. Smout, *A Century of the Scottish People 1830–1950*, p. 171.
[22] Murdo Murray was recorded by MB while visiting his home in Mt Pearl, Newfoundland, Canada, 9 October 1999.

gained currency, this was very much the exception rather than the rule. Such arrangements were generally frowned upon in Scottish communities. There is nothing new under the sun, however, as our forebears had an ancient system of preparing couples for the lifelong partnership of marriage. '*Handfasting*', once commonplace all over Scotland, allowed a couple to declare their intention at a simple formality that usually took place at the Lammas fair, then live together publicly for a year. If all worked out favourably they were married a year and a day after they handfasted. In 1609 the 'Statues of Icolmkill [Iona] announced the abolition of handfast marriages in the Highlands, in an effort to bring all of Scotland under the control of the Scottish Parliament.[23] The custom was eventually wiped out with more than a little help from the church, yet it probably existed in the first place because of the scarcity of clergy in rural communities. Compared to the difficulties involved in travelling to remote settlements to perform individual marriages, it was much more practical for a priest from Melrose Abbey to attend a Lammas fair in the Borders and formally marry a number of couples who, after successfully handfasting for a year, had returned to formalise the marriage the next day. The rules that governed handfasting, and especially the care of any children born to such a union, were, however, firmly established: custody and care were the responsibility of the father, and the reputation of the mother was not in the least held in question. By contrast, the current century offers no such security to unwed mothers and their children who may find themselves the subjects of long legal debates, to say nothing of the village gossip they might have to 'live down'.

Martin Martin
Western Isles, *c.* 1695

It was an ancient custom in the islands that a man should take a maid to his wife, and keep her the space of a year without marrying her; and if she pleased him all the while, he married her at the end of the year, and legitimated these children; but if he did not love her, he returned her to her parents, and her portion also; and if there happened to be any children, they were kept by the father: but this unreasonable custom was long ago brought into disuse.[24]

---

[23] Register of the Privy Council, vol. ix, pp. 26–30. See e.g. Erskine Beveridge, *North Uist*, pp. 304–05.
[24] Martin Martin, *Description*, p. 114.

Revd Donald MacQueen
Kilmuir, Skye, 1774

The hand-fasting of the southern part of Scotland has put me in mind of an omission in [Thomas Pennant's *Tour*]. It was an ancient practice among the men of rank especially to take an year's tryal of a wife, and if they were mutually satisfied with one another in that time, the marriage was declared good and lawful at the expiration of it. But when either of the parties insisted upon a separation, and that a child was begotten in the year of probation, it was to be taken care of by the father only, and to be ranked among his lawful children, next after his heirs. He was not considered as a bastard, because the cohabitation was justified by custom, and introduced with a view of making way for a happy and peaceable marriage. One of the great Lords of the Isles took such a tryal of a nobleman's daughter upon the continent, got a son by her, and after separation settled an extensive fortune upon him in lands *tenendus de me, et heredibus meis,* the greater part of which his honorable posterity possess to this day. Such was also the power of custom, that this apprenticeship for matrimony brought no reproach on the separated lady; and if her character was good, she was entitled to an equal match as if nothing had ever happened.[25]

Meigle SWRI
Meigle, Perthshire, 1931

An old custom which was general in pre-Reformation days, and was participated in by a progenitor of a local family of standing, was that of marriage by handfast.

By it a couple agreed to live together for a year and a day. If at the end of that year they so desired it, they could separate, each going his or her way without loss of prestige. On the other hand, if they decided that they could go on through life together, then they were married in the usual way. Sounds rather like goods on approbation! A one-time popular form of marriage was the 'Penny Bridal,' but before a wedding could take place the couple had to become betrothed. This was marked by great ceremony, part of which was that of the couple licking the thumbs of their right hands and sticking them together in a solemn vow to keep faith. A few decades ago, this custom of licking and sticking thumbs together still prevailed among school children.[26]

---

[25] Written on 17 November 1774 by Revd Donald MacQueen, Kilmuir, Isle of Skye and published in Appendix XI of Pennant's *Tour*, vol. II, 1776, p. 432.
[26] Meigle SWRI, *Our Meigle Book*, p. 127. See also, 'The Custom of Hand-fasting', in E.T. Guthrie, *Old Scottish Customs*, pp. 46–9.

Betrothal Ceremonies

Revd George Low
Orkney, *c.* 1774

There was a custom among the lower class of people in this country which has entirely subsided within these twenty or thirty years. Upon the first day of every new year the common people, from all parts of the country, met at the Kirk of Stainhouse [Stennis], each person having provision for four or five days they continued there for that time dancing and feasting in the kirk. This meeting gave the young people an opportunity of seeing each other, which seldom failed in making four or five marriages every year; and to secure each other's love, till an opportunity of celebrating their nuptials, they had resource to the following solemn engagements: The parties agreed stole from the rest of their companions, and went to the Temple of the Moon, where the woman, in presence of the man, fell down on her knees and prayed to the god Wodden (for such was the name of the god they addressed upon this occasion) that he would enable her to perform all the promises and obligations she had and was to make the young man present, after which they both went to the Temple of the Sun, where the man prayed in like manner before the woman, then they repaired from this to the stone marked D [Stone of Odin], and the man being on the one side and the woman on the other, they took hold of each other's right hand though the hole, and there swore to be constant and faithful to each other. This ceremony was held so very sacred in those times that the person who dared to break the engagement made here was counted infamous, and excluded from all society.[27]

Iain Nicolson
Uig, Skye, 1988

MB *Were they still holding the réiteach [in the 1920s and '30s] when you were young?*
IN Réiteach? Oh, yes, yes, yes, yes, yes, yes . . . Well that was [held after] they were both together for a long time, and [they were getting close to] the time that they were going to marry. Oh well, bha seachdain na réiteach ann. So [the people involved] came [to the house of the young woman], well they took an offer. Well, I never heard of anything going wrong at all, but they would say at times it would, you know – they would break up and, och no, they never married; the réiteach finished. [For example], they weren't agreeing, something would come up, you

---

[27] G. Low, *A Tour Through the Islands of Orkney and Shetland in 1774,* Intro., p. xxvi.

know, and it was dismissed. Oh yes, oh the réiteach, ah yes. It was customary.

TM What would happen at a successful réiteach?

IN Oh well, you would get married; the day was appointed. The réiteach was first, whatever you do after that. Och aye, och that was quite common then. Oh aye. Oh very common.[28]

Dolly Wallace
Harris, 1985

Born and brought up in Harris, Dolly Wallace (née MacKenzie) regarded her local customs as part of the way of life. Over the years, she saw (and regretted) many changes in the traditional ways, including the disappearance of the *réiteach*. When her own daughter, Mórag, was about to get married in 1985, Dolly (then living in Skye) held a réiteach for the young couple.

DW Well, it was a fortnight before the wedding. That was in the old days before engagement parties came into it.[29] Now it's an engagement party when they get engaged. But I call it a réiteach, because to me it's tradition that counts. What I remember about it is it was an informal gathering where the bride's hand was asked for in marriage. A third party asked . . . He talked about something quite different. He didn't ask for the woman. When Morag's réiteach was here [May 1985] Iain MacDonald from Milivaig asked for her hand, it was a ewe lamb . . . He got up and he said that he had heard that Jim [her father] had a ewe lamb that was inclined to stray, and that he would be glad to take the ewe lamb off his hands and put it into a safer place, and that we wouldn't need to worry about the ewe lamb then because it would be in its own fold as it were. Jim replied 'Yes', he was quite happy to let him have the ewe lamb because he knew it was going into good hands.

MB *Back to the first réeiteach that you were at in Harris, can you remember what was asked for there?*

DW No!, but it was something on the same lines. He would have – whatever it was he had asked for, a boat or whatever was the case, he would have replied that he had this boat that had never been used by anybody else. . . . And that he was welcome to take her, and sail her in calm waters . . . I suppose it goes by the trade of the bride's family.

I was at one earlier but I was only eight. And that was my cousin that was getting married . . . It ran along the same lines. Her father was asked for the bride and he

---

[28] Iain Nicolson was recorded at Cuidreach, Isle of Skye, on 9 December 1988 by Thomas A. McKean and MB. SA1988/65.

[28] In his book *The Tolsta Townships*, Donald MacDonald notes that in his village in Lewis engagements did not exist until after the First World War. See pp. 64–6.

replied 'Yes'. Now I'm sure it was a sheep that was asked for there; he was a crofter. And when that was over there was a set meal . . . Oh they'd have the usual chickens and – it was a fork and knife affair. And the women would have been baking for days before it – cooking for days before it . . . The mother of the bride and all the neighbours would have helped. The best man and the bridesmaid would have been there, not in an official capacity but just as mere guests. It was better than a wedding. There was songs and dancing and music into the wee small hours. Accordions and fiddles, yes, and if there was a piper available he played.

It was all traditional singing, which was much, much nicer. They used to form a ring on the floor and everybody got into this – like a Paul Jones sort of thing – and joined hands and they sang . . . In 'the room'[30] really, because the kitchen would be fully occupied with pots and pans and dishes.

There was one in fact had a room off the end of the house, which was supposed to be a loom shed. But I don't think the loom even got the length of it. It was solely for weddings I think! It had no furniture. It had a seat. A wooden form round it; a cement floor. Well, it was just a shed really, but it was on the end of the house.

MB *So that was one particular réiteach . . . normally in a Harris house it would be in the part of the house they called 'the room'?*

DW Yes! That was used. That's where the food was.

MB *And was that where they kept all the best things? The best china. The seldom-used things?*

DW Oh yes! And the other room, which might have been a bedroom, was used for the singing and the dancing and whatever . . . Lots. And all the old songs that you don't hear anymore . . . and it went on until the wee small hours.

The first one I was at, we weren't that far away, we all walked home. And the next one it was buses . . . Och! 19— I was 17. That's 32 years ago. 1954?

The réiteach then was dying out; it's certainly died out at home now, because everybody that gets married gets married in a hotel, has the reception anyway in a hotel. And it's not the same. There's no house weddings now . . . It's very few of them that could remember a réiteach.

Well [in Skye] it's just similar to what I remembered being told about it, and what I remembered seeing myself, [except the] cuach-phòsda . . . That's a traditional Skye custom. And nobody living today remembers it being presented . . . It's got to be made of local wood by a local craftsman . . . George MacPherson made it [for Morag and Allan] from a piece of Hamara pine . . . from what his father told him.

MB *Is he still alive?*

DW Yes! And he's 86. George is in his 50s and his father, Alec Eirdsi, told him.

---

[30] 'The room' is the term used in both Gaelic and English for the best room in the house. In daily life it was seldom used, as it was normally kept for special occasions such as New Year celebrations, weddings, and funerals.

MB *Now, at what point in the evening's proceedings was it presented?*

DW . . . It was George, the man that made it [who] gave it to Morag and Allan, jointly.

MB *As a token of their betrothal?*

DW Yes!

MB *And from then on what happened?*

DW We had a great time! . . . And really it was fantastic. There was somebody playing an accordion. There was no room to dance. The children sang. The two wee girls and Colin sang 'Brochan Lom' in Gaelic for us . . . And . . . jokes were cracked and stories were told. They gave all sorts of advice to the young couple. And there was lots of stories told, all evening . . . Before and after . . . about various bridal couples.[31]

Robert Jamieson
Shetland, 1869

Before describing a Shetland wedding, we may step aside into a cottage by the banks of a quiet voe in the parish of Walls. . . Mary, whom the occasion has invested with a temporary importance, is awaiting the visit of her Jamie, who is coming that night to 'speer' for her. The house and its inmates are in the best of order; and while all are seated round the firefire, a tap is heard at the door, which is opened by the youngest member of the family, who, by dint of listening and reasoning, has formed a pretty correct idea of what is about to take place. In walks Jamie, remarkably confused. He does not know what to say, or where to look; but if he can at all manage it, he makes an awkward sally on the floor, and slips a small bundle into a box-bed which stands opposite the door – a bundle which everybody knows to be a bottle of excellent whisky, the 'speering bottle.' He advances to the fire, and shakes hands with all except Mary whom he does not seem to notice; while she, covered with blushes, does not seem to notice him. Tea over, every facility is put in his way for having an interview with the father; but he takes no hint, and appears blind to all the little plans and arrangements which Mary's sisters have made and are making. However, as the night advances, one of the sisters whispers to him, that if he 'wants to speak to da,' he would better do so now, as he has just gone to the barn to thrash the straw for the cow's supper. Go now he must; but when face to face with the man whose consent he must ask, his former awe of him having painfully increased, his mind becomes a blank, and he forgets every word of the neat little speech he had been prepared to

[31] Dolly Wallace was recorded on 23 July 1985, at Ramasaig, Isle of Skye, by MB. SA1985/156.

deliver, and can only stammer out bluntly that he and Mary are going to marry, and he wishes to ask his consent. When the father consents, and wishes them many happy days, Jamie comes jumping out of the barn, feeling as light as if a hill had been rolled off his shoulders, and is for the remainder of the night the heartiest, happiest, chattiest fellow alive. The bottle is drunk at breakfast next morning (Sunday); and in a few hours the whole district is informed that 'Jamie O'Houll speered for Mary O'Clingrigarth the streen.'[32]

Rosie and Dougald Campbell
Badenoch, 1992

RC They usually went together for years; it wasn't a few weeks! [laughs]

DC They still asked for the girl, oh yes . . . Oh yes, it was quite an occasion going and asking for the girl's hand in marriage.

MB *Are you talking from experience?*

DC Yes. [laughs] I had to ask for her!

RC [laughs]

MB *What actually happened?*

DC Well . . . the night seemed to be set aside, or at least by the couple anyway, but I think it was organized in the bride's home as well, in the girl's home . . . And on that evening the couple would go into the room where her parents were, and in due course you would ask for the girl's hand in marriage.

MB *Were you nervous?*

DC Very much so! [laughs] I suppose we were at that time. [laughs] . . . I suppose you were always under the impression that there might be a negative answer, and what would you do then?

RC We were told we were too young, weren't we?

DC Yes, we were told we were too young! Now what age would I be then?

RC You were going [on] 27 and I was 26. [laughs]

DC Yes, I was going 27 [laughs]. A few months later I was in active service during the war. And that was me too young!
     . . . We didn't get married till 1940.

RC Yes, were engaged two years.

DC . . . [After the engagement] the bottom drawer was always a great feature of the preparation. Everything went into the bottom drawer, building up a kind of household stock – tablecloths, towels, sheets, and that sort of thing – gifts that were presented once the couple were engaged . . . household items, so that this was a start-off in the new house.

---

[32] From an essay written by the teacher at Sandness, Robert Jamieson, chapter IX in John T. Reid's *Art Rambles in Shetland*, 1869, pp. 59–60.

MB *So you kept a bottom drawer?*

RC Oh yes! Actually I had one of the deep ones in the old-fashioned, big chest of
drawers, and everything went in there . . . Well, if you were away and you fancied
something, you maybe bought it and put it in. My sister and I had a habit that if
one of us was away for the day anywhere we bought something for ourselves and
brought the same back for the other one at home . . . Because we were both
engaged about the same time and there was just a year between us getting married.
She was the oldest so she was married first.[33]

Feet Washing and Other Good Clean Fun

Captain Edward Burt

Inverness, 1726

At a young Highlander's first setting up for himself, if he be of any
consideration, he goes about among his near relations and friends; and from
one he begs a cow, from another a sheep; a third gives him seed to sow his
land, and so on, till he has procured for himself a tolerable stock for a
beginner. This they call the *thigging*.

The evening before a wedding, there is a ceremony called the *feet-washing*,
when the bride-maids attend the future bride, and wash her feet.[34]

Samuel Hibbert

Shetland, 1822

Marriages, which are chiefly contracted during winter, serve to draw together
a large party, who not many years ago, used to meet on the night before the
solemnity took place. It was then usual for the bridegroom to have his feet
formally washed in water by his men, though in wealthy houses wine is used
for the purpose. A ring is thrown into the tub – a scramble for it ensued, the
finder being the person who would be first married.[35]

---

[33] Rosie and Dougald Campbell were recorded on 15 March 1992 at their home in
Newtonmore by MB. Rosie, b. 1914, is from Laggan and Dougald, b. 1913, is from
Knapdale, Argyllshire.
[34] Capt. Edward Burt, *Letters*, vol . II, pp. 188–9 and p. 207.
[35] Samuel Hibbert, *A Description of the Shetland Islands, Comprising an Account of their
Geology, Scenery, Antiquities, and Superstitions*, p. 554. There are relatively recent
accounts from oral tradition of a ring in the wash tub, for example, in 1969 Fred
MacAulay recorded a Gaelic-speaking woman in Fearn, Easter Ross, telling of a
'nighe nan cas' [feet washing] where several items, including a wedding ring, a half
crown and a sixpence, were put in the tub of water, along with cinders and hair.
After the girl's feet were washed, her friends scrambled for the ring to see who would
marry that year. SA1969/185.

Revd Walter Gregor
North-east, 1874

On the evening before the marriage there was the 'feet-washing'. A few of the bridegroom's most intimate friends assembled at his house, when a large tub was brought forward and nearly filled with water. The bridegroom was stripped of shoes and stockings, and his feet and legs were plunged in the water. One seized a besom and began to rub them lustily, while another was busy besmearing them with soot or shoe-blacking, and a third was practising some other vagary. Such a meeting could not take place without the board of hospitality being spread.

John H. Dixon
Gairloch, 1886

Among old customs still remaining in Gairloch are those connected with marriages and funerals . . . The marriage customs are a relic of the remote past. They consist of the washing of the feet of the bride and bridegroom at their respective homes on the evening before the wedding, and the putting to bed of the married couple on the night of the ceremony . . . Some of the younger people shirk these proceedings, especially in the more accessible parts of the parish, but as a rule they are strictly observed to the present day.[36]

Norman Kennedy
Aberdeen, 1991

MB *Norman, you were telling me you were at a feet-washing . . .*

NK Oh yes! Oh, dear, dear, dear! Well, this was more than twenty-five year ago, but the lad, a friend o mine – he wis a piper, and his father was a piper – and this was aboot two nights before the weddin, an we went oot for a drink, a whole bunch of us. And a couple of them had cars, you know – och, they would drink and drive no bother in those days. So we got real happy, an we decided – well, we'd *arranged* – to tell you the truth, we'd the stuff with us to do it – tae gie him a feet-washing, ye see. So we got into the car eftir the drink, an he had *no idea* what was going on – or if he did, he kept quiet. And we went doon tae the beach, doon on the sands in Aberdeen, an a bunch o us grabbed him an held him doon, an pulled off his troosers. An we had brown boot polish and black boot polish. So we took one leg and it was a' black; this one [slaps his right leg] was black, and the left one got

---

[36] John H. Dixon, *Gairloch*, 1886, p. 115.

brown! An eh, [laughs]] one ball was one colour an the other, let me tell you, it really wis! We did the whole works, you know, we did it all over! Oh he wis stretchin aboot, wrestlin aboot.

We got him into the car again an took him home, an we were goin to dump him at his folk's door, but they wir really old-fashioned folk, you know, an they knew this wis goin to happen. So they opened the door. 'C'm'on in, c'm'on in, boys!' So, oh, 'whit a mess!' his mother wis laughin. 'Oh, into the bathroom! Go on 'n wash yersel!'

An they had san'wiches made, an tea, an whisky, an we'd a good night eftir that. An poor laddie, his hands had been stood on an things like that, but he took oot his practice chanter, an his father too, an they played the tunes an that. I remember the neighbour doon the stairs – he was a policeman – an he knocked up 'cos o the noise, an we jist [both feet in heavy boots STAMP! STAMP! STAMP! on the floor], *everybody* in the room thumpin! The guy jist stopped, you know. So that wis one o the feet-washins. An then of course there wis my brother an sister-in-law. Oh, that wis rowdy!

MB *When was that one?*

NK Well, they were married twenty-five year ago. Noo this wis in my sister-in-law's mother's hoose, an we went across, cos they'd been across in my father an mother's hoose just tae meet our relatives an we went tae meet *their* relatives . . . oh, nice people . . . So anyway, we went across, an my sister-in-law, some o her aunties said 'C'm'on we'll make a cup o tea, c'm'on an gie's a hand.' An they went into the scullery and the door slammed shut! An her mother said 'Oh, my God! Not again,' she says, 'they jist did this last night, they feet-washed her wi cocoa, an it took me a day,' she says 'tae get the floor cleaned.' Ye see, so, there's pandemonium goin on! 'Oh, No! Let me go!' [the sister-in-law shouts], an then pots bashin, an then my mother says tae mi brither – he's jist sittin listenin tae a this, quite alarmed, you know. She says 'Oh, John, dinna sit there! Go an gie the lassie a hand.' I wonder if she meant it, you know, cos she *knew* what wid happen!

So he went in, an the door slammed shut again! An the door opened an oot cam his jacket, cos he wis dressed, ye know – oot cam his jacket. An there's pandemonium! 'Oh! you bugger!' he was shouting like that. An then one o the aunties cam flyin oot – cos they wir big, strong women – an her hands jist covered with boot polish, an she says, 'Throw my coat ower my shoulders,' she says, 'I'm gettin oot o here! An my brother cam oot pullin up his trousers, an grabbed her by the neck, and WHSSSHT! right in! I mean, her feet left the ground! Slammed the door, an jist hollerin an laughin! An another one cam oot, an as I say, they thought my brother wis straight-laced. An this woman burst oot, cam up tae my mother an she says 'So, ye thocht yer laddie wis a bittie straight-laced, eh? Look at this!' An she lifted her skirt right up, an he'd took two hands, an right up here all doon her [inner] thighs [were covered with black boot polish].

But I'll tell ye this, they thought a lot more of him because he wisnae sae straight-laced. But oh, you should have seen the shambles that kitchen wis in! Whit a shambles! An here's ma brither, he'd got a basin, an ordinary scrubbin brush, an he's washin himsel, an here's my poor sister-in-law waitin for him tae finish with the basin. And oh, I says, 'Is this a sign o things tae come? You've tae take second chance, you know!' But I'm sure they do that a lot in some places yet.[37]

James and Ina MacQueen
Gargunnock, Stirlingshire, 1982

IM I quite believe in my mother's day they had more fun than what we really had, they played more tricks. Because I remember one of my uncles, and his bride was down in our house and I remember they got her on the table and they were trying to make her eat soap . . . Of course they'd blackened her feet, and someone was trying to put the soap in her mouth . . . I've seen some of the girls in Stirling decorated with streamers and balloons, that's later on [in more recent years].

JM You get that with the factories . . . there's hardly a Friday night in Stirling but there's some of the factory girls, about a dozen or so, and they've got em all dressed up, balloons and what not.[38]

Maureen Jelks
Dundee, 1992

MJ If a girl wis gettin married, especially in the mills, then they dressed her up in old curtains or anythin, an one o the other women would dress as the man, an they would all go through the town, singin, and collectin money . . . I think the girl got to keep it, but they didna go into pubs or nothin like that, they jist walked. I can remember just them walkin doon the Overgate, they'd mebbe walk up an doon, up an doon, a' singin an huvin a cerry-on , an that wis that; an it wis good.

MB *Did they carry anything?*

MJ You know I really can't remember but people say they did, but I can't actually visualize this. An certainly when I saw this recently in Dundee she wasn't carrying

---

[37] Norman Kennedy from Aberdeen was recorded in Vermont, USA by MB, 14 August 1991.

[38] Mr and Mrs James MacQueen were recorded in Gargunnock in 1982 by Catherine Nichols who, at the time, was a student of Scottish Folklife Studies at Stirling University. Supervised by Dr Emily Lyle, she made extensive recordings of elderly people in Stirlingshire, almost all of which have customs that compare to the ones contained in this collection. Copies of her tapes are deposited in the Archives of the School of Scottish Studies. SA1982/37.

anythin – they jist huv white lace curtains fur their veil, the other lassie would huv a man's suit on an a top hat, and then the rest o them, the mill lasses, some o them dressed up wi funny hats or they'd carry balloons an follow them, just singin.

MB *What kind of songs would they sing?*

MJ Anythin. 'Ah'm gettin married in the mornin' and they still sing that song aboot, you know, 'Jessie's gettin married.' That's still [sung]! I couldn't believe that, actually, when I heard them singin that [even nowadays, in the 1990s]. Ah mean it wis just great![39]

The song 'Jessie's Gettin Merried', also known as 'The Spinner's Weddin' was composed early this century by former Dundee jute mill worker Mary Brooksbank when she was a young woman. She was born in 1898 and was recorded by Hamish Henderson when she was seventy years old.

Mary Brooksbank
Dundee, 1968

MB
    Oh the gaffer's lookin worried
    An the flett's a' in a steer;
    Jessie Brodie's gettin married,
    An the morn she'll no be here.

    Chorus
        Hurrah, hurro, a daddie o,
        Hurrah, hurro, a daddie o,
        Hurrah, hurro, a daddie o,
        Jessie's gettin married o.

    Oh the helper an the piecer
    Gaed doon the toon last nicht
    Tae buy a wee bit present
    Jist tae mak her hame look bricht.

    They bocht a cheeny tea-set,
    An a chanty fu o saut,
    A bonnie coloured carpet,
    A kettle, an a pot.

[39] Maureen Jelks was recorded at the School of Scottish Studies on 2 April 1992 by MB. SA1992/02.

Oh the shifters they're a' singin,
The spinners dancin tae;
The gaffer he's fair worried
But there's naethin he can dae.

Here's best wishes tae ye, lassie,
Stannin at yer spinnin frame.
May ye aye hae full an plenty
In yer wee bit hame.

Oh ye'll no mak muckle siller,
Nae matter hoo ye try;
But hoard ye love an loyalty,
That's whit money cannae buy.

I put the words on the basis o what really happened – they gaithered up an gave her a present, an they danced an they sang, an made life unbearable that day for the gaffer, till she got married. It wis a happy time, though.

HH When did you make that song, Mary?

MBr Oh, years an years ago . . . no in mi teens actually . . . it wis eftir an incident like that took place, but I jist canna mind the year. But I put the words, an I sung them tae some o the lassies, you know. They used tae dress her in auld lace curtains an gie her a cabbage as a bouquet, an escort her hame.[40]

Nan Courtney
Glasgow, 1991

MB *Did they ever get a hold of the bride or groom before they were married?*

NC Yes, they had a night for the bride, an the bridegroom had his friends an usually they got a very rough passage. An' at my particular time in life when girls were getting married they usually worked in a factory, and the girls in the factory wid all be asked up tae the house tae what they called the 'show o' presents'. And then they would take the bride an dress her up in ribbons an bows an take her out ontae the street and parade her up an doun the street an huv pots an pans an rattles an thingmys like that. An then they would sit her doun, an they usually hud a chamber pot – noo a very, very auld Scotch custom, they used to fill it wi salt an dance round about the bride . . . She'd sit on the chamber pot, an it was full o salt for

---

[40] Mary Brooksbank was recorded on 22 May 1968 in her home in Dundee by Hamish Henderson. SA1968/317. On this recording she omitted verse 3 'They bocht a cheeny tea-set . . .' but I have included it here as it is commonly sung by many singers and is also printed in several song collections. The rest of the transcription is just as she sang it, and is not, therefore, identical to other printed versions.

luck . . . an they wid dance on the street, dance around, and they wid parade her up an doun, an she had to carry this chamber pot, you know, or 'chanty' as we would call it.

MB *What would occasion her sitting down?*

NC They wid jist, eh, dance round about her – jist plop her doun an hold her doun, you know – a lot of fun! An tie balloons an . . . They'd dressd her up . . . mebbe old curtains, in a mock bridal array . . . Oh, net curtains, an mebbe a bunch o flowers or mebbe a bunch o vegetables fur a prank, you know. An a' these sorta things, an balloons tied a' roon about her, you know. But the men, really, when they went tae toun, they gave some of the bridegrooms a very rough passage! Sometimes they tarred an feathered them – they got up tae all sorts of things, ye know. But eh, they got many a sore crack, you know! Mebbe chained tae a lamp post . . . a' sorts o pranks, you know!

MB *What would he be wearing?*

NC Well, usually they wid have him dressed up, an sometimes their suits got quite a lot of rough handlin, you know. I think they'd be very well advised no tae go very well dressed up tae thir night out. But there wis really some fun! Ah there's been different things happen; sometimes serious accidents happened at these sort a thing. But wi the girls it wis mair sort a jovial, but the bridegrooms, they played some terrible pranks on them, you know. But oh, customs is a' changed noo – you still see them in Glasgow right enough – ocasionally, mebbe there's still a night they go on tae the street an that, but it's no as hectic as it used tae be – you know when they used tae have them a' dressed up in big lace curtains an that, wreaths roon thir heid, an balloons a' tied all o'er them, you know. An thir jackets mebbe a' sewn up when they went tae pit on thir coat, when they were leavin the work thir jacket wid be a' sewn up an if they wir in the factory, oh there wis a' sorts o thing, fancy things done tae them . . . fancy streamers, ribbons an everything, you know. Oh aye, it was good fun! . . . An drink was taken by a'! [laughs]

MB *Did the girls have a drink too?*

NC Oh aye! Very often. Oh they used to call it a 'bottlin'. In some parts o Scotland they used to say they're 'Gaun tae a bottlin'.

MB *How well in advance of the wedding did this take place?*

NC Well the bridegroom, it wis really the night before his marriage, an the girl, mebbe a day or two, you know. Durin the week which she was gettin married. Mebbe about the beginnin o the week havin the show o presents, you know, then this would happen.

MB *There were maybe one or two weddings with sore heads?*

NC Very, very many sore heads! An some just could make it to the marriage ceremony an no more! [laughs] Ah yes! I've heard o some funny things happinin, they jist didnae know how they wir gaun tae make it, but they usually did, you know, they usually made it tae the altar!

MB *What a way to start!*

NC Well, this is it: this is customs – this is custom in Scotland you know![41]

Pat MacNab
Comrie, Perthshire, 2004

MB *You told me once about the herds down Glenartney –*

PM Oh, aye, it was a big day, that. They used to hide and everything else, the men that were getting married, away to my mother's. And one was there one night, and they came in and hauled him out of my mother's house.

MB *Roughly what year that would be?*

PM Oh, I would be about twelve, I remember them hauling him out the back door – around 1924. I was born in 1912.

MB *Why was he hiding?*

PM Because they tarred and feathered him. They had him out there, and they stripped him off – it was cold weather too – completely naked, and tarred him a' doon then flung a whole load of feathers. There was feathers in yon green for days afterwards.

MB *Did they actually use tar, or some other black substance that would be less drastic?*

PM Oh tar!

MB *So what was his fate after he was covered?*

PM Oh, well, he was there – and you see in these days you had no baths and everything else, you had to boil water and everything to try and get yourselves clean. He was chocolate coloured for days afterwards. You could see his arms and everything where they had done him, and he'd scraped and washed it off as best he could. But that was quite common in these days.

MB *How long before his wedding was that?*

PM That one? Oh, that one we're talking about was just nights because he'd escaped everything till the day before . . . Well, he got married in Abernethy. He went away across there, on a pushbike, to Abernethy Church.[42]

Margaret Wilson
Lilliesleaf, 1990

MW Here it was the custom to blacken the bridegroom's feet the night before [the wedding] with shoe polish. Some of the young ones would catch him unawares and they would get a hold of him, take his shoes and socks off to blacken his feet – it's

---

[41] Nan Courtney, Glasgow, was recorded by MB on 7 July 1991.
[42] Pat (aged 91) was recorded in Comrie, Perthshire by MB, 5 April 2004

supposed to be lucky. Now it has got out of hand. At the stag night in the pub they strip all his clothes off, *the lot*! They blacken anywhere they can get a hold of, and then they turn him upside down and mark the ceiling with his feet. Another thing they would do the day before the wedding, if the mother would be in on it and let them at the packed case: They got a hold of the bride's nightie and sew up the bottom and fill it with confetti, or possibly they'd sprinkle confetti into the case among the clothes. They did things like that for fun.[43]

Jim Rendall
Papay Westray, Orkney, 2002

JR We didn't have blackenings in Papay till about fifty year ago when a fellow from the Mainland (Orkney) was getting married and he said he'd need to be blackened. We had no bother obliging, with tins of boot polish – and that was the night afore his wedding![44]

Elizabeth Stewart
Mintlaw, 1988

MB *What is the blackening?*
ES Oh, they mak a right mess o ye! They would plan to get a hold of the bride either comin from her work or whatever she was doing, and get a hold of the groom the same way. Just sort o trap them intae something so you could get a hold of them and really make a mess o them!
MB *What would you put on them?*
ES It could be anything – tar, syrup, treacle, feathers, chocolate, anything, like cocoa . . .
MB *And did it matter what they were wearing at the time?*
ES Not at all!
MB *If they were wearing their Sunday best you'd still do it?*
ES Yes, oh yes! Even better! I just happen to know a family not long ago – my nephew was one of them. Oh, it's terrible, it was ridiculous! They actually stripped him and he had nothing on but a pair of [under]pants, and they took him all through the streets of Ellon . . . He's a musician, this boy, and he was really dressed up to go away to do some teaching this night, and they caught him and put him in a lorry.

---

[43] Margaret Wilson was recorded in Lilliesleaf by Susan Huntly in 1990. SA1990/18.
[44] Noted from Mr Rendall during a discussion on customs held after a talk by MB in the village school, Papay Westray, 2002. 'The blackening' occurs in most parts of Scotland, sometimes under another name, and with a range of regional variations. See M. Bennett, *Local Dimensions in Oral Tradition*, 1991.

Of course I was on top of the lorry with them, holding him down! All through the streets of Ellon! [laughs] They poured syrup, treacle, feathers, eggs, flour . . . Fit else, Michael? [to her son] You wis there! Aye, they mixed everything you could get in a kitchen into big bowls – sauces, salt, spices, anything!

MB *And you'd call it 'a blackening' even though it wasn't necessarily black?*

ES Oh aye. And soot! Long, long ago it used to be soot!

MB *Did they do this to the girl as well?*

ES Oh yes![45]

In some parts of Scotland it is only the men who get blackened, such as the poor victim I saw in Kingussie one icy December night. He was tied to a lamppost on the main street, wearing only underpants (which were hardly visible) and covered head to foot with car oil and feathers. As he waited to be rescued by a benevolent relative or friend, he was, nevertheless, much more fortunate than the off-shore worker who spent the night before his wedding on the deck of an oil rig, clad only in used engine-oil and the feathers from a pillow plastered on his naked body by an enthusiastic crew of drillers who left him at the mercy of the elements. As some folk say, 'There's no end to the fun you can have at a blackening or foot-washing, provided you're no the victim!' There are, however, other pre-wedding customs which amount to a 'real guid night for everyone', despite certain risks that accompany all of them – headaches, hangovers, loss of memory, broken limbs – the choice is limitless!

Bill McBride
Bathgate, 1992

BM In our area when somebody's getting married some of the local lads climb onto the roof and tie a flag, a Saltire or whatever, onto the chimney or some projection of it. And the first one to do it gets a bottle of whisky.

MB *Is this the night before the wedding?*

BM Yes, in fact it happened in the case of my own son, three or four years ago.

MB *Which town is this done in?*

BM Well, I come from Whitburn [West Lothian]; certainly in Blackburn. I don't know where else, but I've seen it done in both these places.

MB *Any idea where it comes from?*

BM Not really. Just one of those things![46]

---

[45] Elizabeth Stewart was recorded at the School of Scottish Studies while a guest at a lecture given by MB. SA1988/25.
[46] Bill McBride was recorded in Bathgate on 3 March 1992 by MB.

John Jack
St Monans, Fife, 1858

A [wedding] flag or ensign embellished with many figurative representations, such as hands joined, hearts united, and other fanciful devices, all emblematic of the matrimonial union [was raised]. This bridal concomitant has almost fallen into total [disuse], except amongst the seafaring population, who still maintain the practice, and preserve it from literally vanishing.[47]

Wedding Presents

Peigi Stewart (Bennett)
Isle of Skye (and Balquhidder) 2004

MB *Did you have a show of presents when you were married?*

PSB Oh good gracious, yes! That would always take place a week or so before the wedding, in the bride's house, usually in a bedroom. But I was married in Glasgow, in 1940, so it wasn't in my mother's house [in Glenconon, Skye], but in my mother-in-law's house, in Glasgow. Compared to today, you only got small presents[48], and you would have them all laid out on a bed.

MB *What sort of presents did you get?*

PSB It was a custom that the chief bridesmaid always gave the bride a china tea-set, like, my sister Effie gave me my wedding tea-set. You wouldn't get any furniture or anything like that – not even a stool. Table lamps were very popular, so were table cloths. Bedspreads, quilts, blankets, often from the parents, and pillows and boxed sets of pillow cases and all sorts of linen – bed linen, towels, usually boxed sets. And cheval sets – wee dressing table sets, usually from a neighbour, or a girl you worked with, she would give you a wee thing like that. And another thing was chair-backs, and chair-arms – antimacassars, as they're called, but I only read that word in a book, and the first time I read about antimacassars I didn't know I actually had some! And cushion covers. Ornaments, vases, glasses – I got a crystal sugar and cream. Teapots. Fireside sets. Cutlery, cake-stands, and anything you'd use in the kitchen, mostly not a big thing – a toasting fork, there were no toasters,

---

[46] *County Folklore*, vol. vii, *Fife*, p. 164, quoted from a note in John Jack, *The Key of the Forth*, p. 60.

[48] In Joyce Rankin's anthology about her Scottish-Cape Breton mother and grandmother, her poem 'Wedding Gifts' paints the picture: 'Small offerings from neighbours/ when a girl became a wife . . . On her wedding day she got:/ a black-iron biscuit tin / 2 tin bread pans/ and 2 more that came later / (not quite the same size), / a flour sifter . . . / a rolling pin – a rock maple chunk her father carved by hand . . .' *At My Mother's Door*, p. 31.

you made your toast over the open fire. Did I mention tongs? And you might get an odd picture. Some people gave money, but of course the money was never on show, it was just an envelope with the person's name on it. And of course you always thanked the people who gave presents.

MB *And who would attend?*

PSB It was all women who went to the show of presents, mostly the close relatives and neighbours and girls you worked with. You'd have a cup of tea and lots of home baking. And at my show of presents, a friend of mine read the cups – she was a landlady we had, and she used to read tea-cups. Of course it was all loose tea then, not such thing as teabags. It was just for a bit of fun. And it was always in the evening because a lot of people were working, especially during the wartime. You see, before the war, once a woman got married she left her work – in a lot of places they weren't allowed to work, except maybe widows, and sometimes the women who cleaned might be married supporting a family.

MB *And at the show of presents, were there any men at all?*

PSB Oh, no, anything like that would be cissy! Men wouldn't wash a cup in those days, and they wouldn't even push a pram or do anything that was women's work. Really, it was a different world.

Wedding presents are usually brought to the reception nowadays, (apart from items too big to carry), though it was formerly the custom to deliver the present to the bride's parents' house several days before the wedding. Today's lavish presents (often requested by the bridal couple via their chosen department store) bear no resemblance to typical gifts from the past.

Before the Second World War, wedding presents were often a contribution to the wedding feast. Gifts such as oatmeal, butter, whisky, dried fish, salted mutton, pieces of stoneware or small household items were frequently given, while the most common gift of all was a hen for the feast. Then, a few nights before the wedding, the bride, her mother, sisters and female friends got together to pluck and prepare them and to prepare the entire bridal feast. The hard work was made light by the hilarity and banter among the women – thus the origin of the 'hen-party' of the late twentieth century, which has become another commercial venture for twenty-first century business opportunists.

Dolly Wallace
Harris, 1985

MB *What happened between the réiteach and the wedding?*

DW Oh, just the plucking of the hens for the wedding [feast]. The 'hen wedding' it was called, when they went up a couple of days before the actual wedding and plucked all the hens that were handed in by various neighbours . . . And they cooked all the meat and all the hens . . . And there was tea going all night.

MB *Was there a wedding cake?*

DW Oh, yes! That was always bought – even in my mother's day, I think. But I made Morag's engagement cake for the réiteach.

MB *Did you put any trinkets in it?*

DW No . . . but in the old days it would be sixpences and buttons. The one that got the button would end up a bachelor, be it men or women. And the one that got the sixpence of course, would get the fortune – that never materialised!

Hen Nights and Stag Parties

Louise MacVicar and Joan Mann
Glenalmond, Perthshire, 2002

MB *Looking back over these years to before you were married, you had at least one – what did you call it?*

LM Hen night.

MB *Why is it called a 'hen night'?*

LM I've absolutely no idea.[49]

MB *And who arranged it?*

LM The girls from work . . . in Edinburgh. There was a crowd of girls from work, and my family – yourself and Mum, and my sister . . . The girls from work had me all dressed up. They had made a board with L-plates [on the back] and a little pot for collecting money – a cup, sort of thing, which they attached on to the placard board, which I wore, and the idea was to collect money, which I had never heard of before, but apparently that's the tradition. And it had condoms and all sorts of horrible things attached to it . . . And round my head I had a garland of silk flowers, like you'd be presented with if you went Hawaii, strung together with elastic, and I wore them like a daisy crown! And I think I ended up with your Statue of Liberty glasses as well!

---

[49] Several earlier writers describe the importance of hens in wedding preparations, not only for the wedding feast, but also the 'thigging', saving the feathers for pillows, etc. (e.g., Revd Walter Gregor, 1874)

MB *Where were you working at the time?*

LM *The Scotsman* newspaper. It was all the glamour girls from the advertising department and they were just riotous . . . Great fun! . . . We went to [a restaurant in the Grassmarket] and had a meal.

MB *Can you remember the hilarity at the meal?*

LM Yes, I can. It was great fun! I remember being presented with a bouquet – the best one I've ever had! Basically a banana, with two broccoli florets – is that what you call them? – surrounded by other vegetables, all tied up nicely with ribbons – and some chickweed trailing, instead of gypsophila. It was hilarious! Just hilarious! I do remember you turned up in a very fetching pair of bright yellow sunglasses!

MB *And even your mother found it amusing?*

LM Oh, yes, I think that's one of the most amusing things about my hen night – the first time you ever see your mum in that situation. I don't think I'd ever been in the pub with Mum until that point, and I thought, if somebody had been telling me afterwards of Mum, I'd have thought 'Oh, she'll be horrified!' But in fact she thoroughly enjoyed it and joined in all the fun. She though it was really good crack!

MB *Even laughed at the off-colour jokes?*

LM Oh, yes, whereas before I'd have expected her to go, 'Hmm! That's terrible!' [*laughs*] She didn't quite tell any herself but she certainly joined in with the laughter.

MB *Were you embarrassed at any of them?*

LM No, I don't think so.

MB *Can you remember any of the jokes?*

LM [*helpless laughter*] I can, but I couldn't possibly repeat them! [*laughs*]

MB *Ones told in front of your mum?*

LM Oh, jings! [*laughs*] I hope they weren't told in front of my mum!

MB *Who told them?*

LM I think maybe the girls from work.

MB *That bad?*

LM Oh, terrible! But then, this is a crowd of girls who'd dance on the top of the tables in a public restaurant after one glass of wine. They're just hilarious and I couldn't possibly repeat any of the jokes.

[Louise's mother joins the conversation]

MB *Joan, what do you remember about Louise's hen-night?*

JM Just the hilarity, and taking over this whole restaurant, everybody looking to see what all the fun and games was all about. I remember being extremely embarrassed by her aunt's phallic posy [*laughs*] with the vegetables.

MB *Embarrassed by that? It was just a bunch of vegetables!*

JM Extremely embarrassed – it was so suggestive!

LM Of course I was very innocent. I'd never seen anything like that – I didn't know why it was suggestive at all! [*laughs*]

MB *I remember Joan laughing so much her mascara ran down her cheeks!*

LM Yes, so do I! And thinking 'What's Mum laughing at? She probably doesn't even know what they're talking about!'

JM I remember feeling very privileged that I was invited to my daughter's hen party. And, to tell the truth, I had never been to a hen party before that.

MB *Do you think it's a good idea?*

JM Very good idea, just a time to let her hair down. And then after we had our meal the youngsters all went off by themselves, and the older ones went home to bed.

MB *It sounds from all reports that you and I shouldn't have been in the second part of it anyhow!*

JM No, we wouldn't want to know!

MB *After you got rid of the mother and the aunties, where did you go then?*

LM We went on and got riotously drunk, basically. And the idea was to kiss as many blokes as you could get round in the evening . . . We went on to Harry's Bar in the West End where we got chatted up by loads of blokes and I'm sure I ended up nearly slapping some guy because he was just, oh, awful. Blokes seem to think that when you're on your hen night and you're wearing L-plates or whatever, that they can get away with whatever they like.

MB *Really? What sort of things?*

LM Touching you up and kissing you when you don't want a kiss and just general lewd behaviour.

MB *So did you set them straight?*

LM Oh, absolutely! Short of raising my hand to one of them I just basically told them to get lost. Or raising my knee, but I'm quicker with my hands! And I seem to remember we were home and in bed by one o'clock in the morning which is unusually early for a girls' night out, but I think by then we'd all drunk so much that we were all unable to go anywhere else. We didn't walk home because we lived in Portobello at the time so it would've been an awful long walk, but I don't remember going home. I do remember we couldn't get into a nightclub because we were all so drunk, and that's the point at which we went home.

MB *At least you had sense enough to do that – presumably in a taxi.*

LM Yes, although my second hen night I did walk home because it was in Lochearnhead.

MB *A second one? Was that quite different?*

LM It was different. In some ways that was more fun because I wasn't dressed up, it was just a crowd of friends and it was actually mixed company. What happened was, it was the weekend of Alan's stag night and his friends had all come over from Ireland. So I was on my own, and I went up to stay at Mum and Dad's, and all my friends from home said, 'Come on out to the pub, you can't sit in on your last weekend of freedom.' . . . There was a band playing in the Clachan

[Lochearnhead] and we had a rip-roaring night! As I say, it was boys and girls, so, although I say it was my second hen-night some people might just say it was a night out. But, because Alan wasn't there, and it was probably the last night I had on my own before I got married, I'd say it was my second hen-night.

MB *Did you really feel a sense of liberty for the last time, or anything like that?*

LM In a way, but then again, I wouldn't be the sort of that would take to extremes. You do hear of some girls who think it's the end of their freedom and will go, you know, get themselves a lumber for the night, sort of thing, but that's not my cup of tea, and to me it's just a bit of a laugh. It's tradition, you know, to go out and have a bit of a party, make a fool of yourself.

MB *Did Alan have a stag night?*

LM He had a stag night in Edinburgh – all his friends came from Ireland and they all went out in Edinburgh – his brothers too. And I think it ended at midnight when Alan had to take the best man home cos the best man was so drunk – I'd say they were all extremely drunk by midnight. But thankfully there were no strippers and he wasn't tied to any lamppost and there was nothing like that! So that was good . . . You look forward to your hen-night or your stag night so much, cos it's such a big thing, that it always has the potential to be a real let down, a real anti-climax. And I think that's why my Lochearnhead second hen-night was such good fun, because it was really impromptu.

MB *How long before the wedding?*

LM I think my hen-night was three weeks before the wedding and Alan's stag night was two weeks before the wedding.

MB *So, there was plenty time to recover.*

LM Oh, yes, nowadays I don't think you'd risk doing it the night before, as is tradition. But then that's because there's such a strong emphasis on getting full out your mind that you just wouldn't risk doing it the night before. Nothing worse than walking down the aisle with a hangover – or maybe *not* being able to walk down the aisle! You hear horror stories of people whose husbands have been down the aisle then thrown up all over his wife's wedding dress! No! You wouldn't risk that!

MB *No word of blackening you?*

LM No, I had all the girls warned that there was to be none of that – that if they tried to attach me to a lamppost or get me a stripper I was out there, I wouldn't stay. As soon as I said I wouldn't hang about at all, I think they realised I was quite serious, so they didn't do anything but have this placard board thing which was just fun, really.[50]

---

[50] Recorded by MB, 4 April 2002.

Margaret Bennett
Diary entry, 4 July 2003:

Flying from Dublin to Prestwick we discover a new meaning for 'in-flight entertainment'. A bunch o lassies board the plane in high spirits, coming home after a hen night – or weekend. The bride-to-be sporting an outrageous pink wig, a very flimsy tartan skirt showing old-fashioned white bloomers rather than sexy knickers, and the most awful set of grotty false teeth. Several of her pals wear tartan 'Jimmy' hats, and some have opted for the teeth as well. They're having a great time, and plan to make it last as long as they can. At Prestwick, they're rounded up by one of the group so that I can take a photo. 'Fabulous time,' she tells me, handing me her business card in case I know some other lassies who fancy a hen night in Dublin

Margaret Bennett
Diary entry, 22 February 2004

Sunday night flight from Edinburgh to Dublin – here we go again, a hen party, with the traffic in the opposite direction. The Dublin girls have had a great time in Edinburgh – 'great craic altogether!' My two companions (both professors of art) make hilarious quips about the get-ups. The outside temperature is freezing, the bride-to-be is wearing a scanty crop-top skin-tight over her '48 triple E's', as she tells her pal. As she negotiates the aisle the banter escalates. More hilarity in Dublin as we wait for the luggage. A photo? 'Of course', says she, grabbing Will MacLean's arm. 'Take one of me with your husband!' We're helpless with laughter. I attempt to rescue Will, 'Oh, that's OK, just yourself, he's getting our luggage.'

'Fabulous place, Edinburgh,' she tells us, and Will tells me that this so-called research of mine could get folk in bad trouble.

Joe McAtamney
Glasgow, 1992

JM Stag parties? Oh dear, you don't really want to know! . . . This is one of the earliest
    times I remember ever being at a stag party . . . Now this stag party was held in the
    Covenanters' Hotel up in Aberfoyle. Ah'd went up with a group; we all went up in
    a big bunch o cars and vans, and we proceeded wi the stag party – laughing, joking,
    drinking as much as we could, singing a few songs, and then drinking more than
    we could. So this went on until obviously I reached oblivion. I remember waking
    up the next morning in bed – and the 'uniform' [fashionable dresswear] at that

time, I forgot to say, was usually a charcoal grey suit, and a white collar and everything else. So I woke up the next day an I looked out the side o the bed, and I thought 'Oh dear God!' I couldn't remember where I had been or anything else, how I got home. I looked down an here's this beautiful white shirt, black! Full of clay an you name it, whatever, an everything that I had on, the whole suit was jist a shambles of earth, dirt, tattie peelins and God knows what.

I'd no idea where I was, so I had this paranoia, I wis scared to ask anything for while. I eventually got up courage and phoned up one o ma friends an says, 'Last night, how did I get home?' He says, 'You mean how did we all get home?' He says, 'We were all in the back o Bob the Bell's fruit van, an it was a fu o sacks of potatoes an everything else, an we were all that drunk that every time he's drivin down the road at 80 miles an hour, you see, an we were all rollin among all these potatoes an everything else.' That was my first experience of a stag party.

MB *It wasn't your own one, then?*

JM No, not my own. I remember less about it, except I woke up the next mornin wi frilly knickers in my pocket, an packets of condoms – planted, of course! [*laughs*]

SS Did nobody every tell you that condoms don't grow?

JM Huv you not heard o rubber trees, no?[51]

'Jumping the Chanty' in Kilmarnock, Ayrshire

Audrey Bain
Kilmarnock, 1989

'Jumping the chanty' is a ritual which brides-to-be in Kilmarnock have practised for at least ninety years.[52] The actual jumping of the chanty (chamber pot) takes place at the 'pay-off' of the girl in question, and is normally held on the last Friday at work before her wedding. The girl's workmates, however, prepare for the occasion several weeks in advance.

An old coat is acquired, usually from the girl's mother, and workmates meet secretly at lunchtime in the ladies' toilets at work or after working hours at each others' houses to make paper flowers from coloured tissue (sometimes coloured toilet roll is used, though this is not usual!) with which to decorate it. The girl's female workmates also decorate a hat, shoes and a chanty with brightly coloured paper roses and these are laid aside for her special night out. While

---

[51] Joe McAtamney, from Glasgow, was recorded by MB on 22 March 1992. The quip at the end [SS] is from Joe's step-son who was in the company at the time.
[52] The custom is also familiar to several other towns and villages, not only on the west coast of Scotland but also in parts of the Lothians.

some women churn out small paper blooms by the dozen, and some are busily stitching these to the coat, others are feverishly scribbling small verses peppered with lively innuendo concerning the wedding night which are tied to the chanty or put inside it. From the typical examples that follow it is obvious that the ladies have a great deal of fun concocting them:

Two white pillows edged with lace,
Bride and bridegroom face to face,
Everything in its proper place,
TALLY HO!!!

When you get up in the morning,
Don't blush with shame,
Remember your mother before you,
Did the very same.

Love is a thing that no man knows,
It touches the heart,
And tickles the toes,
Six months of pleasure,
Three months of pain,
A fortnight in bed,
And a bonnie wee wean!

Long and thin goes too far in
And doesn't please the ladies
Short and thick does the trick
And manufactures babies!

Love is like a mutton chop
Sometimes COLD,
Sometimes HOT!!

There's a marriage game called 'Ten Toes,'
It's played all over the town;
The girls play with ten toes UP,
The boys play with ten toes DOWN!

Honeymoon Drink
1 Long John
2 High Balls

The taxman takes your tax,
The rent man takes your rent,

> Your husband knows what he's going to take,
> And he knows his money's well spent!

Thus adorned, the chanty is then filled with salt. Until about ten years ago a real china chamber pot was used, but since these are now become scarce and often very expensive, and also because they were fairly heavy objects, many people now use basins or large bowls, still referred to as chanties. Filled with salt the chanty is now ready to receive 'lucky pieces' and coins on the day of the pay-off.

When the day of the pay-off finally arrives, the girl is taken by her workmates into a small room or the ladies' toilet shortly before stopping work and dressed up in the special costume they have painstakingly prepared for her, though in some factories such as Jaeger in Kilmarnock, the bride-to-be has to sit at her machine all day dressed in her flowery outfit or some other fancy dress outfit. The girl is then handed the salt-filled chanty and throughout the presentation, she acts with the degree of surprise considered appropriate on such an occasion though I have been told many times that 'the lassie kent fine well whit wis going tae happen'. Next the workmates of the girl take her round the factory or office – sometimes on her feet, sometimes in a barrow – so that all the other workers from the tea-boy to the managing director can wish her luck, give her a kiss, and put some silver in her pot. Sometimes the well-wisher will also 'take a lick o' salt for luck'. Chanty salt was believed to be very lucky at one time, and people with ailments such as backache put this 'lucky salt' on a plaster and placed this over the affected area. This belief was so strong that even cuts were treated in this manner, and this is one of the reasons why even today women keep their chanties intact.

Only silver coins are put into the chanty, and they are pushed deep into the layer of salt so that the contribution is anonymous. In this way, everyone, regardless of their financial status, is able to contribute something without embarrassment. Several significant small items are also put into the chanty, and these differ slightly from pay-off to pay-off these days, but the main objects to which all form of weird and wonderful other things can be added are a baby doll, a dummy teat, safety pins, vaseline, condoms and syrup of figs.[53] The condoms are not a new element introduced as a result of today's open attitudes to sex and contraception as I at first assumed. The buying of the condoms is itself an integral part of the tradition, and it always has been. Condoms, or 'French letters' as they were once commonly known, were not always as easy to purchase as they are today because few shops in the town

---

[53] Health warning: in other circumstances, keep vaseline away from condoms; petroleum jelly dissolves rubber.

actually stocked them. One shop which did sell condoms was the local herbalist, and the lady assigned the unenviable task of buying the embarrassing articles – she was chosen by picking straws or drawing names from a hat – would always be at great pains to stress to the assistant that it was 'for a chanty', and a knowing look would pass between them.

Before work is over for the day, the girl is led by her workmates to an appointed place in the centre of the factory or office where she jumps her chanty three times, supported on either arm by two of her girl-friends. All the girl's workmates shout 'Bosola' and 'Hurray' as she jumps, and if they have tools they clang these on their machines. Kilmarnock women reserve the word 'bosola' especially for this occasion; for some of them it refers to the event, while to others it is the name for the bedecked bride-to-be on this unique day. So begins the pay-off, and to the sound of rousing cheers the group proceeds out of the place of work to begin the grand tour.

The bride-to-be and her female workmates plan a route which will ensure maximum exposure to the public. They choose the main streets and the busiest roads as places to jump the chanty, singing and shouting as they go for people to 'Come and see the bosola!'. Each time the girl jumps her chanty at an appointed place she must jump it 'three times for luck'. Mrs Mary Bain of Kilmarnock stressed the importance of the three jumps:

> If you jumped the chanty twice and a bus came you would have to wait till the bus went past – bearing in mind you jump the chanty in the centre of the main road, you don't do it on the pavement, you do it in the centre of the main road – so if you jump twice and a bus comes, of course, you've to move away to let the bus pass. Everybody on the bus waves out to you, they are quite used to that kind of thing happening, and they enter into the spirit of the thing. Only recently, just the other week, I was in a bus and this same thing happened. Somebody was jumping the chanty and they'd to remove the chanty from the centre of the road till the bus went past. The passengers all waved and then she had to put the chanty back into the middle of the road and complete her third jump. So its significant that it's three times – three times for luck – that's part of the tradition.

While this is certainly true of some pay-offs, many now stop the traffic, and buses, cars and lorries just have to wait until the 'bosola' has completed her third jump before carrying on with their journey.

The men of the town all have to kiss the girl and put something in her chanty. Before decimalisation it was an old-fashioned threepenny piece, but nowadays it is normally at least ten pence. Sometimes the procession will even shout 'Ten pence for a kiss!' as they come down the High Street. There is no doubt, according to the consensus of opinion voiced by Mrs Jean Reid, as to which sector of the male population gives most generously:

> The auld guys – see in thae wee pubs, the auld guys, well, they were queueing up.
> Mibbie the sowels are, ken, a wee bit frustrated mind you! They were gien the
> fifty pence an the pounds wis comin oot. Young fellas, they seen you an they rin.

At some point in the proceedings the women go to a butcher and ask for a large link sausage. The butcher, seeing that it is for a chanty, is only too happy to oblige with one of the largest in his shop, free of charge. He will often keep a supply of these specifically for chanties. The girls sometimes go to Ferri's chip shop for 'a penny's worth of chips' or a black pudding for the chanty (an alternative to the large link if there are no butchers nearby).

After the visit to the butcher, the ladies go round many other shops in the town where they receive gifts to put in the chanty. Women on pay-offs are infamous in the town for causing havoc in the shops they choose to visit. On one occasion very recently a young lad working in a local chemist had a very red face when, after inflating some condoms and exclaiming that they were not large enough, a bunch of rather over-exuberant ladies on a pay-off requested that he come down from his ladder and 'try them for size'!

Until twenty years ago the ladies confined themselves to the main streets of the town and remained outside the public houses, cheering, singing and ringing a 'school bell' borrowed for the evening until the men came outside and made their contributions. Nowadays the 'pub-crawl' aspect of the tradition is as important as any because a special practice has grown with it – the 'penny pint'. Before the late sixties the ladies would have made their way to the home of the bride-to-be and feasted on sandwiches, a piece of bun, and, if they were lucky, a small glass of port. This 'spread' was provided by the girl's mother who would welcome the party at the door when they arrived after their procession around the town, stay long enough to serve all the girls tea, and then go off to bed leaving them to have their little celebration. These days it is not uncommon for a mother to attend her daughter's pay-off, joining in on all the fun and games, and though several years ago the girl would endeavour to 'lose' all the embarrassing articles her friends had put in her chanty before going home lest her parents should find them, the bride's mother often openly enjoys the smutty atmosphere of the celebration today. The tradition of the 'penny pint' involves the handing over of a penny for a pint of beer. The girl about to be married receives one 'penny pint' in each pub she visits, and each member of the pay-off party must take a sip from the pint thus pledging that they will share with their friends the joys and pains of her life to come.

In the days before the 'pub crawl' became an integral part of this tradition, the women would be home before ten o'clock. Nowadays a pay-off lasts as long as the ladies can stay standing, as they are known to share more than a sip from the penny-pint! The head barman at The Auld Hoose in Kilmarnock confided that women on pay-offs come into the pub in various states, not always on their feet. 'Some come in in wheelbarrows, some in shopping trolleys, and some are carried in,' he said, 'but the favourite seems to be the supermarket trolley – there's always a big row of them outside Fine Fare across the road there, and usually the girls steal one and wheel the lassie up the road in that.'

Once inside the pub, and with a few drinks inside them, the girls delight in thoroughly embarrassing any male who comes within a five mile radius of them, and usually there is a certain amount of recounting of incredible stories concerning those attending the pay-off, and general, good-humoured 'slagging off' of each other. A competition is held to determine who knows the dirtiest joke, and various smutty songs are sung. This process is repeated as the girls travel from pub to pub, the 'bosolaa' receiving kisses and money from all the men she meets on the way, and all those she meets in the pubs she is taken into. The chanty is normally jumped a few times when travelling from one pub to another, for if the distance between stops is not too far the girls walk from pub to pub singing as they go.

After the ladies feel that they have visited enough pubs they usually move to a discotheque and end the night dancing, and if the 'bosola' wants to dance, no matter how hot it is, she must keep her costume on, and sometimes even take her chanty onto the dance-floor with her. To remove her costume before the end of the night would be a great insult to the girls who had painstakingly designed and decorated it for her – she simply would not dare![54]

Celebrating the Marriage

Anon.
Logierait, Perthshire, *c.* 1811

As recently as 1811 the following curious marriage custom was kept up at Logierait, eighteen miles from Kenmore. After arriving at the church, and just immediately before the celebration of the marriage ceremony, every knot about the dress of both bride an bridegroom, such as garters, shoe-strings, stings of petticoats, etc., was carefully, loosened. After leaving the church the

---

[54] 'Jumping the Chanty' is excerpted and edited from a student research paper in Scottish Ethnology submitted by Audrey Bain from Kilmarnock.

whole company walked round it, keeping the church walls always on the right hand. The bridegroom first, however, turned aside with a friend to tie the strings of his dress, while the bride retired with her friends to adjust the disorder of hers.[55]

Revd James Napier
Renfrewshire, 1879

The ceremony was generally performed at the minister's residence, which was often a considerable distance off. The marriage party generally walked all the way, but if the distance was unusually great, the company rode the journey, and this was called 'a riding wedding'. There were two companies – the bride's party and the bridegroom's party. The bride's party met in the bride's parents' house, the best man being with them, and the groom's party met in his parents' house, the best maid being with them – the males conducting the females to their respective parties. At the time appointed the bride's party left first, followed immediately by the groom's party – each company headed by the respective fathers. They so arranged their walk that both parties would reach the minister's house together.

As soon as the ceremony was concluded, there was a rush on the part of the young men to get the first kiss of the newly-made wife. This was frequently taken by the clergyman himself, a survival of an old custom said to have been practised in the middle ages. This custom is referred to in the following old song. The bridegroom, addressing the minister, says:

> It's no very decent for you to be kissing,
> It does not look weel wi' the black coat ava,
> 'Twould hae set you far better tae hae gi'en us your blessing,
> Than thus by such tricks to be breaking the law.
> Dear Watty, quo Robin, it's just an auld custom,
> And the thing that is common should ne'er be ill taen,
> For where ye are wrong, if ye hadna a wished him
> You should have been first. It's yourself is to blame.

The party now returned in the following order: first, the two fathers in company together, then the newly-married couple, behind them the best man and the best maid, and the others following in couples as they might arrange. There were frequently as many as twenty couples.[56]

---

[55] *The Celtic Magazine*, vol. x, No. cxx, 1885, p. 542.
[56] J. Napier, *Folk Lore*, pp. 48–9.

Revd Walter Gregor
North-east, 1874

The marriage was commonly arranged between the two without the knowledge of the parents. At times the mothers might be let into the secret, but it was only after all the arrangements were completed the subject was broken to the fathers. The marriage day was either Tuesday or Thursday, more rarely Saturday, during the increase of the moon, and any month except May. It was, however, unlucky for two of a family to be married during the same year.

In the interval between the final contract of marriage and its celebration the young woman was busy getting in order all her *providan* for her future home. One or more days were given to the thigging of wool from her friends and neighbours. If she had been thrifty, her feather bed, bolster, and pillows, blankets, sheets, etc., had been for some time ready in anticipation of the coming event. On a day some weeks before the marriage the affianced, accompanied by the bride's mother or sister, went to a neighbouring village to buy the *bonnie things*, that is, the bridal dress, etc., when it was the custom for the young man to present dresses to the mother and sisters of her who was to be his wife. Besides the *providan* already spoken of, the young woman brought a chest of drawers, or, if that was too costly, a *kist*. All the *providan* was sent to the future home a few days before the marriage, and it was sent unlocked and unbound. To have sent it locked or bound would have entailed difficult travail.

The guests were invited by the bride and bridegroom. The bride, commonly alone, sometimes, however, attended by her who was to do the office of 'best maid', called on her friends, and gave them a personal invitation. She chose two young men to lead her to church. The bridegroom, sometimes alone, and sometimes accompanied by the young friend who was to stand as his 'best man', gave personal invitations to his party, and at the same time asked two young women to lead him to church.

The invitations were all given and all the arrangements fully made before the minister was invited. To have done otherwise would not have been lucky. A present of a hat was made to the minister by those in better circumstances. It was customary for each guest to make a present to the bride and bridegroom. It usually took the form of something required for the marriage feast, as a fowl, a few pounds of butter, a bottle of whisky, etc. The present was often reserved till the morning of the marriage-day, when there was a rivalry who should give *hansel*.

Great preparations were made for the feast, and from the brewing of the bridal ale and the baking of the bridal bread omens were drawn. With respect to the ale, if the wort boiled up on the far off side of the pot, it was accounted unlucky; if in front, lucky. If it fermented strongly, or, as it was expressed, if it was strong on the barm, good fortune was augured. It was the same if the ale was strong when presented at the feast. In baking the cakes, great care was taken with the first cake lest it should be broken – a broken cake portending unhappiness.

On the Saturday evening previous to the Sunday on which the proclamation of banns, called the *beuckin nicht*, was made, the bridegroom, if at all possible, presented himself at the house of the bride. A few friends were also present, and a small feast was given. Along with the bride's father, or brother, or it might be with a friend, the young man went to the Session-Clerk to give in the names for proclamation of banns, or, as it was called, to 'lay doon the pawns'. The banns were proclaimed three times either on three, two or one Sundays. For the young woman to have appeared in church on the Sunday on which the banns were published would have been the cause of troubles of many kinds during the married life. Between the Sunday on which the banns were published and the day of the marriage it was customary for the young friends of both bride and bridegroom on meeting them to 'rub shoulders' with them, as if to catch the infection of marriage.

The state of the weather on the marriage day was watched most narrowly, and omens were drawn from it. There might be heard on all sides such expressions as 'He's gloomin gey sair on in,' if the day was gloomy; 'He's blinkin fell cantie on ir,' if the day was alternately bright and cloudy; or, 'She's greetin unco sair,' if the day was rainy, although a show of rain was propitious:

> Happy's the corpse, an happy's the bride
> It gits a shoor i' thir side.

A bright sunny day indicated as much happiness as can fall to the lot of man in time:

> Happy's the bride the sun shines on,
> Happy's the corpse the rain falls on.

The bride was usually dressed by her maid, and every article of dress must be new. The bridal dress could on no account be fitted on. When it came to be put on, if it did not fit, it could not be cut or altered, but adjusted the best was possible. If the marriage shoes were too little, evils of many kinds were foreboded. Something borrowed must be worn. A ring was accounted of most virtue.

If it was a younger sister that was married, she had to give her elder sister green garters.

The guests arrived at an early hour – those invited by the bride at her home, and those invited by the bridegroom at his. Breakfast was served up, and consisted of two courses – oatmeal porridge made with milk, well overlaid with sugar, and curds and cream. In later times a tea-breakfast was served. After breakfast it was no unusual thing for all to join in dancing till the hour of going to church came.

Two men, called the *sens*, were despatched from the house of the bridegroom to demand the bride. On making their appearance a volley of fire-arms met them. When they came up to the door of the bride's home they asked:

'Does — bide here?'
'Aye, faht de ye wint wi ir?'
'We wint ir for — ,' was the answer.
'Bit ye winna get ir.'
'Bit we'll tack ir.'
'Will ye come in, in taste a mouthfu o' a dram till we see aboot it?'

And so the *sens* entered the house and got possession of the bride.

Both parties arranged their departure from their respective homes in such a way as to arrive at church about the same time – the bride's party always having the preference. The bride, supported by the two young men formerly chosen by herself, walked at the head of her party, and when she set out she was on no account to look back. Such an action entailed disaster of the worst kind during the married life. The bridegroom, supported by two young maidens, walked at the head of his party. On leaving, a few old shoes and besoms or scrubbers were thrown after both bride and bridegroom. In each party there was one that carried a bottle of whisky and a glass, and there was another that carried bread and cheese. The person first met received a glass, with bread and cheese, and then turned and walked a short distance. Great attention was paid to the *first fit*. A man on horseback, or a horse drawing a cart, after the introduction of carts, was deemed most lucky. Each party was accompanied by pipers, and a constant firing of guns and pistols was kept up.

The church door had been opened by the beadle or bellman, who was in attendance to lead the bridegroom to the *bride-steel* – that is, the pew that was set apart for the use of those who were to be married. The bride was now led forth and placed beside him, and great care was used to have her placed at the proper side. To have placed her improperly would have been unlucky in the extreme. Next to the bride stood her 'best maid'. This office, though accounted an honour, was not unattended with risk. If the bride was *enceinte*, the maid would within a year fall into the same disgrace. Three times a bridesmaid was the inevitable prelude of remaining unmarried. Next to the bridegroom stood 'best young man'. On no account could the bride and bridegroom meet on the marriage day till they met on the bride-stool. Such a meeting would have been followed by some calamity or series of calamities. After the celebration of the marriage the minister frequently kissed the bride. In certain districts, the bride pinned a marriage favour to the minister's right arm. The two received the congratulations of all present.

The bridegroom paid the beadle his fee, usually a sixpence. It was no unusual thing for one of the party to go round the guests, and make a collection for him, in addition to his fee, when each contributed a half-penny or a penny.

The procession was again formed, led by the bride, supported by the two *sens*. Then followed the bridegroom, supported by the bride's two best maidens; and with music and the firing of guns and pistols, the two parties, now united, marched along the ordinary road to the home of the bridegroom. On no account was it lawful to take any bye-roads, however much shorter they might be, either in going to church or in returning from it. Bread and cheese and a *dram* were given as before to the *first fit* on the homeward journey. On coming near the house, a few of the swiftest runners of the unmarried set out 'to win the kail' and he or she who did so was the first of the party to be married.

When the bride arrived, she was welcomed by the bridegroom's mother, if alive. If she was dead, the welcome was given by one of the bridegroom's nearest relatives. When passing over the threshold, there was held over the bride's head a sieve, containing bread and cheese, which were distributed among the guests. They were sometimes scattered around her, when there was a rush made by the young folks to secure a piece. At times an oatmeal cake was broken over her head. In later times a thin cake of 'short bread', called the bride-cake, was substituted for the oatmeal cake. It was distributed among the guests, who carefully preserved it, particularly the unmarried, who placed it below their pillows to 'dream on'. In some districts, when the sieve was in the act of being placed over the bride's head, or the bread broken, it was the bridegroom's duty to snatch her from below it. She was led straight to the hearth, and into her hands was put the tongs, with which she made up the fire. The besom was at times substituted for the tongs, when she swept the hearth. The *crook* was then swung three times round her head, in the name of the Father, Son, and Holy Ghost, and with the prayer: 'May the Almichty mack this umman a gueede wife.' The last act of her installation as 'gueedwife' was leading her to the *girnal,* or *mehl-bowie,* and pressing her hand into the meal as far as possible. This last action, it was believed, secured in all time coming abundance of the staff of life in the household.[57]

Revd W. (Bill) Pollock
Isle of Mull, 2002

In the fifteen years I've ministered on Mull, I've conducted weddings in the couple's home, in the manse, and in their local church – all fairly traditional – but I've also been asked to conduct weddings in some most improbable places: under a bridge, on a ferry crossing, at a motor rally, atop a mountain. Even a church can be an improbable place if it's in a remote location, approached by miles of mountain road, by a footpath deep in mud, or even by small boat. I've been asked to conduct weddings for people from enormous distances who've found Mull on the internet and even by commercial wedding organisers who have never even seen the place. What is going on?

Simplifying enormously no doubt, I suspect a number of trends. Guest lists for conventional weddings have lengthened, causing the church to replace the home and manse almost completely. Perhaps as the social and spiritual significance of marriage has decreased for many couples, or perhaps as social competition has increased, some couples have sought new and further-reaching ways of making their weddings occasions to remember. One common response is to transport a large number of guests to a distant and romantic setting. Some couples opt out of the trend to large weddings and may seek to make their ceremony memorable by linking it with something they know will give them a kick – like being on top of a mountain. Others similarly flee the social pressure for a large gathering, but still want a religious or spiritual emphasis – and so travel to a distant place to marry privately in church.

While the marriage itself may (or may not) succeed, efforts as described towards the longed-for perfect ceremony are often, sadly, perhaps inevitably, self-defeating. The more distant and unfamiliar the setting, for example, the more confident we can be that some pitfall will have gone unnoticed. Thus I've seen a white bride and her guests in a small boat carrying umbrellas which were useless in the wind; guests in their finery running for a train; others at a candle-lit service in the falling dark without a torch to leave the church, a woman wearing her fur coat right through a chilly reception in an otherwise idyllic castle. And don't think that professionals always get it right

---

[57] W. Gregor, *Echo*, pp. 108–19 and *Notes*, pp. 87–93.

– I've known expensive caterers, far from home, unwittingly summoning the fire brigade; and wedding organisers who kept us starving so long that a guest ate the decorations. Such aberrations may not ruin the day - and one or two can add to the fun – but there must come a point where they outweigh the benefits sought through the choice of location.

It is almost impossible to do marriage preparation with couples at a distance. And with so many couples unfamiliar with their religious heritage, there's an increasing need for theological preparation too. I've had such varied sources as *Winnie the Pooh* and a Muslim prophet suggested for the principal readings in a Christian ceremony. And on one occasion no one seemed to notice a chorus was missing from the hymn sheet – so the bride lustily led her guests in singing every second verse to the chorus tune and thus worked her way from verses 1 to 6 and then back from 6 to 1 before the organ stopped. The minister or the couple or both are becoming physically and metaphorically distant from the service they should be preparing together.

There may thus be much to be said for updated versions of the old-style weddings in house or manse. They can be social affairs but are constrained by the settings from excessive numbers, extravagance, or show. They are in familiar places where unforeseen problems should easily be managed. Appropriate counselling and guidance should be available locally. There should be maximum time and opportunity to discuss, prepare and think through the true purpose of the exercise, and minimum distraction from it when the great day comes.[58]

Alexander Polson
Caithness, 1907

In Caithness, as elsewhere, it is believed that only they who are stark mad marry in May. All other months, however, are lucky. Notwithstanding the fact that people well know the marriage rhyme:

> Monday for wealth,
> Tuesday for health,
> Wednesday the best day of all,
> Thursday for crosses,
> Friday for losses,
> Saturday no luck at all.

---

[58] I attended a house wedding conducted by the Revd Pollock in Mull, 8 February 2002. In the total absence of the frills and falderals, froth and hype that one has come to expect at modern church and hotel weddings, it struck me that the true meaning of marriage could be seen more clearly in this simple, dignified setting. After discussing this point with the minister, he kindly responded to my request that he write this piece.

Yet Friday is in Caithness by far the most popular wedding-day. The only explanation given of this is that Caithness people are economical, and as wedding feasts always take end on the Sunday a great spread has not to be provided. When the day arrives, the bride ought to be careful to put on her right shoe first, as to put on the left spells bad luck; and as to her dress, she must wear 'something old and something new, something borrowed and something blue.'

Elsewhere it is necessary to carry a silver coin in the pocket, but a Caithness bride prefers to carry it inside her stocking.[59] The bridegroom ought to have at least a groat in coppers in his pocket, to throw away among the crowd of youngsters at the church (or house) door, as he emerges with the bride on his arm (preceded, of course, by a luck-insuring married couple). While on the homeward way, it is bad to be caught in a shower of rain, but it is infinitely worse to meet a funeral. When the wedding cake is cut he who strikes the ring hidden in it is considered immune from ill luck for at least a year.

Of course, the bride expected a sunshiny day for her wedding: 'Happy is the bride that the sun shines on!' And when she left her father's house, after the ceremony, to proceed to her new home, she had old shoes flung after her, and some corn or rice – indulgences common to other counties. It may be observed here that originally the newly-wedded pair had to sleep the first night on a shake-down bed, to teach them due humility, at the start of life.[60]

Isobel Colquhoun
Armadale, 1992

IC The wedding rhyme in Armadale [West Lothian] is:

> Monday for health
> Tuesday for wealth
> Wednesday no luck at all
> Thursday for losses
> Friday for crosses
> Saturday the best day of all.[61]

---

[59] There are still instances of brides wearing a silver sixpence inside one of their shoes. Norman Kennedy cited a recent example from his niece's wedding in Aberdeen, 1991.
[60] Alexander Polson, 'Folklore', pp. 96–7.
[61] Isobel Colquhouln was recorded in Bathgate, West Lothian, on 3 March 1992 by MB.

Margaret Wilson
Lilliesleaf, 1990

MW   Married in white, you've chosen all right

Married in blue, love ever true,

Married in brown, live out of town,

Married in grey, live far away,

Married in green, a shame to be seen.

My mother didn't like wearing green, she attached bad luck to this; I don't know why. Mind you, green has always been a colour that has suggested envy. . . .[62]

They used to say it was unlucky to make your own dress, though that doesn't seem to hold nowadays. The bridegroom isn't supposed to see the outfit before the service, and you're not supposed to look in the mirror fully dressed. But of course that's simple because they always used to say you had to wear a fancy garter – supposed to be lucky; so all you had to do was leave that off and add it after . . .

It's lucky to have white heather in the bouquet. I did have a bit of wild heather growing in the garden and if someone was getting married, I often cut a piece and sent it to her.[63] I like the white heather, and I could give it to a bride because I know a lot of them feel that this is lucky; but I cannae see that it would bring you any more luck than what is happening . . . They said it's lucky to see a sweep on the way to church . . .[64]

Doris Rougvie
Huntingtower, Perthshire, 2004

MB *When did you first begin to do flowers for weddings?*

DR I always wanted to be a florist, but the first time was my own wedding . . . in Almondbank, in St Serf's Church, 15 July 1967 . . . but I wouldn't be officially a florist till the early eighties and then I ran a shop in Perth.

MB *Is there a style of wedding flower arrangement that could be considered traditional?*

DR Well, it has varied a lot, but very nicely things have come full circle and it's come back to the traditional loose arrangements – not these when everything's wired, which are beautiful, but it's come back to what it was many years ago. Lots of

---

[62] The colour green also has a strong association with the fairies.

[63] Mrs Wilson was well known in her village as a very skilled craftswoman. She was often called upon to sew dresses or make floral decorations for local weddings. She was particularly skilled at dressing the handball in honour of a marriage, and each year at Shrovetide she would carefully 'dress the ba'' to remember local weddings in the traditional manner. [Video-recorded for the School of Scottish Studies Archives by Neil MacQueen and MB. Mrs Wilson died in August 1991.]

[64] Margaret Wilson, Lilliesleaf, recorded by Susan Huntly. SA1990/18.

greenery and hand-held posies . . . . the roses would still be my favourite and I would go for pinks and white myself.

MB *Are there any taboos about colours or flowers?*

DR Lots of people are superstitious about yellow – yellow is forsaken. For weddings and for funerals . . .

MB *Is that only yellow, or even yellow included in the arrangement?*

DR Yellow included.

MB *Any other taboos?*

DR You never put red and white together, because I think it was to do with when the barber poles were red and white and the barbers used to do amputations many years ago. People associate it with death.

MB *Is it OK to have red and white and another colour?*

DR And another colour, yes, red, white and blue or mauve, that's OK. But it's the red and white alone. You would never put out a bouquet from your shop with red and white. I remember getting one when I was principal boy in a pantomime . . . and my mother was appalled and she insisted that we had to have the white flowers in one room and the red flowers in another.

MB *And you wouldn't bring them to somebody in a hospital then?*

DR No. Oh, never! Never!

MB *Are flowers in the church important?*

DR Yes, pedestals have always been very popular and altar arrangements . . . That hasn't changed very much, although nowadays it's the fashion to have the pew-ends decorated. Every pew has a posy tied on to the end of it.

Joseph Laing Waugh
Thornhill, 1903

In 1714 the session enacted and ordained that such as are married in their own houses and not in the church should pay a fine of £2 Scots, the same sum to be given to the poor. If this fine had been zealously enacted the poor's fund would have been a large one, as it is only within the last twenty years that a marriage has been celebrated in the new Parish Church. Beddin the Bride is an obsolete custom now, but very common long ago. After the festivities the guests followed the bride to her new home and put her to bed. Her health was drunk, after which she flung her stocking among those assembled, and whoever she thus struck first would be married first.[65]

---

[65] J.L. Waugh, *Thornhill and its Worthies*, p. 30.

Revd John Lane Buchanan
Western Isles, 1782

Marriages among the gentlemen are attended with no greater pomp than among the better sort through Great Britain; they are commonly attended by their friends, who make merry on the happy occasion. Contracts are only known to few. But it is not so with the common people. They invite the friends on both sides, to make up the contract of marriage; and as all the poor people retain that part of their former importance that entitled them to the honour of gentleman, *duine uasal*, at least in words, it is supposed that the lady's parents will not make a trifling offer of portion to their intended son-in-law. A pompous promise, if they fail in the performance, adds much to the dignity of the match. Being present at one of these meetings of friends, I observed that the friends of the young man began with a set speech, by informing the parents of the cause and design of their meeting, which was, to pave the way for an alliance with the family to which the woman belonged; and then launched out at considerable length on the great and good qualities of the young man who aspired at the connection. Meanwhile, they remarked, that the friends of the gentleman were such as ought not to be received with indifference. It ought, they proceeded, to be esteemed a very happy turn of Providence to cast such a hopeful youth, and good friends to back him, to solicit their friendship. They hoped, therefore, they would make an offer of such a portion to the young woman, as might do honour to themselves, and worthy of so promising a young man.

The portion formerly was paid in cows, sheep and goats, these being more valuable to them than money; and this old practice is continued in full force. Even if the parents should have none, they must name a number of cows, and a handsome number too, otherwise the young man would think his dignity suffered in the eyes of the neighbours. Twenty cows are among the most moderate portions promised, and many of them considerably above that number. If the young couple had reason to be satisfied with each other during the courtship, the affair is generally settled to the satisfaction of the parties, after which they begin to make merry. They eat, drink, dance and sing, etc. But as their cows are but few, they must take, at the time of payment, a kind of representative value of it. Accordingly I was told that a year old cow stood for one; three ewes for another; a spinning wheel for a third; two blankets for a fourth; a small chest for a fifth; and so on until the number agreed upon was completed.

On the Saturday evening after the contract is settled, their names must be given to the parish clerk to have the banns published in the church the following day.[66] This piece of ceremony they are truly averse to, as private marriage is more eligible, and they wish much not to have their names called. They pretend to be ashamed on these occasions: for I believe the true cause is the fear of alarming others of the sweet-hearts, who might step forward to claim a *prior* right, and perhaps occupancy. I myself have seen the proceedings stopped by the opposite party, while the publication of the banns was going forward.

However, when there is no interruption made, they appear before the clergyman, when the ceremony is regularly performed. After the ceremony is finished, the parson calls to the bridegroom to remember his duty to the bride; and as an earnest of obedience to his reverence, the swain gives her a hearty kiss. A very rough scramble follows among the other men, who try which will have the good fortune of getting the next kiss from the blushing bride: after which she is led home in triumph, with a large bag-pipe playing some cheerful march, and other tunes composed for the purpose.

One would naturally wonder that women of easy virtue, as we before described, should not find it difficult to meet with helpmates: yet so it is, that many instances can be produced, when the men strive to get their favourite in spite of what may be alleged against her virtue.

They make large weddings, and they frequently spend more money than their promised portion on the occasion; though they should want in the after part of life. It is customary for both the bride and bridegroom, just before their marriage ceremony, to untie their shoes, garters, and some other bandage, to prevent witchcraft, of which they are much afraid on these occasions, and think this an antidote against it.

In many parts of Scotland a practice prevails which not only lessens the expense of the weddings but even makes them so profitable as to enrich the young couple. That is what is called *penny-weddings*, at which the bridegroom prepares a feast, and invites the whole country. Every man, and every woman, pays a shilling, which, voracious as they may be, is twice as much as the value of what they eat. The men drink four or five shillings a-piece, so that (to such poor people) a great sum is collected. These penny weddings, and all promiscuous meetings, it is said, contribute much to population.[67]

---

[66] The calling of marriage banns in church was a legal requirement in Scotland until 1971.

[67] Buchanan, *Travels*, pp. 163–8.

Highland Weddings

Captain Edward Burt
Inverness, 1726

When a young couple are married, for the first night the company keep possession of the dwelling-house or hut, and send the bridegroom and bride to a barn or out-house, giving them straw, heath, or fern for a bed, with blankets for their covering; and then they make merry, and dance to the piper all the night long.

They have a penny-wedding; that is, when a servant-maid has served faithfully, and gained the good will of her master and mistress, they invite their relations and friends, and there is a dinner or supper on the day the servant is married, and music and dancing follow to complete the evening.

The bride must go about the room, and kiss every man in the company, and in the end every body puts money into a dish, according to their inclination and ability. By this means, a family in good circumstance, and respected by those they invite, have procured for the new couple wherewithal to begin the world pretty comfortably for people of their low condition. But I should have told you, that the whole expense of the feast and fiddlers is paid out of the contributions. This and the former are likewise customs all over the Lowlands of Scotland . . . they do not use the ring in marriage as in England.[68]

Soon after the wedding-day, the new-married woman sets herself about spinning her winding-sheet, and a husband that should sell or pawn it, is esteemed, among all men, one of the most profligate.[69]

---

[68] Wedding rings have also undergone changes in fashion for, although a gold band is the recognised symbol of today, during the fifteenth, sixteenth and seventeenth centuries gold rings with two clasped hands were common. Until the seventeenth century 'spousing rings' were worn on the right hand and, although they remained part of the wedding ceremony in the Catholic Church, during the Reformation no rings were exchanged at weddings – this was evidently still the case in Burt's time. During the reign of Charles I, the custom of exchanging rings began to be re-established, with the left hand as standard throughout Britain, though in St Kilda (for example) wedding rings were not part of the ceremony even in the twentieth century.
[69] Captain Edward Burt, *Letters*, vol. II, paragraphs excerpted from pp. 188–9 and 207 have been rearranged for this anthology.

The Inverness Courier
1820

The editor of the *Edinburgh Literary Journal* lately drew a moving picture of the insipidity of most modern marriages – stating that a few soft looks, a walk, a squeeze of the hand, a popping of the question, a ring, a clergyman, etc. made up the whole of the commonplace affair. Our friend, the editor, like the public, will be glad to hear that they managed the affair much better in the Highlands. The following instance of old-fashioned mirth and jollity in the present dull, disastrous times, is really, as Mr Jeffrey says, 'quite refreshing'. Last week a wedding was solemnized in the wild but beautiful Glen of Urquhart, near Lakefield, betwixt George Anderson, the blacksmith of the district, and Marjory May Macdonald, a decent young damsel, who belonged to the same parish. As the 'Gobhadh-òg-a-Ghline', or blacksmith, is still a personage of some importance in the thinly populated straths, a vast concourse of people assembled on the joyous occasion, and numerous presents were made from all quarters, that there might be a competency of good things of this world available at the ceremony. The younger members of the families of Lochletter, Lakefield, and Corrimony graces [*sic*] the scene with their presence, and there were in all four hundred persons assembled. All the maidens displayed their snoods and plaids, about ninety of the young men were dressed in full Highland garb. The preparations for the feast would not have disgraced an English corporation dinner or vestry meeting. There were 200 Scottish pints or 100 English gallons of whisky; 15 Scots or 60 English gallons of homebrewed ale; 2 cows; 18 Highland wedders; 12 salmon; 3 dozen hens; 40 ducks; and 6 turkeys; 30 brace of muirfowl; and 6 black cocks; 50 stones of cheese; 7 stones of butter; 6 bolls of meal baked into cakes; 50 cogs of croudie; with milk in all varieties of preparation, and eggs 'thick as the leaves of Vallombrosa'. The distribution of the native beverage was entrusted to the management of a Highland Caleb Balderstone called 'Sogan Buie' (hearty, jovial fellow), and he performed the important functions with such success, that there was not one of the guests upon which he did not confer the degree of hilarity, so admirably defined by his Celtic cognomen. As merry-makings of this sort do not occur every day, even in the Highlands, the guests wisely resolved to make the most of the occasion, and they accordingly kept up the festivities from Tuesday till Saturday night. Among many diversions resorted to for amusement, the athletic and national sport of putting the stone was the favourite, at which a man named 'Ian-mor-na Cunn', about 6ft 6in high, the Goliath of the Glen, outdistanced all his competitors, except one, while throwing the stone kneeling upon one knee. Dancing was kept up with occasional short intervals, day and night – the mountain dew circulated with a twelve horse power of rapidity, while the pipers 'hotched and blew with might and main'. The local band of pipers and fiddlers was led and the dancing was conducted by an eccentric, well qualified master of ceremonies, named 'Murrach na Gaelich' or 'Murdo of the Moon', a sobriquet originating in a Munchansen [Munchausenian] feat, which Murdo boasts of having performed with a favourite rifle – namely, having with one shot brought down an enormous earn or eagle, and fractured at the same time a piece of the moon. On the whole, 'sic dancing and deray', has not been witnessed for many a long year in the Glen of Urquhart, and as the Gaelic bards are invoking the great lost power of song to celebrate the event, there can be no doubt but the nuptials of 'Gou-òg-a-Ghlinn', and the bonny May, will be sung and remembered to the latest posterity.[70]

Duncan 'Major' Morrison
Stornoway, Isle of Lewis, 1996

DM The eldest brother . . . he could play the melodeon. He taught me all the dance tunes and I was playing for the dances with these, that I learned from him and Bella, the teacher – she taught me to play the harmonium. And when I was old enough, I was playing the harmonium. Oh, the brother who played the melodeon really well, he was in great demand to play for 'dannsa rathaid . . . Bheil fhios agad mu dheidhinn dannsa rathaid'? [dances at the crossroads – do you know about them?] They would have to go down all the way to Sandwick to get enough space to do eightsome reels – and he was the best player of the melodeon . . . [That was] Neil – Oh he was full of music and he used to teach me the reels and that's how I learned. And then I would go and play in the castle, play the grand piano at the castle – these reels that I heard from the 'dannsa rathaid' . . .

MB *Did you get going down to Sandwick yourself?*

DM Oh no, I think I was too young. You might be run over by a horse! There were no cars in that day, but at the crossroads somewhere there was evidently a square place of size of a ballroom. And Neil was in great demand for playing, but when we played here together [in Ness], I played the organ. Oh, I never got to Sandwick. I was considered too young.

MB *Can you tell me that lovely story about the wedding?*

DM When I was a little, a very small boy [in my grandparents house in Habost, Ness[71]]

---

[70] I am grateful to Janette French of the Highland Folklife Museum in Kingussie for drawing my attention to this newspaper cutting from one of the files stored in the museum's archive.
[71] The house is now known as 'Taigh Dhonnchaidh' (Duncan's House), an arts centre for music, song and dance classes, céilidhs and other arts activities.

I was looking through the porch and I saw this wedding procession coming that had already walked two miles . . . and they were going up to the church, which was another mile away. And the girls were singing a song and the boys were whistling – 'Mòrag bheag nighean Mhurchaidh an t-saoir', a song that my great-granny knew . . . Years later I tried to play an arrangement of what they sounded like. And that's what I played when I was invited to play in London [where all the other young musicians were performing for the Marchioness of Londonderry]. And I got away with it.

MB *You mean, it was a resounding success?*

DM (Laughs) And I had called it 'The Lewis Bridal Procession', which was rather grand, you see!

MB *And indeed, that's what it was.*

DM But the words of 'Mairi's Wedding' became very popular.

MB *I still hear people calling it, 'the Lewis bridal song'.*

DM Oh its still called 'the Lewis bridal song' . . . [Till then], there was never such a thing as the 'Lewis bridal song'. It was just a little ditty that the girls sang – 'Morag bheag nighean Mhurchaidh an t-saoir' . . .

MB *And so that's what captured the heart of Lady Londonderry, is it?*

DM Yes . . . And when I played it to the Duchess of York she said, 'I would love to have a copy of that!'

And I said, 'But ma'am, it's in my head.'

But Lady Londonderry said, 'It must come out of your head. You'll come and write it down just as you played it!'

And that's what I did [Pause then laughs]. Now – I'm frightened to say it, but Sir Hugh Roberton pinched the tune and called it 'Mairi's Wedding' . . . But the popular words of 'Mairi's Wedding' became very popular.

MB I still hear people calling it, 'The Lewis bridal song':

Step we gaily on we go
Heel for heel and toe for toe,
Arm in arm and row on row
All for Mairi's wedding . . . .[72]

DM Oh its still called – that's [more or less] what I called it. But [when I was young] there was never such a thing as the 'Lewis Bridal Song'. It was just a little ditty that the girls sang.[73]

---

[72] The words were composed by Sir Hugh Roberton, who published his own arrangement of the song in his book, *Songs of the Isles*, (1950), pp. 20–21. The chorus noted here is added to Duncan's text.

[73] Duncan was recorded by MB shortly after his ninetieth birthday, July 1996.

Alexander MacDonald
Inverness-shire, 1914

Marriage was not at one time the hard and fast institution it has now become. Long, long ago, as is well known, the ceremony was frequently negotiated under pressure of all sorts and conditions of circumstances. Handfast unions were quite common, and it is probable that, in some instances, marriage was, with very little formality entered into. In later years, marriage came to be much more religiously observed; but till within recent times the festivities connected with the institution as a rule extended over a number of days. A wedding was then the occasion of genuine jollification to everyone, relatives and non-relatives alike; though there was always evidence of the little spitefulnesses that union ever seems to engender. We have all heard of the pretty old proverb which says:

> Ma tha thu 'g iarraidh do mholadh faigh bàs,
> 's ma tha thu 'g iarraidh do chaineadh pòs.
> (If you want to be praised, die,
> If you want to be traduced, marry).

Our wedding of the olden time was invariably preceded by the 'contract' – an institution of long standing and great importance. This function took place in the house of the bride's father, to which the bridegroom and a small party of chosen friends repaired, usually on a certain appointed Friday evening. The proceedings were interesting. One of the party, probably a near relative, introduced himself and his companions as wanderers, seeking a night's lodgings, and the bride's father, if matters were agreeable to all concerned, received the would-be strangers hospitably. In due time a mere form of contract was entered into by the prospective bride and bridegroom, in the course of which proceeding they for the first time that evening saw each other. On those occasions, as a general custom, there was excellent cheer, all of which was supposed to be provided by the bridegroom. It was not common to have a dance at those contracts, but songs were sung, tales were told, and there was also much good-natured fun. Omens were watched carefully in connection with all that pertained to the marriage. People never liked a drinking glass to break between any two of the parties present; nor did they look without grave apprehension upon such an accident as the light going out.

As soon as possible after the contract, the marriage came off, for which great event certain days of the week were always preferred to others. The month of May has always been in our country, as elsewhere, allowed to witness very few marriages; a favourite time being between the November term[74] and the New Year.

---

[74] The November term day is usually called Martinmas. It was formerly November 11, and in 1886 it was changed to November 28.

A wedding properly began on the night before the marriage, when the time-honoured custom of '*Glanadh-nan-cas*' ('feet-washing') fell to be observed. A number of the relatives of both the bridegroom and bride assembled at the respective homes of these parties, and were entertained in a manner that in most cases rendered this function most enjoyable. At the same time as the process of washing the feet went on, efforts were persistently made to blacken them with soot. Sometimes the legs, and even the face, came in for a rubbing, and thus, washing and blackening alternated, until, after a while, the fun was discontinued, and music and dancing were indulged in, and kept up till an early hour. In good time in the morning all were astir, and the preparations for the great event of the day became general, not only in the homes of the contracting parties, but practically all over the neighbourhood . . . Marriages most frequently took place in the church, and by a well-understood pre-arrangement, every effort was made to have the bride's party first there; it having always been considered unlucky that the bridegroom should have to wait for her. Just when leaving her father's home there was generally thrown after the bride an old boot, or some such article, thus observing a custom, in some shape or another, peculiar to many peoples.

The marriage ceremony over, the two parties issued by different doors from the church, just as they had entered. Outside, after cordial hand-shaking, refreshments were served, and the toast of the newly-wedded couple was proposed and joyfully responded to. It was not uncommon to engage then, for a time, in dancing, even, as sometimes happened, when snow lay deep on the ground.

The marriage dinner was always a most interesting event. This repast was usually set in the bride's father's barn. There was a superstition to the effect that it was not lucky to have it in his house.[75] The bridegroom sat at the end of the long table, his best man and maid, one on each side of him; the bride at the other end between her best man and maid. When the guests could not all be served at once, as many sittings were arranged as might be required, the bride and bridegroom keeping their seats throughout, as, without their presence, the feast would not be so much enjoyed. And the young would not be overlooked; they were specially provided for, sometimes in a place by themselves.

Dancing usually took full prominence at weddings. After the dinner the barn was cleared, and the guests took their places on the floor. The music, frequently supplied by both pipes and fiddle, was invariably of excellent quality. The tunes were those strathspeys and reels known as *dance music*; but

---

[75] Any bride or mother of the bride who has cleaned up after a 'house wedding' might heartily endorse this 'superstition'.

latterly some South-country dances were being introduced, and *Lancers, Schottisches, Quadrilles,* etc. were in evidence.

There was a custom, the observance of which was a matter of great moment, and much interest centred in it. The procedure was romantic in its way. During the small hours of the morning, as the fun was at its height, the bride's maids stole away with the bride, and as it was considered of great importance that nobody should see her being 'spirited' off, the undertaking had to be carefully managed. Thus, when a dance was well on, and everybody's attention absorbed in it, advantage was taken of the general abandon, and the bride was smartly driven off the floor, and with all speed hurried home. In a little while afterwards the bridegroom was snatched away in a similar manner. As soon, however, as missed they were followed by a number of persons from the barn, who found their way inside, when a great uproar prevailed. All available articles of dress, belonging to the married couple, were thrown about in all directions, and a great scramble followed; the belief being that the first to catch hold of any of those should be the next to get married. When order was restored a refreshment was served round, and the company returned to the barn, to prolong, till a later hour, the enjoyment at their disposal. In the morning, when all the people had left, there was a wedding breakfast. There was a belief to the effect that the young couple should not appear outside without having had something to eat, otherwise ill-luck might follow after them. Breakfast, as a rule, closed the wedding festivities. But, in some cases, those who attended visited the relatives of the married parties on their way home, and recommenced a series of pleasures which were kept up till all concerned become well-nigh physically exhausted. It was thus, when nature could go no farther, that an end was put to the fun, which, as will be readily imagined, often lasted for days.

It will occur to the reader that such an event as we have just described could not possibly have come off, even in the olden time, except at considerable expense. But there was in vogue an excellent provision against this. It was a standing rule that the expenses of the wedding should be born by the bride's father, or, in his absence, by her relatives or guardians; and towards this expenditure very material assistance was extended in the shape of butter, milk, cheese, fowls, meat, and drink, somewhat on the same lines as the marriage presents of later times. Indeed, it was no uncommon result to find a considerable supply at the credit of the function when all was over.[76]

---

[76] Alexander MacDonald, *Story and Song from Loch Ness-side*, Inverness, 1914, pp. 143–8

William Mackay
Inverness-shire, 1914

Marriage was regular or irregular, for life or for a more limited period. The contract – *an leabhrachadh*, or 'the booking' – was signed or otherwise concluded a short time before the date fixed for the marriage.[77] Its common form ran thus: – 'We, Donald Mac Homish, and Mary daughter of Ronald Mac Rory, bind ourselves to marry each other within the space of forty days hence under the penalty of £40 Scots payable by the party failing to fulfill this engagement to the party willing to perform the same.' The money (equal to £3 6s 8d sterling) was placed in neutral hands, usually in those of the Session Clerk, who entered the contract in a book which he kept for the purpose. The document was, however, more elaborate with people of consequence, and it sometimes contained strange provisions. The contract of Hugh Rose of Kilravock and Joneta, daughter of Sir Robert Chisholm, Governor of Urquhart Castle, on Loch Ness, dated 1364, after binding the parties to marry each other in face of Holy Church, provides: 'From the date of the marriage the said Sir Robert shall keep and maintain his said daughter (the bride) for three whole years in meat and drink, but the said Hugh (the bridegroom) shall find and keep her in all necessary garments and ornaments.'

In 1482 a treaty was entered into by Lachlan Mackintosh of Gallovie, in Badenoch (brother of The Mackintosh) and Donald, son of Angus Mackintosh, in connection with the estate of Kilravock, which he tried to capture from Rose. It contains the provision that, 'For the mare kyndness, traistnes, and securitie,' Donald shall marry Margaret daughter of Lachlan; and, as they are within the forbidden degrees, Lachlan shall bring a dispensation from the Pope. Until the dispensation arrives, the young people are to be handfast, and the lady's father binds himself to make thankful payment of forty merks of tocher to Donald; to clothe his daughter honestly, and to hold and sustain her in his own house, 'twa years giff it please the said Donald that she shall remaine so long with her father.'

A similar treaty between Donald, son of Cameron of Lochiel, and Agnes,

---

[77] A considerable number of ancient Scottish marriage contracts still survive, many of which indicate the lengthy and elaborate details involved in such a contract. For example, see *The Book of Dunvegan*, vol. I, which gives the full transcription of the 'Contract of Marriage between William MacLeod and Agnes Fraser 1540', (pp. 51–9), and *Charters and Other Records of the City and Royal Burgh of Kirkwall*, which gives the full transcription of the 'Marriage Contract between King James III of Scotland and Princess Margaret, Daughter of King Christian I of Denmark and Norway, 1468' (pp. 96–102, with translation from Latin, pp. 102–9).

daughter of the Laird of Grant, entered into at Urquhart Castle in 1520, in presence of Lord Lovat, Grant of Glenmoriston, the Prior of Beauly, and the Vicar of Kilmonivaig, binds Donald to marry Agnes as soon as a dispensation rendered necessary by some canonical impediment is obtained from Rome. Meantime, as in the case of Gallovie, the rules of the Church yield to the worldly interests of the parties, and until the dispensation arrives the young couple are to live together without the sanction of religion – an arrangement calmly acquiesced in by the pious prior and vicar. 'And if it shall happen that the said dispensation come not home within fifteen days after Martinmas the said John the Grant is bound and obliged to cause them to be handfast and put together, his said daughter and the said Donald, for marriage to be completed, in the default of the dispensation not coming home at the said time.' There is danger that after the handfast period of probation, Donald may decline to tie himself indissolubly to the young lady. To meet this risk, Lord Lovat and other two gentlemen become sureties that the marriage will be completed, under the penalty of £1,000 to be paid to Agnes in the event of Donald refusing. It is satisfactory to state that the dispensation came, and that the regular marriage was solemnised. From the union has come the present race of Lochiel.

I show you, as a specimen, a post-nuptial contract, dated 1592, between my own ancestor, Duncan Mackay of Achmonie, in Glen Urquhart, and Margaret, daughter of The Chisholm.[78] It is a business-like Latin document, six inches long, and it provides that in the event of Duncan predeceasing his spouse, she will have the revenue of the estate of Achmonie during her life. As a contrast to it in length, I also show you the contract, dated 1710, between my great-great-grand-uncle, Alexander Grant of Shewglie, in Glen Urquhart, and Margaret Chisholm, also a daughter of the Chisholm of the day, consisting of a roll of paper four feet long. The deed of 1592 was written by a priest; that of 1710 by a professional lawyer! One of the witnesses to the deed of 1710 was Donald Murchison, the famous factor of Kintail, who defeated Government troops at Ath-nam-Muileach, in Affaric, in 1721, and whose signature I give.

D. Murchison Witness

There was as a rule excessive conviviality at marriages, the rejoicings extending sometimes over a week. Until comparatively recently a wedding

---

[78] This essay was originally presented orally at the meeting of the TGSI in Inverness. Mr Mackay obviously brought the document to the meeting to show his audience. He did, however, reproduce the signature in the published version of his talk; see next citation.

that did not last three days was a poor wedding indeed. Among the humbler classes the guests subscribed towards the cost of the entertainment; hence the name 'penny wedding.' The marriage usually took place on a Thursday, and the festivities lasted until the bride was kirked on the following Sunday. The Sunday afternoon was devoted to feasting and dancing. The clergy did their best to stop these extravagances. In February, 1640, the Synod of Moray: 'In respect of ye gryt disorders yat haw fallen out in dyverse parts off ye land by drunkenness and tuilzieing [fighting] at pennie brydalls, therefore it is ordained that thair be no pennie brydalls maid on ye Sabbathe.' This ordinance was ignored by the Reverend John Marshall of Dundorcas, as appears from the following minute of October, 1640: 'Mr Johne Marshall being founde to have maid a marriage on the thursday, and wt ye same persones keiped a pennie brydall on ye nixt Sabbath day, hawing a minstrell playing to ye churche and from ye same befoir them, is sharplie and grawlie rebucked in ye face of ye Synod.' In 1675 the Bishop of Moray made an effort to regulate penny weddings. The following are his rules:

1. That the usual excessive number be limited to and restrained to eight persons allenarlie [only] on each side of the married persons.

2. That all piping, fiddling, and dancing without doors of all whomsoever resorting these meetings be restrained and discharged [prohibited.]

3. That all obscene, lascivious, and promiscuous dancing within doors be discharged.

4. That the two dollars consigned at the contract of the married persons (which is also ordained to be deposited not only as pledges of performing their intended purposes of marriage, but also of the civil and sober deportment of all those that shall countenance their marriage feast) remaine in the Sessione Clerk's hands until the Lord's Day after the marriage, that in case of contravening one or other of the foresaid articles by any whomsoever, then and in that case the foresaid two dollars shall be confiscated to the common good of the parish church, and this by and attour the public censure to be imposed upon the transgressors of the foresaid articles.

These rules, however, were not respected, and in 1709 and 1710 the excesses, which still prevail, are again alluded to. In time the entertainment was gradually modified, but penny weddings still continued, and as late as 1870 I myself attended one within two miles from Inverness and contributed my mite towards the expense.[79]

---

[79] William Mackay, 'Life in the Highlands in the Olden Times', *TGSI* 1914, pp. 4–7.

Trefor M. Owen
North Uist, 1953

Before the banns were announced, the bridegroom-to-be used to have to ask permission of the girl's father at a 'reiteach' or an 'arrangement' on the Friday evening. He would bring three or four friends with him. They were always men friends, usually close relatives of all ages. The bridegroom would bring half a gallon of whisky and some port wine with him. The bride-to-be would also invite some neighbours and close friends and relatives. When the party all sat down at the table, one of the groom's friends or neighbours would serve round the whisky. The friend chosen would usually be a good speaker and a wit. Then they start on the meal and after that is over a second round of whisky is served and the speaker for the groom rises to his feet to speak. The groom himself is not called upon to speak at all. His spokesman would say why they had come and would make many references to the proposed marriage. When he had finished, the girl's father rises to reply; his remarks are generally limited to wishing the couple every success and to saying how glad he is at the match. The proposed marriage is approved before the 'reiteach' is held so that the father is sure to wish them well. When he sits down, the company drink a toast to the couple.

All this takes place in the sitting room, but after this toast the company divides in two groups. All except the bride and groom and their parents or brothers and sisters (usually the fathers or a brother if the father is dead) move to the kitchen where they pass the time in conversation and drinking. The groom and his party remained in the sitting room to talk over matters relating to the forthcoming wedding. The date would already have been fixed but they still have to decide who is to be invited to the marriage and to the wedding. The groom would also be told what the dowry was; he would know nothing about this until the girl's father told him at the reiteach, but this custom has ceased during the last forty or fifty years. When the arrangements were completed the two parties would reunite and the singing, talking and drinking would continue perhaps until five or six in the morning. The groom did not always bring his parents with him – often they were too old – but the girl's father was, of course, always there.

Reiteachs are very rare now, and when they occur they are on a very much smaller scale. Only the groom, his best man, the bride and her bridesmaids attend. It is not a formal party nowadays in the sense that nobody gets up to speak. Local people believe that the reiteach originated during the period when the bride and the groom only met each other for the first time in these meetings following a match arranged beforehand by their parents.

The banns are read in the Church of Scotland for all the inhabitants whatever their affiliation. The following day preparation begins in the bride's home. Tables are set up in the sitting room. They are not ordinary tables but are made especially by a handyman or a joiner and are set up in the room, making up the three sides of a square. Chairs are placed on the inside and the outside of the square. Table and chairs are covered with cloths. While these arrangements are taking place the invitations are sent out by friends of the bride. Sometimes the groom sends out friends from his own home to give out invitations, especially if he lives in another district. Usually, however, he arranges with the bride in the reiteach for her to be responsible for all invitations being sent out. The friends who take round the verbal invitations are sometimes given a glass or two of whisky before they set on their way. The townships are divided among them, each individual visiting those townships allotted to him by [the groom] himself. On his return to the bride's home each friend is given a meal and another couple of whiskies. There is no party after the invitations are all handed out, for the bearers all return individually.

On the Monday also a small outbuilding is cleared out and a fire made. Some women gather to pluck and cook the fowls, which are to be served to visitors on the following day (Tuesday). Three or four wethers are killed on the Monday and are cooked on the Tuesday or Wednesday in preparation for the Thursday feast. In this way, all the cooking will be over before Thursday morning. The women who come to help are usually from the same township as the bride or from a neighbouring township. They are paid in money or partly in money by the bride's family.

On Monday evening the groom calls round at the bride's home and brings with him two or three bottles of whisky and some bottles of wine to serve to the helpers and to the people who bring presents on the following day.

The guests to the wedding call at the bride's home on the Tuesday and Wednesday and bring their gifts with them, often baskets of food. They call at any time of the day or night up to midnight and hand the food to the bride or her mother who put it on one side. The guests are taken to see the bride's dress and to view the presents which are usually of an utilitarian kind. They are displayed in a room by themselves. The guests are then taken to have a meal in the sitting room. There would often be ten to twelve of the guests in the house at the same time so that the bride's family would be kept busy throughout the day and late into the night on the Tuesday and Wednesday. A party of the bride's friends clear out one of the outbuildings, usually the barn, in readiness for the dance on the Thursday evening. Seats are fixed up round the inside of the barn to seat people during the dance.

On Thursday morning the tables in the sitting room are re-set; and the wedding cake planted in position. The service in the Church generally starts about two or three o'clock in the afternoon. The bride's parents and the people of the house usually take their meal before leaving for the church. On arrival at the church the groom and best man sit in front of the pulpit on the right hand side of the Church. The bride and her father (or a brother) then enter, followed by the bridesmaids, and take their place on the groom's left hand side. The service opens with a psalm followed by a reading from the Bible and a prayer. The minister then descends from the pulpit and questions and advises the couple before marrying them. The best man hands the ring to the groom, who in turn gives it to the minister. The minister then talks about the significance of the marriage bond and the meaning of the ring as a symbol of marriage – 'a thing without an end'. He then hands the ring back to the groom and asks him to put it on the bride's finger. After pronouncing them man and wife, the minister then gives out another psalm followed by a prayer. The married couple then sign the certificate. At the end of the service the bride and groom march out of the church followed by the best man and the bridesmaid. They stand at the church door until all the guests have left the church and shake hands with them as they pass. Outside they are greeted by confetti and rice and by the noise of two or three shots from a gun.

The marriage guests, who are usually the close relatives and most intimate friends of the couple, return to the bride's home and sit down to a meal in the sitting room. When the meal for the marriage guests is over, the wedding guests begin to arrive and are given a meal before the dancing and merrymaking begin. Drink is supplied by the bridegroom – generally seven to nine gallons of whisky – and is brought to the bride's home the previous night. The dancing starts in the evening and carries on throughout the night and intermittently throughout the following day.

'Highland' weddings of the type described above are not common nowadays. Catering for the guests became a difficult problem when rationing of foodstuffs was introduced at the beginning of the war. Many, indeed most, persons marry on the mainland nowadays and have a reception in a hotel in the usual urban manner. On their return to the island the married couple visit all persons in the locality who have given them presents and sent telegrams of congratulation. A bottle of whisky is brought by the groom on this round of visits, and the health of the pair is drunk by the people of each house. The visits are, of course, spread over several nights.[80]

---

[80] While based at the School of Scottish Studies in 1953, Welsh folklorist Trefor M. Owen conducted research into the economy, religious organisation, and social status in North Uist. This excerpt is from the Appendix to his 'Abstract of Report on Field Work in North Uist, Western Isles'. Mr Owen notes it is 'based on an account given by an informant and supplemented by material from other, oral sources.'

Christina Stewart

Urray, 1991

By the beginning of the twentieth century, many of the traditional aspects of Highland marriages were things of the past and most of the associated beliefs and superstitions either forgotten or deliberately set aside. Peigi Grant, my grandmother, who was born Margaret Carmichael in Sheildaig, Torridon, and was brought up in Fasag, has seen many of these changes, not only in marriage customs, but throughout the pattern of life in the Highlands.

> Everything changed . . . My grandmother never was in school. There were no schools. My mother was in school, and I went to University; that's three generations. It shows you how quickly things moved.

Widespread education and ease of travel and communication accelerated the changes in perceptions and beliefs; superstitions became old wives' tales. Nevertheless, centuries of tradition do not disappear en masse overnight. Some areas hang on to their customs longer than others, and some customs are more durable than others. My grandmother's own wedding, just after the First World War, was a simple affair:

> There was nothing elaborate about it. It was in Kyle Hotel . . . your grandfather's people belonged to Skye. They were all near Kyle, and my friends, the few that I had there, they came by train, so it was a nice place to have it in. My boss gave me away . . . it was in a hotel, not a church. There weren't many people there.

Nor did they have a reiteach beforehand. Such occasions were already very rare in my grandmother's day, but despite never having been to one, she is quite well aware of what went on.

> The reiteach was as big a thing as the wedding . . . but I don't think they were such open affairs. I think they were friends of the bride and bridegroom that went to the reiteach. It was to ask the father for the bride, for his consent . . . they approached it in an out of the way habit. They said 'I believe you have a very precious jug' or something in the house like that, and they would go on arguing about this jug, or a car, or something they had. They would never say the girl first – until the whole thing ironed out and came to an agreement. And then the bride was taken out, I think she was in the other room, and she was taken in and handed to the man . . . And then there was singing . . . a little party. I remember the reiteach all right. I never was at one, nor do I remember my mother going to one. There weren't many weddings [in our community]. By that time the young

people started to go away for work, you see, and they married elsewhere. There weren't many local weddings . . . I suppose they would have reiteachs in my mother's time, och yes, they had them . . . I suppose they died out by degrees.

In her early years in Torridon, she only went to one wedding, and that was of a couple 'not in their first youth'. The bride was a MacGregor who lived next door to the Carmichaels in Fasag, and her groom a MacLean, also from the Torridon area. They were married around 1905 and while their wedding lacked many traditional Highland features, it resembled no more closely what we would recognise as a standard modern wedding today. They had no reiteach, but nor did they go away on a honeymoon, going instead straight to their new house in Annat. The elaborate white dress and veil which today's fashion magazines describe as 'traditional' did not appear, rather the bride wore a tweed suit. The couple married in Corry Church, some two miles from Fasag. All the guests walked in procession to the church and back, led by a piper. This procession would have included the entire adult population of the locality, as a wedding was regarded as a great social event to which there was no need for a formal invitation. It was equally accepted that all would share in providing the food – an aspect which interested the children much more than the church service.

> Oh, we children didn't go to the wedding, we were only interested in the dancing and the big feeds they had. Everybody in the village gave a hen when there was a wedding. They contributed it to the feast. Fortunately, when this woman got married there was a house just newly built, but it wasn't occupied and there was no furniture in it. So, they allowed them to have the wedding there . . . You never waited for an invitation to it – you just took it for granted that you were welcome there! If your mother gave a hen! . . . They cooked them, some of [the women] cooked them, and they had them cold. But I don't think we got any of them. I don't remember getting any of them at that wedding – we got scraps!

Nowadays there is a great industry of books and magazines which specialize in the correct procedures to be observed, from anything up to six months previous to the wedding, through the event and its attendant celebrations and so into the honeymoon.[81] Sometimes the only feature to distinguish a Highland wedding from any other in the western world is the piper at the door of the church who plays as the guests enter and exit. All the same, it is not unheard of for wedding parties to take place in the home of the bride's parents, or for the food to be

---

[81] Six months is a conservative estimate, as many weddings are arranged well over a year in advance. From a general, verbal survey of friends, I am told that if the reception is to be held in a popular hotel the management generally require advance booking of a year or more.

provided by the guests, but these are exceptions rather than the rule, and are sometimes dictated by considerations of finance rather than choice. A few occasions, such as a reiteach-of-sorts I attended in 1988, are simply echoes of traditions which were already disappearing at the beginning of the century, and which seemed to become lost in the confusion of the two world wars and the general upheavals the Highlands have undergone this century.[82]

Weddings in the North-east Fishing Villages

Revd Walter Gregor
North-east, 1874

> When Jamie vowed he wud be mine,
> And wan frae me my heart,
> O, muckle lichter grew my creel.

Early marriage rules among the fishing population. Their occupation calls for this. Much of its work, such as the gathering of the bait, the preparing of it, the baiting of the fishing lines, the cleaning and curing of the fish, and the selling of them, is done by women.

The mode of bringing about and arranging the marriage is not uniform. Here is one mode. When a young man wishes to marry, his father is told. The father goes to the parents of the young maiden on whom his son has fixed his fancy, gives a detail of what he is worth as to his worldly gear, and recounts all his good qualities. If the offer is accepted, a night is fixed when the two meet along with their friends, and the final arrangement is made. This meeting goes by the name of the 'beukin nicht', or the 'nicht o' the greeance'.

Of an evening shortly before the marriage day, or on the evening before the marriage, the bride and bridegroom set out in company often hand in hand to invite the guests. The bridegroom carries a piece of chalk, and, if he finds the door of any of his friends' houses shut, he makes a cross on it with his chalk. This mark is understood as an invitation to the marriage. A common form of words in giving the invitation is: 'Ye ken faht's adee the morn at twal o'clock. Come our in fess a' yir oose wi ye,' or, 'Come ane, come athegeethir.' The number of guests is usually large, ranging from forty to a hundred or a hundred and twenty.

On the morning of the marriage day, the bride, after being decked in bridal

---

[82] I am grateful to Christinal Stewart, former student at the School of Scottish Studies, for taking up my suggestion that she should record her grandmother, and also for writing this essay, which includes her own perception of Highland weddings. The recordings are Christina's. Mrs Grant died only months after she was recorded.

array, goes the round of her own friends in company with her 'best maid', and repeats her invitation to such as she wishes to be of her party. The bridegroom, accompanied by his 'best man', does the same, and repeats his invitation to those he wishes to be of his party.

If the bride and bridegroom are of the same village, and if the church is within convenient distance, the marriage ceremony takes place in it. The bride with her party heads the procession to and from the church. If the church is at too great a distance, and if there is a schoolhouse or a public hall in the village, the ceremony takes place in it. It is, however, often performed in the house of the bride's father, During the time the guests are absent the feast is spread, and by the time they return everything is ready.

If the bride and bridegroom live in different villages, the two companies commonly meet in some convenient house between the two villages, and in it the marriage rite is performed. The bride and her company continue their journey to the house of the bridegroom's father, or to the bridegroom's house, where the marriage feast is spread. In days gone by, in some of the villages the bride put a sixpence or a shilling into her stocking or her shoe.

In one, if not more, of the villages, when the marriage takes place at the home of the bride, after the rite is concluded the whole of the marriage party makes the circuit of the village. The bride is married in full travelling attire, and all the women present are in the same costume. Special notice is taken of the *first fit*, and the success of the future life is divined from it. A man with a white horse is deemed most propitious.

When a sailor is married, immediately on the conclusion of the rite the two youngest sailor-apprentices in the harbour at the time march into the room carrying the Union Jack. The bride is completely wrapped in it along with the youngest apprentice, who has the privilege of kissing her.

When the bride is entering her future home, two of her female friends meet her at the door, the one bearing a towel or napkin, and the other a dish filled with various kinds of bread. The towel or napkin is spread over her head, and the bread is then poured over her. It is gathered up by the children who have collected round the door. In former times the bride was then led up to the hearth, and, after the fire had been scattered, the tongs was put into her hand and she made it up.

It is usual, at least among the well-to-do fishermen, for the bride to bring to her new home a chest of drawers, a *kist,* a feather bed, four pairs of white blankets, two pairs of barred, two bolsters, four pillows, sheets, one dozen towels, a table-cloth, all the hardware, cogs, tubs, and a *sheelin coug.*

The young maiden begins commonly at an early age to collect feathers for her bed and pillows, and her admirers or her affianced lends help by shooting wild-fowl for her. Out of her first earnings is bought a *kist,* and she goes on adding one thing to another till her *providan* is complete.

The husband's part is to provide the chairs, tables etc., and all the fishing gear.

The bride's *plinisan is* taken home with as much show as possible, and in some villages always much after the same fashion. There are two carts, however poor it is. In the one cart are placed, and in the following order, the chest of drawers, over it the bed, over it the blankets, and on top of all the bolsters and pillows. In the other cart are carried the *kist,* tubs, etc. The carts are followed by a train of women, each carrying something that cannot be put on the carts without the danger of being broken, as a looking-glass, a picture, a chimney-ornament.

Kind friends commonly make presents. In one village, the day after the marriage, the wives or mothers of those who sail in the boat with the bridegroom present themselves, each with a basin filled with oatmeal.

In others of the villages, when the bride is taken to another village, her female friends and well-wishers make their appearance at her home on the day after the marriage, carrying their creels, which contain the little gifts they are to present. These gifts consist of dried fish, meal, pieces of stoneware – whatever is needed for household use. The bride entertains them to tea, and tradition has it, at times, to a cup more cheering than tea, and that the company of wives, before separating, have also been known to take to the green to dance when music could be got.[83]

Shetland Weddings

Robert Jamieson
Shetland, 1869

All weddings in Shetland must commence with [a] new moon, otherwise the marriage will be an unlucky one. The week succeeding the 'speering', after which the young couple are called bride and bridegroom, they proceed to Lerwick to purchase their 'wedding needs'. The bride's eldest brother, and the bridegroom's eldest sister, accompany them. Jamie is no miser on such an occasion: he has, perhaps, had a successful season at Davis' Straits, or returned home from a voyage to Australia or California, and is in possession of money. He buys a white muslin dress, white shawl, and two beautiful caps, tastefully trimmed with ribbons, for his bride, with some 'braw' for each of his and her sisters, and a suit for himself. He will think nothing of laying out

[83] W. Gregor, *Echo*, pp. 126–31 and *Notes*, pp. 97–101.

£20 on his wedding. 'It is a poor heart,' he says, 'that never rejoices; let the money go; as long as I keep my health, I have no fear.' On Saturday the bridegroom's family and friends meet by invitation at the house of the bride's father, to celebrate the contract feast. The bride awaits their arrival, and must kiss every invited guest as they enter. The sumptuous 'tea' which follows consists of bread, butter, and fresh mutton, two or three fat sheep having been killed that morning. The bottle is sent round freely. The night is spent in discussing the crops, the fishing, and the condition of the country in olden times. Tales of voyages and shipwrecks and of hair-breadth escapes on returning from the haaf, are told; and after a late but plentiful supper they separate.

The wedding-even at the bride's house is a day of great bustle and preparation. Two women are employed from morning till morning[84] baking oatmeal cakes – vast ones, about three feet in circumference, and cut in halves, – care being taken, in setting them on the wedding-table to have their cut edges next the fire. The men are engaged in bringing home sheep from the hill, and slaughtering them; and the young women in cleaning up the house, and putting the finishing touches to their caps and dresses.

The 'best man' must sleep with the bridegroom on the wedding-even. About six o'clock, the 'aff-gang', or bridegroom's breakfast, is put on the table, and his men, who have been invited, assemble; and about the same time the bride's maidens, twelve or fifteen in number, meet at her house. Breakfast over at the bridegroom's (generally a work of three hours), he and his men walk to the bride's house, draw up in line before the door, and fire a shot. The door is shut, and no response is made. A second shot is fired; still silence. After a third shot, the door is opened, and the bride, leading all her maidens in single file, walks to the spot where the bridegroom and his men are standing, when every lad must kiss every lass. On re-entering the house, an ancient and peculiar custom is observed. The bride, with her maidens, on coming out of the house, does not walk direct to the spot where the bridegroom is standing, but turns to the left, and goes so as to form a half-circle, following the course of the sun; and on re-entering, the circle is completed. Observing an order of procession as old as the hills, they walk to the manse. There is a married couple at every wedding, called the 'honest folk', whose duty it is to walk before the bride and bridegroom in procession, bridal, and attend to the comforts of the whole company. There is also a fiddler, who walks at the head of the procession on every occasion, playing

---

[84] The text was reprinted as 'morning till night' in G.F. Black & W. Northcote, *Examples of Printed Folk-Lore Concerning the Orkney and Shetland Islands*, p. 208.

TOP. 'I wis born in a wee bow tent on the bank of the River Tay . . .' Belle Stewart in conversation with Margaret Bennett, June 1992. (Thomas A. McKean)

LOWER LEFT. 'Oh, listen tae this, May!' Nan Millar plays back MB's recording, Glasgow, 2003. (MB)

LOWER RIGHT. Agnes and Joe McAtamney, Glasgow, 2002.

WHEN THE BAIRN'S ASLEEP

TOP. In an Orkney cottage: the box-bed on the right has doors, 'ye jist slid them along'. The old lady sitting in the Orkney chair is wearing a mutch. Early twentieth century. (School of Scottish Studies Archive)

LOWER. 'No prams in them days . . .' but the mother can sing a lullaby and rock the cradle while knitting. Note the cruise lamp on the wall to her left. Late nineteenth century. (Highland Folk Museum Collection, Kingussie)

LEFT. At Stobhill Hospital, Glasgow, one nurse holds the new baby while the other holds the little visitor, Janet Price. (George Bennett, c. 1930)

BELOW LEFT AND RIGHT. 'Oh, he had such a lot of patience . . . and she would sing to the little ones.' John and Flora Stewart, haymaking, Glenconon, Uig, Skye, c. 1953. (George Bennett)

TOP LEFT. Pat MacNab with his sister Mary in Glenartney c. 1917. 'It was taken after the family left the Isle of Eigg . . .

TOP RIGHT. Pat MacNab, aged ninety, sits by the hingin' lum at the Long House, Moirlanich (near Killin). 'I went there at the age of sixteen to do the lambing . . .'

LOWER LEFT. May Anderson, Glasgow, 2002

LOWER RIGHT. Bill Innes: 'Old Mrs. Bowie had brought up a family of ten in that little house in South Uist . . . She was pure gold as far as we were concerned.' (2003)

LEFT. Nettie (Mrs George) Price, pushes her pram up Muir Street, Glasgow. Her twins are Alex (left) and Janet (right). (George Bennett, early 1930s)

BELOW. Five generations: Belle Stewart sits holding her great-great grandson, Damien. Her daughter Cathy is on the right, grand-daughter Sheila on the left, while great-grand-daughter Karen (Damien's mother) holds her sister Jade (Sheila's baby) in the centre. June, 1992. (Thomas A. McKean)

TOP LEFT AND RIGHT. Sandy Stanage at the Christening Well near Carnbee Church, Fife. (MB, 2004)

LOWER LEFT. Captain and Mrs John A. MacLellan with their daughter Kirsteen at her christening in Rogart, Sutherland, 1956. She is wearing her christening robe, hand-knitted shawl and her bonnet is trimmed with swan's down. (Bunty MacLellan's family collection)

LOWER RIGHT. '*The Lord bless thee and keep thee . . .*' Mia Kathleen Galanti with her godmother, Margaret Bennett. Her christening shawl was knitted by her great-grandmother, Peigi Stewart. (Bishopbriggs, 2004)

TOP. 'We wet the baby's head in Dunkeld . . .' Ardella Hurd demonstrates the custom to her daughter-in-law in Texas, 2002.

BOTTOM. Nan Courtney at home in Glasgow, 1989, with School of Scottish Studies tape recorder and microphone dominating her sitting room.

Keeping the bairns amused: 'Rashie rattles' and other toys made by Sandra Miller's grandfather, Orkney. (MB, 2001)

TOP LEFT. Rosie and Dougald Campbell, Newtonmore, 1992. (Thomas A. McKean)

TOP RIGHT. Rose MacDonald, aged 92, Glasgow, 2003. (MB)

BELOW LEFT. George Bennett, born in Glasgow in 1917. (Charlie West, Halifax, Nova Scotia, 2002)

BELOW RIGHT. Charles and Gladys Simpson from Keith, Banffshire. (MB, Skye, 1991)

TOP LEFT. 'Just great fun!' Louise Mann at her hen night in Edinburgh, 1992. (MB)

TOP RIGHT. 'Edinburgh's some place! You should have seen us!' Apparently none the worse of February's freezing temperature, the bride-to-be arrives home in Dublin airport, 2004. (MB)

LOWER. 'That was some hen party!' The Glasgow girls arrive home from a weekend in Dublin, July 2003.

ABOVE. Caught! A fortnight before his wedding, Gavin Wilson is 'blackened' by two friends in Kingussie, June 1992. (Ian MacKenzie)

LEFT. Lucky to get off so lightly, Gavin, joins friends in the pub for his stag night in Kingussie, June 1992. (Ian MacKenzie)

ABOVE. The *cuach phòsda* presented to Morag MacKenzie and Alan MacDougall at their *réiteach* in Glendale, Skye, May 1985. (Approx. 6" across, including the lugs.)

UPPER RIGHT. Morag and Allan MacDougall on their wedding day, June 1986 – the *réiteach* was just as memorable.

LOWER RIGHT. 'Slainte mhath!' Morag's mother, Dolly Wallace, raises her glass to the couple on their wedding anniversary, 1991.

TOP. Wedding procession in Colonsay, led by a piper (1930s). (School of Scottish Studies, postcard collection)

ABOVE. 'Roping the bride and groom': Steven Allan ties the gate and will open the rope after the groom, Phil McCall, hands over some money on behalf of himself and his new bride, Hazel Law. Outside Ancrum Church, Borders region, March 1970. (Dan and Sheena Allan's family collection)

LEFT. Marriage lintel of 1694, Falkland, Fife. (MB, 2004)

UPPER AND MIDDLE RIGHT. Paying their last respects, relatives and friends gather at the funeral of Jimmie Higgins, Blairgowrie, June 11, 1992. His sons lower the coffin, then, finally, his wife Cathy throws in a handful of earth as mourners leave the cemetery. (Thomas A. McKean)

LOWER LEFT AND RIGHT. Floral tributes (made by Doris Rougvie) to two custodians of tradition: Willie MacPhee (2001), traveller, piper, storyteller (Perth) and Tam Reid (2003), 'bothy ballad king'. Two gentlemen and friends, 'the kirk wis filled tae overflowing baith times . . .' (MB)

LEFT. Edged in black, the Order of Service to remember Captain Duncan Campbell of the Black Watch, killed in action, 1915. A regimental piper played 'The Flowers of the Forest', 'The Last Post' and 'Lochaber no More'. 'The family was from South Hall, Colintraive . . . he was an only son . . .' (Thanks to Alastair Kissack in Comrie for sharing his family papers.)

BELOW. Carrying the coffin: a Roman Catholic funeral attended by men, women and children, Isle of Barra, 1953 (Frank G. Vallee, School of Scottish Studies Archive)

BOTTOM. Funeral procession of the Rev. Kenneth MacRae, Free Church of Scotland, 1974, Stornoway (men only). (Alexander Fenton)

TOP LEFT. Lest We Forget: all over Scotland memorials such as this one at Spean Bridge remember service men and women who did not return from war. (Bill Innes)

TOP RIGHT. Brevig cairn, memorial to the fishermen of Back, Brevig, Coll and Tong (Isle of Lewis) who drowned in Broad Bay and the Minch. (Ian MacLellan)

LOWER LEFT. Miners' memorial in Muirkirk to eighty comrades killed in Ayrshire pits, sculpted by Kirti Mandir, 2004. (MB)

LOWER RIGHT. Remembering the football fans lost at Ibrox stadium in the disasters of 1902, 1961 and 1971 on 'Stairway thirteen'. (MB) energetically. On the conclusion of the ceremony, which is generally performed in the manse kitchen, the 'honest man' goes round with a bottle of wine or brandy, offering each of the company a glass, and the 'honest woman' follows with a basket of biscuit or cake. There is always a 'gunner' in every company and on returning from the manse, shots are fired as fast as the gun can be loaded, while with every shot there issues from the throat of each man a vociferous 'hip – hip – hurrah.' As they approach the bride's house, her mother and one or two female relatives meet her, carrying in a clean white cambric napkin a cake baked with seeds and sugar, called the 'bride's-cake' or 'dreaming-bread,' broken into small pieces, which she throws over the head of the bride. Dinner is now on the table – a dinner, I believe, peculiar to Shetland weddings. The fire has been removed from the centre of the floor, and the table, formed of chests, extends the whole length of the house, and is covered with white cotton. The dinner consists of a savoury dish of 'stove' made of five or six fat newly-slaughtered sheep, cut into small pieces with an axe, and boiled in the largest 'kettle' in the neighbourhood: it is seasoned with salt, pepper, and caraway seeds, and served boiling hot in huge dishes, around each of which are laid a number of cow's-horn spoons. The company are seated each opposite his own partner; grace is said; and fortunate is he who has secured a spoon with a long handle, since in a few minutes the short-handled ones become encased in a mass of mutton-fat. Oatcakes are eaten along with the 'stove,' and a glass of whisky concludes the repast. Tea, or the 'bride's piece,' is generally over about six o'clock; the floor is cleared, the fiddler is elevated on the top of a chest, and dancing commences. About nine o'clock, commotion and whispering being observed among those nearest the door, the fiddler stops, dancing ceases, and the 'honest man' informs the company that the 'guisers' have arrived. On the best man's announcing that there is plenty of both meat and drink for all comers – five gallons of whisky, it may be, yet untouched – the fiddler is told to 'play up the guisers' spring.' In walks a tall, slender-looking man, called the 'scuddler', his face closely veiled with a white cambric napkin, and on his head a cap made of straw, in shape like a sugar-loaf, with three loops at the upper extremity, filled with ribbons of every conceivable hue, and hanging down so as nearly to cover the cap. He wears a white shirt, with a band of ribbons around each arm, and a bunch of ribbons on each shoulder, with a petticoat of long clean straw (called 'gloy') which hangs loosely. The moment he enters he gives a snore, and having danced for a few minutes, another enters, called the 'gentleman,' somewhat similarly attired: he, too, having danced, a third, called the 'fool,' appears, and so on till all are in. And it is really a strange sight to see six tall young men dressed thus fantastically, and dancing with so much earnestness.

They are careful to speak not a word lest they reveal their identity; and not a sound is heard but the music of the fiddle, the rustle of the straw petticoats, the thud of their feet on the earthen floor, the laughter of the 'fool,' and the whispers of the bride's maidens guessing who the guisers may be. Dancing is kept up by the company till far on in the small hours, and supper is at last announced – a simple repast of sowans and milk, after which they retire for the night. About ten a.m. they reassemble, have breakfast, walk in procession for two or three hours, take dinner, and then finally separate.[85]

Don Ratter (b. Lerwick, 1912)
New Zealand, 2002

MB *In your parents' day [before the First World War], would the groom be saving up for the wedding?*

DR Oh, maybe for a year or two they'd save up, you know and have a real good do.

MB *And would the couple go away after they married?*

DR Oh, they would've gone to Edinburgh . . . the ferry took them to Edinburgh – It took them to Leith.

MB *Ah, that's a long sail.*

DR Yeah well, [the boat] took them to Aberdeen and sometimes they took them to Kirkwall, then Aberdeen and then Leith.

MB *Are we talking about say, twenty-four hours later?*

DR Yes, yes, about that, yes . . . And, there's lots and lots o Shetlanders that lived in Edinburgh. And lots lived in Leith.

MB *Yes indeed. And did they call it a honeymoon?*

DR They called it a honeymoon, yes . . . And there was one fellow, he couldn't remember, he said they wir gone on their honeysuckle!

MB *[laughter] And when they returned, was it just back home to hard work?*

DR Oh yes, very hard work.[86]

---

[85] Robert Jamieson's essay in John T. Reid, *Art Rambles in Shetland*, pp. 60–62.

[86] Don Ratter, aged 90, was recorded by MB in a retirement home in Masterton, New Zealand, 30 October 2002. Having emigrated in the 1950s, he retained clear memories of home.

[87] Carrying the bride over the threshold is still done, if only for fun, and usually without any understanding of its origin.

Feastin' and Dancin'

Revd James Napier
Renfrewshire, 1879

The wedding party proceeded to the house of the young couple, and in some parts of Scotland, at the beginning of the century, the young wife was lifted over the threshold, or first step of the door, lest any witchcraft or 'ill e'e' should be cast upon and influence her.[87] Just at the entering of the house, the young man's mother broke a cake of bread, prepared for the occasion, over the young wife's head. She was then led to the hearth, and the poker and tongs – in some places the broom also – were put into her hands, as symbols of her office and duty. After this, her mother-in-law handed her the keys of the house and furniture, thus transferring the mother's rights over her son to his wife. Again the glass went round, and each guest drank and wished happiness to the young pair. The cake which was broken over the young wife's head was now gathered and distributed among the unmarried female guests, and by them retained to be placed under their pillows, so that they might dream of their future husbands. This is a custom still practised, but what is now the bridescake is not a cake broken over the bride's head, but a larger and more elaborately-prepared article, which is cut up and distributed immediately after the marriage ceremony. Young girls still put a piece of it under their pillows in order to obtain prophetic dreams. In some cases, this is done by a friend writing the names of three young men on a piece of paper, and the cake, wrapped in it, is put under the pillow for three nights in succession before it is opened. Should the owners of the cake have dreamed of one of the three young men therein written, it is regarded as a sure proof that he is to be her future husband. After drinking to the health and happiness of the young couple, the wedding party then went to the house of the bridegroom's father where they partook of supper, generally a very substantial meal; and this being finished, the young people of the party became restless for a change of amusement, and generally all then repaired to some hall or barn, and there spent the night in dancing. It was the custom for the young couple, with their respective parents and the best man and the best maid, to lead off by dancing the first reel. Should the young couple happen to have either brothers or sisters older than themselves, but unmarried, these unfortunate brethren danced the first reel without their shoes. Probably this has its origin in the old Jewish custom of giving up the shoe or sandal when the right or priority passed from one to another. For an instance of this [see] Ruth 4:7.[88] Having danced till far on in the morning of next day, the young couple

---

[88] 'Now this was the manner in former times in Israel concerning redeeming and concerning changing, for to confirm all things; a man plucked off his shoe, and gave it to his neighbour; and this was a testimony in Israel.'

were then conducted home. The young wife, assisted by her female friends, undressed and got to bed, then the young man was sent into bed by his friends, and then all the marriage party entered the bedroom, when the young wife took one of her stockings, which had been put in bed with her, and threw it among the company. The person who got this was to be the first married. The best man then handed round the glass, and when all had again drunk to the young couple, the company retired. This custom was termed *the bedding,* and was regarded as a ceremony necessary to the completion of the marriage; and there can be little doubt that it is a survival of a very ancient ceremony of the same family as the old Grecian custom of moving the bride's coronet and putting her to bed. This particular form of ceremony was also found in Scotland, and continued to comparatively modern times. Young Scotch maidens formerly wore a snood, a sort of coronet, open at the top, called the virgin snood, and before being put to bed on the marriage night this snood was removed by the young women of the party. This custom is referred to in an ancient ballad:

> They've ta'en the bride to the bridal bed,
> To loose her snood nae mind they had.
> 'I'll loose it,' quo John.

On the morning after, some of the married women of the neighbourhood met in the young wife's house and put on her the *curtch* or close cap *mutch,* a token of the marriage state. In my young days unmarried women went with the head uncovered; but after marriage, never were seen without a cap. On the morning after marriage the best man and maid breakfasted with the young couple, after which they spent the day in the country, or if they lived in the country, they went to town for a change. Weddings were invariably celebrated on a Friday – the reason for this preference being, as is supposed, that Friday was the day dedicated by the Norsemen to the goddess, Friga, the bestower of joy and happiness. The wedding day being Friday, the walking-day was a Saturday; and on Sunday the young couple, with their best man and best maid, attended church in the forenoon, and took a walk in the afternoon, then spent the evening in the house of one of their parents, the meeting there being closed by family worship, and a pious advice to the young couple to practise this in their own house.

If the bride had been courted by other sweethearts than he who was now her husband, there was a fear that those discarded suitors might entertain unkindly feelings towards her, and that their evil wishes might supernaturally influence her, and affect her first-born. This evil result was sought to be averted by the bride wearing a sixpence in her left shoe till she was *kirked;* but should the bride have made a vow to any other, and broken it, this wearing of the sixpence did not prevent the evil consequences from falling upon her first-born. Many instances were currently quoted among the people of first-born children, under such circumstances, having been born of such unnatural shapes and natures that, with the sanction of the minister and the relations, the monster birth was put to death . . .

Dr Jamieson says: 'When a woman of the lower class in Scotland, however poor, or whether married or single, commences housekeeping, her *first care*, after what is absolutely necessary for the time, is to provide *death linen* for herself and those who look to her for that office, and *her next* to earn, save, and *lay up not put to interest* such money as may decently serve for funeral expenses. And many keep secret these honourable deposits and salutary *mementoes* for two or threescore years.' This practice was continued within my recollection. The first care of the young married wife was still, in my young days, to spin and get woven sufficient linen to make for herself and her husband their *dead claes*. I can well remember the time when, in my father's house, these things were spread out to air before the fire. This was done periodically, and these were days when mirth was banished from the household, and everything was done in a solemn mood. The day was kept as a Sabbath. The reader will not fail to observe in some of these modern customs and beliefs modified survivals of the old Roman practices and superstitious beliefs.[89]

Revd Walter Gregor
North-east, 1874

> An' there was a waddin'! Sic vivers an' drinks,
> Sic fiddlin' an' pipin', sic dancin' an' jinks;
> The haggis e'en hotched te the piper its lane.

Now followed the feast, which was laid out in the barn. All the tables belonging to the household were called into use, and a few might be borrowed. If these were not sufficient, deals were placed on barrels, or masons' trestles, or boxes. The seats consisted of deals laid on chairs, or the old naves of cart-wheels, or, in corners, on two bags of corn or bere laid on their sides, one above the other. The dishes and spoons were very varied, for they had been gathered in for the occasion from friends. The bride got the seat of honour, the head of the table; and the guests arranged themselves according to their fancy. Those, however, who were accounted more honourable, were placed nearest the bride. The bridegroom did not take his seat at table. His charge was to serve and to look after the comfort of all the guests.

---

[89] J. Napier, *Folk Lore*, pp. 51–2.

The feast was abundant. First came a course of milk-broth, made of barley; barley-broth, made from beef or mutton, or fowls, formed the second course. The third consisted of rounds of beef, legs of mutton, and fowls by the dozen. Last of all came puddings, cooked in every variety of dish, and eaten from saucers, and swimming in cream. Home-brewed ales flowed in abundance from first to last of the feast. When the tables were cleared, big bottles full of whisky were brought in, along with punchbowls, each holding a punch ladle made of wood, and placed before patriarchs renowned for their skill in making punch. With a firm hand each laid hold of a bottle and poured into his bowl for a time. He then looked at the quantity in the bowl, and to make sure of the quantity he held up the bottle before him, and measured with the eye what he had poured in. Then he slowly added the sugar, scanning carefully what he cast in. The water was poured boiling over the whisky and sugar. The mixture was stirred till the sugar was melted. He then took a glass and poured a little of the mixture into it, and tasted it with a knowing smack of the tongue. The glass was handed to another connoisseur of the delicious beverage. It was pronounced good. All the glasses were filled and handed round. The health of the bride and bridegroom was proposed. The glasses were drunk off at once, and the toast received with 'a' the honours three'. Round after round was drunk, each to a toast or sentiment, and the glass emptied at each; bowl after bowl was made till the hour for dancing came. The tables, with their contents, were moved away, and the seats were ranged round the wall, so that the whole area of the barn was left clear for dancing.

The dancing was begun by the *shaimit reel*. This dance was performed by the bride, the bride's maidens, the bridegroom, and the best young men. The music to which it was danced was called the *shaim-spring*, and the bride had the privilege of choosing the music. The male dancers then paid the musician his fee. Another dance was performed by the same six, after which the floor was open. In some districts the *shaimit reel* was danced by the bride and her best maid, with the two *sens* as partners. After it was danced the bride fixed a marriage favour on the right arm of her partner in the dance, and the best maid best maid fixed one on the left arm of her partner. The two *sens* then paid the fiddler. Frequently the bride and her maid asked if there were other young men who wished to win favours. Two jumped to the floor, danced with the bride and her maid, and earned the honour on the left arm. Dancing was carried on far into the morning with the utmost vigour, each dance being begun and ended by the partners saluting each other.

At intervals the dancing ceased, and all seated themselves, when bread and cheese and home-brewed ale and punch reeking hot were served round. Punch flowed most freely during the whole night, and, to keep up the supply of it, a few old man established themselves commonly in the best room, or *but ein*, and, if the party was large, the *firlot* was substituted for punchbowls, and there the patriarchs sat and brewed and pledged each other's health, and with grasped hands again and again swore eternal friendship, and dealt out the inspiriting beverage in large decanters to young women, who carried it to the barn to the dancers, and who, every time they returned empty-handed, reported the progress of the mirth. The old men would go and satisfy themselves that the young folk were behaving in a manner worthy of the occasion and their fathers. Under the influence of punch and music and example they forgot their years, and were back again to the days of youth. Each jumped to the floor with a young maiden in her teens, and saluted her with a kiss that made the kaibbers of the barn echo. When all were ready, they shouted to the fiddler to play up, and away they sprang as if they were but 'sweet ane and twenty', snapped the fingers, and hooched 'Till reef an' rafters a' did dirll'.

The time for separating came. It was in vain the bride retired in secret. No sooner was she missed than there was a rush to the bridal chamber, which was burst open and filled in an instant to perform the ceremony of *beddan*. After the bride was in bed a bottle of whisky, with a quantity of bread and cheese, was handed to her. She gave each a 'dram' and a piece of the bread and cheese. One of her stockings was then given her, and it she threw over her left shoulder amongst the onlookers. Strong and long was the contest for it, as the one who remained possessor of it was the first of that company who would be married. The guests then retired.

The one who fell asleep first was the first to die. 'My ane's awa noo,' an aged woman was heard to say not long ago, with the tears in her eyes, 'an I myne weel he fell asleep first. A speert at — (another widow) gehn she mynt filk o' them fell asleep first, bit she said she didna myne.' In other places it was augured that the one who awoke first was the first to depart.

If the husband arose before the wife, he carried the pains and sorrows of child-bearing.

The *kirkin* was usually attended by a considerable company. But time reduced the company to the bride's maids and the best young man. The party never under any consideration took a bye-path to church, however much shorter or more convenient it might be than the ordinary 'kirk road', nor did they enter church till the service was well begun. To have done otherwise would have entailed misfortune. If two bridal parties were in church at once, it was an endeavour which should get out first, as the one that left last did not enjoy success and happiness. The party was entertained to a feast by the newly-married pair.[90]

---

[90] *Ibid*, pp. 120–5 and pp. 93–7.

Iain Nicolson
Uig, Skye, 1990

IN But things wasn't so easy got then [just after the Second World War[91]] as it is now. The drinks were scarce at times. But I got so much [i.e. a certain amount], you know, on the quiet. Mm.

TM How many were at your wedding?

IN Oh, there would be a hundred anyhow, oh, there would be, in Portree. Of course I had to, I butchered two sheep myself and put them up to the hotel because you wouldn't get meat at that time. But I had the sheep here, you know . . . on the quiet. [The sheep] went up there and they cooked them there [with] whatever they had over and above that. Aye.

TM And that was the same day as the queen got married?

IN Aye, right! Aye, aye, the twentieth of November, [1948]. Oh yes, I had an anniversary here, three or four years ago, in Portree [laughs]. . . . I was there, just the same. Well, it was alright!

TM Were there a lot of Uig people at the wedding?

IN Oh yes, quite a lot, yes. Well of Glenconon and . . . Earlish and Glenhinnisdale. Oh yes . . . we got plenty of telegrams anyhow, heaps of them there. Yes.[92]

Wedding Cakes and Favours

Although commercial bakers have mostly taken over the baking of wedding cakes, it was generally done by one of the women, who gave it as a gift. Tradition dictated it had to be as rich a fruit cake as they could afford, and decorated with icing and symbols of good luck, such as small ornamental silver horse-shoes and white heather. After the ceremonial cutting of the cake, it was the custom to give these ornaments, known as 'favours', to selected female guests at the wedding.

At my sister's wedding in 1968 – a Highland wedding in Glasgow – one of my duties as bridesmaid was to distribute the 'favours' to a very specific number of female guests. When the bride and groom cut the cake the favours were set aside – a dozen or so small silver horseshoes, each with a sprig of white heather tied on with a little ribbon. When they were handed out, the recipients all seemed honoured to receive one.

Thirty years on, at the close of the twentieth century, this custom was fast disappearing and new practices emerging.

---

[91] The rationing of food and clothing was still strictly enforced into the 1950s.
[92] Iain Nicolson was recorded at his home in Cuidreach, Skye, by T.A. McKean. SA1990/108.

Doris Rougvie
Huntingtower, Perthshire, 2004

MB *Doris, when you got married in the sixties, were there favours on your cake?*

DR There were . . . Well, the ones I had were a little gold ring with a dove – that was my favourite one, and then there was a little spray of silk flowers with pearly centres . . . You had a three-tier cake with four on each, and you had a little basket with the extras in it. And people were given them – aunts, cousins, close female relatives – and granny if you had one . . .

MB *So, only a limited number of favours?*

DR Yes, I'd say ten or twelve. The men didn't get anything. Nowadays they get a little bottle of whisky but that's a fairly recent thing, and nowadays all the women at the wedding get something . . . There's a new thing that came in the eighties – sugared almonds. But I think that came from the Greek tradition.[93] Well it was a Greek wedding I first did it for. You made the favours – it was a wee piece of net.

MB *And the florist made the favours?*

DR Yes, yes, and these went with the flowers . . . The first time they said they wanted a little net parcel tied with a ribbon to match the dresses and there was five almonds in each. [In those days] they would have had about twenty of these . . . not one for everyone.

MB *So when did this come in, having a favour for everybody at the wedding?*

DR Within the last ten years [1990s]. All the women get something. It varies, sometimes it's a little parchment giving the date, with fresh rose petals inside – there's all kinds of things they do now.[94]

MB *And when did the men start getting favours?*

DR Again, very recently. I think it came in from America because it certainly was never ever a tradition in Scotland.

MB *Indeed. I actually looked this one up on the internet and the first response I got was, 'Do you mean FAVOR?' A bit of a give-away, it didn't take to my request for British spelling, 'favour'! Now this is big business in the UK – if you read the web-ads incorporating the buzzwords 'Scottish Highland wedding' you find a good many are based outside Scotland – London seems to do a roaring trade. These favours have little or*

---

[93] Sugared almonds are common in Italian tradition, and Scotland has a significant Italian population.

[94] Among the so-called traditional favours advertised by specialist companies are the following items: candles, matches, fortune cookies, sweets, dragees, cameras, sparklers, cufflinks, boxer shorts, candies, soaps, bookmarks, champagne glasses, swans, princess slippers, and ceramic keepsakes. Most items can be personalised with the names or initials of the bride and groom and although some are even advertised as 'Scottish Highland' there seems to be no mention of horseshoes or white heather. 'Men's Favours' include personalised miniature bottles of Scotch whisky, brandy, vodka or wine.

nothing to do with Scottish tradition and everything to do with capturing a very lucrative
mail order market. An order can set you back several hundred pounds even if you don't
buy the personalised whisky miniatures![95]

J.J. Vernon and J. McNairn
Hawick, 1911

Bridals were more often of a public than of a private nature, and the occasion
of much hilarity and merriment. Publicity pervaded the whole arrangements,
the invitations being numerous and almost indiscriminate. In many instances
it was customary for the guests to contribute towards the cost of the
entertainment – in most cases so liberally as to leave a considerable surplus,
which formed a 'nest egg' towards furnishing the house of the happy couple.
In families who could afford the expense, it often happened that several days
were spent in feasting and revelry. The names having been 'given in',
proclamation followed, the fee for which was 7s 6d if it was to be made three
Sundays in succession; if for twice the first, and once the second Sunday, 10s
6d was the fee imposed; but if all three times of asking had to be done in one
day, then a guinea was charged. It was considered unlucky for a woman to
attend the church on those Sundays when she was to be 'cried'.

An indispensable preliminary to marriage was the preparation by the bride
elect of her blankets and sheets, which were all of home-made yarn, the
spinning and preparing of which had employed her during the long nights of
several winters, and in the quantity and quality of which an excusable pride
was felt. The wedding was usually deferred till the Friday after the last
proclamation. On the Tuesday evening previous to the marriage, on the
invitation of the bride, all her young friends gathered for the last time ere she
changed her name, and were entertained to supper. After supper, a tub three
quarters full of warm water was introduced, into which was thrown a ring
from the finger of one of the married women present, which had the double
merit of communicating some secret virtue to the water, and ensuring the
speedy marriage of the party who first got it. Then followed the time-
honoured ceremony of 'the feet-washing,' with its attendant pranks and
frolic. Some of the wags of the company had an impression that candle grease
and soot were the proper detergents to employ, so that the feet were more
soiled when withdrawn than when put in, and the operation had to be done
over again with soap and water. As every one present had to give the bride's
feet a rub, and at the same time every one was anxious to find the ring, we

---

[95] Doris was recorded by MB.

may imagine the sport and merriment which ensued, especially as the fortunate finder of the ring sometimes concealed the fact, in order to keep the fun going a little longer.

The eventful day having at length arrived, it was the custom of the bridegroom's friends to assemble at his house and proceed to that of the bride, where she was waiting with her friends. When the time came they all, headed by a fiddle playing some merry air, set out in gay procession to the house of the minister who was to perform the ceremony. The bride, on her way to be married, was forbidden to look back; to do so was to ensure a succession of disasters and quarrels in the married state. Entering the manse, the ceremony was duly performed, at the conclusion of which the procession re-formed, the fiddler resumed his office, accompanied them back to the bride's parents' home, and to the bridal feast. A plentiful repast was provided, the principal dish being the 'bride's pie', as it was termed. All were merry and full of good wishes for the young couple; a large thick slice – the 'first cut' – of the bride's-cake was reduced into small pieces, each of which was passed through the wedding-ring and distributed among the company. These tiny pieces were much valued, especially by the young women, who were sure to behold their future husbands in dreamland. The evening soon passed away with music and dancing.

The natural sequence to a wedding a hundred years ago was the 'infare' or homecoming of the bride, which was made the occasion for more jollification. Those who could afford it would indulge in a short holiday, spent in visiting some friend in the district. On the return of the newly-married couple, they proceeded to their future home, where had gathered a number of their more intimate friends who had been present at the wedding. Here the bride was welcomed by her husband's mother, who, as the bride crossed the threshold, broke the infare cake of shortbread over the head of the bride, the remaining portions of the cake being distributed among the company present. The remainder of the day was given up to feasting and merriment once more. On the following Sunday the couple, attended by the best man and the best maid, were 'kirked'. The kirking was considered the final act of the ceremony, after which they were considered man and wife in the ordinary sense of the term, and treated accordingly. On such occasions the minister was almost certain to give out the 128th Psalm:

> Thy wife shall as a fruitful vine
> By thy house sides be found;
> Thy children like to olive-plants
> About thy table round.

It was the exception in the days of our grandmothers to find a woman unable to spin, and it was no uncommon custom for the young wife during the winter months following her wedding to spin the thread which, when woven into a fine linen web, was fashioned into her 'dead claes'. These were carefully hidden away in some drawer against the day for which they would be required, and only taken out to be aired when no one was about who might take notice.[96]

Racin' and Ropin'

George Penny
Perth, 1836

The country weddings were celebrated in a manner similar to those in the towns; only the invitations were more numerous. Sometimes the whole parish were invited; and when the company had far to ride, the cavalcade had a very imposing appearance. Many of the farmers had their wives mounted behind them, and the lads their sweethearts. The moment the bride started, all the old shoes about the house were thrown after her, fire arms were discharged, and the gridiron was rung with a thundering noise. There was a halt made at every public house on the way, and a quantity of spirits distributed . . . But the most extravagant custom was that of riding the broose – a practice replete with hazard, and often attended with serious accidents. When the returning party approached within a mile or two of the bridegroom's house, the more reckless and better mounted set off on a sort of steeplechase; the winner having the honour of welcoming the wedding party with a dram.

The writer was present at a scene of this kind at Fossaway. The bride's house was on one side of the Rumbling Bridge, and the bridegroom's on the other. At this time the bridge had no ledge, and was scarcely broad enough to admit the passage of a cart; and the danger was further increased by an abrupt turn of the road, close upon the bridge The party being a little elevated, a number set off for the broose, before crossing this dangerous pass. It was truly terrifying to see the horses, even those which were double mounted, rushing across this awful chasm, which is upwards of two hundred feet in depth. There were two cripple dominies present, one of whom distinguished himself on the occasion. He was mounted on a strong horse, with his wife behind him. In rushing past a rival in the race, the wife unfortunately lost her hold. He was called on to stop and take up his wife, but he pushed on, crying

---

[96] J.J. Vernon and J. McNairn, *Pictures from the Past of Auld Hawick*, 1911, pp. 93–7.

out, 'Let the devil stop and take up his own.' The dominie's horse, like the post-boy's in John Gilpin, right glad to be relieved of so much of its burden, sprang forward with increased speed, and succeeded in winning the broose. Fortunately the wife had received little injury, and was taken up behind one of the more sedate of the party.[97]

Revd James Napier
Renfrewshire, 1879

On coming within a mile or so of the young couple's house, where the mother of the young good man was waiting, a few of the young men would start on a race home. This race was often keenly contested, and was termed *running the brooze or braize*. The one who reached the house first and announced the happy completion of the wedding, was presented with a bottle of whisky and a glass, with which he returned to meet the marriage procession, and the progress of the procession was generally so arranged that he would meet them before they arrived at the village or town where the young couple were to be resident. He was therefore considered their *first foot*, and distributed the contents of his bottle among the party, each drinking to the health of the young married pair, and then bottle and glass were thrown away and broken. The whole party then proceeded on their way to the young folk's house. To be the successful runner in this race was an object of considerable ambition, and the whole town and neighbourhood took great interest in it. At riding weddings it was the great ambition of farmers' sons to succeed in winning the *braize*, and they would even borrow racing horses for the occasion.

The origin of this custom of running the *braize* – it was so pronounced in the west country – has long been a puzzle to antiquarians. Probably it is the survival of a custom practised by our Scandinavian forefathers. A Scandinavian hero or warrior considered it beneath his dignity to court a lady's favour by submitting the matter of marriage to her decision. When he saw or heard of a beauty whom he decided to make his wife, he either went direct and took her away by force from her home, or he gained the right to make her his bride by success in battle with his opponents. Often, however, one who was no hero might gain the consent of the parents to his marriage with their daughter, she having little or no voice in the matter; and when she and her friends were on their way to the church, some heroic but unapproved admirer, determined to win her by force of arms, having collected his followers and friends who were ever ready for a fight, would fall upon the

---

[97] George Penny, *Traditions of Perth*, pp. 31–2.

marriage cortege, and carry off the bride.[98] Under those circumstances there was often great anxiety on the part of both the groom's and bride's relations, who remained at home when they had reason to apprehend that such attack might be made, and so, whenever the marriage ceremony was over, some of the company hasted home with the glad news; but commonly youth stationed themselves at the church-door, ready to run the moment the ceremony was over, and whether on foot or horseback, the race became an exciting one. He who first brought the good news received as a reward a bowl of brose, and such brose as was made in those days for this occasion was an acceptable prize. Although the necessity for running ceased, the sport occasioned by these contentions was too good and exciting to be readily given up, but it came to be confined to those who were at the wedding, and many young men looked forward eagerly to taking part in the sport. The prize, which originally was brose, came to be changed to something more congenial to the tastes and usages of the times, viz., a bottle of whisky. In this way, I think, we may account for the custom of 'running the braize.'

Tom Ovens
Morebattle, 1984

TO   There was a race that used to be run after a wedding called the braize . . . It was just a short race, really, and the winner got a kiss from the bride, that was his chief reward.

EL   *Did you see this?*

TO   Yes, I've seen it.

EL   *Where did the race start?*

TO   Well, the only time I can remember seeing it was at a wedding at Frogden, just held in a cottage at Frogden, and it was at night, after dark, so I couldn't really tell you how far it was away that they started. I was just a boy.

EL   *Where was the bride?*

TO   Just waiting at the door.

EL   *Just waiting at the door of the house?*

TO   Yes, but the men who were taking part just went away. I don't know how it was started or who started it . . . It was just a short distance, just a couple of hundred yards, maybe, at the most, just a short sprint.

EL   *And you couldn't actually see the start, could you, because of the dark?*

TO   No, it was dark.

EL   *And the first one that came . . .*

---

[98] In his *Lindores Abbey and its Burgh of Newburgh*, Laing refers to 'riding the broose' as a 'mock capture of the bride [which] continued in [that part of Fife] to about 1820'. See p. 386.

TO He was the winner.

EL *And gave the bride a kiss?*

TO Yes.

EL *Did they actually run at the bride?*

TO Well, just ran forward to the door and, as I say, the winner got his reward.

EL *Were these people who had been at the wedding?*

TO Oh yes, they were all guests of the wedding.

EL *Is that the only time you've actually seen it?*

TO As far as I can remember.

EL *But you've heard about it?*

TO Yes, oh yes. It used to be the regular thing at a wedding.

> . . . You know the church at Morebattle? . . . Well, when there was a wedding on, the bride and the bridegroom used to come along the path from the church to the gate and they wouldn't let the happy couple out until the bride-groom had forked out something for a drink for those that were roping and then they were allowed out.

EL *Have you been involved in that?*

TO No, I was never allowed to take part in that.

EL *Did someone disapprove of it?*

TO Well, my mother never allowed me to go near it. But it's a funny thing, it seems as if it's almost begging, that, you know, and yet the married couple would be disappointed if there were nobody there doing it . . .

EL *After the wedding, you were saying . . .*

TO The bride and bridegroom used to throw out a few handfuls of ha'pennies in those days and the children were all there waiting to gather them up.

EL *And how did this connect with the roping?*

TO No, that was nothing to do with the roping. The roping took place at the church gate.

EL *And where was this other thing?*

TO Well, usually from the house that the bride and bridegroom went to after the ceremony.

EL *So the roping would be as they left the church, and the 'scramble', did you call it, was later?*

TO Yes.

EL *Did they call out anything when they wanted the money, the children?*

TO Yes, they used to sometimes call out 'Poor oot! Poor oot!' . . . [The roping] was mainly to get money to go for a drink. Money was scarce in these days, of course, and, whoever did the roping, he and his friends went to the pub to get rid of the money as soon as possible.[99]

---

[99] Tom Ovens, aged 76, remembering Morebattle, was recorded in Hawick by Emily Lyle, on 8 June 1984. SA1984/33.

Walter Culbertson
Morebattle, 1984

WC The bride and bridegroom had got married and come out o' the church, and the church had quite a long walk out there. Then at the church gate the children usually had a scramble – pennies thrown, you know; that's for the children – and they waited until that was finished and then the young men that could run used to line up and run. Somebody started them off and they ran tae a certain other man – that would be a hundred yards or something like that – and the one that won it got to kiss the bride. It was run from the [chosen] point back to the bride, back to the church. They started in the middle of the village, what they call the toon gate there, and they run to the church gate. Well, it's a good hundred yards you know and the one who got there first got to kiss the bride, and that was it.

EL *And there was something about roping too, was there?*

WC Yes, that was before they came out of the church gate there. They came down the walk at the gate and they put a rope across the road and the bridegroom had to give the ropers a donation of some kind. This usually meant a pound even in the harder days – even in them days, it meant a pound! And then the men that weren't at the wedding retired all down to the pub and spent the pound. And that's it; that's how the pound went.

EL *So it was men doing this?*

WC Yes, that's right. The men wouldn't let the children in to have anything to do with it. They wouldn't let any children in – it was the men only.

EL *And you weren't married in Morebattle yourself, or were you?*

WC Yes, I was married at Caverton Mill, anyway, down near Morebattle.

EL *Did this happen to you?*

WC I wasn't married in the village, ye see, but they roped me when I come back.

EL *Oh, did they? Tell me about that.*

WC Well, you'd a house ready and when they knew you were comin back they were all keyed up ready for comin' back, and then they used to rope you before you went into the house, and put the rope across the house door and you didna get in until you'd paid and that cost me a pound.[100]

[100] Walter Culbertson, aged 83, was recorded by Emily Lyle at Morebattle in 1984. SA1984/33.

Dan and Sheena Allan
Ancrum, 1991

SA Now here you just used to tie the gate – before you let the bride and groom out you just used to tie the gate and they would have to pay some money over to you to open the gate and let them out.

MB *Oh that's nice!*

DA It's no so nice when ye've tae stand up a fiver afore ye get oot! [laughs!] It's the wee boys [that] tie a wee bit string on the gate. Ye could have opened it, knocked it open, but ye hud tae gie them a few pennies; it's a tradition, and they opened the gate and let ye oot.

MB *Does that still go on?*

SA No, it's . . .

MR A They'd be havin a scramble now, and you want pennies and ten pences and chuck them out.

EL But this happened to you?

DA Uh huh! Yes!

MRS A Yes, aye, tie the gate! We had tae hand something over when we were coming oot.

MB *Where were you married?*

SA St Boswells [laughs] He wis there too! [laughs!]

MR A That's a lang time ago! [laughs]

SA Thirty-six years this month just past.

EL Who were these people tying the gate?

SA Just village boys, just locals. Oh, ye know it's going tae happen!

MB *So you're not stuck without the purse?*

DA No, no!

EL Have you ever done it to anyone else?

SA Oor sons have, up at the church [in Ancrum]; I've got some photographs o them gettin their money.[101]

Anna Cunningham
Edinburgh, 2002

Reading your book . . . I was interested in the 'Ropin' custom following a wedding. I first saw this custom seven years ago in the south of Poland – south of Katowice in a small town called Szczyrk, south-west of Bielsko

---

[101] Mr and Mrs Dan Allan, Ancrum, were recorded by Emily Lyle and MB on 16 June 1991. SA 1991/37.

Biata. The young couple kept being stopped by a rope across the road and had to pay to get through. I thought nothing of the custom at the time but just two weeks ago I was at a Polish Dance Performance of a Sieradz wedding (Sieradz is just west of Warsaw) where the same roping custom was performed at the end of the 2–3 day wedding ceremony.

Many Scots emigrated to Poland from the sixteenth century on and in the nineteenth century many of them to'd and fro'd between Poland and Scotland.

It would be interesting to know if this custom existed in other parts of Europe or whether it was Scottish exported to Poland or vice versa.[102]

Scramblin an Scatterin

Bill Douglas and Bill Kirkwood
Niddrie and Glasgow respectively, 1973

BD The weddings were generally held in the home and the minister, of course, come to the home and then all the ones that were invited to the wedding were brought there in cabs – there were no cars in these days and it would be hansom cabs with a horse. And the boys used to ride on the back axle there but they put spikes across there and that kept the boys off of there – but they used to go and pick up the guests. The guests were brought by the best man, and he used to ride up beside the cabbie and he went to the guests' home and picked them up and brought them to the house where the wedding was bein held, and all the kids from all over the district would be at the house, swarms o' them, and they'd be there shoutin. Their war cry was: 'Poor oot, ye dirty brute, ye canna spare a ha'penny!'

And the best man had always a pocket full of coppers and silver and he used to shower this among the kids and the kids dived on the money and then the guests got clear to get into the house.

BK As Bill was sayin, the wedding used to take place from the house itself and, as the people were going away from the house to go to the church, either the bridegroom or the bride as they were leaving they used to open the windows of the cars and throw this money out and if the kids who were waiting around waiting for this money didn't think they'd thrown enough money out, as they pulled away they used to shout after them 'Rusty pockets! Rusty pockets!' in the hope that by the time the car got to the end of the street they'd chuck a few more pennies out.[103]

---

[102] Letter, prompted by discussion after a talk I gave to the Braid Circle, Morningside, Edinburgh, October 2002.
[103] Bill Douglas of Niddrie and Bill Kirkwood of Glasgow were recorded by Emily Lyle in 1977. SA1977/31.

Revd Walter Gregor
North-east, 1874

In some of the villages it was usually the custom for children to assemble round the door, and demand *ba-siller*, when a few coppers were given them. *Pieces* however, were ordinarily given.

A good many beggars commonly gathered together, and they were regaled most plentifully, and if any of them had a hankering after punch of whisky, it was not spared.[104]

Joseph Laing Waugh
Thornhill, 1903

The 'baa' was a *largesse* of copper coins flung among the children on the street. We still hear Thornhill children cry at weddings: 'If ye don't gie's a baa/Ye'll hae nae weans ava.[105]

Margaret Wilson
Lilliesleaf, 1990

We used to go along to the church for the scatter, when the money was thrown out after they came out of the church. The bridegroom would throw out pennies from the car and the children would scramble; it's supposed to be lucky. At one time they used to put a rope across the street to stop the car coming down. They let the car go after the money was thrown out . . . We used to get old boots and tie them onto the car, and I've seen them tying old tin cans and everything, making a big din; they took off with all this clatter at the back. The boot, that's supposed to be lucky.[106]

George Bennett
Halifax, Nova Scotia, 2003

In the old days in Glasgow – the twenties and thirties – it was always a horse-drawn vehicle that carried the bridal couple at their wedding. There were very few cars used before the war. As they came out of the church they were showered with confetti and rice, and they'd be driven to the reception, usually in a house or a hall. There would be a meal and then the couple would usually

---

[104] W. Gregor, *Echo*, p. 119 and *Notes*, p. 93.
[105] J.L. Waugh, *Thornhill and its Worthies*, p. 30.
[106] Margaret Wilson, Lilliesleaf, recorded by Susan Huntly. SA1990/18.

slip away while the reception was still in full swing. Just as the horse and carriage drew away, the groom usually scattered pennies, ha'pennies and farthings for the children. But if he didn't do that right away, the kids would all run after the carriage shouting 'Hard up! Hard up!' as if to challenge the groom about his worldly wealth, his means of supporting his wife. And then he'd open the window and out would come this shower of coins for the big scramble.

Now when David and Florence got married in 1970, obviously things had changed. They were showered with confetti coming out of the church, St George's Tron, but when they left the reception, there were no pennies or money thrown. So Granny, who was in her eighties by then, ran after the taxi shouting, 'Hard up! Hard up!' But nobody understood, and no pennies were thrown – they probably wondered what in the world she was doing. But that was the custom in her day, and in mine too.[107]

Arranged Marriages and Elopement

Over the centuries, courtship and marriage patterns in Scotland have varied widely depending on social class, religion and region. The age-old custom of 'arranged marriages', if acknowledged at all, is sometimes regarded as belonging to another culture, or, if it did exist in Scotland, then only in the dim and distant past, between the families of lords and ladies, kings and queens. Scottish history books, romantic novels, classic ballads, poems and songs cite many examples where land inheritance and family titles were at stake, and some record the fact that children as young as twelve were married under Scots law. While time has obscured the actual identity of the majority of those who figure in the ballads, there are, nevertheless, songs dating back several centuries, which still preserve precise details. 'Griogal Chridhe' [The Glen Lyon Lament], for example, dates to the early 1570s when the daughter of Campbell of Glenstrae defies her father's plans of an arranged marriage and runs away to Glen Lyon with the man she loves, Gregor MacGregor. Her disobedience results in Gregor's murder at the hands of her merciless father and brothers.[108] Several Scots ballads have equally cruel and tragic endings when young lovers defy the parents' wishes: 'Andrew Lammie' is a particularly heart-rending case in point.

Within living memory, and recorded in oral tradition, are comparatively

---

[107] My father, George Bennett, who lives in Halifax, e-mailed this to me.
[108] There are many versions in oral tradition, in print and on recordings. The one from my mother's family is on Martyn Bennett's *Glen Lyon* (Footstompin Records, CDFSR1714).

more instances of arranged marriages, and attempts to thwart or avoid them.
There seem to be few happy endings if we are to judge by songs such as
'Oran Chaluim Sgaire', composed in the early 1850s by Malcolm MacAulay
from Lewis, who planned to elope with his sweetheart, Margaret MacLeod.
When the attempt failed, her parents forced her to marry a man she didn't
love. One of her descendants takes up the story.

Muriel Mayhew
Lennoxville, Quebec, 1992

MM The first time I heard the story of Calum Sgaire [Malcom, son of Zachary
MacAulay] I was on a visit to Scotland with my mother in 1957. We visited a
cousin of my father's . . . living in Bernaray . . . the old home where she once lived
. . . She had lots of stories, and one of them was the story of Calum Sgaire. And I
think it was my grandmother's ancestor – my ancestor too, as far as that goes – and
it was her aunt who was the Margaret in the story. Anyway, they were lovers and
they wanted to get married and he [Malcolm MacAulay] was considered much
beneath this family who didn't want her to marry him because he was a sailor
[fisherman]. And Malcolm had come home, he had come back to get her, and they
would go away together [elope]. And [secretly] they planned to meet one particular
night. And she went out to meet him on the moors and a fog came up and she lost
her way, and he thought she had decided not to come, and she, I guess, thought
that he hadn't come to meet her, and then he made up the song after that, was
what I was told. And his name was Malcolm and her name was Margaret, and he
was Calum Sgaire. And in the end her parents made her marry a person they had
chosen for her, [the local merchant, an older man, with whom she would have a
more prosperous life]. And she married him with her hands behind her back. She
wouldn't give him her hand in marriage, and I think it was a few months or a year
later she died. She was supposed to have died of a broken heart . . .

Later on I think he came to Canada [Quebec]. If I'm not mistaken, he married
somebody else anyway – but he had made this song for her . . . Now the name
Sgaire is very common around here, the MacAulays . . . the descendants of Calum
Sgaire . . . My mother was related to them somehow.[109]

---

[109] Muriel Mayhew was recorded in her home in Quebec in 1993. See also,
M. Bennett, *Oatmeal and the Catechism: Scottish Gaelic Settlers in Quebec*, p. 243.
Another version of the story was recorded by Francis Collinson in Bernera, Lewis, in
1954, although there is no mention of Malcolm going to Quebec; see *Tocher*, 9, pp.
34–5. A revival of interest in the song is probably due to the recording of the 1936
National Mod gold-medallist, Kitty MacLeod of Lewis (1914–2001), who composed
the tune.

No doubt the heartbreak of the young lovers and the ensuing course of events soon led to untold sorrow for the bride's parents and, most likely, the man she was persuaded to marry.

Elopement was usually the solution to avoid an arranged marriage, or to escape the wrath and disapproval of families. In most cases, parents who arranged a marriage for their daughter did so because wealth and prestige were the main factors, regardless of the feelings of the young woman concerned. Come what may (even a lifetime of misery with a man she did not love), some were determined to see their daughter make a 'sensible choice', often one which might better the position of the family in general.

Nevertheless, the old saying 'Love will find out the way' has frequently been borne out by couples who have successfully eloped. In days before rapid communication systems, it was not too difficult to run away and get married in another town, village or island before parents could catch up. When there was no complex network of police to help trace runaways, for some young lovers it was simply a matter of getting from one place to another, finding a clergyman who would perform the marriage, and then hoping that things would eventually calm down so that the couple could return home.[110] For others, elopement meant running away to the ends of the earth, such as the oft-told story of two young lovers from Skye and Uist.

William MacKenzie
Skye, 1930

Donald, one of Hugh [MacDonald of Mogstad]'s sons [in Skye], was enamoured of Jessie, daughter of MacDonald of Balranald in Uist, and she returned his affection. Balranald objected, and favoured the suit of a wealthy factor, a Mr Cooper. The family were at Rodel, Harris, probably on a visit to Mr Cooper. On the night of the 15th February, 1850, Donald, with a crew of eight strong lusty fellows, crossed the Minch to Tarbert, Harris, and made their way to Rodel, where by some sign their presence would become known to the young lady. As no response was made to their knocking, the doors were forced and the lady was carried off. Arriving at Tarbert their boat was soon beyond pursuit. Donald MacDonald, one of the principals in the abduction, was tried before the High Court of Justiciary at Inverness on the 14th August, 1850, and was discharged not guilty. The young couple emigrated to Australia. Mrs MacDonald (Miss Jessie of Balranald) died at Hartfield, near Melbourne, on

---

[110] For one such example, where the daughter of Donald of Islay eloped from one island to another, see Donald Budge, *Jura, An Island of Argyll: its History, People and Story*, pp. 197–9.

the 18th May, 1896. The elopement, on account of the position of both families, made a great sensation at the time, and for many years it was recounted by the peat fires in Uist and Skye. The writer remembers having seen two of the band, and the last survivor is believed to have been Donald MacKinnon, who lived in Linicro, opposite Mogstad. It is not surprising that the episode found expression in song. A nephew and niece of Miss Jessie live in Skye.[111]

Scotland has also been the destination for couples from England (and elsewhere) who elope to escape the stricter rules governing the 'age of consent' for marriage. Under English law, they are required to wait till the age of eighteen to obtain parental consent, or to twenty-one to be free of it altogether, but under Scots law couples can marry at the age of sixteen.

The town of Gretna Green, just over the Scottish border, has a long-standing, worldwide reputation for performing marriages at the old blacksmith's forge. In the nineteenth century, however, runaway couples sometimes eloped to Edinburgh, which also offered facilities.

Thomas Pennant
Traveller, 1774

At a little distance from the bridge, stop at the little village of Gratna [sic], the resort of all amorous couples, whose union the prudence of parents or guardians prohibits; here the young pair may be instantly united by a fisherman, a joiner, or a blacksmith, who marry from two guineas a job, to a dram of whisky: but the price is generally adjusted by the information of the postilions from Carlisle, who are in pay of one or other of the above worthies; but even the drivers, in case of necessity, have been known to undertake the sacerdotal office. If the pursuit of friends proves very hot, and there is not time for the ceremony, the frightened pair are advised to slip into bed; are shewn to the pursuers, who imagining they are irrecoverably united, retire, to leave them to 'consummate their unfinished loves'.

This place is distinguished from afar by a small plantation of firs . . . a sort of land-mark for fugitive lovers . . . The church of Scotland does what it can to prevent these clandestine matches, but in vain, for those infamous couples despise the fulmination of the kirk, and ex-communication is the only penalty it can inflict.

---

[111] William MacKenzie, *Skye: Iochdar-Trotternish . . . Traditions, Reflections and Memories*, p. 101. The songs associated with the incident are quoted and discussed, pp. 102–4.

Robert Chambers
Edinburgh, 1869

The oldest house known to have been used in the character of an inn [in Edinburgh] is one situated in what is called Davidson's or the White Horse Close, at the bottom of the Canongate . . . This house, supposed to have been styled *The White Horse Inn* . . . would be conveniently situated for persons travelling to, or arriving from, London as it is close to the ancient exit of the town in that direction . . . A large room in the *White Horse* was the frequent scene of the marriages of runaway English couples, at a time when these irregularities were permitted in Edinburgh.[112]

The Herald
Glasgow, 2004

Feb. 15, 'Record-breaking day for Gretna', report by Jenifer Johnston

Registrars and ministers at Gretna Green worked flat out for twelve hours yesterday as a record-breaking ninety-seven couples chose St Valentine's Day to get married at the famous town.

There was a party atmosphere, with pipers, photographers, stretch limos and horse-drawn carriages.

Forty-four of the weddings were performed by ministers, mainly in traditional fashion over the anvil in the old blacksmith's shop. Twenty-six were held in the registry office and another twenty-seven at 'approved venues' for civil ceremonies.

'We have never been so busy,' said registrar Sheila Wallace, 'a record ninety-seven weddings – fourteen more than last year. We have seven registrars and marriage celebrants on duty. Although it's non-stop work, there is a lovely atmosphere. Romance is alive in Gretna.'

A spokeswoman from Dumfries and Galloway Council said: 'Couples come here from all over the world.'

The custom of arranged marriage is still an issue in Scotland among Scots-Asians who retain the custom in the present day. Discussions within Scotland's Asian communities reveal that, in common with the ancient practice in their adopted country, there are accounts of both happy and unhappy outcomes. According to the Incompatible Marriage Project run by the Edinburgh-based Council of British Pakistanis in Scotland, 'almost half of Scots Asians end up in unhappy

---

[112] Robert Chambers, *Traditions of Edinburgh*, pp. 187 and 191.

marriages because of arranged weddings with a spouse who is incompatible . . . Set up three years ago [2001], the project has seen more than 200 Scots-Asians seeking help . . . Around 90per cent had been married to a spouse from the parents' country of origin and many of them found they did not speak the same language or share the same values.' Nevertheless, a young woman from Edinburgh whose Bangladeshi parents arranged her marriage to her Scots-Asian husband commented, 'I was happy for my parents to arrange it because I know they wanted me to be happy and I would not be forced into anything.' After they met, the couple (both born and brought up in Scotland), were given a year to get to know each other before their marriage. Now happily married, she explained that hers was an *arranged* marriage, and not a *forced* one. Her parents would have accepted her decision if she had refused the man they had chosen for her, there being a world of difference between arranging and forcing a daughter to marry.[113]

Weddings and Honeymoons During Wartime and the Depression

James and Ina MacQueen
Gargunnock, 1982

JM Some weddings might have only half a dozen guests, but where it was going to be a wedding with a reception and a dance . . . they had to know just how many exactly were going to be there.

At the time when I went dancing it was all old-time dancing, and except for the quickstep and foxtrot and tango, it was all old-time . . .

IM Eightsome reels, quadrilles, lancers . . .

JM . . . They always started with the Grand March and the Circassian Circle. . .

IM . . . They tied on tin cans, old boots, to the car . . . anything to make a noise. Balloons, anything. . .

JM A 'Just Married' placard. While they were getting them into the car . . . rice and confetti would be thrown at them. Rice was cheaper and easier to get than confetti.[114]

IM You had to go to Stirling to buy confetti.

JM Horseshoes were given to the bride for good luck.

IM Not so many horseshoes until after the war . . . when we were children, not so much of that. The toffs might carry the bride over the threshold, but in our village it was more ploughmen . . . they didn't do anything like that.[115]

[113] Reported in *The Herald*, Glasgow, 22 March 2004.
[114] The throwing of rice is also a much more ancient custom. See Napier, *Notes*.
[115] Mr and Mrs James MacQueen were recorded in Gargunnock in 1982 by Catherine Nichols. SA1982/37.

Nan Courtney
Glasgow, 1991

NC There's big, big changes in weddings. It's a very expensive thing now, a wedding.

MB *Is it any more enjoyable?*

NC Oh, I think the Scotch folk always enjoy thirsel, as a rule, at a wedding. Usually at an English wedding it's very sort of tame compared to what we – we let wir hair doun, you know! [Laughs] . . . Just the usual sorta readin the telegrams, an the bride an bridegroom, when they're gaun away there's usually the 'stooshie' as we call it – you know, the tying the cans, doin a lot o funny things. Then if they know or if they could get access to the bridal home they made up beds wi peas, an different things, thistles, you know whit ah mean, or mebbe make the bed that it would collapse! [Laughs] Just sorta tricks, ah don't know if they get up tae them noo or no – pranks!

MB . . . *What arrangements did people use to make for the wedding reception?*

NC Well, a lot depended on what they could afford. There usually wis a hall hired . . . Ah can remember bein at a weddin, I wis just a wee girl, an the minister came tae the house, an the weddin reception was held in the house, an that was that. I would just be aboot four year old, that wid be practically in the First World War, because I was born in 1913 and the First World War started in 1914, and I remember my mother's cousin bein married. She lived jist up the street from us, an ah wis thrilled! Ah wis always waitin till they kissed the bride! I thought this wis the highlight o everybody's life when they kissed the bride! [laughs] And they lifted the veil tae kiss the bride – but eh this cousin wis married in the house, that wis the first weddin that I remember being at, you know. An then gradually, you know they hired a hall. There was the Co-operative usually did the weddin reception. It wis quite famous fur doin purveys, for the wedding receptions, an City Bakeries for the cake an a' these different things.

MB *Was the reception a sit down meal or was it a buffet?*

NC Always a sit down meal.

MB *Did they have any standard expectation of the food?*

NC Well, pre Second World War, it wis usually steak pies. They didnae huv much varieties – steak pie, or mebbe some kinda cold meat. Oh, salads werenae just sae fashionable then; no, they werenae intae the health food. And the bride cut the cake, and then there wis a band hired, and they danced – and they had wee fights! Oh yes, they had wee fights! Wan side mebbe wisnae speakin tae the other side! [laughs] And then sometimes it wis a very jovial occasion – very jovial! Oh I've been tae some great weddings . . .

MB *What about the fashions? White weddings are popular today, but was this always so?*

NC Not always . . . well if it was what we usually term a 'big weddin' it was usually a white bride, an the veil, an bridesmaids, trainbearers, flower girls, eh, just one or two, and no jist so elaborate as what they have today, because they go to a very,

very great display now when they're having big weddings. I wouldnae like to be footin the bill for some o them!

MB *Were there any other colours popular?*

NC Very often powder blue – Ah wis married in powder blue, jist a robe wi silk cord around it; my bridesmaid was in lilac. I had no flower girls, and we had our reception in the Corn Exchange and then we all went to the theatre afterwards, and Tom Mix[116] was on the stage that night with his horse – that was on the 28th of October, 1938, Tom Mix was in Glasgow!

MB *The whole wedding party went to the theatre?*

NC Yes.

MB *Who got the tickets?*

NC Well, we had to – my auntie [Nan's guardian] had to pay for all the tickets for everybody.

MB *Was that a common idea, that everybody went to the theatre?*

NC Yes, quite. I mean mines wisnae a great big wedding party; it was mebbe a weddin party aboot thirty, over thirty people you know. But it was so that there'd be entertainment for people that couldnae take part in dancin or anything like that; there was a lot o elderly people, you know.

MB *Which theatre was that?*

NC . . . The Empire Theatre.

MB *After the theatre was over, what happened then?*

NC After the theatre was over – well one couldnae afford a honeymoon because we had bought all the furniture for the house, we bought everything, so we just came home . . . to wir own house, and my husband brought his best man with him [laughs] jist fur company! [laughs]. So, we came home in a taxi . . . to this house: . . . fifty-two years in here.[117]

Rose MacDonald
Glasgow, 2004

RM I was married in Glasgow in 1934.

MB *And after your marriage did you have a weekend away or a honeymoon?*

RM No, straight back to our own wee house which we loved, because we never actually lived in it. This was us going home, for the very first time, you know, and what could be nicer than that? On Paisley Road . . . we'd rented it and had it all ready for stepping into. So that was as good as anything, we really enjoyed that.[118]

---

[116] Tom Mix was the star of several Western films popular in the cinema of the 1930s. He rode a white horse.
[117] Nan Courtney, Glasgow, was recorded by MB on 7 July 1991.
[118] Recorded by MB in Glasgow, 16 February 2004.

Ann Pollock
Glasgow, 2004

AP We were married in Glasgow, 1940. And we went away for a week. My husband had an uncle that lived in Kinlochleven. People didn't go away so long then, or so far. The scenery was nice too . . . It was a three-storey house, and when you opened the back door you saw the salmon going up the river. It was really nice.

MB *Folk seem to go abroad nowadays.*

AP The sun's all right, but when the sun goes in abroad, everything looks dull . . . and cheap.[119]

Pat MacNab
Comrie, 2004

PM I was 27 year old, shepherding in Glenartney, when we were married in 1940. The banns had been called for three weeks and everything else ready, for the wedding to be held in the village o Comrie. And this day, I came home from the hill and the post had been, and there was a letter for me to report for service twelve o'clock the next day. And all our banns had been called and everything else, and I didn't know what to do. And it was at mid-day, and of course she was working at Gask, down near Perth. So I got on a pushbike, I came down to Comrie (16 miles), collected the papers, and cycled out to Gask and took her by surprise, because she had no idea when I got there. So, meanwhile, I'd gone to the church and it was an Irish minister and his two sisters, and he was busy digging in the garden. And he came out and said he would do the service, and 'Come in.' And we did, into the church at Gask, and he conducted it –

MB *You mean on that self-same day?*

PM Aye, the self-same day!

MB *You mean Isobel had to drop things and down to the church?*

PM Aye, down to the church. And she had all her wedding affairs, clothes, wedding gear up at home, my home in Glenartney. Anyway, the minister came out of the garden and he couldn't be nicer, and his sisters, they were witnesses, the two sisters. And we got married and we went back to Gask and they had a huge, what we call a 'dust-cart' affair, and they'd it all laid wi' carpets and threw the pair of us in there, and gave us a whirl right round about Gask House. And then a big tea.

MB *How long did you have to prepare the tea?*

PM Oh, they had the tea prepared for us coming back from the church –

MB *In that short shape of time.*

---

[119] Recorded by MB in Glasgow, 16 February 2004.

PM Aye. And afterwards we started off and cycled back to Glenartney the pair of us. Then it came bucketing rain, and she had on a linen frock and here, it started tearing wi' the rain, wi' the bike.

MB *Surely not the two of you on one bike?*

PM No, no, two bikes. And we came back to Thomsons up there at the Glenartney road-end and I threw a stone up to the window. Now this is away about half past one in the morning, and Peter came to the window, and he says to Annie, 'Oh, that's Pat and Isobel.' And down they came, and they were there, and of course it was oot wi the bottle.

MB *So you told them you'd just got married?*

PM Aye, just got married – and they gave Isobel something else to wear, and then we'd to cycle to the top of the glen after that, right up to Staghorn.

MB *How many miles was all that?*

PM Oh, about fifty and more. Oh, mercy, aye. Cycled up there, and my mother and dad were in bed. So we went to the spare room, and I was away in the morning, and I wasn't back for six months after that. That's a fact.

MB *That was some wedding night! I'd better not ask any more!*

PM Aye, some wedding! And I was away on the train the next morning, away to Blackpool, to do square-bashing. And that was me . . . Aye, we were married for 47 years . . . Isobel died in 1988.[120]

May Anderson
Glasgow, 2004

MA I was married at the church on Polmadie Road, St James's, in 1947. My husband was in the army. An' I made my own suit, because I'm a machinist. It was blue, navy-blue with inverted pleats an' my sister was in green. We went to the church an' then we got a taxi into the town and went to the theatre . . . the Pavillion to see Jack Milroy. There was just the four of us.

MB *And then?*

MA After that we got a bus, down to my mother's place – my maw had a hut, we called it a hut, in Meadowpark in Troon. It was a [converted] bus.

MB *Yes. Like what they'd call a caravan now?*

MA Yes. Eventually they built a hut – this was a bus, an' we went there, you know, on my wedding night . . . Through Troon and Irvine.[121]

---

[120] Pat was recorded in Comrie, Perthshire by MB, 5 April 2004.
[121] Recorded by MB in Glasgow, 16 February 2004.

Nan Millar
Glasgow, 2004

NM I was born and brought up in this area (Ibrox) . . . And I was married in 1951.

MB *And your husband was serving in the forcres?*

NM Uh, huh. He was in the RASC – the Royal Army Service Corps, at the time of the Korean War . . .

MB *Did you plan ahead a long way for your wedding?*

NM We were goin' tae get married in the December, an' we were savin up for a weddin', you know. An' he came home in the August . . . on embarkation leave, and he said he was goin abroad, to Korea. So I said, 'Do you want to wait till you come back or – ?' He says, 'No, I want to get married.' So that's what happened. Scared he'd lose me! [laughs]

We got married on the 31 of August. We had to declare banns in the church three weeks in advance, then we were married a week and he went away. In fact he didnae want to go, and I'd visions of him getting shot an everything. Eventually he went away and that was that. And the weddin? He didn't want to get married in the army uniform, he wanted a new suit, so wi the money we'd saved up we got a new suit for him, and by the time we bought an outfit for me the money was gone, you know. I wore a blue suit. Blue's my favourite colour. Pale blue. It was lovely. I've got photos, you know – it wasnae a heavy suit. It was nice material. And it had lovely wee pleats here, and these kind of [decoration on the lapels]. And my bridesmaid, she was in the same suit in pink. There's a saying about the colours, 'Married in blue, your love is true; married in red, you wish you were dead; Married in brown, you'll have your ups and downs . . .' (And black is taboo).

MB *And where was the wedding?*

NM It was the St James's Church in Pollok, cos we lived in Pollok then. That's where we were married, and it wisnae even built right. It was in the vestry. An I fell in the church, skint a' ma knees [laughs] cos I was that excited, you know. [laughs] And I said 'I do' before the minister finished. [laughter] And he used to say, he used to go, 'Ah, you couldnae wait to get me!' You know. (He'd a great sense of humour.) Oh, gosh, see when you think back! [laughter]

So, anyway, after the weddin' we didnae want to stay in my Mum's house that night, cos my Mum, she done the purveying an' everything – it was just aunties uncles an cousins an a' that there, but in the house. An' the photographer came an' took photos an' a' the rest o it. An' my brother had a wee single en' in Scotland Street. So my brother said, 'Well, you can have oor wee single en', and we'll go up to my Mum's wi the weans,' you know.

When we went down to my brother's, we got a taxi. An' it was a laugh, you know. My brothers were a' runnin at the side o the taxi and they were kiddin' on they were gonnae jump in – a lot o daft carry on, you know. An' we went doon to this wee single en', you know, an we went in. An' we wanted a wee cuppie tea, you know, an he went in, an' ma sister-in-law, she didnae leave any matches, so he'd to go oot, an' he'd to climb up tae get a light off the gas light in the close!

I felt very shy . . . for in those days most girls were so innocent before marriage – no just shy, but folk respected their parents. An' it was much better for everybody concerned . . . I think it's a' gone crazy noo . . . They don't even know who the fathers o the babies are noo, an' some couldnae care less! Anything goes and nobody cares. Well, you didnae do that kin' o thing, in thae days. Folk respected themselves. It used to be a joke, sayin' 'Were you at yer mammie's weddin'?' But no noo! It's reality. That wasnae how it was our day . . .

Anyway, my husband went away the following week . . . He was away about a year an three months – aye. It was like eternity, you know. And I thought I'd have a wee babbie for him comin back, you know. I was sure! [laughter] An I was that surprised when I wisnae expectin. I wis that positive – you know. I was positive! [laughs]. See, when you look back![122]

Divorce

Revd George Low
Orkney, *c.* 1774

It was likewise usual, when husband and wife could not agree, that they both came to the Kirk of Stainhouse [Stennis], and after entering into the kirk the one went out at the south and the other at the north door, by which they were holden legally divorced, and free to make another choice.[123]

The Bible

Deuteronomy, 24: 1–5

When a man hath taken a wife, and married her, and it come to pass that she find no favour in his eyes, because he hath found some uncleanness in her: then let him write her a bill of divorcement, and give it in her hand, and send her out of his house.

And when she is departed out of his house, she may go and be another man's wife.

---

[122] Recorded by MB in Glasgow, 16 February 2004. Nan, May, Ann and Rose are members of the Kinning Park Over-Sixties club, which meets weekly in Ibrox Library. They were recorded MB as part of an oral history project, exhibited in the library, entitled 'See When you Look Back!'
[123] *A Tour Through the Islands of Orkney and Shetland in 1774*, Intro., p. xxvi.

And if the latter husband hate her, and write her a bill of divorcement, and giveth it in her hand, and sendeth her out of house; or if the latter husband die, which took her to be his wife;

Her former husband, which sent her away, may not take her again to be his wife, after that she is defiled; for that is abomination before the Lord: and thou shalt not cause the land to sin, which the Lord thy God giveth thee for an inheritance.

When a man hath taken a new wife, he shall not go out to war, neither shall he be charged with any business: but he shall be free at home one year, and shall cheer up his wife which he hath taken.

Matthew, 5: 31–32

It hath been said, Whosoever shall put away his wife, let him write her a bill of divorcement:

But I say unto you, that whosoever shall put away his wife, saving for the cause of fornication, causeth her to commit adultery: and whosoever shall marry her that is divorced committeth adultery.

Matthew 19: 3–11

The Pharisees came unto him, tempting him, and saying unto him, Is it lawful for a man to put away his wife for every cause?

And he answered and said unto them, Have ye not read, that he which made them at the beginning made them male and female,

And he said, For this cause shall a man leave father and mother, and shall cleave to his wife: and they twain shall be one flesh?

Wherefore they are no more twain, but one flesh. What therefore God has joined together, let not man put asunder.

They say unto him, Why did Moses then command to give a writing of divorcement, and to put her away?

He saith unto them, Moses because of the hardness of your hearts suffered you to put away your wives: but from the beginning it was not so

And I say unto you, Whosoever shall put away his wife, except it be for fornication, and shall marry another, committeth adultery: and whoso marrieth her which is put away doth commit adultery.

His disciples say unto him, If the case of the man be so with his wife, it is not good to marry.

PART III

Death and Burial

Death and Burial

> Nowhere, even in modern times, do religious ritual and custom retain a stronger hold on the majority of mankind that at the crisis of death and burial.[1]

It is no accident or coincidence that death customs have long since been established in every community; they are essential to the stability of life. Their existence allows the community to fall back on the security of established order at a time when the bereaved cannot possibly have the inner resources to organise anew the entire procedure from the moment of death to the last farewell of burial.

The customs which surround death and burial are generally determined by the community in which the subject of the occasion is located. Regardless of whether it is urban or rural, large or small, built over centuries (such as an ancient town or village) or constructed to plan on a particular site within a matter of months (such as a modern hospital), each community has its own traditions, which will usually be followed by its members. Individuals may find themselves to be members of more than one group, such as the fisherman's daughter who becomes a nurse in a city hospital, or the city advocate's son who decides to 'get away from it all' and become a crofter in the Highlands – when faced with death, those who become responsible for arranging the burial or participating in the arrangements will more than likely find themselves observing the customs which have been established by that community. The nurse in hospital will follow exactly the routine she has been taught by her tutors, while at home she will find herself fitting into family tradition; the city advocate may, in the course of duty, be called upon to preside over legal matters demanded by his profession, yet he may also find himself sharing a glass of whisky with complete strangers if he happens to be visiting his son when a death occurs in that neighbourhood.

Death, we're told, is the only thing in this life we can all be sure of: 'Oor

---

[1] Reidar Th. Christiansen, 'The Dead and the Living', *Studio Norvegica*, no. 2, 1946, p. 4.

first breath is the beginnin o daith.' is re-echoed in the Gaelic proverb 'Am fear as fhaide bha beò riamh, fhuair e 'm bàs,' [the oldest man that ever lived, died at last]. The absolute certainty is affirmed in 'daith is deaf, an will hear nae denial,' and again in 'amaisidh an dall air an reilig' [a blind man will find his way to the burial ground]. When a death occurs suddenly or unexpectedly we may hear folk remark that 'daith comes in an speirs nae questions,' or 'it's no particular who it taks awa.'[2] Whatever the circumstances, wherever the bereavement, the most frequently heard saying must surely be the universal cautionary advice: 'Ne'er speak ill o the dead.'

Death Omens

Revd Walter Gregor
North-east, 1874

'Oh! C'est triste, et je häis la mort.'

Three knocks were heard at regular intervals of one or two minutes' duration. They might be heard in any part of the dwelling-house, on the entrance door, on a table, on the top of a *bunbed*. Their sound was quite different from any other. It was dull and heavy, and had something eerie about it. A similar omen was the *deid-drap*. Its sound resembled that of a continued drop of water falling slowly and regularly from a height, but it was leaden and hollow. Such sounds were heard at any time during night or day. Night, however, was the usual time when they were heard. They were heard first by one, and could not be heard by a second without taking hold of the one that first heard them. This was the case with all the sights and sounds that prognosticated death, and lasted for any length of time.

Before the death of one of the household, there was at times heard during the night the noise as if something heavy were laid down outside the door of the dwelling-house. It was the sound of the coffin as it was laid down outside the door, before it was carried into the house.

A murmur as of many human voices was sometimes heard around the door of the dwelling-house. It was the harbinger of the murmur of the voices of those who were to assemble for the funeral.

---

[2] While almost all of the proverbs and proverbial expressions in this book are from written collections (or simply from personal memory), this one was noted from traveller Willie MacPhee in March 1992. He had just told me of the death of a young member of his family, and in response to my solemn condolences he replied with characteristic resignation, 'Aye, it's no particular who it taks awa.'

A picture or a looking-glass falling from the wall portended a death. If one's portrait fell, death was not far off.

A death was often made known by the light called a *deid-can'le*. It was seen moving about the house in which the death was to take place, and along the road by which the corpse was to be carried to the grave. Its motion was slow and even. The light was pale-bluish, wholly unlike any made by human art.

A crop more than usually good foreshadowed the death of the goodman, and went by the name of a *fey-crap*.

A white dove was seen sometimes approaching and hovering over one that was soon to leave earth. Such a thing has been seen in the early morning when a few were travelling together.

The crowing of a cock before twelve o'clock at night was heard with fear and trembling. It was usually regarded as the death-warning of a member or relative of the family. The roost was immediately inspected to ascertain in what direction the bird was looking, and whether his comb, wattles, and feet were cold. If they felt cold to the touch, the death of one of the household, or of one nearly related, was not far distant. The fowl's look was directed towards the abode of the one who was so soon to depart.[3]

The crowing of a hen was regarded with special dread, and as the sure indication of death in the dwelling. Speedy death was the fate of the bird that thus belied her sex.

A dog howling at night portended death, and the grim king was to seize his victim in the direction towards which the animal was looking, and at no great distance.[4] The same superstition prevails among the Arabs, who fancy that the dog is then seeing Azrael, the angel of death. It was believed that a dog would not approach a sick person, if the sickness was unto death; and most minutely did the inmates of the house watch the conduct of the dog with any one of their number that might fall ill.

The apparition of the person that was doomed to die within a short time was seen wrapped in a winding-sheet, and the higher the winding-sheet reached up towards the head, the nearer was death. This apparition was seen during day, and it might show itself to any one, but only to one, who generally fell into a faint a short time afterwards. If the person who saw the apparition was alone at the time, the fainting fit did not come on till after meeting with others.

---

[3] For a fuller discussion on the subject see also Anne Ross, 'Birds of Life and Birds of Death', *Scottish Studies*, vol. 3, 1963, pp. 215–3.

[4] There are also instances of more than one dog howling when death is nigh; William MacKenzie notes that 'nearly all the dogs in the vicinity kept howling all night' when a heavily laden boat carrying nineteen passengers form Portree to Culnancnoc overturned in 1812, and 'nearly every family in the township lost one or two members.' See *Skye: Iochdar-Trotternish*, p. 39.

Three drops of cold blood falling from the nose was the sure indication of the death of one very nearly related to the one from whose nose the blood fell.

It was regarded as an omen of death, either of himself or herself, or of one nearly related, if one showed more than ordinary joy.

If the sick person did not sneeze, the disease would end in death. Sneezing was accounted the turning-point towards recovery.[5]

Margaret Wilson
Lilliesleaf, 1990

My mother was very superstitious; there seemed to be an awful lot of things that were foreboding something. I mean, I've heard my Mum say a bird hitting the window was bad news – I just see these things as logical, that the bird thought it was an open space. My mother hated crows hanging around; she always said it was the sign of a death in the house or family. A picture falling [off the wall] was terrible; really they were annoyed [troubled] about it, they felt it was foretelling a death. A lot of people in the community, friends and relatives, held the same beliefs; they'd talk about and agree that this picture falling was a terrible thing.[6]

Pat Christie
Shetland, 2002

I heard this from Lorna Christie from Aith, Cunningsburgh:

If a craa is seen fleein ower da hoose makin a noise dan som een is gyan tae be very ill or mibe dee.

Warst of aa birds is da coarncrake – hit's a fey bird. If hit comes in closs or taks on aroond da hoose dan som een will dee in da nixt twall munt. My fedder said dat da year wir bridder Johnie deed [aged 3], dan a corncrake cam aroond da hoose, hit geed 'Craak, craak!' an Johnie wis dead afore lang.[7]

---

[5] W. Gregor, *Echo*, pp. 132–5 and *Notes* pp. 203–4.
[6] Margaret Wilson was recorded in Lilliesleaf by Susan Huntly. SA1990/18.
[7] E-mailed by Pat Christie, while a student in one of my classes on Cultural Studies (Orkney College).

John Firth
Orkney, 1920

Even the most common phenomena were looked upon with dark foreboding, for when

> They saw the new moon
> Wi' the auld moon in her arm,
> They feared they'd come to harm.

In every district there were certain elderly women who 'had a way with' sick folk, and these women invariably professed to be gifted with the prophetic eye. In cases of sickness they were always called on for advice, and their ministrations at a death-bed or chesting were indispensable. Whenever one fell ill or died suddenly, they were never surprised, for they had dreamed dreams and seen visions. On visits of condolence these death warnings were gone over in detail, and never failed to impress the listeners, especially young people whose minds, owing to the surrounding conditions, were in their most susceptible mood.[8] The most common death warning was 'the dead jack'. This sound was, by some people, described as the tick of a watch, and by others as the intermittent fall of drops of water. Anyone who has listened intently to the working of the wood-worm knows that it is capable of producing a great variety of noises in addition to those two distinct sounds. This omen is widely believed in even at the present day, and, owing to his secret methods of working and the infrequency with which he shows himself, it is difficult to convince the superstitious mind that those sounds are produced by natural means.

The dreams that foretold the passing of a soul were legion. To dream of seeing a ship on dry land betokened the seeing of a coffin soon after. The losing of a tooth meant the losing of a relative. In connection with this a curious incident was related of a man in whom the writer never, on any other occasion, found the slightest leaning towards superstition. The man in question, when a boy of twelve, dreamt that a number of his teeth had fallen out and were lying at his feet on a grassy knowe. He regretted his misfortune keenly, but for his own satisfaction counted them. Unaware of the signifi-cance of his dream, he told his mother on the following day that he had dreamt he had lost a dozen of his teeth. With great solemnity she said, 'Ah,

---

[8] Not only did people interpret signs which appeared 'naturally' but there was also a strong tradition of actively trying to find out who was going to die. See Calum MacLean, 'Death Divination in Scottish Folk Tradition', *TGSI*, vol. XLII, 1965, pp. 56–8.

boy, boy! a tooth's a friend, bit twal's ower many.' Strangely enough, the figures exactly corresponded with the number of persons, including four of his relatives, who, she subsequently learned, had perished in a boating accident in the String on the day following the night of his dream. A feeling of itch in the nose always called forth the remark, 'We'll sune be hearin' dead news,' and the same belief was held regarding a ringing in the ears or 'dead bells', as the term ran. Another certain sign of death was the appearance of a white cabbage-stock in the kail-yard. This freak was the more noticeable in that the old Orkney cabbage was of a dark colour, resembling the pickling cabbage of modern days, and rarely forming into hearts until late in the season, usually about Hallowmas. The crow of a cock after dark, or the howl of a dog during the still hours of the night, struck fear into the hearts of the listeners, for these were the portents of a death in the near vicinity, or if the two ends of a rainbow reached earth in the same district, someone within the distance o'erspanned would shortly pass away.[9]

Iain Nicolson
Uig, Skye, 1988

IN I've seen people going and pulling me off the road, seeing a funeral passing. I couldn't see it. They were seeing it . . . Well, I think it was myself and A — B — , he pulled me aside. 'What's that?'

'Do you see,' he says, 'people passing with a coffin?'

'Ach away, no. I didn't see nothing of it.' But they were saying people that was born at midnight [have second sight] . . . if that's right, I don't know, I know nothing about it. But I heard if it was midnight [you were born], that you were apt to see these things. But I know of one that was in Skudiborg, A — Bh —, a brother of J — G — that was in Baile nan Cnoc there. They were in the hotel . . . [in Uig, Skye. A man] gave him a glass of whisky and he saw the grave clothes on him. And he was shivering; takes the glass out of his hand. But the man lived maybe a month or two after that – but he saw it! Aye, it's a thing that I wouldn't like to have, eh! [*laughs*]

MB *What Gaelic word did they have for that?*

IN An e samhla? [Is it a spectre?] Well, what we saw and would call a 'samhla' now, was just an imaginary [vision] . . . I would say that a 'taibhse' is what I see in the air. Well, there used to be talk [of the supernatural] but many a time I would be feared of going out of the house, when I knew all the tales that was there. Oh my God, it's a good thing they [the stories] went. Because I wouldn't get anybody to go . . .

---

[9] John Firth, *Orkney*, pp. 81–2.

WN It scares me anyway.

IN You wouldn't get anybody to go for a pail of water or anything [peats] to burn at that time, with the tales I heard about the samhla and the ghosts that was there and things . . . And that was prevalent among everybody in the houses. 'And he saw the samhla of this one, and he saw the ghost of that one!'

MB . . . *or three knocks? Did you ever hear stories about people hearing a knock?*

IN Aye, at the door; yes, and seen the chair jumping. I've seen the chair jumping right enough. But these chairs were going under a coffin.

MB *And did a funeral happen afterwards?*

IN Oh . . . I've seen it happening in our own home, before my father died, um, went . . . I've seen them jump, right out – the chairs were there. But I heard one time, I came down out of bed, oh, everything had fell in the kitchen. I went down, nothing was there, but I was imagining then . . . that you were preparing and washing the body and all that, [with the things] that would be about the fire. But I was in Glenhinnisdail there when the old man died that was there then. Well, I used to have a trap, in the closet there where a rat happened to be there, and I didn't get the rat at all. Well, there was two planks across there in one place, shelves. Oh I heard a BRAG![10] [slaps hands] like that. 'Oh shiorruidh, the rat is in his trap, I know!' I went down. The trap was there all right; nothing there at all. Within a fortnight the old man died. And I know, I can imagine it now, Calum, M — M —'s father there, it was him that put the body right then. I wonder how he will get any planks to put under the body you know to keep it stiff, you know to keep it straight. I went down to the closet there and got the two planks. That's all I can account for. So it must be me taking out the planks there and the noise was the forerunner of it. I could never place it otherwise and that's because there was nothing moved, but you'd hear the [slaps hands] as [if they] were just getting the hammer, two or three of them. Oh, I thought it was the rat, [but] it wasn't. I know that much. But that's all I have seen of anything, myself. But I've seen the chairs like that, as I was glancing out of the corner of my eyes. But they didn't move [from] where they are. But that's always the case you know when you are putting the dead body on it, or something like that might be a forerunner of it.[11]

---

[10] Gaelic onomatopoeic word pronounced suddenly like brack! and said simultaneously with a loud clap of the hands.

[11] Iain Nicolson was recorded in his home in Cuidreach, near Uig, Isle of Skye, by MB and T.A. McKean, December 1988. His son Willie was also in the company, cited WN in the transcription. SA1988/65.

Murdo MacLean
Portree, Isle of Skye, 1994

MM A joiner in Portree kept the 'carrying board' as they called it – it had big handles in the middle and the shorter ones at the end so that people wouldn't trip when they were walking, you see . . . but they would carry it for miles . . .

Now my granny lived three mile out of Portree, and my uncles and my aunties were there. And when she died we were over at her house. Now what they did in these days – it wasn't like today, you pick your coffin today, you get either 300, 400, 500 – but in these days the joiner had to come up and measure the body and he went [back to his workshop] and made the coffin. And then when it was ready – it took about a day – they would walk it up . . . But the joiner worked in Portree, you see, and when he came up and he measured the body, the length and width, he made it in the joiner-shop and when he was finished he carried it up and, eh, it was left for the next day to be carried to the graveyard.

So, with my granny – I was only young, and in those days they had cattle, and the byre was up a bit from the house, and [so was] the stack yard. But when my uncles came, they put the carrying-board at the end of the gable. So when I came out I says to my uncles 'Well, Auntie will be going to milk the cows about nine, and it's not nice to see that, so you'll need to hide it somewhere else – now this is true what I'm telling. So they says 'Where'll we put it?' So there was a stack-yard just behind the byre, and eh, we thought we'd hide it there, you see. And nine o'clock, Auntie Annie went to milk the cow, but she wasn't long away when she came back, and we says to her, 'You weren't long.'

She says, 'I didn't reach the byre at all.'

And I asked her why.

'Well, I seen it three nights ago in the barn, this thing sticking out, but I passed it by. But tonight I got a fright [for I could see clearly what it was].'

Now she didn't know we put it there, and it didn't matter what they did, they couldn't hide it. The stacks weren't very big. So she seen it three nights there before it came at all. Now I'm telling you a true story of what I know was there, and it sticks in my mind because in the first place it was me suggesting to put it [away] from the gable of the house, into the stack yard . . . but she saw it three nights before that. And that's true . . . That was in my own family . . .

MB *How can anyone explain this kind of experience?*

MM I believe myself in my own experience in life . . . there are signs given before death, and there are signs given after death. And I believe there are signs given for the living too.[12]

---

[12] Murdo MacLean, aged 82, was recorded by MB at his home in North Kessock, Black Isle, in 1994.

Anne MacDonald

1992

My grandmother would never have snowdrops in the house because she said they 'brought death in with them'. She said she always had a 'ding' in her ear when someone she knew died, and she had many other experiences such as three knocks which were premonitions of death. One night she was in bed in her cottage in Tiree and she heard three knocks at the door but when she got up to answer it there was nobody there. This happened three times that night and in the end she thought that it must have been the wind. In the morning, however, she heard the three knocks again so she went to the door where she found her neighbour whose husband had just died, coming for help. On another occasion she heard banging coming from the kitchen so she went to investigate the noise. It appeared to come from two kitchen chairs, as she heard a bang on one chair and then a bang on the other. The next day a neighbour came to borrow two chairs to lay a coffin on.[13]

Alexander Polson

Caithness, 1907

It seems strange that the howling of a dog at night is still regarded as one of the certain signs of death's coming, just as it has been in most countries from the earliest times. Besides this, a cock that persistently crows through the night shows that death is near to some one who lives in the direction to which the fowl turns.

Birds tapping against a window pane, and the screaming of an owl in the neighbourhood of a house, are also ominous. Willie Badenoch, gravedigger, Bower, was sitting in his house one night with a friend when there came three taps to the window. Quietly turning to his companion, Willie uncannily said: 'At's 'e usual warning I get! I'll be asked till dig a grave 'e morn.'

When horses on a road which they know quite well appear to be in terror from some cause which the driver is unable to understand it is thought that the fear comes from a phantom funeral seen by the animal, whose senses are more acute than those of any human being.

Village carpenters have often averred that several days before a coffin is required there is often a rattling noise to be heard among the deals set apart for the making of coffins. Others affirm that they can always foretell the death

---

[13] This is excerpted from an essay by Anne MacDonald, Scottish ethnology student, 1992.

of a friend by a loud cracking heard among the house joists.[14]

Christina [Ciorstaigh] Docherty
Kingussie, 1992

MB *Did anyone ever talk of foretelling a death?*

CD Oh, I've done it myself . . . Before my husband died, I told my cousin six weeks before he died that something dreadful was going to happen in the house . . . I could feel it; I could feel it in the house, but I didn't know it was him . . . he was thirty-seven. I could feel it. And before my father died, I wasn't well and I was going away and the doctor and the priest more or less demanded that I went away for a couple of days. And I said to the doctor, 'If I go I'll never see my father again.' I told him. And the priest actually came to meet me at the station when I came off the train. And my father had died two hours before I arrived home . . . And he had said to the doctor, 'What'll I say to her?' and the doctor said, 'She knows, she told me before she left.'

MB *Had he been ill?*

CD No, not any more than, I mean he was an old man, and he was on the go; he actually died outside. He was pottering about outside when he dropped dead . . . But you can feel death . . .

MB *Are there any sayings around here about animals or birds associated with death?*

CD Yes, if a cockerel crows at night, during the night – but if you believe that, then they would be dropping off like flies, cos mine crow every night! [*laughs*] But if a cockerel crows before daybreak it's supposed to foretell death, or bad news. And also if you dream of flowers out of season: that's another one my mother had. Or if a frog comes into the house. And to this day I believe if a frog comes into the house it foretells misfortune or a death; I hate frogs in the house . . . I was never allowed to take tadpoles in[to the house as a child] in case they hatched! [*laughs*] I know that's going a bit far, but they could come as far as the door, but they had to stay at the door. [*laughs*]

. . . My mother was full of superstition, you know, coming from the island, you know. Mind you, I've never seen a frog in Barra, so I don't know where she got the [one about the] frog from!

MB *Anything about flowers?*

CD Oh, red and white, never, ever, ever red and white flowers, yes, or death! Another thing, my mother wouldn't take in lilac. She wouldn't take in lilac and she wouldn't take in primroses into the house, and if you came anywhere near the house with broom or the may blossom you were hounded. You just weren't allowed anywhere near the house with anything like that.

MB *Was it just bad luck, or did it mean death?*

---

[14] Alexander Polson, 'Folklore', pp. 97–8.

CD Oh it was death, it was destruction. You weren't just allowed in the door with anything of those. Broom especially.

MB *Gosh! I've taken a bunch of lilacs to you myself.*

CD Och, I take lilacs in all the time. [*laughs*] But she wouldn't let you come into the house – or primroses. And I love primroses, one of my favourite flowers, and she wouldn't let you take primroses over the doorsteps. Mind you, there are a lot of primroses in Barra. Oh no, she was funny about flowers – red and white flowers in a vase together. Mind you a lot of people believe that – in hospitals they wouldn't put red and white flowers together in a vase; no. But I think it's a bit stupid, really, I mean, what harm are flowers going to do you?

Fiona Hunter
Glasgow, 2001

My Mum won't have any red and white flowers in the house. She says it's tempting fate and is bad luck. If anyone gave her some, she would throw them out straight after the person had gone . . . My grandmother was from South Uist.[15]

Wilma Forret
Kirkcaldy, 1992

WF The Polish servicemen arrived here when I was in my early teens, about 1940, and we thought they were very continental. For example they had this way of giving flowers to girlfriends, and they used to give bunches of red and white flowers because red and white were their national colours. But of course this is a 'no-no'; you wouldn't put them together in the same vase, because in Fife of course red and white flowers mean a death.[16]

It is commonly (and erroneously) thought that stories of second sight, apparitions, wraiths, fetches and other premonitory experiences are common only in the Highlands and Islands. These phenomena are not only known all over Scotland, in both rural and urban settings, but are also encountered all over the world. Some strange stories could be told of these mysterious appearances, of which the following is only one example of several well authenticated cases' retold by William Wilson.

---

[15] From Fiona's essay written for my folklore class at the Royal Scottish Academy of Music and Drama, 2001.
[16] Wilma Forret told me about this when I visited Kirkcaldy as a guest lecturer on 19 March 1992. Recorded by MB.

William Wilson
Sanquhar, 1904

The late Peter Hastie, who lived in the Lochan, Sanquhar, told me of a remarkable apparition which he saw when he was a youth. He said he was brought up in the village of Kirkconnel, and that he had a school companion, a lad named Thomas Blacklock, who, like himself, was put to farm service after leaving the schoolmaster's hands, Blacklock to the farm of Nether Cairn and Peter to Kelloside, a distance of about three miles separating the places. One day in the spring of the year Peter was engaged in carting manure from the farm steading to one of the fields near the public road, and about one o'clock, when he was going with his first load after dinner, he saw, just before he reached the gate, his friend, Thomas Blacklock, coming down the road to meet him, which made him wonder what could be bringing him there at that time of day. Being by this time at the gate leading into the field Peter caught hold of the bridle to lead him in, but the beast was startled at something; one of the wheels struck the gate posts, upsetting the cart, and Peter had a narrow escape of it falling on him. The people in the field, seeing his predicament, ran to his assistance, and quickly put things to rights. His friend, Blacklock, however, instead of lending his help, stood quietly looking on, a proceeding, or lack of action rather, that Peter could not reconcile with his views of friendship, but being busy at the time, he only gave the matter a passing thought. On all being put straight he looked round for his old friend, but he was nowhere to be seen, nor had any of the field workers seen Blacklock. That evening when returning from their day's darg, Peter and his fellow-servants were met by a man belonging to the Cairn, who told them that that day about one o'clock Thomas Blacklock had been accidentally killed. It appears that at Nether Cairn Blacklock had, like his friend, been carting manure. He had taken one load after his dinner, and was in the act of returning, sitting in the empty cart, when the horse took fright, ran away, and threw him out. His head struck a large stone, and he was killed on the spot. The time of Thomas Blacklock's tragic death corresponded exactly with the time Peter Hastie witnessed the appearance of his old companion, and when he himself had had an accident to his own cart.[17]

---

[17] William Wilson, *Folk Lore and Genealogies of Uppermost Nithsdale*, pp. 79–80. Among other accounts of wraiths, Wilson also tells of an incident where a couple who were sleeping in bed heard a 'loud crash, as if part of the house had fallen.' Like Iain Nicolson of Skye, they got up to investigate and, finding nothing out of place, they returned to bed. The next day at work, the man was victim of a mining accident, 'when he was suddenly buried under a heavy fall from the roof.' See pp. 77–9.

Revd James Napier
Renfrewshire, 1879

It is not surprising that the solemn period of death should have been surrounded with many superstitious ideas – with a great variety of omens and warnings, many of which, however, were only called to mind after the event. In the country, when any person was taken unwell, it was very soon known over the whole neighbourhood, and all sorts of remedies were recommended. Generally a doctor was not sent for until the patient was considered in a dangerous state, and then began the search for omens or warnings. If the patient recovered, these premonitions were forgotten, but if death ensued, then everything was remembered and rendered significant. Was a dog heard to howl and moan during the night, with his head in the direction of the house where the patient lay; was there heard in the silent watches of the night in the room occupied by the sick person, a tick, ticking as of a watch about the bed or furniture – these were sure signs of approaching death, and adult patients, hearing these omens, often made sure that their end was near. Many pious people also improved the circumstance, pointing out that these omens were evidence of God's great mercy, in as much as He vouchsafed to give a timely warning in order that the dying persons might prepare for death, and make their peace with the great Judge. To have hinted, under such circumstances, that the ticking sounds were caused by a small wood moth tapping for its mate, would have subjected the hinter to the name of infidel or unbeliever in Scripture, as superstitious people always took shelter in Scripture.

Persons hearing a tingling sound in their ears, called the *deid bells*, expected news of the death of a friend or neighbour. A knock heard at the door of the patient's room, and on opening no person being found, was a sure warning of approaching death. If the same thing occurred where there was no patient, it was a sign that some relation at a distance had died. I was sitting once in the house of a newly married couple, when a loud knock was heard upon the floor under a chair, as if some one had struck the floor with a flat piece of wood. The young wife removed the chair, and seeing nothing, remarked with some alarm, 'It is hasty news of a death.' Next day she received word of the death of two of her brothers, soldiers in India, the deaths having occurred nearly a year before. There was no doubt in the mind of the young wife that the knock was a supernatural warning. The natural explanation probably was that the sound came from the chair, which, being new, was liable to shrink at the joints for some time, and thus cause the sound heard. This cracking sound is quite common with new furniture.

Again, if someone were to catch a glimpse of a person whom they knew passing the door or window, and on looking outside were to find no such person there, this was a sign of the approaching death of the person seen. There were many instances quoted of the accuracy of this omen, instances generally of persons who, in good health at the time of their illusionary presence, died shortly after. Another form of this superstition was connected with those who were known to be seriously ill. Should the observer see what he felt convinced was the unwell person, say, walking along the street, and on looking round as the presence passed, see no person, this was a token of the death of the person whose spectre was seen. I knew of a person who, on going home from his work one evening, came suddenly upon an old man whom he knew to be bed-ridden, dressed as was formerly his wont, with knee breeches, blue coat, and red nightcap. Although he knew that the old man had for some time been confined to bed, so distinct was the illusion that he bid him 'good night' in passing, but receiving no reply, looked behind and saw no one. Seized with fright, he ran home and told what he had seen. On the following morning it was known through the village that the old man was dead. And his death had taken place at the time when the young man had seen him on the previous evening. This was considered a remarkably clear instance of a person's wraith or spirit being seen at the time of death. However, the seeing of a person's wraith was not always an omen of death. There were certain rules observed in relation to wraiths, by which their meaning could be ascertained, but these rules differed in different localities. In my native village a wraith seen during morning, or before twelve noon, betokened that the person whose wraith was seen would be fortunate in life, or if unwell at the time, would recover; but when the wraith was seen in the afternoon or evening, this betokened evil or approaching death, and the time within which death would occur was considered to be within a year. This belief in wraiths goes back to a very early period of man's history. The ancient Persians and Jews believed that every person had a spirit or guardian angel attending him, and although generally invisible, it had the power of becoming visible and separating itself for a time from the person it attended, and of appearing to other persons in the guise of the individual from whom it emanated. An excellent example of this superstitious belief is recorded in the Acts of the Apostles. When Peter, who was believed to be in prison, knocked at the 'door of the gate' of the house where the disciples were met, the young woman who went to open the door, on recognising Peter's voice, was overjoyed, and, instead of opening, ran into the house, and told the disciples Peter was at the door. Then they said, 'It is his angel' (wraith). Thus the whole company expressed their belief in attending angels. The belief in wraiths was prevalent throughout all Scotland. It is beautifully introduced in the song of 'Auld

Robin Gray.' When the young wife narrates her meeting with her old sweetheart, she says, 'I thought it was his wraith, I could not think it he,' and the belief survives in some parts of the country to the present day. If a dying person struggled hard and long, it was believed that the spirit was kept from departing by some magic spell. It was therefore customary, under these circumstances, for the attendants to open every lock in the house, that the spell might be broken, and the spirit let loose.[18]

Preparing the Body, Layin' Out and Kistin'

Revd Walter Gregor
North-east, 1874

At other times [in the North-east] the dying person was removed from the bed and laid on the floor of the apartment, as it might happen that there were wild fowls' feathers in the pillows or bed, a cause at all times of a hard struggle in death. This notion about wild fowls' feathers did not exist among some of the fishing population that used the feathers of all kinds of birds except those of the pigeon.

In the very moment of death all the doors and windows that were capable of being opened were thrown wide open, to give the departing spirit full and free egress, lest the evil spirits might intercept it in its heavenward flight. The Esquimo have the same custom.

Immediately on death, a piece of iron, such as a knitting wire or a nail, was stuck into whatever meal, butter, cheese, foodflesh, or whisky were in the house, to prevent death from entering them. The corruption of these articles has followed closely on the neglect of this, and the whisky has been known to become white as milk.

All the milk in the house was poured out on the ground. In some of the fishing villages all the onions and butter were cast forth.

The chairs etc. in the house were sprinkled with water. The clothes of the dead were also sprinkled with water, and it was the common belief that they always had a peculiar smell.

If there was a clock, it was stopped. If there was a looking-glass, it was covered, as were also the pictures.

All the hens and the cats were shut up during the whole time the body was unburied, from the belief that, if a cat or a hen leaped over it, the person who was the first to meet the cat or hen that did so became blind, not perhaps at

---

[18] J. Napier, *Folk Lore*, pp. 56–9.

the time, but assuredly before leaving this earth.

The neighbours did not yoke their horses, unless there was a running stream between the dwellings. In the fishing village of — , on the north-east coast of Aberdeenshire, not a single spadeful of earth was moved within the village during the time the corpse was lying unburied.

When the death took place a messenger was despatched for a wright, who hastened to the house of death with his *strykin beuird*. The body was washed, and, after being clothed in a home-made linen shirt and stockings, it was *strykit* on the board brought by the wright, and covered with a home-made linen sheet. Many a bride laid up in store her bridal dress, to be made into her winding-sheet, and her bridal linen and bridal stockings, as well as her husband's, to be put on when life's journey was ended.

When the eyelids did not close, or if they opened a little after being closed, an old penny or halfpenny piece was laid over the eyes.

On the breast was placed a saucer or a plate containing a little salt, to keep the evil spirits away, because they could not come near Christ's savour of the earth.

To prevent swelling in the bowels, any small dish with a little mould was at times placed on them. If this had been neglected, and swelling made its appearance, a small green turf was cut and placed upon them, when, it was alleged, the swelling immediately disappeared.

A candle or two were kept constantly burning beside the body. It has happened that the candle has been overturned and the grave-clothes set on fire and the body burned. This took place only in the case of those who were believed to have possessed during their lifetime more than human skill and power, which they had obtained at the price of their souls from the Prince of Evil, or of those whose lives had been more than ordinarily stained, either openly or secretly. Such an untoward accident was spoken of in whispers, and was looked on as the dark omen of the future state.

In one instance, at least, the time of the death was observed:

> Gehn the gueedeman o' a toon
> Dee i' the fou' o' the moon,
> His family 'ill be rich
> Till the wardle be doon.

The bodies of those who drowned, but were not recovered, were supposed to come to the surface of the water on the ninth day. It was the weight of the gall that kept the body at the bottom. On the ninth day the gall-bag broke, and the body, being relieved of the weight, floated.

A mode of discovering a body drowned in a stream or river was to put a loaf into the water at the spot where the unfortunate fell. The loaf floated down the stream till it came above the body, when it began to whirl round and round.

If one committed suicide by drowning, it was believed the body did not sink. It floated on the surface.

The opinion prevailed till not very long ago, and even yet lingers, that in a case of murder, if the murderer touches the corpse, blood flows from the wounds.

The coffin and grave-clothes were made with all becoming speed. When all were ready, a day and an hour were fixed for the *kistan* that is, for laying the body in the coffin, and a few of the most intimate female friends and nearest relatives of the deceased were invited to attend. At the appointed time they came, usually dressed in mourning clothes, and assisted in placing the body in the coffin, and in making suitable preparation for the funeral. The board of hospitality was spread, when the qualities and deeds of the departed formed the subject of conversation.

To the other female acquaintances that had not been present at the *kistan*, invitations were sent to come and take the last look of the dead – 'to see the corpse'.[19]

Sir John Lauderdale of Fountainhall
1683

Apr. 5. – At the funeral of the Duke of Lauderdale at Haddington, while the usual dole money was being distributed among the beggars, one, named Bell, stabbed another. 'He was apprehended, and several stolen things found on him, and he being made to touch the corpse, the wound bled afresh. The town of Haddington who it seems have a sheriff's power, judged him presently, and hanged him over the bridge the next day.'[*]

Margaret Ann Clouston
Orkney, 1985

In her role as local midwife, Margaret Ann Clouston was also called upon to wash, dress and lay out the body of a deceased member of her family or

---

[19] W. Gregor, *Echo*, pp. 136–41 and *Notes* pp. 206–9.
[*] Robert Chambers, *Domestic Annals of Scotland*, p. 334. Quoted from the MS of Sir John Lauderdale of Fountainhall, 1848. [There was an ancient belief that if a person were guilty of causing death their guilt would be revealed if, when they touched the corpse, it began to bleed.]

community. Long before she was asked to perform this task, however, she vividly remembered having to acknowledge her own mortality when she was just a little girl at school.

MB *And who laid out the bodies at death?*

MC They wir jist dressed by the oldest woman of the family.

MB *Did they have special grave clothes?*

MC They had all white things, cotton . . . it was a shroud. I hed mine lyin years – and mine's no been used yit!

MB *I hope not! Who made yours?*

MC I made it mesel. I made it when I wir gan tae the school. I sewed it wi me hands, all hand-stitched.

MB *Did all the boys and girls do that?*

MC Boys nivvir did it, jist the girls . . . I made it and I've hed it for years . . . the teacher likely shapit it. It was common, very common.[20]

John Firth
Orkney, 1920

As soon as the body had been *taen aboot*, that is dressed and laid out, a small plate of salt was placed on the chest of the deceased to prevent swelling. When the straiking was completed, refreshments were handed round and arrangements made for the wake. In those days a much longer time was allowed to elapse between the death and the burial than is now considered sanitary. It was looked upon as a mark of disrespect if the funeral took place before the usual time – eight days – and no matter how loathsome or infectious the fatal complaint had been, this custom was strictly adhered to. After the laws of hygiene began to be better known, one poor old woman's brother was, in her absence from home, buried before the usual time had elapsed. This proved a standing grievance to her; and, whenever afterwards his decease was referred to, she never failed to shed tears and lament that they had not kept him a week.[21]

---

[20] Margaret Ann Clouston, aged 105, was recorded in Kirwall, Orkney, on 24 May 1985, by MB, accompanied by Gail Christie. SA1985/146.
[21] John Firth, *Orkney*, p. 84.

Gladys and Charles Simpson
Keith, Banff-shire, 1988

MB *What about funerals at home with you in Keith?*

CS We're talking about the 1920s. Well they were always held from the house, at home. But nowadays it's all church funerals.

MB *And who made the coffin?*

CS O, just the local joiner.

GS He was a joiner and undertaker.

CS The cheapest ones were the plain white wood with black cloth covering. Or if it was a very young [person], a white cloth covering. But then they started making them oot o elm.

MB *Did men have more to do with funerals than women?*

CS Oh, yes. Women didn't go to funerals. They went to the service in the house, but they never went to the churchyard.

MB *Did they do the laying out of the body?*

CS There was one woman that usually . . . a sort of a near neighbour, really, well, from the way it was workit in Keith . . . I remember the first dead person I saw was my grandfather – my father's father. And it was the woman that laid him out that took me up to see him. And it was one of these old-fashioned kitchen tables that the coffin was on, in the room, you know. And I had to stand on a chair to look in.

MB *Did the person get laid out in their best clothes or in a shroud?*

CS Just in a shroud . . . in fact the man that made the coffin had a board that they called – it was for streikin them oot on – the streikin board . . . And you would see them goin into Johnny Cormack's at Keith. That was the undertaker, goin down with the board underneath his arm. I don't know what it was for unless it was just because there was nothing long enough in the house for a body to lie on . . . It was probably to keep the whole body straight. It was just the shape of a coffin.

MB *And would that go into the coffin after?*

CS Oh no, no! [It was just used during the preparation.]

GS It was the custom that the dead person would be laid in the best room. And friends would come and visit, and go through and see them. They would usually lay a hand on them or touch them in some way.

CS After the funeral, after the burial took place they had a sort of spread of high tea sort of business. I ate so much cheese that I was sick! (So that brought [the memory] back to me!) But it was always that. Most of the folk, the relations anyway, came back to the house and they had this meal.

GS [After the funeral the women] stayed at the house. And usually a few neighbours came in to be with the relatives who were left. And they would prepare this tea for the men coming back from the cemetery.

CS It was all walking in these days – with horse-drawn hearses, of course. And the hearses had a pair of horses. I never saw them carrying them from the house. They carried them into the cemetery, of course, and up into the cemetery. But never from the house as they used to do here [in Skye].

MB *Were there flowers at funerals?*

CS I can't remember flowers in the early days.

MB *What about mourning clothes?*

GS Oh, everything in black. Well, I have a recollection that it was six months that a widow had to wear widow's weeds as they called them . . . And my granny, in fact I think both my grannies were always in black.[22]

Betty Stewart
Orkney, 1985

Betty Stewart is a retired midwife who moved from Aberdeen to the Orkneys before the Second World War. She has distinct memories of the prevalent customs in Aberdeenshire in the 1930s.

BS I remember my granny once showed me, she'd two brown paper parcels in the bottom drawer of a chest of drawers, and when she opened them there was this beautiful shroud, all hand-sewn . . .

Usually when the body was all laid out some of the neighbours would go there and put the body into the coffin and this was called 'the kistin'.[23]

Douglas Neally
Stornoway, 1992

DN *[At home during the holidays I asked one of the older men about death customs . . .]*

LM In my young days there was someone to arrange the body, to lay it out and to dress it, wash it. Today that's done mostly in hospital or by professional people. My father was one of these who used to go and make up men's bodies if they were friends . . . And [for] women, of course, there was always women who did the same thing.

DN *So it was usually the men who did it for the men and the women for women.*

---

[22] Charles and Gladys Simpson were recorded at Ardvasar, Isle of Skye, on 5 May 1985 by MB. SA1985/141.

[23] Betty Stewart was recorded in Kirkwall on 24 May 1885, by MB and Gail Christie. SA1985/146.

LM Usually. All men wouldn't do it, just certain members of the community who knew what to do and how to do it.[24]

Burial

Revd Walter Gregor
North-east, 1874

> The storm that wrecks the winter sky
> No more disturbs their deep repose
> Than summer evening's latest sigh
> That shuts the rose.

The barn was cleared, swept clean, and fitted up with seats – deals placed on anything and everything capable of supporting them. On the middle of the floor was placed a table covered with a table-cloth, at the head of which was set an arm-chair for the minister. On the table was a quantity of bread and cheese, as well as of cut tobacco, with a number of new tobacco pipes. Beneath the table were bottles and jars of whisky, with ale.

The people had been invited to the funeral, or *warnt*, by a special messenger a few days before the funeral took place. On arriving, they were received by the nearest relative of the deceased and conducted to the barn. Each, as he entered, if he was a smoker, laid hold of a pipe, filled, and lighted it. When all arrived, and usually the arrivals lasted from one to two hours and even longer, prayer was offered up by the minister, and in his absence by an elder or any other that 'had the gift'. When the prayer was ended, the whisky was brought forward, and toddy was made in bowls, if the company was not very large, or if the friends of the departed were poor; but, if the company was large and the deceased well-to-do, it was brewed in the firlot. There have been those who were famous for their joviality in their lifetime giving strict orders on their death-bed regarding the quantity of whisky to be used at their funeral obsequies. When the toddy was made and tested, all glasses were filled and handed round. They were emptied to the memory of the departed. Bread and cheese followed. The glasses were again filled and drained to the toast, 'Consolation to the friends of the deceased'. Then came more bread and cheese, and a glass or two more of toddy. Such as preferred 'a drap' o'

---

[24] Edinburgh University divinity student Douglas Neally recorded a family friend, an older man who did not wish to be named. [Local Man = LM] The recording was part of his Scottish Ethnology project, recorded in his own home on the Isle of Lewis, March 1992.

the raw geer,' or ale to the toddy, received it. When all had eaten and drunken in a manner befitting the station and means of the dead, prayer was again offered; not, however, always. It was then announced, 'Gehn ony o' ye wis t' see the corp, ye'll noo hae an opportunity.' The company thereupon left the barn, and one by one went into the apartment of death, uncovered his head, and gently and reverently laid his hand upon the breast or brow of the dead, frequently making a remark on the appearance of the body, as 'He's unco like himsel,' 'She's a bonnie corp,' or 'He's sair alert', or on the character of the departed, as 'She'll be a sehr misst umman,' or 'He wiz a gueede freen t' mony ane.' It was believed that unless the body was touched the image of it haunted the fancy.

If the body was soft and flabby when the coffin lid was closed, it was a sure indication that another corpse would at no distant period of time be carried from the same dwelling.

When the last look had been taken by all the coffin lid was closed. Before this was done part of the winding sheet, commonly one of the corners, was cut off, and preserved with tender care beside a lock of the hair of the dead one. Sometimes it was made into a napkin, which was worn only on the occasion of a *kistan*, or on a Communion Sunday. When all was ready, or, as it was expressed, 'fin the beerial wiz ready t' lift,' two chairs were placed in front of the door of the dwelling-house, and the coffin was tenderly borne forth and laid upon them. The spokes were then adjusted under it. The coffin was covered with the mort-cloth, or, if the friends of the deceased were too poor to pay for it, with a plaid. The coffin of a boy or a girl was often covered with a sheet, and a child's almost always. The coffin of a full-grown person was carried on spokes by eight bearers, who relieved each other, not at regular intervals, but as fancy struck them, the one nearest the coffin retiring. In the Highlands the coffin was sometimes carried shoulder-high, as the more honourable mode of being borne to the grave. The *first lift* was taken by the females of the family and near female relatives of friends that were present.

In some of the fishing villages the coffin of a young unmarried woman was carried to the grave by her young companions, dressed in white, with a black ribbon round the waist.

The chairs were overturned as soon as the coffin was lifted off them, and were allowed to lie, in some places till sunset, and in others till one of these that had attended the funeral returned, when they were lifted and carefully washed. If not overturned, the spirit returned from the unseen world.

On the funeral leaving – 'the beerial liftin' – all the animals, such as the horses and cattle belonging to the farm, were loosed from their stalls and driven forth. The funeral has been seen to be followed by the cattle in amazement with wide nostrils, wild eyes, and much lowing. Such an occurrence was looked upon with awe, and was set down as an indication of brute sorrow and sympathy for the departed.

The funeral procession on no account took byeways, or moved a foot from the common path, but moved along the *kirk-road*. The road which the deceased had walked to God's house must be the road along which the mortal remains were carried to God's acre.

In some parts the bellman went in front of the procession and tolled a hand-bell, kept by the kirk-session for the purpose. In other places the church-bell was tolled as the procession neared the churchyard.

If the churchyard was at a distance, whisky was carried; and on the road was usually a fixed spot for resting and partaking of it. At this spot there was in some places a big stone, called *the ristin stehn*, on which the coffin was laid. Fame has it that the quantity now taken in addition to what was formerly taken not infrequently put not a few of the coffin-bearers into a state far from seemly, and that even old scores have been paid off by broken heads and faces.

When the grave was again covered over with the green sod, whisky was in many cases partaken of, when each took his way home. A few of the nearest relatives and intimate friends of the dead returned to the house, where a dinner was prepared.

The weather on the day of the funeral was most carefully observed. A shower on the mould of the open grave – *the meels* – was taken as an indication that the soul of the departed was enjoying happiness. A hurricane told of some foul deed done, but never brought to light, or of a bad life, however fair to the eye, or of a compact with Satan.

A coffin more than ordinarily heavy was remarked; and there have been coffins of 'a heavier weight than lead', which were with the utmost difficulty carried to the graveyard. Such a thing was spoken of with awe.

In the case of those who were supposed to possess in their lifetime other power than their own, a white dove and a crow have been seen to make a dash on the coffin in contest which should reach it first. Sometimes the dove gained the victory, and sometimes the crow, that came with such violence that it broke through the lid of the coffin. The dove was the emblem of the Spirit, and the crow that of the Prince of Evil.

In B —, the night after the funeral, bread and water were placed in the apartment in which the body lay. The dead was believed to return that night and partake of the bread and water. Unless this were done the spirit could not rest in the unseen world. This curious custom seems to throw light upon what have been called 'food vases,' and 'drinking cups,' found in round barrows and in the secondary interments in long barrows, supposed to be of the 'bronze age' and of the ancient British period.

A burial ought not on any account to be looked at from a window. The one that did so would soon follow.

Peculiar horror was manifested towards suicides. Such were not buried in the churchyard.[25] It is not much over half a century since a fierce fight took place in a churchyard in the middle of Banff-shire, to prevent the burial of a suicide in it. By an early hour all the strong men of the parish who were opposed to an act so sacrilegious were astir and hastening to the churchyard with their weapons of defence – strong sticks. The churchyard was taken possession of and the walls manned. The gate and more accessible parts of the wall were assigned to picked men. In due time the suicide's coffin appeared, surrounded by an excited crowd, for the most part armed with sticks. Some, however, carried spades sharpened on the edge. Fierce and long was the fight at the gate, and not a few rolled in the dust. The assailing party was beaten off. A grave was dug outside the churchyard, close beneath the wall, and the coffin laid in it. The lid was lifted, and a bottle of vitriol poured over the body. Before the lid could be again closed, the fumes of the dissolving body were rising thickly over the heads of actors and spectators. This was done to prevent the body from being lifted during the coming night from its resting place, conveyed back to its abode when in life, and placed against the door, to fall at the feet of the member of the family that was the first to open the door in the morning.

The self-murderer's grave was on the boundary of two lairds' lands, and was marked by a single large stone or by a small cairn, to which the passing traveller was bound to cast a stone.

It was the prevailing idea that nothing would grow over the grave of a suicide, or on the spot on which a murder was committed.

After the suicide's body was allowed to be buried within the churchyard, it was laid below the wall in such a position that one could not step over the grave.[26] This was done under the belief that, if a woman *enceinte* stepped over such a grave, her child would quit this earth by its own act.

The instrument by which the unfortunate put an end to life was eagerly

[25] In *Closeburn (Dumfriesshire): Reminiscent, Historic and Traditional*, R.M.F. Watson tells a distressing story of a motherless young girl who committed suicide after the death of her father. Despite the tragic circumstances of her death, she was not buried beside her father, but was 'committed to the earth at the boundary of Lanarkshire and Dumfriesshire, according to the custom then prevailing in the case of a suicide'. See pp. 220–8.

[26] According to the Revd Norman MacDonald, Skye, recorded by Paterson in 1975, a suicide's coffin should be taken to the grave head first. SA/1975/81.

sought after, as the possession of it, particularly the knot of the rope, if death was brought about by hanging, secured great worldly prosperity. This notion about the knot of a rope by which one was hanged did not attach simply to a suicide's rope, but also to a criminal's.

Stillborn children and children that died without baptism were buried before sunrise, from the belief that, unless this were done, their spirits were not admitted into Heaven, but floated homeless through the regions of space. In some places they were buried in such a position that one could not step over their graves.[27]

Florence Clow
Dumfries, 1985

Florence Clow trained as a midwife and neo-natal paediatric nurse in the Royal Maternity Hospital, Glasgow and is now a lecturer at a community college in Dumfries. Here she recalls some of the more sensitive moments from her career as a midwife:

MB *When you were nursing in Rotten Row[28] I remember that you mentioned . . . that some mothers . . . would urge you to baptise a baby, in spite of the fact that you were possibly not of the same faith or had absolutely no religious training.*

FC Yes, this did happen . . .

MB *Was it usually in the case of a weakly baby, or just any baby at all.*

FC It was usually a baby that had been stillborn . . . Yes, even a dead baby, if they wanted it baptised . . . If it was one that was sickly we always had a priest's telephone number, and normally we would phone the priest. But if it was a baby that had been born dead then the mother would simply ask us to baptise it . . . I did baptise a few babies, because it was the mother's wish. And I feel strongly that when a mother has some request it's very important to her. And I feel that it's an important part of a nurse's duty to carry this out.

MB *Did you do it under the mother's instruction?*

FC Yes, I did. I found that if the baby was of a Roman Catholic mother she would want her baby baptised. It was important to her. If there was a Catholic nurse then she would baptise the child . . . She would just get some water and put it on the baby's head, and . . . 'In the name of the Father, the Son and the Holy Ghost, I baptise thee,' and the name of the child.

MB *Did [any of the mothers] express any fear that if this didn't take place something dreadful might befall the child?*

---

[27] Ibid. pp. 144–51 and pp. 210–14.
[28] The Royal Maternity Hospital on Rottenrow, Glasgow, is generally referred to as 'Rottenrow'.

FC No, they didn't, and I didn't question it. I don't feel it's a time to question a
mother when she's upset about her baby.

MB *Nowadays there's quite a controversy over the burial of stillborn babies and miscarried*
foetuses. Did you ever come across anything like that while nursing in Scotland?

FC Yes. There are different views. Some mothers obviously felt that although their
babies had been born dead, they had been a part of them; they had been
alive . . . so they were quite sure that they wanted their child buried like a baby
which had been born alive and had died. But there were many mothers whose
husbands wanted to protect them from the trauma of a funeral, so their babies were
just buried in a grave.

MB *Ever incinerated?*[29]

FC No, never.

MB *Even an aborted foetus?*

FC No, they were just put into a grave that had been opened.[30]

MB *Just any grave do you mean?*

FC I'm not quite sure, but I think there was a special part of the cemetery that they
used to keep for stillbirths.[31]

Regardless of the circumstances of death, bereaved relatives and friends
share a basic human need to pay their last respects in a manner they
consider fitting. They also need to ensure that every measure is taken to
maintain the dignity and peace which belongs to the final resting place. At
no time in Scottish history did this become a greater issue than in the days
of the so-called resurrectionists, here referred to by James Thomson.

James Thomson
Aberlour 1887

The watch-house is associated in the writer's memory with a host of incidents
that left a deep impression of the horrible deeds done by resurrectionists. Few
at the present day can remember the agitation caused in Scotland when the
dreadful deeds and doings of Burke and and Hare were made public. Horror
and dread became epidemic, and the whole country was in a fever of agitation

---

[29] This is sometimes more euphemistically referred to as 'cremation' in hospitals.
[30] The policy and attitude varies from hospital to hospital. In 1992 the Department of
Health issued guidelines to all hospitals to 'tighten up' on procedures followed in
cases of stillbirths or spontaneous abortions and to make sure that hospitals would
treat stillbirths and miscarriages as a human life rather than waste products of an
operation.
[31] Florence Clow was recorded in Dumfries by MB on 6 January 1985. SA1985/130.
See also *Carmina Gadelica*, vol. 3, pp. 3–5 for traditions surrounding stillbirths.

at the thought of having the remains of a wife, a mother, or father dragged from their grave and carried off . . . the very thought of such a thing roused the people in many places to desperation . . . They rose up, determined to baulk the resurrectionists of their prey. A watch-house was erected in many graveyards; indeed, very few in the north-eastern counties were without an erection of some kind to shelter the watchers of the dead, and their ruins may be seen in many graveyards at the present day.

A short description of a watch-house well remembered by the writer may interest the reader. The one referred to was built of rough stones, and was about ten feet square. It stood on a spot that overlooked the whole graveyard. On either side of the door was a narrow slit or window, that opened and closed with strong wooden shutters. Through these apertures the watchers could reconnoitre unobserved, and, if need be, fire their guns upon the desecrators of the grave. The fire-place was opposite the door, and over it hung two claymores that had done service at Culloden; upon a small table in the centre of the apartment lay an open Bible, a snuff-mull, pipes, and a bottle of *usquabae* also stood there to refresh the wary watchers. Had the staunchest teetotaller been there, he would have been sorely tempted to fill the quaich and taste the contents of the bottle. Few at the present time have any idea of the hardships entailed upon the male population of a small parish, in having to watch over the remains of their friends and neighbours for six weeks. That was the prescribed time necessary. The watch-house in some cases was occupied the whole of the winter months, if an epidemic was prevalent in the parish.[32]

Revd Donald MacQueen
Kilmuir, Skye, 1774

Traitors were put to death in the Isles, being, according to custom that prevailed among the *Norwegians*, first gelded and both their eyes pulled out. Incestuous persons were buried in marshes alive, and bankrupts, without entering into a consideration of the nature of their misfortunes, were stripped of their all, clad in a party-coloured [*sic*] clouted garment, with stockings of different sets, and had their hips dashed against a stone in presence of the people by four men, each taking hold of an arm or a thigh. This punishment they called *Tòn Cruaidh*: and cowardice, when not capitally punished, was accompanied with perpetual infamy.[33]

---

[32] James Thomson, *Recollections of a Speyside Parish*, pp. 65–6. See also Alexander Stewart, 'The Resurrection Trade' in *Reminiscences of Dunfermline*, pp. 53–4.
[33] Written on 17 November 1774 by Revd Donald MacQueen, Kilmuir, Isle of Skye and published in Appendix XI in Pennant's *Tour*, vol. II, 1776, p. 421.

Death and Burial in Dumfries and Galloway

J. Maxwell Wood
Dumfries, 1911

When that sure hand called Death knocked at the cottar's or laird's door, or stalked with unhalting step into moorland farm or upland home to beckon away some weary inmate, the actual decease, or passing, was of itself associated with significant observance.

The nearest relative bent down to the dying face to receive the last breath. The door was kept ajar, although not too wide, that the spirit might be untrammelled in its flight.

The spirit fled, the poor dead eyes were closed, also by the nearest relative, and generally kept so by means of copper coins placed upon them.

The looking-glass in the death-chamber was covered with a white cloth. The clock was stopped, or at least the striking-weight removed. The daily routine of work was discontinued, such days of enforced idleness being known as the 'dead days'. On the farm, for example, no matter the season, the appropriate labour of ploughing, seed sowing, or even harvest, at once ceased. The household companions of dog and cat were rigidly excluded from the stricken house; indeed, it was not uncommon for the cat to be imprisoned beneath an inverted tub, for it was believed that if either of these animals should jump or cross over the dead body, the welfare of the spirit of the deceased would certainly be affected.

The body was then washed, and dressed in its last garments, the hands of females being crossed over the breast, those of the other sex being extended by the sides. Last of all a plate of salt was placed upon the breast, either from the higher idea of future life being signified by the salt, which is the emblem of perpetuity, or from a more practical notion, however unlikely, that by this means the body would be prevented from swelling.

Of the curious custom of 'sin-eatings' – that is, the placing of a piece of bread upon the salt by a recognised individual known as the sin-eater, who, for money reward, at the same time partook of it, thereby, as it was believed, absorbing to himself all the sins of the deceased – there is little to be gleaned in this district. The term 'dishaloof' still exists, however, as a vestige of the custom in lowland Scotland.

There falls to be mentioned here a quaint superstition associated with 'bee folklore', as described by the late Patrick Dudgeon, Esq. of Cargen, Kirkcudbrightshire, who specially studied this matter. The custom was, when a death took place, to at once go to the bee-hives, or skeps, and whisper the tidings of the sad event to the bees. This was followed by 'putting the bees in mourning' – that is, attaching black ribbons to each of the skeps.

Mr Dudgeon, in a paper on the subject, observes that 'the custom was very general some time ago, and several of my correspondents mention instances of old people having seen it observed. It is not altogether extinct yet.'

The last toilet completed, it was the usual custom for friends and neighbours to manifest their sympathy by watching, or 'waulking', the dead. Through the long hours of night, by the glimmering candle-light at the silent bedside, this was really a service that called for some resolution, as tales of dead bodies coming back to life were fully believed in these superstitious days. Occasionally special candles were used for 'the watching', known as Yule candles. These were the remains of specially large candles burned at Yule, and extinguished at the close of the day, what was left of the candle being carefully preserved and locked away, to be burned at the owners' own 'wauking'.

Visiting the house of the dead for the sake of seeing the corpse was a regular practice, and, it may be added, that to touch the corpse was considered a sure safeguard against all eerie dreams of death and ghostly trappings, as well as a counter-influence to illness and disease.

With the encoffining, or 'kistin' of the dead, a further stage was reached. The ceremony was apparently religious, and one of deep solemnity, the minister, or one of his elders or deacons, attending to see the remains of the deceased placed in the coffin, to offer up prayer, and generally to console and sympathise with the bereaved. In reality, the official presence of the minister, elder or deacon, was directly due to an Act of Parliament,* actually framed

---

* In the second session of the first Parliament of James VII, held at Edinburgh, 1686, an Act was passed called the 'Act for Burying in Scots Linen,' in which it was ordained, for the encouragement of the linen manufactures within the kingdom, that no person whatsoever, of high or low degree, should be buried in any shirt, sheet, or anything else, except in plain linen or cloth, of Hards made and spun within the kingdom, and without lace or point. There was specially prohibited the use of Holland, or other linen cloth made in other kingdoms; and of silk, woollen, gold, or silver, or any other stuff than what was made of Hards spun and wrought within the kingdom, under the penalty of 300 pounds Scots for a nobleman, and 200 pounds for every other person for each offence. One-half of this penalty was to go to the informer, and the other half to the poor of the parish of where the body should be interred. And, for the better discovery of contraveners, it was ordained that every minister within the kingdom should keep an account and register of all persons buried in his parish. A certificate upon oath, in writing duly attested by two 'famous' persons, was to be delivered by one of the relatives to the minister within eight days, declaring that the deceased person had been shrouded in the manner prescribed; which certificate was to be recorded without charge. The penalty was to be sued for by the minister before any judge competent; and if he should prove negligent in pursuing the contraveners within six months after the interment, he himself was liable for the said fine. *Life and Times of Rev. John Wightman, D.D., of Kirkmahoe.*

and passed, incongruous as it may appear, for the 'improvement of Linen manufacture within the Kingdom.' The clerical representative was present in the house of mourning, to be fully satisfied that 'the corpse was shrouded in home-made linen, and that not exceeding in value twenty shillings per ell.'

This curious Act had as curious a sequel, for, prompted by an evident spirit of fair dealing, the Linen Act was rescinded in the first Parliament of Queen Anne in favour of a 'Woollen Act', insisting upon the exclusive use of 'wool' as a material for shrouds, under exactly the same pains and penalties as the previous Act laid down to compel the use of linen. In course of time such rigid intrusive conditions, despite the law, came to be disregarded, and people shrouded their dead as they thought best, and in material of their own choice. It was, however, usual for the undertaker to safeguard those concerned in any such infringement by charging half the statutory fine in his account, taking credit to himself for the other half as being the informer against himself. This was usually entered as the first item of his undertaking expenses, being expressed in his bill against the relatives as: 'To paying the penalty under the Act for burying in Scots linen'.

The custom of relatives and intimate friends being at the encoffining or 'kistin' is to some extent associated with the 'lykewake', or 'latewake', of Roman Catholic usage. Although now quite unknown among adherents of the Scottish Presbyterian Church, such wakes were at one time common enough, even after the Reformation. They were, however, attended by such unseemly behaviour that in 1645 the General Assembly passed an edict to suppress them.

That the custom still continued is brought out by the knowledge that in 1701 it was found necessary to revive and enforce the statute against the practice.

The culminating feature of the rites of bereavement, the funeral ceremony, was in these old days (particularly between the years 1700 and 1800) an occasion altogether outstanding in social importance. It was an occasion, however, very often marred by the profuse liberality and use of stimulants, lavish hospitality in the house of mourning being too frequently followed by ludicrous and extraordinary results as the body was being conveyed to its last resting-place. 'A funeral party,' for example, 'had wended their way for miles through deep snow over Eskdale Moor, bound for Moffat Churchyard. On arriving at the burial-ground it was actually discovered that they had dropped the coffin by the way, the back having fallen from the cart on which it was being conveyed.'

Ten o'clock in the morning saw the commencement of the funeral ceremonies, this being so generally understood that no special hour was mentioned in 'the bidding to the buriall.' The setting-out for the churchyard, however, or the 'liftin',' as it was termed, did not, as a rule, take place for several hours later, and in many instances not until well on in the afternoon. This delay, as well as giving ample time to partake of refreshment, was really meant to enable all the guests to gather together, many of them travelling long distances, which were not made shorter by bad roads or inclement weather. A precaution sometimes taken before the company moved off was to send someone to the top of the nearest height to signal when the horizon was clear and no more guests in sight.

The place of entertainment was usually the barn. Planks laid along the tops of wooden trestles formed a large table, on which were piled up a superabundance of food and drink, while a constant feature of the entertainment was an imposing array of tobacco pipes already filled by the women who had sat beside, or watched, the dead body. It was not considered seemly for the women of the house to mingle with the male guests. The usual custom in Galloway and Nithsdale was for the women folk to sit together in a room apart.

As the company gathered they formed themselves into relays – for the number of guests as a rule exceeded the accommodation of even the largest barn – and entered the place set aside for refreshment. This took the form of what were known as 'services', and these in their usual order, after each guest had been proffered a pipe of tobacco:

(a) Bread and cheese, with ale and porter; (b) A glass of whisky, with again bread and cheese; (c) A glass of rum and biscuits; (d) A glass of brandy and currant bun; (e) Wine and shortbread (or burial bread).

It was not, be it mentioned in passing, a very unusual thing for some of the company to enter the barn again, and undertake the 'services' a second time.

The natural consequence of all this is obvious, but to a certain extent the situation could be saved by the use of a private receptacle called the 'droddy bottle', into which the liquor could be poured to be taken home, or at least carried outside. Before partaking of each individual 'service' it was solemnised by the minister offering up an appropriate prayer, a clerical task which must have been trying in the extreme.

As instancing the prodigality of preparation in the way of food, notice may be taken of a funeral in the parish of Mochrum, where two bushels (160 lbs.) of shortbread were provided, and it is quite unnecessary to suggest that the supply of spirits would be in proportion.

The following account of funeral expenses, drawn from a Wigtownshire farmer's book of expenses in 1794, may here be included, as it affords an excellent illustration of how the expenses of an ordinary funeral were swelled by the amounts paid for alcoholic liquor:

Mrs G. – One gallon brandy	0	18	1
5 gills gin	0	7	0
To bread	0	5	9
J.C. for biding and walking and other attendance	0	4	0
J.S. for whiskie and ale at sitting up	0	3	1

Of the expenses of funerals in a higher rank of life those incurred on the deaths of Grierson of Lag and his third son, John Grierson, afford full and interesting information. Mr John Grierson, third son of the Laird of Lag, died early in 1730, and to one Jean Scott the purveying of the meat and drink considered requisite for the friends attending the funeral was entrusted. The bill came to about £160 Scots. When the Laird himself died, on the last day of the year 1733, there was a repetition of the feasting and drinking at the house of the deceased, at the kirkyard, and at an adjoining house, which had evidently been requisitioned for the accommodation of several of the gentlemen, among whom were Lord Stormonth, Sir Thomas Kirkpatrick, Maxwell of Carriel, and others who had come from a distance to assist. The account begins two days before the death of the Laird, and ends on January 14. In round figures the cost of the meat and drink consumed at the Laird's funeral come to £240 Scots.

The following are the detailed accounts:

Accott. of the Funerals of Mr John Griersone. 1730. To Jean Scott.

Feb. 23rd. 2 bottels clarit to these as set up all night wt ye corps	£0	3	0
do. 1 bottel of brandy for do.	0	1	6
Feb. 24th. 1 bottel of clarit when the sear-cloath was put on	0	1	6
do.1 bottel clarit when the grave-cloaths was put on	0	1	6
do. At the in-coffining where the ladys was, 1 bottel clarit, 2 bottels white wine, and 1 bottel Cannary	0	6	2
do. In the bed room wt the Gentelmen before the corps was transported – 2 bottels white wine	0	3	0
do. When the company returned – 10 bottels clarit	0	15	0
do. 2 bottels brandy for Gentelmen's Servts.	0	3	0
do. 2 bottels clarit to Sir Robert's Servts.	0	3	0
Feb. 26th. 1 bottel clarit to Sir Robert's Servts.	0	1	6
Mar. 2nd. 1 bottel clarit to Sir Robert's Servts.	0	1	6
Mar. 4th. 1 bottel clarit to Sir Robert's Servts.	0	1	6
Mar. 5th. In the two rooms when at meat 22 bottels clarit	1	13	0
do. ffor the Servts. and Gentelmen's Servts., 4 bottels of brandy	0	6	0
do. at night when the Gentelmen returned – 25 bottels of clarit	1	17	6

do. 2 bottels brandy to Rockhall wt bottels	0	3	0
Mar. 6th. 2 bottels clarit at dinr wt Sr Walter Laurie and Cariel	0	3	0
do. Ale from the 23rd of ffebr., till this day	1	19	6
do. To 1 baccon ham	0	9	0
do. To a rosting piece of beef	0	6	6
do. To a rost pigg	0	2	6
do. To 2 rost gease	0	3	0
do. To 1 rost turkey	0	4	0
do. To a calf's head stwed wt wine and oysstars	0	3	6
do. To 2 dish of neats' tongues	0	8	0
do. To 2 dish of capons and fowls	0	6	0
do. To a passtie	0	7	0
do. To a dozn. of tearts	0	6	0
do. To 2 dozn. of mincht pys	0	8	0
do. To 1 quarter of rost mutton	0	3	6
do. To rost veal	0	3	6
do. To 1 barrel of oysters, 6 limmons, and other pickels	0	4	0
do. To eating for Tennents and Servants	1	0	0

A notable exception to the practice of the period was the funeral of William Burnes, father of the National Bard, who was borne from Lochlea to Alloway Kirkyard, a distance of twelve miles, not a drop of anything excepting a draught of water from a roadside stream being tasted.

The funeral festivities, however, did not end with the lowering of the dead into the grave. There yet remained the final entertainment at the house of the bereaved. If within reasonable distance at all the funeral party returned from the churchyard to partake of the entertainment known as the 'draigie,' or 'dredgy.' Again the drinking was long and deep, with results that can only too readily be imagined.

But it must not be assumed that such scenes and proceedings passed without protest on the part of the Church and those who had the welfare of decency and morality at heart. The Presbytery of Penpont, for example, in 1736 issued the following warning to their own district:

Yet further how unaccountable and scandalous are the large gatherings and unbecoming behaviour at burials and 'lake-wacks,' also in some places how many are grossly unmannerly in coming to burials without invitation. How extravagant are many in their preparations for such occasions, and in giving much drink, and driving it too frequently, before and after the corpse is enterred, and keeping the company too long together; how many scandalouslie drink until they be drunk on such occasions; this practice cannot but be hurtfull, therefore ought to be discouraged and reformed, and people that are not ashamed to be so vilely unmannerly as to thrust themselves into such meetings without being called ought to be affronted.

Despite protest and counsel, however, the custom of supplying refreshment to mourners in the form of 'services' lingered until well into the nineteenth century.

After the funeral, certain old rites and customs were carried out. On the death of a tenant the mart, or herezeld (heriot, or best aucht) was seized by the landowner to substantiate his title. The bed and straw on which the deceased had lain were burned in the open field. Concerning this practice, Joseph Train, in a note to *Strains of the Mountain Muse*, describes how, 'as soon as the corpse is taken from the bed on which the person died, all the straw or heather of which it was composed is taken out and burned in a place where no beast can get near it, and they pretend to find next morning in the ashes the print of the foot of that person in the family who shall die first'.

A short reference may here be made to the custom of burial without coffin.

The spirit of economy went far indeed in these older days, for burial, particularly of the poor, took place either without a coffin at all, or they were carried to the grave in one of common and general use, from which they were removed and buried when the grave-side was reached.

A doubtful advance upon this method was the introduction of the 'slip-coffin,' which permitted of a bolt being drawn when lowered to the bottom of the grave. A hinged bottom was in this way relieved, which left the poor dead body in the closest of contact with mother earth. The motive, of course, was economy, and its use practically restricted to paupers.

On the authority of Edgar, author of *Old Church Life in Scotland* (1886), it is gratifying to note that none of these uncoffined interments had taken place in the South of Scotland for at least 150 years.

. . . Before the days of hearses the coffin was borne to the grave on two long poles or hand-spokes. Over the simple bare coffin the 'mort-cloth' was spread, for the use of which the 'Kirk-Session' made a charge, the money received being devoted to the relief of the poor of the parish. As superstitious custom refused the rites of Christian burial to those who died by their own hand, so was also the use of the 'mort-cloth' withheld.

Until comparatively recent days the bodies of suicides were buried at the meeting of four cross roads, or at all events at some lonely, unfrequented spot, the remains having not unusually the additional indignity of being impaled by a stake practised upon them. It is of interest to note that the name of the 'Stake Moss', Sanquhar, may be traced to this callous practice.

A superstition of the churchyard itself that still lingers and is worthy of notice is that the north side is less hallowed than the other portions of 'God's Acre.' The origin of this comes from the Scriptural description of the last judgement (Matthew xxv), which tells how: 'He shall set the sheep on His right hand, but the goats on His left.'

A recent local writer has thus embodied the idea and its probable derivation:

> This superstition (he says) is said to have originated in the New Testament story of the Day of Judgement, when the Lord on entering His house (the entrance of the old churches being at the west end, or on the south near the west) would separate the sheep from the goats – the former to His right hand, the south; and the latter to His left, the north. Our forefathers would not see their dear ones among the goats, 'for evil,' said they, 'is there'. This credulous imagining is not exemplified in the kirkyard alone. Many of our old pre-Reformation churches exhibit evidence of the superstition in the entire absence of windows in their north walls; and in general it would appear that in mediaeval times there was a common belief in the evil influence of the north, and that thence came all kinds of ill.
>
> In Sanquhar Kirkyard it is evident that the superstition prevailed until comparatively modern times, for there are no headstones on the north side of the kirk earlier than the beginning of the last century, all the older monuments being to the south of the kirk, and at its east and west ends.

To the simple earnest dweller in the country there comes at times the thought that brings with it a comfort all its own, that after 'life's fitful fever' they will be quietly laid to rest underneath the green turf, within the shadow of the kirk itself. Of this the origin of Carsphairn parish, in the uplands of Galloway, gives telling proof; for in the year 1645 complaint was made to the Scottish Parliament that in the parishes of Dalry and Kells numbers of people had to be buried in the fields, because the houses in which they lived and died were twelve miles from a churchyard. The issue of this was that the district of Carsphairn was erected into a separate parish, and the indignity of such burials came to an end.

Before closing a chapter devoted to 'death custom' and 'funeral ceremony,' the use of the 'dead bell' must certainly be referred to.

In these old days when methods of conveying news and information were restricted, it was the routine practice when a death occurred for the 'beadle' (sexton) to go, bell in hand, around the district, pausing at intervals to ring the 'passing bell' more particularly in front of the houses of friends of the deceased, announcing at the same time not only the death but also the day of burial. The usual form of his intimation which, with uncovered head, he delivered was:

Brethren and sisters, I hereby let ye to wit that our brother (or sister), named (name, address, and occupation), departed this life at — of the clock, according to the pleasure of Almighty God, and you are all invited to attend the funeral on —.

Particular reference to this custom in the town of Dumfries is given in the Itinerary of John Ray, naturalist, who visited the town in August, 1662:

Here (he says) . . . we observed the manner of their burials, which is this: when anyone dies the sexton or bellman goeth about the streets, with a small bell in his hand, which he tinkleth all along as he goeth, and now and then he makes a stance, and proclaims who is dead, and invites the people to come to the funeral.

On the day of the funeral it was again customary for the 'beadle' to ring the bell, walking in front of the funeral procession, ringing it as he went. This is also noticed by Ray, who notes that: 'The people and ministers . . . accompany the corpse to the grave . . . with the bell before them.' This usage has passed to a form, common enough to this day, particularly in the country, of tolling the church bell as the funeral cortege approaches the churchyard.

In the scarce *Book of Galloway* it is recorded how 'the beadle had rung the "passing bell" on the bellknowe of Penninghame, and it was heard again when the mourners approached the graveyard.'

The ringing of the 'dead bell' had its origin in the superstitious idea that by this means evil spirits were held at bay.[34]

Emily Smith
Sanquhar, 2001

If someone had died in the village, all of the houses would close their curtains when the hearse came into the village, and open them when it went away. My Dad was always told that if you see a funeral procession you must stand still and show respect. I have also heard that you must touch something black if a funeral procession passes you. And of course, you wear black or dark colours if you ever go to a funeral.[35]

---

[34] J. Maxwell Wood, *Witchcraft and Superstitions Record in the South-Western District of Scotland*, 1911, pp. 216–21, 223–29, 234–37, 239–43.
[35] From Emily's essay, written while a student (aged 19) in my folklore class at the Royal Scottish Academy of Music and Drama.

Death and Burial in an East Lothian Mining Community

Marianne Holligan
Newcraighall, 1993

MH Some of my earliest memories are about death. Not just about the wakes and funerals, but people dying. It was all around us. Pneumoconiosis and TB. The terrible hacking coughs. The same story at the Bath St School and the same at the Creamery. There were many diseases and the mortality rate amongst my school friends was high. Within a single fortnight two of my cousins died of TB. I heard them say once that a man was pushing a wheel-barrow along one day and the polis stopped him. They wanted to know where he was going. He told them he was just off to bury his dead child.

I remember coming in from the school one day and there, lying on the floor, was the long bearded figure of my Uncle Jim; he was like Jesus, stretched out on the carpet. He'd been killed in the pit. That was that. You had to clean and wash them yourself, that was all your responsibility. We held a wake that went on for a week and on funeral day all the people drew down their blinds. Nobody does that now. When somebody died in the village we had the wake and then the funeral and then the mourning.

Then, I was in my granny's a couple of doors down in Newcraighall. She was sitting in the big chair specially reserved for the man of the house, when in came a party of miners down from the pit, with my second grandfather, Robert Wood, on a rough made stretcher. Dead. The blood was still running out of him. He'd fallen over an incline in the Klondyke pit and had been killed. He was just laid out on the carpet, there was no ceremony.

After the death of my dear second grandfather, granny was mourning. [Grandfather] Wood had converted to the Faith. A good man and a member of so many societies, Temperance and the like. It had been a good life with him. I remember my granny was rocking backwards and forwards. She wasn't going to live long, [she'd say] 'Ah think ah'm gonnae dee.' I'd run home to tell my mother. [And she'd say] 'Och, yer granny's always sayin that.'

Granny would walk up and down on the living room floor, dump herself, put her pinny up and go, 'Oh my!' I stayed with my granny for four years. Mother would say, 'Come on now, your granny will be waiting on ye.'

I wanted to go and play. I think that I was maybe five or six years old for I was in Class 2 at the school. I had to go over and kneel down at the table with my granny, whilst she said the rosary. Then when it was time to go to sleep with her, I'd hear the rustling of the brown paper on my granny's chest.

One day I was sent over to get a sharp knife for granny who was making tablet for a charity. I was to come down early that night because she thought that she was going to die. It came close to the time when I was to go to granny's to say the rosary. I wasn't going to go, no, I was going to go out and play instead. Mother was angry. Now that was the first time that I can recall disobeying my mother. Something told me not to go down that night. In the morning, my granny was found dead. She was maybe sixty years old.

In the village, news of a death went around like lightning. If the fella that had died was maybe poor, they'd get up a collection for his funeral. Sometimes they'd be lucky to get threepence for someone, but everybody gave. Two women rapping on a door.

'Huv ye anything tae gi us fi Mr Pride's funeral?'

Then there were the wakes. My granny and my mother told me everything. Everybody would try to get into the wake house. It wasn't for the love of the man in the bed but for the eats. My granny lent out her two linen sheets for the wake house. She'd fix one sheet up over the wall with a washing pole and rope, the other one went over the corpse. Sometimes the houses were in a terrible state. The sheet that went over the wall would cover up the dirty green dado walls, once they'd been a light and dark green, now they were all grimy with smoke. My mother said that she could smell bugs in a house. Well, in one case the beasts were crawling all over the white sheet. So at the wake the body was supposed to be lying there for seven days whilst folk came in to say their prayers for the dead. It was, 'Wull now go doon on wur knees and say a prayer for [the deceased].'

Prayers for the dead. Since Vatican Two [1962], now we'd say prayers for the dying, the sick, and the dead. Vatican Two has changed all that. But anyway, they were there because they were going to say a prayer and because they were fond of the corpse – but, no, no! They had their eyes on the banked up slices of bread. That was it, and of course in many cases people were hungry, they couldn't wait to get stuck into the food and drink. Those with the better wages, they didn't come, but the oncost men and the Irishmen working in the potato fields did.

When you stepped into the wake house, on a table set with two brass candles and decorative white fancy cut paper, there'd be all this food and drink. There were pieces with corned beef, jam and cheese. I think the corned beef was threepence per quarter. Then there were saucers of snuff, cigarettes, a few clay pipes and thick black pipe tobacco. Along with the food, there was the drink. Whisky, which my dad was always sent down to Joppa to get. Then there was cheap beer that we called 'porters'. There wasn't enough drink for them to get drunk though. Those who didn't take a drink had tea and cocoa. They'd all kneel down and say about two prayers, [then]: 'Eh well, I think we'll stop now and we'll have a little sandwich and a little bit of water.' It wasn't water, it was the sixpenny gill – whisky!

So this big fellow says about his father, who hadn't treated his wife too well, 'Wull now go down on our knees and say a dacoit of the rosary for my father who is a bright angel in heaven.'

Now a 'dacoit' is a bandit, he should have said a decade, ten 'Hail Mary's of the Rosary. When it was all over and they'd gone home my mother or granny would say, 'Did ye hear that, a bright angel? Never worked a day in his life and always hitting her. Well if that's a bright angel, we can get in any time!'

There were a couple of other things about wakes too. My granny when she was lifting a corpse would say, [if] this corpse's wrists are too supple, there will be another one to follow.

I had to touch them. In those days Catholics were laid out in their habits. Shrouds. These were brown with a cowl, people who had lain there for ages with the wee peaked nose, no teeth and all yelly and parched, 'Come on here and touch its brow . . . and ye'll no dream aboot them.'

Well I was frightened, frightened. When I was out running a message in the dark – for there wasn't any [street] light – I thought that they were going in front of me.

The 'corp' as my daddy called it, after about a week of lying there he would say, 'talked back at ye'. Many's the smell that wasn't too nice either. Sometimes you'd be in there and you would see the corpse's chest moving – as if he was breathing – but it was all in the head. When I went into the house, the beds as I've said were just deals or dales, long planks against the wall with legs and a bit spar. They with bigger families or poorer would burn up the odd deal. Maybe they were waiting on the half ton of coal. For a mattress, they had ticking and straw or a flock one. That might be down the hole at the back, so it was bolstered up with other things.

Now at one of these wakes, granny and mother told me about a man, Mr Pride? He had lain a long time, he was one of these emaciated crowd. They were asked around to the wake because the man's wife, well, she couldn't get his knees to go down. See, he'd died with his knees up, I think that was because he slept that way. They couldn't get enough purchase to get them down because they couldn't push too hard for he lay on about three deals.

After a struggle, my mother got one of Paddy Carr's wooden tubs and put that on, they moved a little, then she went back and got her wringer and she put that into the tub. Well, it was crowded in there and somebody went to sit down on a deal for a wee rest. There weren't enough deals for they'd burnt one up. This corpse just about catapulted up into the air as if he was still alive. Total panic. People were screaming that the man in the bed wasn't dead at all, 'Holy murder!'

They all ran out of there and into their own houses. Eventually somebody ventured back to see what had happened. Then a bright spark went down to Niddrie Mill to get Joiner Wilson. It's the Craigmillar scheme now. Wilson was the undertaker, wheelwright, joiner, carpenter and blacksmith. He was everything. He came down on his bike. It was rigor mortis. He just snipped the legs under the knee at the tendons and they went down fine.

People wore mourning for years after, they were terrible for that. They were always in deep black for years to come. They didn't wear any colours. Then came funeral day, the day of the funeral. Joiner Wilson would come along with his hearse, and the horses. They were jet black and they had black satin headdresses with large bows, plumes. They really frightened me. Out came the black suits, kept for funerals. Then there were the vicuna shirts, the bowler hats – they cost 2/11d. each. If they didn't have a bowler, they borrowed one. If they were taking part, they wore no bonnet. They that weren't taking part took their bonnets off as the cortege passed.

Everyone's blinds were drawn down on funeral day. If they hadn't any blinds, then curtains were hung over the windows. The men that had them assembled in striped trousers and brown boots. It was never black boots, just these brown things with basket woven uppers, they were light coloured. A whole line of miners. The funeral took place either at Liberton, or at Mount. Vernon . . . They'd walk away behind the hearse, up the Craigmillar Road by the castle. When they came to Speed's pub on the corner, the corpse could go where it liked. They stayed there and drank; they were tired from all the walking.

Sometimes the driver couldn't wait, for there was a time limit, so the hearse would go away into the cemetery with nobody – bar a few relatives. No women, oh no. The Canon wouldn't allow it – only men went to the funeral. You could tell what like of a funeral it was by the coffin. An orange box meant that they were being buried on the parish. The box was draped over with a piece of mauve coloured brocade. My mother would say, 'Oh my, a parish funeral.' It was a great scandal if you were buried on the parish. See, it cost about a fiver to get buried and the collections that were held didn't often raise that kind of money. They were weeks and weeks after it paying for the funeral. If anybody died, they were too poor and they were going to be buried in parish ground, my granny would let them into her ground. Oh aye, they're all mixter-maxter in Mount Vernon. I've all my people in there, that grandfather, right far back. All my people are up at Mount Vernon, layers and layers and layers. Catholics have to get cremated nowadays for there isn't the ground. We have to go the modern way, though it used to be that we didn't get cremated for if you were, your soul wouldn't go to heaven.[36]

---

[36] Marianne Holligan was recorded in Portobello by Alan Bruford with Chris Higham who transcribed the tapes after Dr Bruford's death in 1996.

Funerals in the Outer Hebrides

Douglas Neally
Stornoway, 1992

DN Lewis funerals are always very well attended . . . How did you manage to tell people about death?

LM In the country [when I was young] two young boys, say twelve, thirteen years old, were asked to go round the village to tell what time the coffin was to be lifted away. As a matter of fact [when we were boys] we were guilty of waiting for someone to die so we could earn two or three pennies for doing it, usually a sixpence!

LW When a death happened in the village long ago the horn was blown, that everyone could hear, and everyone knew that somebody died, and they would stop working till the funeral was over.

DN What happens nowadays?

LU The undertakers put [death notices] up in the town, so we usually write out about fifteen, and there's various shops in the town that have notices, so if you're passing any day you'll check, 'cos you know that shop usually carries a death notice – you just check up out of interest . . . it gives you the person's name, their address, when the service is on, when the funeral is leaving, and where it's going to, and if there's flowers [or] sometimes they might ask 'No flowers by request' . . . And in the country areas one person is nominated, well, one person in a village is usually in the know about things. If you phone that person they'll tell you when the service is on, if it's going to be from the house or if it's going to be from the church, when it's leaving and where it's going to . . . [news] passes from place to place quite quickly. It's usually well organised in the country areas.

DN What happens between death and the funeral?

LM Well, the curtains are closed in the room where the body is lying . . . The first night the body is coffined it is usually laid on the bed out of which the body came, and some member of the family takes friends in, friends of the person who has died. The tradition is that they view the body and touch it; they put their hands on the forehead. But they say that people aren't very fond of going to do this, but if they don't touch it, it's very, very hard for them to get the sight out of their minds . . . that's the difference.

DN Usually in Lewis the funeral leaves from the house and takes place around lunchtime or early afternoon. Each room in the house is full of mourners attending the service which starts half an hour before the funeral is said to leave. In the town it, however, is not uncommon for funerals to leave from the church, because it is more convenient for all parties involved. The service itself lasts about half an hour, and consists of prayers, reading and singing, in either English or Gaelic. While the service is going on, many more male mourners gather outside the house to join the funeral procession. From my own experience, this is what usually happens: the coffin is brought out of the house and on to the road where the men begin to form a line in pairs; it is only men who join the funeral. In front of the coffin is a group of men known as 'Head Mourners', who are called by the undertaker, or someone in the village, to lead the procession. The coffin is placed on a bearer, and on each side of it there are four positions where the men carry the coffin, thus it is carried in groups of eight. The undertaker calls the ministers, the elders and the cousins to take the first lift of the coffin. The funeral moves away in the direction of the graveyard, and the curtains or blinds in the house are opened just as it is about to go . . . The women of Lewis have a very small part to play when it comes to funerals; they don't join the procession but stay in the house or in the garden and watch it from a distance . . . they usually stay at home and prepare a big meal for the men coming back, and they look after the children.

LM At my father's funeral a family relation from Dingwall who had never seen a funeral in Lewis [arrived]; he couldn't get over the orderliness with which it was carried along. All coffins are carried for about half a mile to a mile; it usually depends on availability of people and the weather. You walk up, there are four abreast. You walk up to the front of the coffin and you move on to the handles of the bearer, and that man comes on to the centre, and the next moves to the handle behind. In that way everyone who comes to the funeral handles the bearer and pays their respects. For all the world you would think they were trained. [This visitor] couldn't get over the orderliness and manners there was in everybody paying their respects on the way to the graveyard.

DN At both ends of the coffin there are two cords that are to be carried by the closest relatives . . . do you know when these cords started to appear at Lewis funerals?

LM I couldn't really tell you, I think they were in the town [of Stornoway] before the war, probably for the society of the town.

DN What about mourning clothes?

LM In my young days [everyone] wore black, they were black from their shoes to their hat. Widowers wore a crepe black diamond or bandage on their arm and a black tie.

DN How long did the widower do this?

LM Usually about a year.

LW Widows go into black, very often for the rest of their lives, like my own mother. They wore a 'fall' long ago, made of black crepe hanging down behind their bonnets.

LM Girls usually went into black clothes, black coat, and boys a black tie. But they've now very much come away from that.[37]

---

[37] Tape recordings were made by Douglas Neally (aged 20) in March 1992 when he was at home on holiday from Edinburgh University. Informants who did not wish to be named are cited as LM: Local Man, LU: Local Undertaker, and LW: Local Woman. I am extremely grateful to Douglas for allowing me to include this excerpt from his essay, 'Customs and Beliefs about Death in the Island of Lewis Today'.

Alexander Carmichael
Collecting in the Hebrides, 1870s

Isle of Barra

In Barra women leave the house along with the *giùlan*, the body, as it is carried, and go a certain distance. When they resolve to go no further they go upon their knees and pray, lifting the head now and then to look after the departing procession, and again intensifying their supplications and crossing themselves. The scene is striking, impressive and picturesque – a woman here and a woman there and another a little beyond, in tartan gown and tartan *guailleachan*, shoulder-plaid, fastened with a silver or a brass brooch, sometimes a tartan shawl over the head, or a high-crowned mutch . . .[38]

Isles of Lewis, Harris and Skye, 1870s (reflecting on pre-1843)

I obtained four or five versions of this poem in Lewis. A sacred and a secular song had become confused:

> Boineid is it agus breacan is féile . . .
> An t-earradh thig sgiobalt air Clanna nan Gàidheal.

> *Bonnet and feather and tartan plaid . . . [3 times]*
> *The dress that sits bravely on the Sons of the Gael.*

The tune was played at funerals in Lewis, Harris and Skye down to Disruption times [1843], I spoke to people who had heard it played at a funeral at Aoidh, in Lewis. They said that the scene and the tune were singularly impressive – the moaning of the sea, the mourning of the women, and the lament of the pipes over all, as the body was carried to its home of winter, of spring and of summer; never could they forget the solemnity of the occasion, where all was so natural and so beautiful, and nature seemed to join in the feeling of humanity.

> Tha mi dol dachaidh leat
> Go do thaigh! Go do thaigh!
> Tha mi dol dachaidh leat
> Go do thaigh geamhraidh.
> Tha mi dol dachaidh leat
> Go do thaigh! Go do thaigh!
> Tha mi dol dachaidh leat
> Go do thaigh foghair is earraich is samhraidh.

---

[38] A. Carmichael, *Carmina Gadelica*, vol. 3, p. 370.

Tha mi dol dachaidh leat
A leanaibh mo luaidh,
Dha do leaba bhioth-mhaireann
Dha do chadal bhioth-bhuain.
Tha mi dol dachaidh leat
A leanaibh mo luaidh,
Go Macan nam beannachd,
Go Athair nam buadh.

I am going home with thee,
To thy home! To thy home!
I am going home with thee
To thy home of winter.
I am going home with thee,
To thy home! To thy home!

I am going home with thee
To thy home of autumn, of spring and of summer.
I am going home with thee,
Thou child of my love,
To thy eternal bed,
To thy perpetual sleep.
I am going home with thee,
Thou child of my love,
To the dear Son of Blessings,
To the Father of grace.[39]

Trefor M. Owen
North Uist, 1992

The date of the funeral is decided by the closest relatives of the deceased and is usually chosen so as to give relatives from the mainland a chance to be present. This is not always possible. Attendance at the burial service is by invitation only, a custom which is not found, for instance, in the neighbouring region of Harris. In North Uist itself the custom is disliked by many church folk who believe that it allows a 'bad-living' man to be given an undeservedly good funeral merely because care is taken to invite as many people as possible, all of whom attend. If the service were not by invitation, the opponents of the practice contend, the number of people present would

---

[39] A. Carmichael, *Carmina Gadelica*, vol. 3, pp. 378–9.

reflect the character of the deceased. This procedure was adopted when the funeral of a Lochmaddy resident took place. This person, though not of a high status, was well known in all parts of the island since his work brought him in contact with many of the inhabitants. For this reason, and because he had few relatives on the island, his funeral was open to all. The township clerks throughout the island were notified of this decision by phone and were asked to inform everybody in their township. More people turned up than had been expected. Everybody had thought that there would only be very few people present and had accordingly made an effort to attend. Shortly after the funeral one of the district councillors was approached by individuals who suggested that the District Council should impress the desirability of this type of funeral. But nothing came of this.

Invitations are sent to the ministers by letter, but for all other persons they are conveyed by word of mouth, generally by a neighbour or cousin of the bereaved family. In the Paible district all the three ministers are invited to the funerals.

Before the funeral, neighbours and friends call at the house to express their sympathy and to see the dead person in his coffin. People used to bring food to relieve the family of the necessity of baking. In the Sollas area visitors bring baskets of food and money; a table is set especially for this purpose and the baskets emptied on it while the visitors are given a cup of tea. Paible folk say this is more like a wedding than a funeral.

The funeral service is held inside or outside the house, according to the weather. Care is taken that the coffin is inside the house if the service is out of doors, or, if the service is held indoors, that the coffin is in another room. The Free Presbyterians in particular are eager to emphasise in every way that the funeral service does not contain any form of prayer for the dead. The presence of the coffin during the service is indicative or at least suggestive of this Roman Catholic practice in the eyes of the stricter Presbyterians. Prayer offered in the house may contain references to the deceased, but the main emphasis is laid on the consolation of his family. The service lasts from thirty to forty-five minutes and includes (in this order) a prayer, a psalm-reading, psalm-singing, a New Testament reading and a prayer. The deceased's minister takes the service but calls on the two other ministers to take the opening and closing prayers respectively.

After the service in the house the funeral procession moves directly to the cemetery. From houses in the townships adjoining the cemetery, the coffin is carried by the mourners . . . many of the mourners are taken by bus. Funerals from Paible used to be on foot, the six bearers changing every hundred yards or so until all had participated; this is still the practice in Tigharry and

Hougharry, which are near the burial ground. During the procession, a cord leading from the coffin is held by the two nearest male relatives of the deceased, one in front of and the other behind the coffin. Women remain in the house after the service and do not follow the procession.

On arrival at the cemetery the coffin is taken from the car or cart and laid across three poles ready to be carried to the graveside. The company waits until all the men have come out of the bus and lined up behind the coffin. A relative or friend then signals to the mourners that they can line up on either side of the route to the grave. The coffin is then carried by the nearest relatives for the first twenty or thirty yards of the way and is then taken over by friends, the nearest relatives now holding the cord at either end. The minister walks behind the coffin and offers a very short prayer at the graveside. The Free Presbyterians object to a prayer at this point; instead the minister days a few words of advice to the mourners and attendees.

The mourners nowadays disperse once the coffin is lowered in the grave, although formerly refreshments were served to all who attended. A friend of the family would call on those present to come to the church wall, where they would be served with whisky and some biscuits. As was pointed out during this study, the custom has virtually ceased in the west side of the island.

Mourning lasts a year, the men wearing a black diamond on the left arm, and the women black dresses. There is no period of half-mourning dress when the year is completed.[40]

Angus Peter Campbell
South Uist, 2003

'Nis, seo an rud Aonghais' thuirt Damhnall Angaidh leam, 's na deoir na shuilean 's e cuimhneachadh mar a chaill e a bhean aige fhein, Nina, o chionn ghoirid as deidh bhith pòsda còrr is da fhichead bliadhna, 'seo an rud Aonghais – tha am bàs cho 'complete', 's ged a bhiodh tu fhein a-nis beò airson mile bliadhna eile, chan fhaiceadh tu an neach sin anns a' cholainn air an talamh seo gu bràth tuilleadh.'

Translation

'This is the thing, Angus' he said, with tears in his eyes, remembering the loss of his own wife, Nina, after forty years of marriage, 'you see death is so complete, and even if you yourself were now to live for another thousand years you would not see that person in the flesh, on this earth ever again.'

---

[40] This excerpt is from the Appendix to Trefor M. Owen's 'Abstract of Report on Field Work in North Uist, Western Isles' and 'based on an account given by an informant and supplemented by material from other, oral sources.'

I was very moved by his words . . . they faced reality full-on, confronted it, named it, stated it and in so doing helped us deal with the awesome loss that now faced us.

We travelled over from Skye to the island of South Uist, from which I came, for the funeral service at St Peter's Church in Daliburgh and thence down to the graveyard of Hàllainn on the machairland. My brother, who's a priest, officiated at the service, surrounded by seven other priests and led for the Requiem Mass by the Bishop of Argyll and the Isles, the Reverend Iain Murray. The bishop has no Gaelic so he only said, 'Hello', then sat down.

The rest of the requiem service, from the prayers to the unaccompanied singing, from the litany to the eulogy, was conducted entirely in my mother's native language of Gaelic. I know she would have been impressed by the occasion. I could almost feel her peering out of her coffin and saying: 'Goodness – all this for me.' But it was true – all this was for her.

Then we went down to Hàllainn, where her husband, my late father, Eaghainn Mac Aonghais Nill Aonghais Iain Bhain, was buried in the spring of 1980. And alongside him – and alongside her now – lie all the great South Uist bards and storytellers and tradition-bearers and pipers of recent centuries:

Donnchadh mac Dhomhnaill 'ac Dhonnchaidh,
His son, Dòmhnall Iain Dhonnchaidh 'ac Dhomhaill 'ac Dhonnchaidh,
Seonaidh Roidean,
Iain agus Seonaidh MacDhòmhnaill 'ic Iain Bhain,
Bean Eairdsidh Raoghaill,
Iain Pheadair
and so on
and so forth, down to

Calum MacIlleathain, Sorley MacLean's brother Calum, who chose to be buried among the people whom he had come to love the most:

'Tha an saoghal fhathast alainn / Ged nach eil thu ann . . . '
'The world is still beautiful / though you are not in it . . . /Gaelic is eloquent in Uist / though you are in Hàllainn Hill /and your mouth without speech . . .

'A nis faodaidh tu a bhith cinnteach as an seo,' thuirt mo bhrathair Dòmhnall Eòsaph an oidhche ron tòrradh – '
'Now you can be sure of this,' my younger brother Donald Joseph, who

still lives in South Uist told me the night before the funeral, 'that when we reach Hàllainn that Alasdair Nill Ruaraidh will be at the front of the queue waiting to grab the spade to be the first to fill in the grave . . .'

And sure enough, come the day, come the man. It was beautiful, crystal clear, with not a breath of wind and as we stood around the grave I found it to be an awesome experience. As I glanced around I saw and recognized, or half-recognized, or remembered, or half-remembered, or imagined I remembered, a host of faces whom I hadn't seen, or remembered or imagined, since the last time I'd stood there at my father's funeral twenty-two years previously. The faces were the faces of the sons and brothers and daughters and mothers and wives of faces I remembered – faces of the sons and daughters of old men and women whom I'd known in my childhood, and who stretched back as far as time itself, beyond the trenches, beyond the Land Raids, beyond the Cathcart burnings, beyond Alexander Carmichael, beyond Napoleon, beyond Culloden, beyond measure or comprehension. It was a very old thing, and a very noble thing.

Once the last formal rites were done, these young ancient men got to work. At that critical final point no one left, as they do on the mainland now, as they even do in Skye now, for the cup of tea. The entire community remained to see the coffin covered with sand, to see the clods of grass stamped down, to see the job, as it were, completely through. There was no individual or communal pretence that death had not happened; no half-turning away as if its finality was not real. Its completeness, as Donald Angie had rightly said, was not shied away from.

It was a very old, a very communal, a very South Uist tradition I was experiencing; I also realize it was a very awesome and a very privileged experience.

Later, the following day, walking through the villages of my childhood, I told my wife Lyndsay who lived in this house when I was a child in the 1950s; and who harvested that field; and whose peat-stack used to stand there; and I realized, perhaps for the first time ever, that it was completely gone, all of it, forever.[41]

---

[41] Angus Peter Campbell from South Uist represented Scotland at the Celtic Congress in Dublin, August 2003. This excerpt is from his speech in which he addressed issues of cultural retention and change in Gaelic Scotland.

Funerals in Badenoch and Strathspey

Elizabeth Grant of Rothiemurchus
1813

Jane and I were taken to Inverdruie. We had never seen a corpse, and the Captain had died so serenely . . . either 84 or 86 years of age . . . he lay there as if sleeping . . . on the bed in the best room; it had a shirt well ruffled, a night cap, and the hands were crossed over the breast. A white sheet was spread over all . . . Two bottles of wine and a plate of seed cake were on one small table, bread, cheese, butter, and whisky on another . . . offered by the solitary watcher, a decent comely woman . . .

I shall never forget the day of the funeral, the fifth day from the death . . . [The widow's] weeds had arrived, and remarkably well she looked in them . . . At length my father arrived with a paper in hand, and it was the list of the pall-bearers . . .

Hundreds attended the funeral. A young girl in her usual best attire walked first, then the coffin, borne by four sets of broad shoulders, extra bearers grouping round, as the distance was a couple of miles at least to the kirkyard . . . all fell in according to their rank without being marshalled – Highlanders never presume, their innate good breeding never subjecting them to a forced descent from too honourable a place . . .

My father gave the funeral feast at Doune. Most of the friends of fit degree accompanied him home to dinner . . . and very merry they were. All sorts of pleasant stories went round with the wine bottles, clergy and all, and the Parsons of Alvie and Abernethy were both there, as well as our own minister of Duthill . . .[42]

Christina [Ciorstaigh] Docherty
Kingussie, 1992

CD My own family were buried in St Kenneth's in Laggan, because that's the Catholic burial ground for the area. So my grandparents and my parents are both buried in St Kenneth's in Laggan . . .

My father used to say that they walked over the hill roads with the funeral procession when he was a young man . . . well, I suppose if it was a non-Catholic funeral, the funeral would start off from the house. And they would walk in

---

[42] Elizabeth Grant, *Memoirs of a Highland Lady: Elizabeth Grant of Rothiemurchus*, excerpted from her detailed description, pp. 304–09, vol. I, 1988 edition.

procession to the graveyard which could be some distance in Laggan 'cos it's quite
scattered. I think St Kenneth's was used for a number of years and then there are
cemeteries at Laggan Bridge and also beside the Monaliath Hotel. It could be a fair
distance to any of them.

MB *What sort of distances are you talking about, say to St Kenneth's from Laggan?*

CD Oh, you're talking about a good ten miles there, I would imagine, yes . . . I
suppose there would be a fair dram drunk on the way too [laughs], I would imagine
so! They would need something to keep them going . . . My father said there was
certain points where they had cairns, wee cairns, you know, where they would put
a stone in the passing. I suppose that's some of the heaps of stones we come across
nowadays, but they had sort of cairns to mark . . . like a resting place. You put a
stone on the cairn on the way past.

MB *What did they wear?*

CD Oh, black. Black, it wasn't even grey, it was black. I remember my mother being
absolutely horrified that I hadn't changed into everything black when my auntie
died – immediately. And that's in the 1960s. You were supposed to wear black for
a couple of months anyway; it was expected . . .

MB *And did you ever see men with arm bands?*

CD Oh yes, my father wore a black arm band for several weeks after all his own family
died. Just took it from jacket to jacket [during his ordinary working days]. Yes, it
was quite common practice. And in the days before telephones, and people
phoning up or putting up notices, they used to have a black-edged letter come in
for a funeral – the white vellum paper with the black edging on the envelope and
the notepaper, to notify you of a funeral. You know, you always sort of dreaded
getting one of those through the post . . . and I haven't seen any of these for years.[43]

Rosie and Dougald Campbell
Badenoch, 1992

MB *How long would the body remain in the house before the funeral?*

RC Well, they were usually three days – about three days, yes, at the most. Say if they
died on the Sunday, there would be Monday, Tuesday, and by Wednesday the
funeral would be.

MB *And who would dig the grave?*

RC Oh well, there was always some men that did that, and just got paid for digging
the grave. Men from different areas, like in Laggan certain ones would come and
dig the grave. The relations seen about paying them, giving them something, yes.

MB *Was it ever so cold and snowy and frosty they couldn't manage?*

---

[43] Mrs Docherty was recorded in her home at Torcroy, near Kingussie, by MB on
15 March 1992. Track B of SA1985/131.

RC Oh yes, but I've never seen them that they couldn't open one, no. But of course another thing they usually got was a half bottle [*laughs*] or a bottle [of whisky], some of them [*laughs*]. Sometimes I've seen my father being afraid that some of the Laggan ones they would be in the grave themselves! [*laughs*] Father watching them, he thought some of them had too much [to drink], he'd be keepin an eye on them [*laughs*] in the old days, that's when I was quite young. I used to flee around on a tricycle and go along by the churchyard, and turn round about along there, and that!

MB *So you saw everything that was going on?*

RC Yes, yes. I was born in the [apartment above the] shop . . . and then the churchyard and that was just along the road from it.

MB *[And you could see all the local funerals?]*

RC . . . My father had what they call a horse van, and let's say [the funeral] was from Catlodge or Balgowan, and the coffin was [in it], after a certain distance they laid it [down], and he just led his horse. And then when they came to near the churchyard – on the other side of the bridge if you were coming in from the Catlodge side of the river [Spey]. They stopped on the other side of the bridge and took the coffin, carried it again to the churchyard – when I was a child [in the 1920s].

MB *Did the men take it in turns?*

RC Yes, in fours they did it . . .

DC Yes, fours: two at the front and two at the back.

RC The next four walk in again . . . and that ones drop to the back till it comes up till their turn again if you had a long way to take it.

MB *Do you see anything like that nowadays?*

RC No, you don't. The hearse goes right to the church gates and sometimes right in.

MB *Did the women go to the grave?*

RC No, not in these days. No, no, no, never. It was a very rare occasion, unless they came from the south, like up on the train with the remains.

DC That was pretty standard, the women didn't go.

RC I can remember when outside the churchyard – I would be along at the front of the shop [very near the church] as a child – there would be bottles of whisky going round. Certain men, you asked certain men to go round with them. And they'd the lid of a biscuit tin with biscuits and cheese. And everybody got that – it was usually Abernethy or Rich Tea, a plain biscuit with cheese on it. I can remember as long as that went on in Laggan . . . *outside* the gates – there was no whisky served *in* the churchyard . . . It's years since I saw that being done . . . up until the war it would have been done . . .

DC I'm sure that was done when Duncan MacPherson of Glentruim died, there was biscuits and cheese went round then . . . He was the last of the real old Highland lairds, really.

RC Were you not at [MacPherson of] Cluny's funeral?

DC Yes, I played at Cluny's funeral.

MB *Was it customary to play pipes at a funeral?*

DC Yes, oh, at a laird's funeral, yes, oh, yes, aye.

RC And at certain people's funerals they still play pipes . . .

DC There was Dr Kenneth MacKay, when his funeral was in Laggan his grand-daughter played the pipes at the funeral . . . at the graveside, after the burial, some of his own compositions, hymn tunes and psalm tunes which he had set to pipe music, she played some of those . . . oh, she's a good piper . . . But the last time it was done in Laggan it was a couple of years ago . . . I played at [that] funeral.

MB . . . *Did people ever have flowers at funerals in days gone by?*

RC Well, more or less there was wreaths always.[44] Since I can remember there would always be wreaths . . . and a lot of people made wreaths themselves . . . Well, it depended on the time of year, of course – heather, and eh, it depended on what flowers were available. They did them themselves, but there was always wreaths as far back as I can remember.

DC Yes, I can remember when my mother died [in Argyllshire] there were several wreaths, and like that, they were made . . . But one wreath that did take my attention – I was only a boy at the time – was one, that being a Campbell, somebody had gone to the trouble of making a wreath out of bog myrtle, you see, because of the Campbell crest and it was very, very nice indeed. Actually, the man who made it was one of Sir James Lithgow's gardeners, so he knew what he was doing, he was quite an expert at it . . . Now that would be about 1923, I would say.[45]

Floral tributes

Doris Rougvie
Huntingtower, Perthshire, 2004

MB *In your time were there always flowers at funerals?*

DR Yes, yes . . . Depending on the season, chrysanthemums were very popular – I think they have a kind of funereal feel about them, it always reminds me of funerals when I smell chrysanths.

---

[44] Though commonplace in Badenoch and in most parts of Scotland, the placing of wreaths and flowers on a grave was by no means standard throughout Scotland. In many of the Hebridean islands, for example, this was virtually unheard of at a local funeral. Wreaths were 'introduced' to many island communities at the end of the First World War, when they began to be placed at local memorials throughout the country as part of Remembrance Sunday, held the second Sunday in November (closest to the 11th), when the entire nation remembers their war dead.
[45] Mr and Mrs Dougald Campbell were recorded at their home in Newtonmore by MB on 15 March 1992. SA1992/01.

MB *So you wouldn't use them in a wedding bouquet?*

DR You would not, no. But you could use roses, and depending on the time, clarkia and things that were out in the summer, and lots of very heavy greenery . . . Wreaths are still probably the most popular, but they have changed a lot – I just love making funeral flowers, and wreaths are very beautiful with lots more flowers on them . . . It's mostly an oasis base . . . I did a special one recently, it was for Andrew Douglas. And [his wife] Sheila knew exactly what she wanted . . . the red roses for the main flower, with a little bit of blue – the colours of – and lots of light greenery, eucalyptus, and she wanted somewhere to have a heart-shape. So I wired individual red roses into a heart and I set it up above the wreath . . . But the shapes that you do, it's a big piece of oasis, and you draw out your shape and cut out the oasis and then you have a mass of flowers to make anything – the Fergie tractor, the John Deer, the horse's head, the car . . . bagpipes, or whatever you want. A thistle is a popular one too. And if you couldn't get the colour, I have to say we went to the car paint shop and got paint we painted the flower the colour we wanted if you couldn't get that colour.

MB *And did you ever dip the flowers, say white carnations, into red ink, so they'd 'drink' the dye and become coloured?*

DR When I first started to work with flowers [1950s], there was a place in Pitcairngreen, a nursery, and there were only white marguerites in those days. This is before the Dutch flowers began to come in and now you get all the wonderful colours. But we picked white marguerites and dipped them in dye the mauve dye, the pink dye, the yellow dye . . . that was the only way you could get the colours . . . I do lots of funerals and a great many for the travellers and they will not allow you to put yellow in at all.

MB *Did you do the bagpipes for Willie MacPhee's funeral wreath? I took the photo but I had no idea who made the arrangement . . . The bagpipes even had drones.*

DR Yes . . . Well, I did all the travellers' funeral flowers.

MB *So you even made the drones too?*

DR Yes. Bamboo, pieces of garden cane, sprayed.

MB *A special tribute for a wonderful piper and storyteller.*

Funeral Customs 'of every rank' in Skye

Macdonald of Kingsburgh

Skye, 1790

On the 5th of March 1790, the ever-memorable Flora departed this life . . . Her death did not take place at her own residence of Kingsburgh, but at Peinduin, a friend's house on the seacoast, about three miles further north.

Flora's remains were shrouded in one of the sheets in which the Prince had slept at the mansion of Kingsburgh. With this sheet, she never parted in all her travels. It was religiously and faithfully preserved by her in North Carolina . . . At length the purpose she intended it for was accomplished, when all that was mortal of herself was wrapt in it by her sorrowing family. Her remains were conveyed under shade of night to Kingsburgh. The coffin was carried shoulder high by a party of stalwart youths procured for the purpose . . . The body lay in state for nearly a week.

At length the funeral day arrived. The procession started at an early hour, as the distance between Kingsburgh and the place of burial is about sixteen miles. The body was interred in the churchyard of Kilmuir . . . The spot is about a mile and a half from the rock . . . near Monkstadt, on which the Prince landed in Skye . . .

The funeral cortège was immense – more than a mile in length – consisting of several thousand of every rank in Skye and the adjacent Isles.

Flora's marriage and funeral, between which there was an interval of forty years, were the most numerously attended of any of which there is any record as having taken place in the Western Isles. Notwithstanding the vast assemblage present, all were liberally supplied with every variety of refreshment. Of genuine 'mountain dew' alone upwards of three hundred gallons were served. About a dozen of pipers from the MacCrimmon and MacArthur colleges in Skye, and from other quarters, simultaneously played the 'Coronach', the usual melancholy lament for departed greatness.[46]

Murdo MacLean and Teenie Stewart

Skye, 1992

MM Mar a bha iad am Portrigh bha àiteachan bha iad a' coiseachd roimh'n bhaile . . . b'abhaist dhaibh bhi coiseachd fad an t-siubhail, ach 'san urram a thoirt dhan a' chorp 's mar a bh'ann choisicheadh iad a mach don drochaid mhór uaireanan 's bha nuair sin a 'hearse' a sin.

---

[46] Excerpted from A. MacGregor, *The Life of Flora Macdonald*, pp. 173–6.

TS Tha feodhainn a dèanamh sin fhathast.

MM Bheil, Teenie? Oh tha. 'It's a [mark of] respect,' och anns an aon àite bha'n duine fuireach.

MB *An robh iad riamh a' gabhail drama?*

MM Oh uill, latha mu dheireadh a ghabh mis' e 's cha robh mi ach gu math òg cho chreid mi nach e athair Seasaidh Mhàrtuinn as na Budhanan . . . bha an tiodhlacadh agus ceann a chladh bha bocsa bhriosgaidean 's e 'water biscuits' a bh'ann 's càise agus an drama. Bha thu faighinn an drama as a' chladh 'son an fheoghain a chaidh fada.

Translation

MM What happened in Portree sometimes they walked through the town . . . they used to walk all the way to honour the body, and what happened, they walked to the big bridge sometimes, and the hearse would be there.

TS Some still do that.

MM Do they, Teenie? Oh, yes, it's a mark of respect, but in the place where the person lived.

MB *Did they ever take a dram?*

MM Oh well, the last time I took one [at a funeral] I was pretty young. I think it was Jessie Martin's father's funeral from the Budhanan [just outside Portree] . . . and at the end of the churchyard there was a box of biscuits; it was water biscuits and cheese, and a dram. There was a dram in the churchyard for those who came a distance.

Iain Nicolson
Uig, Skye, 1988

At the age of 85, Nicolson reflected on funeral customs during his lifetime.

IN Everybody [would be] sympathizing with them so much and even though a neighbour died, the whole place was going idle . . . till after the funeral. Not a turn would be made on any farm or anywhere but what was necessary. No, they would not. They were having respect that way, but not like today – they would be out while they were dead beside them. Aye.

Ach yes, and [in those days] everybody would [help;[47] for example], if I was

---

[47] There are many recordings from all over Scotland of neighbours offering help to the bereaved. Usually it was in the most practical terms, by way of extra furniture, such as lending chairs on which to place the coffin, or by bringing food to the house to help feed the many visitors who arrived. In 1955 Calum MacLean recorded a man in Achiltibuie who described (in Gaelic) a custom of helping a bereaved neighbour by bringing a creel of peats to the house. In his own lifetime he said that all the men in the township did this, but that custom was disappearing as there was less poverty now than in his youth. SA1955/162. Another factor may also be that local funeral customs changed too, and while neighbours once stayed up all night for three days (thus having to heat a house day and night during that time) this was no longer necessary after organised businesses began to take over the procedure.

behind with my farm [harvest], the whole place would come and help me get it in.

MB *How did they send word around [when there was a funeral]?*

IN By post and by [a] local, maybe I would be appointed to go around Earlish to give the word to the people there that [there was] a funeral on such and such a day of such and such a man.

TM And then what would happen in the home?

IN ... Well there was maybe the neighbours who would be going there for the night, watching the remains there and somebody else the next night and third [it] was away; three days you were left. But there was somebody on the wake there; why that is I don't know. Of course they was like this, you know, they were thatched cottages and the doors were open; if a cat would come in he might eat you or do something like that to you.

TM So there was always somebody watching the body?

IN Oh, there would be two; you and I'd be there for the night until the morning, you know, and that was all right.

MB *Would that be in the far room?*

IN Aye, aye. Well, [the body] would be in the coffin right enough. Well, you had to go to the joiner down there in Camus Mór, he was there, MacRaild ... he would be making the coffin, you would send him word ... he knew what [who] you were and he would make the coffin and come up ... Well it was your [MB's] grandmother and Murdo Skudiburgh's mother that put my mother into the coffin. There was no, you know, anybody else or undertaker doing anything like that, but the locals; they were used to it.

MB ... *What sort of grave clothes were commonly used?*

IN Oh, they were putting a shirt ... Oh yes, a white shirt.

MB ... *on men and women both?*

IN Yes, well probably the joiner that was making the coffin would have that.[48]

MB *What cloth was it?*

IN Oh it would be linen ... oh aye, oh yes.

MB ... *down to the toes?*

IN Oh yes down to the toes, yes, yes, and put stockings on too.

MB *White stockings?*

IN Ah hah, well it didn't matter whether white or ... well as long as they were quite

---

[48] Though the joiner would bring a shroud to a house in more recent years when, as 'joiner-undertaker', he took over the responsibility of all aspects of burial, the custom in previous years was that the women of the homes usually kept a shroud in preparation for death. Many women are reported to have been very fine needleworkers who took great care in their preparation. For example, in 1977 D.A. MacDonald recorded (in Gaelic) South Uist sisters Curstaidh and Mairi MacKay describing their mother and other local women who made shrouds beautifully decorated with various shapes, such as scallops, bells and flowers. The custom ceased in the 1930s when shrouds became commercially available. SA1977/49.

good. You were cladding him that way, and you were putting his hands like that [demonstrates by crossing his own forearms].

MB *Across the breast.*

IN [Lying] on his back. Och yes.

MB *And the eyes closed?*

IN Oh yes.

MB *What with?*

IN Oh, they were closed and they were stuck like that.

MB *Did they put pennies on them?*

IN No, I did not notice that. But I've seen them having trouble closing them out, with getting [them staying] open you know.

MB *Did you ever see somebody put the Bible under the jaw?*

IN No, I didn't but I've seen putting a tape right around it here, holding it up to close it. It went like that still you know. But probably when it was there for a time it was frozen up that way.

MB *That's what they did when Lexy, Granny's cousin who lived down in Cùil, when she died. I remember [as a child] seeing her with the pennies on the eyes . . . And the Bible under her chin.*

IN Oh yes, well, that could be then . . . but when it was, when it was cold it would stop [stay] that way.

TM *And then would there be a gathering at the house?*

IN Oh yes, well they['ve] got to come to the house, when they got word that, you know, in such a time . . . [they] made for the house there. [On the day of the funeral], well if it was a good day, you were outside some of you, and some inside. If it was a bad day you were cramming them in the house to keep dry, but now . . . they take you to the church.

MB *Do you think that in those days when the neighbours were involved that it was more meaningful to the family to have somebody they knew [making the arrangements]?*

IN Yes, I think it was and it was showing that there was some sympathy outside your own family, for you, because they was very sympathetic in those days, they were that. Oh yes, they had more respect to one another at the time.[49]

My grandfather, John Stewart, was born in South Cuil, Uig, in 1881.[50] A crofter-fisherman, he lived most of his life in Glenconon, Uig, where he died in October 1973. His funeral is still talked about by numerous individuals

---

[49] Iain Nicolson, *An Sgiobair*, was recorded at Cuidreach, Isle of Skye by MB and T. A. McKean, December 1988. SA1988/65.

[50] His family were cleared from their former home in Glenconon during the ruthless Clearances of the nineteenth century. They were eventually considered for 're-apportionment', which resulted in John Stewart being granted a croft in Glenconon in 1910.

both inside and outside of the family, who invariably comment upon the enormous attendance and remember it as 'the last walking funeral in Uig.' The circumstances and the funeral are recalled here by four individuals who attended, each with a different role, each with a separate point of view.

His daughter Peigi and son Murdo Stewart
Uig, Skye, 1991

PS Bidh cuimhn' agadsa glé mhath a Mhurchaidh air an tiodhlacadh mu dheireadh leis na choisich iad a dh'ionnsaidh a chladh, ann an Uige – tiodhlacadh m'athair.

MB *Ciamar a thachair sin?*

MS Uill, bliadhna no dhà mun do chaochail e, bhiodh e 'n uair sin timchioll air ceitheir fichead 's a deich, tha mi creidsinn; bha mi fhìn 's e fhéin [aig tiodhlacadh] – thug mi 'lift' dha suas gun a [chladh] – chaidh e suas as a chàr còmhla rium. 'A uill,' ars e fhéin, 'B'fheàrr leam fhìn a bhi air coiseachd. Chan eil tiodhlacan an diugh mar a bha iad 'na mo latha-sa.'

'Ach uill,' thubhairt mise rium fhìn – cha d'thubhairt mi guth ris-san, ach bha e bliadhna no dhà beò as deidh sin. Thubhairt mise rium fhìn nam b'urrainn dhomhsa gu faigheadh esan sin – sin a dhèanadh air a shon – gun choisicheamaid a nuas e. Thachair gu robh latha math ann, ach bhiodh a 'hearse' air fuireach nam biodh an t-uisge ann.

MB *. . . Aig an àm nuair a chaochail e, nuair a chaochail Seanair fhéin, an robh 'n eaglais làn?*

MS O bha an eaglais làn.

MB *Có as a thàinig a h-uile duine?*

MS Dìreach as a h-uile cearna – an ìre math as a h-uile cearna dha'n Eilean.

MB *Nuair a thàinig sibh a mach as an eaglais dé thachair? Bha ciste aca nach robh? 'S de thachair a nis?*

MS . . . Tha na nabaidhean a' toirt a-mach na ciste airson a cheud togail.

MB *Agus choisich a h-uile duine?*

MS Choisich. Cha robh sin fad' aca ri dhol, a robh?

MB *'N e sin an tiodhlacadh mu dheireadh leis an robh iad a' coiseachd ann an Uige?*

MS 'Se, tha cuimhne agams' air co dhiubh. Choisich sinn suas bho'n eaglais chun a' chladh.

MB *'S tric a choisich e fhéin e.*

MS . . . 'S e sin e bha e ràdh – gu robh e fada na b'ordaile coiseachd no falbh ann *an* càr – nach e coltas tiodhlacadh a bh'air.[51]

---

[51] Peigi and Murdo Stewart were recorded in Murdo's home in Glenconon, Uig, Skye, in November 1991, by MB. SA1991/99. I am extremely grateful to my mother, Peigi, for transcribing the Gaelic and translation that follows.

Translation

PS You'll remember very well, Murdo, the last funeral that was walked to the churchyard in Uig, Skye – my father's funeral.

MB *How did that come about?*

MS Well, a year or two before he died – he would then be about ninety years of age, I believe, he and I were [at a funeral in Uig] – I gave him a lift to the [graveyard] – he went up in the car with me. 'Ah well' he said, 'I would rather have walked, myself. Funerals today are not what they were in my day.'

'Oh well,' I said to myself – I didn't say anything to him, but he was alive a year or two after that, I said to myself if I could manage it, that he would get that – to do that for him, that we would walk him up [to the graveyard].

[On the day of his funeral], it happened to be a good day, but the hearse would have waited if it had been raining.

MB *. . . When Seanair [Grandfather] died, was the church full?*

MS Oh, the church was full.

MB *Where did everyone come from?*

MS Just from every part, practically from every part of the island.

MB *When they came out of the church what happened? They had the coffin, hadn't they? What happened then?*

MS . . . The neighbours take out the coffin for the first lifting.

MB *And everyone walked?*

MS Yes. That wasn't far for them to go, was it?

MB *Was that the last funeral that was walked?*

MS As far as I remember, anyway. We walked from the church to the graveyard.

MB *Many a time he walked it himself.*

MS That's what he [Seanair] said – that it was a lot more orderly to walk than to go in a car – that that wasn't like a funeral.

Grandchildren who are fortunate enough to enjoy the pleasures of caring, loving grandparents must inevitably face the reality of losing them and the bereavement which accompanies the loss. John Stewart's eleven grandchildren were all young adults when he died, and each one could look back on a childhood made brighter by his life. His death is recalled by one of his grandsons who was 23 years old at the time.

Iain MacLean
Uig, Skye and Munlochy, 1988

MB *The family gathered for days before Seanair [grandfather] died, and there was always someone nearby. After he died who was responsible in Uig for taking care of the body?*

IM Well, it's the district nurse to begin with . . . to clean the body, but the women used to do that at one time. [Then they dressed the body] normally in a white shroud . . . And he was removed to the church . . . oh, it'd be a couple of days, just lying in the church.

MB *Seanair's funeral service of course was all Gaelic, and the psalm-singing and the precenting . . . Growing up in our tradition I would never have been allowed to go to the graveside as a child, or even as a woman – only to the church . . . do you remember after you left the church what was the procedure?*

IM Normally at a funeral nowadays it's the hearse that takes the coffin to the grave, but with Seanair they decided that seeing he had attended so many, and carried so many coffins himself that they would walk to the grave with him. And Murdo was at the head and Peter at the feet of the coffin.

MB *That would be the two sons, his only two sons, the eldest at the head. Would they be carrying a cord?*

IM There would be three at each side and one at each end . . . just attached to the coffin itself, onto the handles, and there'd be a handle at the back of the coffin and at the front. Well in the procession, it was just the head and the feet that the cords were held. The other cords were taken for lowering into the grave . . . held by a succession of relatives.

MB *Were you involved?*

IM I was. And Angus [his eldest grandson] . . . and my brother Alasdair . . . and the closest relatives. Well, it was Alasdair Beag that organised the burial and that. He just called out the names – see, everybody stood around. You don't know whether you're going to be called or not, well, you know there is a chance. He would have consulted Murdo and Peter.

MB *Is he the undertaker?*

IM Well, he was.

MB *Is he also a joiner, a carpenter?*

IM Yes . . . that was the tradition that the joiner is also the undertaker . . . [but] he wouldn't have made that coffin . . . that was long ago.

MB *There was standing room only in the church . . . he was carried by men who had known him . . . And it's hearsay that the whole of the north of Skye virtually would have been at it. What was your own impression?*

IM Of the actual funeral? Oh, it was just overwhelming really – the amount . . . the whole parish of Snizort . . . and the Staffin area, all round that . . . [the procession]'d be nearly a mile [long], around there.

Well, coming out of the church to begin with it's actually the neighbours that carry the coffin out from the church, and it's set outside [on a bier]. It's all the neighbours, his closest neighbours, they do that traditionally. And then you just more or less stand where you can get space . . . See, you set yourself out in sixes up the road to take your turn of carrying the coffin. And some funerals if you've got to carry it quite a distance . . . the gaps are quite far apart so you've got to carry it quite far. But there was so many people there that you only got a few steps really with the coffin and it was handed over to the next . . . that one was carried by the handles . . . Then after you've carried the coffin, well you go away to the beginning of the queue again, and join, and stand in sixes.

To reach the graveyard, oh it'd be more than . . . three-quarters of an hour towards an hour. And I don't think there would be a word spoken really; I don't remember anybody talking. Once you had carried the coffin, after your turn, when you were moving on to the next if you had seen somebody you knew, even suppose you hadn't seen them for a long time, you didn't stop and speak; you would nod and that, but there was no speech at all . . . Oh well, there would have been a lot of people I wouldn't have known there, really. You know their faces from going to communions and that . . . During the service, well, you wouldn't see much emotion; you know you might see straight faces and that, but the thing that stuck in my mind about the service at the graveside was – the minister he was talking about Seanair and his life and that . . . 'What better example?' You know, anybody that took an example from this man couldn't live a better life. And it stuck with me, you know, and you always relate back to that.[52]

Although most people who attended the funeral were from the Isle of Skye, and were therefore thoroughly conversant with local customs and Gaelic, there were several mourners who 'came from away' to pay their last respects to John Stewart. For most of them the funeral was an experience which contrasted with the form of service generally encountered on the mainland.

Iain Johnston
Glasgow, 1991

MB *Iain, you grew up in Glasgow and of course know all about Glasgow traditions, so you can probably . . . notice some differences in the Skye funeral. You once remarked that you attended one that was more memorable than any.*

IJ I know the one you're talking about; that was . . . John Stewart's.

Aye, but the thing I can remember away back in the days when I was brought up in Glasgow [1940s], where they would walk the coffin behind the hearse through the streets, where I was brought up in the east end of Glasgow. But that was pure and simply walking behind a hearse, whereas John Stewart's funeral was totally different, because each and everyone in the village, relatives, the lot, all mixed

---

[52] Ian MacLean, aged 40, from Uig, Skye was recorded by MB in Munlochy, Ross-shire, on 5 June 1988. SA1988/28.

together and helped [to carry the coffin]. The way I see it is they helped take John Stewart to his grave; they took part in it. And you see, funerals today are so impersonal; you go along, it's all done for you, whereas that was everyone taking part. The fact that his [neighbours] went and dug the grave the night before . . . I thought that was magnificent . . .

MB *And you drove up from Glasgow the day of it?*

IJ Aye, but, eh, the memories of that, when folk would come out of the church and line up the big hill for the mile and a half walk to the cemetery.

MB *And they carried him that distance every step of the way?*

IJ Oh aye.

MB *What was it like in the church? Was it full?*

IJ Oh aye. [Packed] . . . And there were three ministers which [to me] is an unusual thing.

MB *What was the [predominant] colour of the congregation?*

IJ Oh, black. They were all in dark mourning clothes, what I would call mourning clothes. I suppose they might have a different name for it . . .   .

MB *Now, he was an old man when he died, he was over 90. Was it a sad occasion or was it something else?*

IJ Oh, there was sadness, there was regret that they'd miss him. Well, as far as I was concerned there was just a few people that I have met in my life that I would say 'I was pleased I knew that person.' and John Stewart was one of them . . . he was a man of very few words, but what he did say was fantastic, eh. He had an aura about him; he was just the last of a race that will never be repeated.

MB *Was the service in Gaelic or English?*

IJ Oh, ninety percent in Gaelic.

MB *[As a non-Gaelic speaker], how did you feel about that?*

IJ Well, that was his language.[53]

MB *Did it make any difference at all to you, or the feeling of the funeral?*

IJ No, there was the last ten minutes in English, but for outsiders like myself, I would imagine. But that was the language that Seanair had worshipped in all his life; in fact it would have been totally wrong to put that service in English. That's the way it was.

MB *Iain, was there a hearse at John Stewart's funeral?*

IJ Of course not; there was no need for one, because the coffin was already in the

---

[53] The importance of language at a traditional funeral is frequently referred to. For example, the last Gaelic funeral service in Staxby, Sutherland, was recalled by Dugald Campbell, who was headmaster in the area at the time of the death of an old man from Melvich. There was no one in the area who could take the service, as the local minister had no Gaelic, so they called on the schoolmaster to take over. I am grateful to Neil MacGregor for this extract from his fieldwork notebook of February 1991.

church when they all arrived. And when folk came out the bier sat [outside the church], and at first I wondered what it was; it was sitting at the foot of the steps.

MB *Was it different to any funeral you'd ever seen?*

IJ Oh aye!

MB *Nothing like anything you'd ever seen?*

IJ Nothing! And then they just brought out the coffin and laid it on [the bier], and if I remember there was Peter, Murdo, his two sons; Murdo 'Tailor', Iain MacLean, that's four; and Angus [Ross] and Alistair MacLean. They were the first six that left, they were the closest. And then I was in the second or third – I think I was in the second lift, the grandson-in-laws . . . we were the second, and when we passed on we walked up to the back of the queue, so it came up to us, and then we took our turn again, and then they walked on up. Yon was some walk for some of the old men, but by heck nobody would be done out of their turn! And it just shows the respect they had for the dead; they would walk him to his resting place.

MB *And walking to the grave, everybody walked the mile and a half. Did everybody there in the whole procession take a turn of carrying it?*

IJ Oh yes, everyone must have had maybe three or four turns. They just lined up the road and you walked maybe twenty or thirty yards and another six [men] took over; they walked twenty to thirty yards and that's how the coffin was carried. Even the old men, seventy odds, took part, because that was their way of showing their respect for the dead . . . I mean he was well liked; people came from all over the island to the funeral, apart from the people and relatives that came from a [further] distance. But it wasn't a sad occasion as such; you know, I've seen mournful occasions, but John Stewart wisnae a mournful type of person.

MB *What about the graveside, when they got to the grave?*

IJ Well, his coffin was carried right to the graveside, and the nearest relatives lowered him into his [grave], and there was a short word at the graveside. The coffin was just laid in. The amazing thing about it is the women who weren't there, who didn't go with the coffin – it was just the men – they could actually see him from the back door of his house where he had lived, [the women could see] him being put into the grave, across the glen . . . The women didn't go to the graveside. It was only the men.

MB *Did anyone ever tell you why that was?*

IJ No, just the done thing.

MB *Where were the women then?*

IJ The women went up to the house to prepare a meal. That's just the way of it.

MB *Did you notice if there were any flowers?*

IJ No, no flowers at all.

MB *Was that a surprise to you?*

IJ Yes, in a way. But in a way I cannae see the place of flowers just to lie at a graveside. It's different if you were to go along later on and over the grave plant some flowers that would be growing as an everlasting tribute.

MB *And afterwards, where do you go?*

IJ Well, all the relatives went back to his house over in Glenconon.

MB *You got a sit down meal . . . and a dram?*

IJ Oh, that was obligatory.

MB *When did you get the dram?*

IJ Oh, after we got to the house . . . But you know, to me that's a totally different attitude to booze . . . in that instance. That was just taking part, a follow-up of the event.

MB *And you went back to Glasgow the same night?*

IJ Aye, aye.

MB *It must have been pretty important to go up to Skye and back in the one day for funeral?*

IJ Not really. If you respect the person, you would do it . . . The whole thing is more personal up there – or was. I'm told that that has gone now, which is a shame, because I'm sure there are people who would like to take part in a funeral.

But just going along to their impersonal crematorium, a few words, coffin disappears, and that's it! It's not the same. I mean, the memory of that funeral will live with me the rest of my life because it was so personal.[54]

The gathering of family and friends after the funeral service and the participation in a meal happens all over Scotland, usually with regional variations. Some have tea and sandwiches, some go to a hotel and sit down to a pre-booked dinner, others proceed to the family home for home-cooked fare. Any of these may seem quite ordinary to those who take part, and it is only when participants cross boundaries and encounter another version of the hospitality that one notices major differences.

Murdo Stewart
Uig

MS Uill . . . tha mi creidsinn gun do ghabh sinn drama, ceart gu leòir . . .

MB *Dh'fhosgladh iad botul nuair a rachadh iad dhachaidh?*

MS Seadh . . .

MB *Agus an nuair sin am biadh?*

MS Tha sin ceart.

MB *Na shuidh sibh mun bhord a ghabhail biadh?*

MS Suidh. Ghabh sinn dinnear direach mar a rinn sinn an diugh. Direach an aon rud, anns an taigh aige fhein . . .

---

[54] Iain Johnston was recorded at his home in Glasgow by MB on 7 July 1991. SA1991/91.

Translation

MS Well . . . I believe we had a dram right enough.

MB *When they all got back to the house they would open a bottle?*

MS Yes indeed.

MB *And then the food?*

MS That's right . . .

MB *Was the meal at the table?*

MS Yes, a proper meal.

MM Just as we had [here] today [Sunday dinner] – same thing.

MB *The same thing: [barley and vegetable broth; home-reared mutton boiled in the broth, turnip and carrots (also cooked in the broth) with boiled potatoes and cabbage; Scotch trifle with whipped cream; tea, home-made fruit cake, and an assortment of bought biscuits.]*

MS The food was down at the house [i.e. the Glenconon home in which John Stewart had lived for over sixty years of his ninety-two years][55]

Watching and Waking

Revd James Napier
Renfrewshire, 1879

After death there came a new class of superstitious fears and practices. The clock was stopped, the looking-glass was covered with a cloth, and all domestic animals were removed from the house until after the funeral. These things were done, however, by many from old custom, and without their knowing the reason why such things were done. Originally the reason for the exclusion of dogs and cats arose from the belief that, if either of these animals should chance to leap over the corpse, and be afterwards permitted to live, the devil would gain power over the dead person.

When the corpse was laid out, a plate of salt was placed upon the breast,

---

[55] This excerpt is a continuation of the discussion (above) recorded in Glenconon just after we had finished Sunday dinner together. My own childhood recollections of Sunday dinner in Glenconon (in a home where fish was more often the mid-week fare) are completely consistent with this; there was always home-raised mutton, as often as not from the barrel of dry-salted mutton that my grandfather kept. The desert or sweet (always referred to as 'pudding' regardless of what it was) usually consisted of fruit (raspberries picked from the bottom of the croft in summertime, or tinned fruit when there were no fresh berries) or jelly, and always with as much cream as anyone wanted, as several pints were set aside from Saturday's milking. The tea with cake and biscuits were also in keeping with what I regarded as 'special for Sunday.'

ostensibly to prevent the body swelling.[56] Many did so in this belief, but its original purpose was to act as a charm against the devil to prevent him from disturbing the body. In some localities the plate of salt was supplemented with another filled with earth.[57] A symbolical meaning was given for this; that the earth represented the corporeal body, the earthly house, the salt the heavenly state of the soul. But there was an older superstition which gave another explanation for the plate of salt on the breast. There were persons calling themselves '*sin eaters*,' who, when a person died, were sent for to come and eat the sins of the deceased. When they came, their *modus operandi* was to place a plate of salt and a plate of bread on the breast of the corpse, and repeat a series of incantations, after which they ate the contents of the plates, and so relieved the dead person of such sins as would have kept him hovering around his relations, haunting them with his imperfectly purified spirit, to their great annoyance, and without satisfaction to himself. This form of superstition has evidently a close relation to such forms of ancestor-worship as we know were practised by the ancients, and to which reference has already been made.

Until the funeral, it was the practice for some of the relations or friends to sit up all night, and watch the corpse. In my young days this duty was generally undertaken by youths, male and female friends, who volunteered their services; but these watchings were not accompanied by the unseemly revelries which were common in Scotland in earlier times, or as are still practised in Ireland. The company sitting up with the corpse generally numbered from two to six, although I have myself been one of ten. They went to the house about ten in the evening, and before the relations went to bed each received a glass of spirits; about midnight there was a refreshment of tea or ale and bread, and the same in the morning, when the relations of the deceased relieved the watchers. Although during these night sittings nothing unbefitting the solemnity of the occasion was done, the circumstances of the meeting gave opportunity for love-making.[58] The first portion of the night was generally passed in reading, some one reading aloud for the benefit of the company; afterwards they got to story-telling, the stories being generally of a

---

[56] There are several fairly recent accounts of this from oral tradition: In 1971 D.A. MacDonald recorded Donald Alasdair Johnson of South Uist telling that he had seen a dish of salt on a corpse but did not know why it was done. He remarked that some people still did this. SA1971/102. This was also recorded in 1977 from several other people in South Uist who said that both Catholics and Protestants were accustomed to doing this, and some still do. SA1977/49 and SA1977/54.

[57] Aonghas MhicAndra of North Uist, recorded by D.A. MacDonald in 1977, confirmed this fact, and explained that the dish of salt and earth were laid on top of the shroud to stop the body from swelling. He had done this himself. SA1977/58.

[58] Match-making, or, in twentieth century terms, 'chatting-up'.

ghostly description, producing such a weird feeling, that most of the company durst hardly look behind them for terror, and would start at the slightest noise. I have seen some so affected by this fear that they would not venture to the door alone if the morning was dark. These watchings of the dead were no doubt efficacious in perpetuating superstitious ideas.

The reasons given for watching the corpse differed in different localities. The practice is still observed, I believe, in some places; but probably now it is more the result of habit – a custom followed without any basis of definite belief, and merely as a mark of respect for the dead; but in former times, and within this century, it was firmly held that if the corpse were not watched, the devil would carry off the body, and many stories were current of such an awful result having happened. One such story was told me by a person who had received the story from a person who was present at the wake where the occurrence happened. I thus got it at second hand. The story ran as follows.

The corpse was laid out in a room, and the watchers had retired to another apartment to partake of refreshments, having shut the door of the room where the corpse lay. While they were eating there was heard a great noise, as of a struggle between two persons, proceeding from the room where the corpse lay. None of the party would venture into the room, and in this emergency they sent for the minister, who came, and, with the open Bible in his hand, entered the room and shut the door. The noise then ceased, and in about ten minutes he came out, lifted the tongs from the fireplace, and again re-entered the room. When he came out again, he brought out with the tongs a glove, which was seen to be bloody, and this he put into the fire. He refused, however, to tell either what he had seen or heard; but on the watchers returning to their post, the corpse lay as formerly, and as quiet and unruffled as if nothing had taken place, whereat they were all surprised.

From the death till the funeral it was customary for neighbours to call and see the corpse, and should any one see it and not touch it, that person would be haunted for several nights with fearful dreams. I have seen young children and even infants made to touch the face of the corpse, notwithstanding their terror and screams. If a child who had seen the corpse, but had not been compelled to touch it, had shortly afterwards awakened from a sleep crying, it would have been considered that its crying was caused by its having seen the ghost of the dead person.[59]

---

[59] J. Napier, *Folk Lore*, pp. 60–63.

Hugh Miller
Cromarty, the Black Isle, mid-1800s

Born and brought up in Cromarty in the Black Isle, Hugh Miller, 1802-56, stone mason, geologist and folklorist, reflected on every aspect of life and death and recorded his thoughts and observations in his many books. In his essay 'The Lykewake' he describes one such event he attended with a friend.

I know no place where one may be brought acquainted with the more credulous beliefs of our forefathers at a less expense of inquiry and exertion than in a country lykewake . . . I once spent a night with a friend from the south – a man of an inquiring and highly philosophic cast of mind – at a lykewake in the upper part of the parish of Cromarty. I had excited his curiosity by an incidental remark or two and, on his expressing a wish that I should introduce him, by way of illustration, to some such scene as I had been describing, we had set out together to the wake of an elderly female who had died that morning. Her cottage, an humble erection of stone and lime, was situated beside a thick fir-wood, on the edge of the solitary Mullbuoy, one of the dreariest and most extensive commons in Scotland. We had to pass in our journey over several miles of desolate moor . . . through a thick, dark wood, with here and there an intervening marsh. The season was in keeping with the scene. It was drawing towards the close of autumn; and, as we passed through the wood, the falling leaves were eddying round us with every wind, or lay in rustling heaps at our feet.

'I do not wonder,' said my companion, 'that the superstitions of so wild a district as this should bear in their character some marks of a corresponding wildness. Night itself, in a populous and cultivated country, is attended with less of the stern and the solemn than mid-day amid solitudes like these. Is the custom of watching beside the dead of remote antiquity in this part of the country?'

'Far beyond the reach of either history or tradition,' I said. 'But it has gradually been changing its character, as the people have been changing theirs; and is now a very different thing from what it was a century ago. It is not yet ninety years since lykewakes in the neighbouring Highlands used to be celebrated with music and dancing; and even here, on the borders of the low country, they used invariably, like the funerals of antiquity, to be the scenes of wild games and amusements never introduced on any other occasion. You remember how Sir Walter described the funeral of Athelstane? The Saxon ideas of condolence were the most natural imaginable. If grief was hungry, they supplied it with food; if thirsty, they gave it drink. Our simple ancestors here seem to have reasoned by a similar process. They made their seasons of deepest grief their times of greatest merriment; and the more they regretted the deceased, the gayer were they at his wake and his funeral. A friend of mine, now dead, a very old man, has told me that he once danced at a lykewake in the Highlands of Sutherland. It was that of an active and very robust man, taken away from his wife and family in the prime of life; and the poor widow, for the greater part of the evening, sat disconsolate beside the fire, refusing every invitation to join the dancers. She was at length, however, brought out by the father of the deceased. 'Little, little did he think,' he said, 'that she would be the last to dance at poor Rory's lykewake.'

We reached the cottage, and went in. The apartment in which the dead lay was occupied by two men and three women. Every little piece of furniture it contained was hung in white, and the floor had recently been swept and sanded; but it was on the bed where the body lay, and on the body itself, that the greatest care had been lavished. The curtains had been taken down, and their place supplied by linen white as snow; and on the sheet that served as a counterpane the body was laid out in a dress of white, fantastically crossed and re-crossed in every direction by scalloped fringes, and fretted into a species of open work, at least intended to represent alternate rows of roses and tulips. A plate, containing a little salt, was placed over the breast of the corpse. As we entered, one of the women rose, and, filling two glasses with spirits, presented them to us on a salver. We tasted the liquor, and sat down on chairs placed for us beside the fire. The conversation, which had been interrupted by our entrance, began to flow apace; and an elderly female, who had lived under the same roof with the deceased, began to relate, in answer to the queries of one of the others, some of the particulars of her last illness and death.[60]

Lewis Grant
Strathspey, 1983

There was a wake, 'caithris' was what they called it . . . when they died, they put pennies on their eyes, and a saucer of salt on the stomach, that was supposed to stop it swelling. The body was kept three days in the house, and they had ceilidhs round the remains, men and women . . . I was never at them but my granny was.[61]

---

[60] Hugh Miller, *Tales and Sketches*, 1869, pp. 169–73.
[61] Lewis Grant, born *c.* 1896 in Strathspey, was interviewed by Neil MacGregor on 29 September 1983. This is excerpted from his fieldwork notebook.

LG . . . And the corpse was in, they sat all night, drink, drink, drink, that was all. It was a great thing that . . . they always had a dram and that.

Well, they put the shroud on the thing; when they died, they used to put pennies on their eyes, to keep them shut, and they put salt on their stomach, to keep them from swelling.

Did I tell you about this young lad – you would have heard – he was working on this farm. The pig died, and the farmer says, 'Well, go up to the grocer's and get a bag of salt.' They were going to salt the pig. They had an old cow, and she died, and oh, up for the salt. And then the old granny died, and the farmer told him to go up for salt. He went, but he never came back, he cleared out and he never came back! He thought, 'What the hell, if they're going to start salting grannies [I'm out of here]!' Oh, that's an old story, that![62]

Revd Walter Gregor
North-east, 1874

The body was sedulously watched day and night, more particularly, however, during night. The watching during the night was called *the lyke* or *the waukan*.

A few of the neighbours met every evening and performed the kind office of watchers. One of them at least had to be awake, lest the evil spirits might come and put a mark on the body. The time was ordinarily spent in reading the Scriptures, sometimes by one and sometimes by another of the watchers. Some of the passages usually read were the ninety-first Psalm, the fifteenth chapter of St John's Gospel, and the fifteenth chapter of I Corinthians. Other passages were read besides these. All conversation was carried on in a suppressed voice.

Sometimes the *waukan* was not so solemn. Practical jokes have been played upon the timid. Some stout-hearted one placed himself within the *bun-bed* beside the dead, and, when those on whom the trick was to be played had entered the house and taken a seat, he began to move, at first gently, and then more freely, and at last he spoke, imitating as far as possible the voice of the dead, to the utter terror of such as were not in the secret.

There was a plentiful supply of new pipes and tobacco, procured especially for the occasion, and hence the irreverent sometimes spoke of the *lyke* as the *tobacco-nicht*.

Whisky was also freely given, and in many cases tea or bread and cheese with ale were served about midnight.[63]

---

[62] Lewis Grant was recorded by Neil MacGregor on 12 September 1984. I am grateful to him for this transcription.
[63] W. Gregor, *Echo*, p.141 and *Notes*, p. 209.

Although many of the nineteenth-century writers suggested that the wake was virtually a thing of the past, there is plenty of evidence throughout the twentieth century that old-fashioned wakes were (and are) still held. Some areas have a long tradition of solemn occasions where the atmosphere is subdued, while other areas report procedures that are considerably more raucous.

Douglas Neally
Stornoway, 1992

DN *Could you tell us a bit about the wake customs?*

LM At the wake the local elders and deacons gather in, and friends and family gather, and they're led in prayer and reading and singing [psalms] as a means of strengthening the family. Regarding death, death does not call for any prayer, but the family do need prayer.[64]

Well, at a wake in my young days, after the reading and the singing, usually the family, the immediate family, were asked to go and lie down. And friends stayed up all night, they didn't sleep and kept the fire going, and they sort of watched over the coffin. Very often the coffin was open for these three days until about an hour before it was carried away . . . and somebody had to be on hand to walk around the house and have a look at it . . . the lights were kept on, or dimmed, in the room where the coffin was.[65]

John Firth
Orkney, 1920

For the wake, a number of young people were chosen to sit all night and watch by the corpse. This they did by turns; and, far from being considered a repulsive duty, it was accepted as an honour. Each relay of watchers consisted of an equal number of young men and maidens; and when 'ilka lassie had her laddie' there is little doubt but that a good deal of flirtation went on, for their vigil by the dead was cheered by a liberal supply of liquor, and card-playing and other games went on merrily.[66]

---

[64] This is reported in many Presbyterian areas. For example, Murdo MacLean (formerly of Skye, now North Kessock) explains that they do not pray for the soul of the dead because the person's life will already have decided the destiny of the soul. If a person has lived 'according to the Word' then prayers after his death will not affect his soul in any way. Prayers for the bereaved family are, however, much in evidence. Recorded by MB (in Gaelic), SA1991/99.

[65] LM (a local man who did not want to be named) was recorded by Douglas Neilly in Stornoway, March 1992.

[66] John Firth, *Orkney*, p. 84. I attended a wake for Mrs Allan MacArthur, a Gaelic speaker, in Newfoundland in 1974. It lasted three nights, spent in the kitchen, while the body was laid out in 'the room' and visited every twenty or so minutes. See Chapter 3 in M. Bennett, *The Last Stronghold*.

Bill Douglas
Niddrie, 1977

BD Now this [is going back to the 1930s]. Old Conn W— died; and he lived in one of the farmer's cottages, and the night before he was buried they held the wake. Now the wake was just similar to a wedding, the bigger the wake the more you were thought of. . . . And I remember we went down to this wake, and they had old Conn sittin up in the bed – they had taken him out of the coffin and sat him up in the bed – the beds were built into the wall like two recesses – and they had old Conn sittin propped up in the bed with the bandage round his head to keep his mouth shut and they had a clay pipe stuck in his mouth – he was dead, this fellow! And on the table for the feed there was 'tatties and dip', and they boiled these spuds in a great big pot . . . and when the potatoes were ready and started to burst their skins they tipped them out onto the table. Now, you get some picture o the table and potatoes lying all over it and dishes of salt and you took a potato and bit the top off it and stuck it in the salt and ate it – tatties and dip they used to call it. And then they had buttermilk to drink for those that were teetotal and whisky or rum for the ones that really enjoyed it. And this went on long enough until they got that drunk they didn't know what they were doin. And in the meantime old Mrs—'s sittin alongside the bed, sittin lookin at her old man with her glass o whisky and she's sippin away and sippin away and she's gettin as drunk as Bacchus and all the time she's wailing: 'Conn, Conn, fye did ye die? To leave your old mother to weep and to cry?' and this going on continuous. I wouldn't be very old at the time but I can still see it. Somebody threw a potato at old Conn and to finish up they had him sittin up there and were beltin him with potatoes trying to stot the pipe out of his mouth! They finished up they got that drunk that it just faded away, but this was quite a common practice. And then they would have dances and musical chairs and games of all kinds, and this went on till daybreak. And then they went home and had a sleep and then the old fellow was put back in his box and nailed down and then they had the funeral the following day. And all the men used to go to the funerals then – there were no women went to funerals – but the men all went in tall hats and swallow-tail coats and strippit black trousers and umbrellas and cuffs and spats and they all walked behind the hearse and went to the cemetery and, once they were buried, instead of comin straight home they went to the pub and they generally came home from the pub blind drunk. That was the end of old Conn.[67]

---

[67] Bill Douglas, formerly of Niddrie, now of N.S.W., Australia, recorded by Emily Lyle. SA1977/31.

Greenock Telegraph
May 1988

After a funeral wake a violent row broke out in a Greenock house, the sheriff court heard.

A father threw ash-trays and cups about the living room, slapped his 20-year-old daughter and head-butted his wife, the court was told.

A— N— (43), of C— Road, admitted breach of the peace and assault. He was fined £150.

His agent, Mr Norman M—, said his client's wife started throwing the objects and N— had said he 'might as well join in and have the rest'.[68]

Paying Respects

BBC News
Sunday 16 April 1989

United in grief, the players in Hearts and Hibs teams all wore black arm-bands at the match to show their respect for the tragic loss of 94 football fans, crushed to death at Sheffield, when supporting their team (Liverpool United) just over a week ago [5 April 1989].

BBC News
Saturday 22 January 1994

Football matches all over the country began with a minute's silence as a mark of respect for football hero Matt Busby, who died earlier in the week.

John Lane Buchanan
Western Isles 1782

Burials are preceded by the large bagpipes, playing some mournful dirge. They continue playing till they arrive at the place of interment, while the women sing the praises of the dead, clasping the coffin in their arms, and lie on the graves of their departed friends. It is common to see women coming out to stand by the way-side, who are strangers, as the corpse is carried along, with

---

[68] *Greenock Telegraph*, Friday 8 May, 1988. Details of names and addresses have been withheld to protect the guilty. Thanks to Hugh Hagan who brought this excerpt from his local newspaper to my attention.

certain mournful ditties in their mouths, and making great lamentations; while they in the meantime ask some of the attendants where the corpse came from, and whether they are men or women.

On those occasions, there is great profusion of meat and drink brought to the place of interment, where the expenses generally bear a proportion to the rank and fortune of the person deceased, to prevent the imputation of meanness; and they seldom separate while the cask contains any spirits to wash down their sorrow: which seldom happens before their griefs are converted into squabbles, and broken heads, which some of them carry home as marks of remembrance for their lost friends.

They seldom display much mirth at late[69] wakes, as they do in many parts of Scotland; but sit down with great composure, and rehearse the good qualities of their departed friend or neighbour. Their grief soon subsides after they are buried; and many have speedily replaced a lost wife by some of their former acquaintance.[70]

Hugh Hagan
Port Glasgow, 1991

MB *Were the walls and mirrors draped for funerals?*

HH That was something that was common, that's still common amongst us. You drape the walls in white cloth and you cover any mirrors or take them doon or whatever. When my Uncle John died there, this summer we screwed the mirror . . . he'd two or three different mirrors in his room, and we screwed them aff, took them oot the room, what he wis lyin in, the bedroom he was [laid out] in. And before he went into the room – I remember it vividly, because we hadn't done it, it's something we forgot aboot and when the body wis taken from the [funeral] parlour to the hoose, one o ma aunties says, 'Ye'll need tae get them mirrors aff, you know, or get them covered.'

MB *What was the reason for covering the mirrors?*

HH I think there's some belief that ye're gonnae see . . . the spirit in the mirror – like ghosts and stuff might appear, that's in the room at the time [but not actually visible], and ye can see them in mirrors – so ye huvtae dae away wi the mirrors cos that affects the passage [of the soul] of the person who's died, if these things are there to disturb the proceedings, ye know . . . I think it's mair or less believed that the spirits are there, but for some reason that I don't know why, you can see them through the mirror.

---

[69] Buchanan adds the following footnote to his text at this point: 'In many parts of Scotland it is customary for the youth of both sexes to sit up by the corpse, and console themselves by whisky and other pastimes.'
[70] Revd John Lane Buchanan, *Travels*, pp.169–70.

MB *What about drawing the blinds?*

HH Oh aye! When someb'dy dies you always draw the blinds – cover the windows anyway, or something. Most places ye jist draw the blinds, but Ould John didnae huv blinds so we jist covered it wi a white sheet. Where did he die? In a hospital . . . Aye, the undertakers took him fae the hospital tae the funeral parlour tae put him in the box and stuff, you know, and then took him up to the hoose.

The coffin wis put intae his bedroom and the four walls were draped in white cloth, and the window wis covered up and a' the mirrors wir taken aff. The only thing that wis in the room wis a wee table – well it wis the dressin table wi the mirror aff it and it wis, it . . . they made up like a wee altar on it, you know – the candles an the wee eh'm . . . it's a special crucifix that ye use for the last rites – it wis a' there, you know. But apart from that it wis jist the body, you know. [The coffin] wis on trestles. [That was] 1990 . . . the coffin wis open right up until he left the hoose tae go tae the chapel tae Mass, ye know.

MB *Did people touch him?*

HH Aye . . . Some o' the older people, some o the women wid actually kiss them on the forehead, ye know, or they would jist touch his cheek, ye know. Ah jist touched his cheek, ye know. But I remember when ma Uncle John died in Ireland, I wis only young at that time – well, youngish, 15 or 16, and I kissed my Uncle John, but ah only done that because everybody in front o me done it, you know! I jist thought, 'Oh my God: I'm gonnae hiv tae kiss him!' An you know I wis quite worried aboot it at the time, but I had never really seen it done before, really . . . It was obviously done loads o' times afore – I jist didn't remember. When I went to Big John's ah kissed him, but anybody else I jist touched them.

MB *After the funeral mass did everybody go to the cemetery?*

HH Most of the funerals I've been at the women didn't go, ye know. They didn't go to Big John's and that wis jist last year . . . Eftir the mass, when the body wis taken oot tae the hearse to go to the cemetery, the women went to the chapel hall to prepare for everybody comin back for the sausages and a' that kinda stuff, you know – the breakfast eftir . . . It's always one o'clock Mass you know, so it's always aboot eleven o'clock.

MB *So you call it 'breakfast'?*

HH Aye, a funeral breakfast, aye, you always have a funeral breakfast . . . sausage rolls, whatever, sandwiches.

MB *You're not talking about cornflakes!*

HH [Laughs] Na! Naeb'dy wid go if it wis cornflakes. [laughs] . . . Normally you always get a drink, you know, so usually it's in a club, and if the person that's died wis a member of a social club then they usually pit it over. And if it's in the chapel hall ye huvtae supply yer own drink cos they don't have a bar. But it's always the done thing tae supply a drink fur everybody – and sandwiches. And ye don't hunt anybody away; you jist sit there and drink, so you could be there for quite a wee while! [Laughs]

MB *It's always held in a hall?*

HH Aye, I've only ever been to wan that wis held in a hoose . . . I mean if it's a big family it's nearly impossible to haud it in the hoose, you know, cos everybody descends at the wan time; it's no like the lead-up to the funeral when everybody's comin and goin – that's fine. But if you've got a whole squad, a hunner odd people turning up ye cannae huv it in somebody's hoose, ye know, ye jist huv it in a hall. And normally, the likes o Big John and people like that ur all members of some club – some Irish clubs, or if they wir in the army or that they mebbe join the artillery club and the club wid pit it over for ye. It's cheaper as well tae huv it in a club if ye can dae it that way.

MB *And this is all in Port Glasgow?*

HH Yeah.[71]

Martin Martin
Western Isles, *c.* 1695

[In Gigha] the inhabitants are all Protestants, and speak the Irish [Gaelic] tongue generally, there being but few that speak English; they are grave and reserved in their conversation; they are accustomed not to bury on Friday.[72]

. . . [In Jura] there is a church called Killearn, the inhabitants are all Protestants . . . they do not open a grave on Friday, and bury none on that day, except the grave has been opened before.[73]

. . . [In Barra] the natives have a remark, that when the cows belonging to one person do of a sudden become very irregular, and run up and down the fields and make a loud noise without any visible cause, that it is a presage of the master's or mistress's death, of which there were several late instances given me. James Macdonald of Capstil having been killed at the battle of Killiecrankie, it was observed that night that his cows gave blood instead of milk. His family and other neighbours concluded this a bad omen. The minister of the place and the mistress of the cows, together with several neighbours, assured me of the truth of this.[74]

When a tenant's wife [on Barra] or the adjacent islands dies, he then addresses himself to Macneil of Barray [*sic*] representing his loss, and at the

---

[71] Hugh Hagan, Port Glasgow, was recorded in Edinburgh by MB on 6 February 1991. SA1991/15.

[72] Martin Martin, *Description*, p. 230.

[73] *Ibid.*, p. 239.

[74] *Ibid.*, p. 156.

same time desires that he [Macneil] would be pleased to recommend a wife to him, without which he cannot manage his affairs, nor beget followers to Macneil, which would prove a public loss to him. Upon this representation, Macneil finds out a suitable match for him; and the woman's name being told him, immediately he goes to her, carrying with him a bottle of strong waters for their entertainment at marriage, which is then consummated.

When a tenant dies, the widow addresseth herself to Macneil in the same manner, who likewise provides her with a husband, and they are married without any further courtship.[75]

[On the Isle of Taransay] there is an ancient tradition among the natives here, that a man must not be buried in St Tarran, nor a woman in St Keith's because otherwise the corpse would be found above ground the day after it is interred. I told them this was a most ridiculous fancy which they might soon perceive by experience if they would but put it to a trial. Roderick Campbell, who resides there, being of my opinion, resolved to embrace the first opportunity that offered, in order to undeceive the credulous vulgar; and accordingly a poor man in this island, who died a year after, was buried in St Tarran's chapel, contrary to the ancient custom and tradition of this place, but his corpse is still in the grave, from whence it is not like to rise until the general resurrection. This instance has delivered the credulous natives from this unreasonable fancy. This island is a mile distant from the main land of Harris, and when the inhabitants go from this island to Harris with a design to stay for any time, they agree with those that carry them over, on a particular motion of walking upon a certain piece of ground, unknown to every body but themselves, as a signal to bring them back.[76]

Between Bernera and the main land of Harris lies the island Ensay, which is above two miles in circumference, and for the most part arable ground, which is fruitful in corn and grass: there is an old chapel here, for the use of the natives; and there was lately discovered a grave in the west end of the island, in which was found a pair of scales made of brass, and a little hammer, both which were finely polished.[77]

---

[75] *Ibid.*, p. 97.
[76] *Ibid.*, p. 49
[77] *Ibid.*, p. 50.

Alexander Carmichael of Lismore
in Tomintoul, 1870

In Tom an tSobhail, Tomintoul, the horse drawing the cart in which a corpse is laid is taken out of the cart three times on the journey. The horse is then turned around sunwise on the road, and re-yoked 'an ainm Athar, an ainm Mic, an ainm Sprioraid,' in the name of Father, in the name of Son, in the name of Spirit. The cart is then drawn forward a few yards by the horse.[78]

Jean Cameron
Tomintoul, 1953

JC [The Corpse Road] wad be aboot six miles from here . . . an they used to carry, there wes no ither, no motorin then, and there wes no horses, nor the like o that, an it wes all done by men just carryin that weight. (It wes from Glenlivet that the road starts) . . . They took the coaffin an the remains in it, they wad set it down, ye see, an rest, an there wes their bread and cheese in their baskets, an whisky, an used to take a refreshment, they wad need that . . . there wes no ither means o motion there, there wes no carriages nor carts nor nothin else, jist kinna sledge-things they had . . . sometimes when thir wad be frost or ice or that, they wad sledge it along on the snow or the ice, bit fir walkin, they jist had to carry everything . . . Sometimes whan they wide be goin for the remains . . . they wad carry, they called them gallon jars, I'm sure ye've seen them, gallon jar of whisky . . . an they'd have bread an cheese . . . croods, curds they wad call it, like . . . an then when they got to the house whaur the remains wes, they wad start feasting again . . .

Protestant an Catholics, oh there wes plenty o them both. They used to walk . . . down from there to this Carmichael Kirk on a Sunday, an they were takin their fishin-rods with them an fish aa down the River Avon, till they wad come to the church; we have photographs . . . ye wad see them wi their fishin-rods over their shoulders an putting them up against the wall o the church, an they went intae the service, take their fishin-rod an away they went.[79]

---

[78] A. Carmichael, *Carmina Gadelica*, vol. 3, p. 370.
[79] Jean Cameron, Tomintoul, was recorded by Hamish Henderson in 1953. SA 1953/241.

John H. Dixon
Gairloch, 1886

Funerals [in Gairloch] are not now accompanied by such striking peculiarities [as in former times]. Until the last few years, when a death occurred all the people of the township ceased working until after the funeral, which was attended by every adult male. Of course drinking was much in vogue, and the well known Irish wakes were closely imitated. Now, only those invited to a funeral are expected to attend, and the whisky is confined to the serving of a dram all round (preceded by a prayer) before the funeral procession starts, with additional 'nips' whenever a halt is made for rest on the way to the place of burial, and these halts are not infrequent. Until quite lately it was customary for each man accompanying the funeral to throw a stone on the spot where the coffin was placed when a halt was made, thus forming a considerable heap; sometimes the number of stones thrown was the same as the years of age of the deceased. This custom has been generally discontinued in Gairloch since the roads were made, though it is still in vogue in the wilder parts of the adjoining parishes of Applecross and Lochbroom. The use of whisky at funerals is not now universal in the parish of Gairloch; some ministers wisely discourage it, partly on account of its generally evil tendency, and partly because the providing of it is a serious burden on the family of the deceased, already weighted by other expenses in connection with the death or previous sickness.[80]

Funeral Expenses

William MacKay
Inverness-shire, 1914

. . . This is the bill for the wake of Sir Donald Campbell of Ardnamurchan in 1651, the money being Scots:

52 gallons of ale at 20s per gallon	£52	0	0
5 gallons and one quart whisky at £16 per gallon	84	0	0
8 wethers at £3 each		24	0
2 pecks salt	2	0	0
2 stones cheese	4	0	0
1¼ lb tobacco	0	11	0
1 cow	23	6	8
Total cost of the feast	£189	17	8[81]

---

[80] John H. Dixon, *Gairloch*, pp. 115–16.
[81] William Mackay, 'Life in The Highlands . . .' *TGSI*, 1914, p. 8.

Alexander Laing
Newburgh, 1876

Sir Michael Balfour of Denmiln died at Denmiln, on the 4th February, 1652, at the age of 72, and was buried in Abdie Church on the 20th of the same month.

The great length of time which was allowed to elapse betwixt Sir Michael's death and burial . . . arose from the custom of entertaining all relatives and neighbours, so long as the body lay unburied, with a profuse hospitality, which was not bounded by temperance. Day after day scenes of conviviality went on, most unbecoming the solemn occasion, and expenses were incurred which often embarrassed the family of the deceased for generations. Instances are on record of two years' rental of large estates having been spent in this wasteful manner at the funeral of the proprietors; and yet, had the family of the deceased set themselves against the custom of the time, they would have been branded as disregardful of their father's memory.[82]

Ian MacDougall
Edinburgh,1992

The Friendly Society, also known as Benefit Society or Box Club, was the earliest type of voluntary organisation formed in Scotland by working people. Some were certainly formed in the seventeenth century, perhaps even earlier, but the numbers of Friendly Societies increased sharply from the later years of the eighteenth century, no doubt a result of the agrarian and industrial revolutions.

Although Friendly Societies were not exclusive to working people, the overwhelming majority of these societies and of their memberships in Scotland consisted of working men and women – craftsmen of all kinds, coal miners, seamen, carters, and others. In 1801 the Poor Law returns indicated that in England and Wales there were then some 9,600 Friendly Societies, with an aggregate membership of about 700,000. A rough estimate based on the number of Friendly Societies referred to in the *Old Statistical Account* of 1790 would suggest that there were around 600 or 700 of these societies with an aggregate membership at 70,000 to 80,000.[83]

Until the first decade or so of the nineteenth century, Friendly Societies

---

[82] Alexander Laing, *Lindores Abbey and its Burgh of Newburgh*, pp. 355–6.
[83] The parish ministers who contributed to Sir John Sinclair's *Statistical Account* of 1790 made frequent and consistent reports on the Friendly Societies of their individual parishes.

were purely local bodies whose memberships were drawn from a single village, town, a particular suburb, or even from a single street. For instance, the Kilmarnock Back Street Female Society (1835–?) consisted *not* of peculiarly oppressed or furtive souls but simply of women living in Back Street, Kilmarnock. By 1874 it was estimated that the total membership of Friendly Societies throughout Britain had increased to around four million, with a total membership in Scotland between 250,000 and 400,000.

A number of local Friendly Societies were composed of craftsmen or other workers in a single trade or occupation within a single town or district. For example, the Leven and Milton Calico Printers' Friendly Society, formed in 1830, had a membership confined exclusively to calico-printers, cutters, drawers, and engravers in that part of Dunbartonshire and Stirlingshire.

From about 1814 through the first half of the nineteenth century, however, there developed large national, or 'affiliated orders' as they were called, of Friendly Societies. These were the Oddfellows, the Foresters, the Shepherds, the Free Gardeners, the Druids, and others. These affiliated bodies based in Manchester, London, Bolton and elsewhere, with many Scottish branches and members, were enthusiastically noted by The Report of the Royal Commission on Friendly Societies in 1874 as: 'The clubs of highest of organization among those invented by working men to suit their own wants, and, at the present day greatly surpassing all others in popularity . . .'

Of the records of Scottish friendly societies, a great mass of rule books, along with a few other items such as balance sheets and quinquennial returns of sickness and mortality survive in the Scottish Record Office, where they have been deposited over the years by the Registrar, or Assistant Registrar in Scotland, of Friendly Societies. Many other records, or fragments of documentation, survive in other public repositories, such as the National Library of Scotland and local libraries and museums.

A few friendly societies were either clandestine trade combinations or unions in those eras (the eighteenth and earlier nineteenth centuries) when the latter were illegal organizations. One remarkable example of such hybrid friendly societies was the Society of Journeymen Wool Combers in Aberdeen, which seems to have flourished from 1753 to about 1760, and many of whose records are preserved in the Scottish Record Office.

But what friendly societies characteristically and most commonly provided was not of course trade union protection but a modest burial grant. That payment was important to working people at a time of rapid industrial development from the mid or later eighteenth century, rapid growth of towns, often appalling living and working conditions, and limited expectation of life. The Edinburgh journeymen stonemasons, for example, calculated in

1849 that their expectation of life was 34 years.

The funeral benefit provided by the friendly societies therefore offered some assurance to the wage-earner, especially to the better paid wage-earner, who could find the penny or so subscription, or to members of his or her family, that they would or might be saved from the indignity of being cast into a pauper's grave.

In many cases, societies extended their range of benefits the longer they survived beyond the eighteenth and into the nineteenth centuries. Many commentators have seen in the friendly societies forerunners of the Welfare State of the second half of the twentieth century.

One such society that virtually developed its own undertaking business in the late eighteenth century was the Ogleface Friendly Society at Avonbridge, near Linlithgow in West Lothian. A surviving document of the Society dated 11 May, 1795 tells us of the conditions on which its hearse was available for hire:

OGLEFACE Friendly Society's HEARSE.

CONDITIONS on which the OGLEFACE FRIENDLY SOCIETY'S HEARSE is Let out.

I. The Body of every Member of the Society, his Wife, or Widow shall be carried to their place of Interment, by the Society's Hearse, free of hire.

II. The Parents of Members entered before the 1st of May 1793, and all the Children of every member still unmarried, shall have their Bodies carried by the Hearse to their place of Interment for the half of the hire payable by others.

III. When the Hearse is let out to those who are not Members, nor entitled to the above Privileges, there shall be Two Shillings and Sixpence paid, in name of Yoking-money: And Six-pence for every Mile that it travels from the place where it is kept, to the place of Interment. And if it be not returned the same day that it sets out, the Yoking and Mile Money shall be charged as on the preceding day. The Money to be paid when the Hearse is returned.

IV. If any Necessitous Family shall stand in need of the Hearse, by applying to the Hearse-Keeper by a Line signed by two or three respectable persons, testifying their necessity; that Family so applying, shall have the Hearse at that time for the Yoking-money, to the extent of Six Miles from the Hearse-house. Those who sign the Line, shall be good for damages.

V. If the Hearse shall be damaged

when let out, the damage shall be appraised, and those who hired it shall make it good.

VI. Whoever shall hire out the Hearse (whether they be Members or not) shall pay One Shilling to the Keeper for cleaning it.

A TABLE of the Computed Distance of the different Places of Interment, in the Neighbourhood, from the Hearse-house of the OGLEFACE FRIENDLY SOCIETY AT AVON-BRIDGE-END.

	Miles	Qrs.
To TORPHICHEN by the Straths,	3	3
To Ditto by Andrew's Yeards and the Wheat Acres,	4	1
To the West end of Ditto Parish , and East to Ditto Churchyard by Craigs,	10	
To MUIRAVONSIDE by Stand-burn and Tirdiff,	4	2
To Ditto by Torphichen,	8	
To Ditto by Boxton,	6	2
To Ditto by GREY-RIDGE,	5	
TO BATHGATE by Torphichen,	6	
To Ditto by by Bridge-house,	5	
To Ditto by Borbachly,	5	2
To the Old Church-yard always One Mile more,		
To WHITBURN by Wheat-acres or Hills,	6	
To SHOTTS by Craigs and Blairmucks,	8	2
To LINLITHGOW by Torphichen,	8	
To Ditto by Tirduff,	7	
To Ditto by Bathgate by Torphichen Road,	11	1
To Ditto by Bathgate by Cairnpapple road,	10	
To FALKIRK by Glenburn,	6	2
To Ditto by Slamannan Kirk,	10	
To Ditto by Torphichen by Maddiston,	10	3
To SLAMANNAN by Pirney Lodge,	3	3
To Ditto by Bulzingdale and Linhouse,	4	
To WEST CALDER by Bathgate and Blackburn,	10	

The SOCIETY have agreed, that the above table shall be the standard by which their hearse shall be let out in future. And when the number of miles travelled by the hearse cannot be counted by the above table, that part of the journey that lies beyond the places specified above shall be left to the computation of the employers.

By Order of the Ogleface Friendly Society,

EASTER STRATH   (Signed) WILLIAM BRYCE

11th May, 1795

There rests in the surviving documentation of Scottish Friendly Societies (voluminous as it is in the case of rule books, less so in other categories of record) a great mass of potential interest for the economic, the local, the social, the labour, the women's, and the health historian. It is a field of Scottish history that has so far remained relatively untilled.[84]

Douglas Neally
Stornoway, 1992

In the Isle of Lewis a lot of people pay into a funeral fund over the years, and if anyone dies away from home, this fund will pay for the expense of having the remains brought home on the boat or flying them back to Lewis.[85]

Captain Edward Burt
Inverness, 1726

After the death of any one, not in the lowest circumstances, the friends and acquaintance of the deceased assemble to keep the near relations company the first night; and they dance, as if it were at a wedding, till the next morning, though all the time the corpse lies before them in the same room. If the deceased be a woman, the widower leads up the first dance; if a man, the widow. But this Highland custom I knew, to my disturbance, within less than a quarter of a mile of Edinburgh, before I had been among the Mountains. It was upon the death of a smith, next door to my lodgings, who was a Highlander.

The upper class hire women to moan and lament [*keen*] at the funeral of their nearest relations.[86] These women cover their heads with a small piece of cloth, mostly green, and every now and then break out into a hideous howl

---

[84] Ian MacDougall wrote this essay, 'The Ogleface Friendly Society's Hearse', in February 1992. I had heard him touch on the subject of friendly societies during a paper he gave at a conference on The Local Dimension of Oral History in Glasgow, 1990. He brought with him some of the archive material, including the Rules of the Ogleface Friendly Society, and having never seen or read anything of this before, I asked if he would write an essay for the book I had just started to prepare. I am extremely grateful to him for contributing this essay on a facet of life which, so far as I know, was hitherto undocumented. For a complete version of his paper, see *Scottish Culture: The Local Dimension*.

[85] Douglas Neally, from the same paper cited above, March, 1992.

[86] There are several recordings from oral tradition of women who were paid to keen at a funeral, such as those reported by Nan MacKinnon of Vatersay, recorded by Anne Ross in 1964. Usually at the death of one of the clan chiefs or a member of his family, the women wailed and beat themselves against the ground, and eulogised the dead. She said that keening stopped in Barra when the MacNeils sold their land. SA1964/78. In 1968 D.A. MacDonald recorded an account of a woman following a funeral who was paid five pounds by one of the mourners for keening. SA1968/153.

and Ho-bo-bo-bo-boo; as I have often heard is done in some parts of Ireland.

This part of the ceremony is called a *coronach*, and generally speaking, is the cause of much drunkenness, attended with its concomitants, mischievous rencounters and bloody broils; for all that have arms in their possession, accoutre themselves with them upon those occasions.

I have made mention of their funeral piles[87] in a former letter; but I had once occasion to take particular notice of a heap of stones, near the middle of a small piece of arable land. The plough was carefully guided as near to it as possible; and the pile, being like others I had seen upon the moors, I asked, by an interpreter, whether there was a rock beneath it; but being answered in the negative, I further inquired the reasons why they lost so much ground, and did not remove the heap? To this I had for answer, it was a burial-place, and they deemed it a kind of sacrilege to remove one single stone; and that the children, from their infancy, were taught the same veneration for it. Thus a parcel of loose stones are more religiously preserved among them than with us, and thence I could not but conclude, that the inclination to preserve the remains and memory of the dead, is greater with those people than it is among us. The Highlanders, even here in this town, cannot forego the practice of the Hills, in raising heaps of stones over such as have lost their lives by some misfortune; for in Oliver's Fort, no sooner was the body of an officer removed from the place where he fell in a duel, than they set about the raising such a heap of stones upon the spot where he had lain. So much for Mountain monuments. . . .

For inviting people to ordinary buryings in all parts of the low-country, as well as here, a man goes about with a bell; and when he comes to one of his stations, suppose the deceased was a man, he cries, 'All brethren and sisters, I let you to wot, that there is a brother departed this life, at the pleasure of Almighty God; they called him &c. – he lived at, &c.' And so for a woman, with the necessary alterations. The corpse is carried, not upon men's shoulders, as in England, but, under hand, upon a bier; and the nearest relation to the deceased carries the head, the next of kin on his right hand, &c. and if the church-yard be any thing distant, they are relieved by others as occasion may require. The men go two-and-two before the bier, and the women, in the same order, follow after it; and all the way the bellman goes tinkling before the procession, funeral, as is done before the host in popish countries.

Not long ago a Highland-man was buried here. There were few in the procession besides Highlanders in their usual garb; and all the way before

---

[87] Cairns, built of stones.

them a piper played on his bagpipes, which was hung with narrow streamers of black crape.

When people of some circumstance are to be buried, the nearest relation sends printed letters, stationery, signed by himself; and sometimes, but rarely, the invitation has been general, and made by beat of drum.

The friends of the deceased usually meet at the house of mourning the day before the funeral, where they sit a good while like quakers at a silent meeting, in dumb show of sorrow; but in time the bottle is introduced, and the ceremony quite reversed.

It is esteemed very slighting, and scarcely ever to be forgiven, not to attend after invitation, if you are in health: the only means to escape resentment, is to send a letter, in answer, with some reasonable excuse.

The company, which is always numerous, meets in the street at the door of the deceased; and when a proper number of them are assembled, some of those among them, who are of highest rank, or most esteemed, and strangers, are the first invited to walk into a room, where there usually are several pyramids of plum-cake, sweetmeats, and several dishes, with pipes and tobacco; the last is according to an old custom, for it is very rare to see any body smoke in Scotland.[88]

The nearest relations and friends of the person to be interred, attend, and, like waiters, serve you with wine for about a quarter of an hour; and no sooner have you accepted of one glass, but another is at your elbow, and so a third &c. There is no excuse to be made for not drinking, for then it will be said; 'You have obliged my brother, or my cousin such-a-one; pray, sir, what have I done to be refused?' When the usual time is expired, this detachment goes out, and another succeeds; and when all have had their *tour*, they accompany the corpse to the grave, which they generally do about noon.

The minister, who is always invited, performs no kind of funeral service for those of any rank whatever, but most commonly is one of the last that leaves the place of burial.

When the company are about to return, a part of them are selected to go back to the house, where all sorrow seems to be immediately banished, and wine is filled about as fast as it can go round till there is hardly a sober person among them. And, by the way, I have been often told, that some have kept their friends drinking upon this occasion for more days together than I can venture to mention.

In the conclusion, some of the sweetmeats are put into your hat, or thrust

---

[88] On the contrary, Martin Martin notes *c.* 1695 that the Hebridean people were very fond of tobacco. See *Description*, p. 91.

into your pocket, which enables you to make a great compliment to the women of your acquaintance.

This last homage they call the *drudgy*;[89] but I suppose they mean the *dirge*, that is, a service performed for a dead person some time after his death; or this may be instead of a lamentation sung at the funeral; but I am sure it has no sadness attending it, except it be for an aching head the next morning. The day following, every one that has black puts it on, and wears it for some time afterwards; and if the deceased was any thing considerable, though the mourner's relation to him was never so remote, it serves to soothe the vanity of some, by inciting the question, 'For whom do you mourn?' – 'My cousin the Laird of such-a-place,' or 'My Lord such-a-one,' is the answer to the question begged by the sorrowful dress. I have seen the doors and gates blacked over in token of mourning. . . .

You will perhaps wonder why I have continued so long upon this subject, none of the most entertaining; but as the better sort here are almost all of them related to one another in some degree, either by consanguinity, marriage, or clanship, it is to them, as it were, a kind of business, and takes up good part of their time. In short, they take a great pride and pleasure in doing honours to their dead.[90]

Alexander Carmichael of Lismore
in Barra, 1870

In 1870 the writer prevailed upon a woman in Barra to do the 'tuiream' as she had heard it when young. The funeral was that of a crofter at Castlebay who had died leaving a young widow and several children. As the funeral procession left the house the woman set up a plaintive cadence. At first her voice was low and tremulous, but gradually rose to a great height. The scene was striking. Below, on a tidal rock, was the castle of Ciosmal [Kishmul], now a roofless ruin, once the picturesque home of the Macneills of Barra, while the Atlantic waves dashed against the rocks, mingling their wailing with that of the 'bean tuiream', weeping woman.

'Bean tuiream', mourning woman, is the term applied to a professional weeper. 'Tuiream' is specifically applied to mourning for the dead; 'tuiream bhais', death-mourning. Similar terms are 'seis', dirge, and 'seisig bhais',

---

[89] While Burt recorded the appropriate term his supposition of the meaning is unlikely. Compare Napier's account in the next excerpt; also, Hamish Henderson recorded James Taylor of Strathdon talking of the 'dredgie' which consisted of tea and drams given after a funeral. SA1955/67.
[90] Captain Edward Burt, *Letters*, vol. II, selected excerpts from pp. 189–214.

death-dirge, death-wail. In Ireland this is called 'caoineadh', weeping, Anglicized 'keening'.[91]

Revd James Napier
Renfrewshire, 1879

Those attending the funeral who were not near neighbours or relations were given a quantity of bread and cakes to take home with them, but relations and near neighbours returned to the house, where their wives were collected, and were liberally treated to both meat and drink. This was termed the *dredgy* or *dirgy*, and to be present at this was considered a mark of respect to the departed. This custom may be the remnant of an ancient practice – in some sort of superstition – which existed in Greece, where the friends of the deceased, after the funeral, held a banquet, the fragments of which were afterwards carried to the tomb. Upon the death of a wealthy person, when the funeral had left the house, sums of money were divided among the poor. In Catholic times this was done that the poor might pray for the soul of the deceased. In the Danish *Niebellungen* [German *Nibelungen*] song it is stated that, at the burial of the hero Seigfried [*sic*], his wife caused upwards of thirty thousand merks of gold to be distributed among the poor for the welfare and repose of his soul. This custom became in this country and century in Protestant times an occasion for the gathering of beggars and sorners from all parts. At the funeral of George Oswald of Scotstoun, three miles from Glasgow, there were gathered several hundreds, who were each supplied with a silver coin and a drink of beer, and many were the blessings wished. A similar gathering occurred at the funeral of old Mr Bogle of Gilmourhill [*sic*], near Glasgow; but when the announcement was made that nothing was to be given, there rose a fearful howl of execration and cursing both of the dead and living from the mendacious [*sic*] crowd. The village of Partick in both these cases was placed under a species of blackmail for several days by beggars, who would hardly take any denial, and in many instances appropriated what was not their own. I am not aware that this custom is retained in any part of the country now.

As the funerals fifty years ago were mostly walking funerals, the coffin being carried between two spokes, the sort of weather during the funeral had its omens, for in these days the weather was believed to be greatly under the control of the devil, or rather it was considered that he was permitted to tamper with the weather. If the day was fine, this was naturally a good omen

---

[91] Alexander Carmichael, *Carmina Gadelica*, vol. 2, p. 292. [paragraphs reversed].

for the soul's welfare. I remember that the funeral of the only daughter of a worthy couple happened on a wet day, but just as the funeral was leaving the house the sun broke through and the day cleared, whereupon the mother, with evident delight, as she stood at the door, thanked God that Mary was getting a good blink. . .

Another custom of olden times, and which was continued till the beginning of this century, was that of announcing the death of any person by sending a person with a bell – known as the 'deid bell' – through the town or neighbourhood. The same was done to invite to the funeral. In all probability, the custom of ringing the bell had its origin in the church custom, being a call to offer prayer for the soul of the departed. Bell-ringing was also considered a means of keeping away evil spirits. Joseph Train, writing in 1814, refers to another practice common in some parts of Scotland. Whenever the corpse is taken from the house, the bed on which the deceased lay is taken from the house, and all the straw or heather of which it was composed is taken out and burned in a place where no beast can get at it, and in the morning the ashes are carefully examined, believing that the footprint of the next person of the family who will die will be seen. This practice of burning the contents of the bed is commendable for sanitary purposes.[92]

The Last Post

Betsy Whyte
Montrose, 1988

BW We used to put caff in the mattress instead of feathers. Sometimes the leaves o the beech tree because they never turned sour nor smelt nasty like other leaves. They keep quite fresh if you're stayin for a while. We could get it when they were threshin.

MB *And was there a custom at death of people burning the mattress?*

BW Oh well, we burned everything personal. All the clothes, bedding, everything that belonged. We still do, but we dinnae burn furniture, anybody can get the furniture. But we burn everything else, even if it's worth a lot o money – like jewellery an things like that. Provided the dead person hasn't given it to somebody when they're alive, or promised it tae them, then it jist goes wi the rest intae the fire or intae the grave wi them. Like rings or things. They'd never take them off. Often though an auld woman'll say tae a lassie who's admired her earrings, 'All right then you can get them when I go.' Then she'll accept them willingly. But if they're offered after

[92] J. Napier, *Folk Lore*, pp. 56–66.

granny's death the answer will be, 'No, we dinnae want them.' Even if it's money, if the person who died was greedy and regarded their money too much, it wouldn't get taken.

MB *What about somebody, say, who was a good piper or a fiddler, what would you do with the instrument left behind?*

BW Oh, they never burned an instrument. Very seldom. Oh no, they couldnae thole tae burn the pipes especially, or an accordion, or a fiddle. These were aboot the only instruments that they used apart frae a tin whistle or a chanter. So that if there was a grand-bairn there that played wi the grandfather, or a son who played, he would expect the instrument to pass to him.

MB *And at a funeral would somebody play the pipes, generally speaking?*

BW Nearly always. Let it be man or woman who was bein buried, the pipes were played. They still do, an a lot o folk says, 'Ah've never seen a woman gettin pipes played at her funeral before,' but we do.

MB *Any particular tune?*

BW If there was a tune that they particularly liked, that would be played, but they always played the Dead March. Then, after that, at the grave-side, they would play the favourite tune.

MB *Regardless of whether it was a happy one or a sad one.*

BW Yes, that's right. It didnae have tae be mournful.

MB *Did they wear mourning clothes, an arm-band or something to indicate mourning?*

BW Nothing! They never indicated mourning. They jist wore what they always wore. If they had to go where there was non-travellers – what we call 'country hantle' – they would try and wear dark things. Most o the older women were used wi wearin dark things anyway so they were practically always in mournin.

MB *Did any of the older women consider it bad luck, say, for a young girl to wear black?*

BW Yes. They could wear maybe a black jumper wi a coloured skirt or a black skirt wi a coloured jumper, but no black stockins. Never all in black. I never, except rarely, wear black.

MB *What would they say now? Black is the fashion nowadays. You see a lot of young girls wearing all black.*

BW That's what I said the other day. I never seen such trollopy lassies! Long black wide coats that hae neither shape nor form. I thought it looked worse than any traveller would wear. My grand-daughter said it was the fashion but I thought it was worse than the worst fashion that we ever went in for. We were cried 'tinks, dirty tinks' and 'trollopy tinks' but we wouldnae go aboot like that. But it is true. Some o them hae these cotton skirts trailin or almost trailin the grund anyway. Nae shape nor form and aa wrinkles. And then this great black coat wi a white scarf. That's the only bit o relief. They'll spend a fortune on stuff that Ah widnae be seen dead in!

MB *What were people buried in?*

BW Well, now and then you'd get one that would want to be buried in his auld kilt – maybe he would be a piper – wi jist a white sark an tie on. Sometimes some o them wanted even to be buried in a suit – jist as they were. But maist o the women liked a white nightie, shroud.

MB *Did they keep shrouds?*

BW Oh no! They never kept anythin like. That would be too invitin to Death. But a lot o the cottar-folk did. They would show you their white shrouds. This is what Ah'm goin tae show ye now. . . . Aye, isn't it lovely? Ma mother would bless hersel when she cam away frae the door. She would probably be sayin that she had never seen nor heard the like of it. Imagine keepin a shroud? What did it matter what ye wore when ye died? No, they wouldnae keep anythin like that – very rarely they would keep three o a thing. If they had two things o the same kind they would think they had one too many, an the first person to come alang would be offered some o this surplus. That's how they carried on.[93]

Captain John A. MacLellan
Edinburgh,1991

MB *In a military funeral was the role of the piper very specific?*

J.McL Oh yes. The whole business builds up from the bearer party, headed by the piper. Or if they hadn't got a piper in the unit they would try to get a piper from somewhere to play the cortege through the centre gates to the graveside. . . . Most regiments have the same sort of system, where they play a part of 'Lochaber No More' – that's the tune that is usually played at the graveside, whereas approaching the grave he plays 'The Flowers of the Forest'. Now how that Lowland tune became incorporated in Highland regimental tradition I don't know. But it's *always* the 'Flowers of the Forest' and then 'Lochaber No More'. And that's played in three parts, and between each part there's a rifle volley from soldiers who make up the guard – they have their rifles with them and they fire a volley between each stanza of 'Lochaber No More'. After that there is the committal with the bugler playing 'The Last Post', and after 'The Last Post' he plays 'Reveille' – I suppose the waking up of the dead again. And then, *after*, the whole cortege marches out – not slow marching, but *marches* out of the cemetery playing one of the regimental marches. And that's the sort of routine that a military funeral always has.

MB *So that's standard . . .*

J.McL Pretty well – in peace time or wartime or whatever. Some regiments might slightly move away from that but by and large that's it.

---

[93] Betsy Whyte was recorded at the School of Scottish Studies while guest at a lecture by MB on April 28, 1988. SA1988/24.

MB *I've heard it said by some military piper that they wouldn't play 'The Flowers of the Forest' at any other occasion.*

J.McL Oh no! Well it's one of these traditional rules that have come down to us. For instance, when King George VI died I was in Redford Barracks [Edinburgh] and when I came out of the barracks I saw that the flag was flying at half mast, so I knew – already we had been warned that if the King died we'd be on our way to London for the funeral. So I had the music to rehearse. Now we *only* rehearsed the tunes on the practice chanter – the pipe band is never taken out to rehearse any of these tunes, and its bad form to play 'The Flowers of the Forest' in public for any reason other than a funeral.[94]

MB *What about Armistice Day?*

J.McL Again, the piper's supposed to practise it in his garret.

MB *He may play 'The Flowers of the Forest' on Remembrance Sunday at the cenotaph, but that's it?*

J.McL Yes.[95]

A Professional Attitude to Death

Beliefs connected with death that appear to have no logical explanation (and are therefore branded by some as 'superstitious') are commonplace, not only in Scotland but all over the world. Regardless of how sophisticated our society becomes, regardless of the growing tendency towards more professional involvement by highly esteemed hospitals and hospices, we can still hear people from all walks of life react to the news of a death with a comment such as: 'Oh my, there goes the first! Just wait, there'll be another two before long – deaths always come in threes.'

What then of the attitude among the professionals? They are all highly trained in dealing with the process of dying, offer great comfort to all concerned, and at the time of death they automatically and meticulously follow the procedures which are standard to the establishment. A number of nurses from several hospitals in the Glasgow area were asked pertinent

---

[94] The Highland pipe tunes played for the procession at the Queen Mother's funeral, April 2002, were 'Mo Dhachaidh' ['My Home'], 'Chi Mi na Mòrbheanna' ['The mist covered mountains'], said to be a favourite of her husband's. After the ceremony, on leaving Westminster Abbey, the massed pipes and drums, which included the Irish Guards, played 'Oft in the Stilly Night'.

[95] Captain John A. MacLellan, founder of the Army School of Piping at Edinburgh Castle and world authority on piping was recorded in Edinburgh on 28 February 1991 by MB. SA1991/06. I am grateful to Capt. MacLellan for going over the transcription with me, and to his wife Bunty for her hospitality and interest. His death (aged 69) in April 1991 has been a great loss not only to the world of piping, but to all who knew him.

questions by a member of their own profession, Howard Mitchell, who was studying ethnology at the time. As an 'insider' discussing aspects of common interest, the replies he elicited to the questions paraphrased here go to show that attitudes and beliefs have more to do with tradition than training.

Howard Mitchell
Glasgow, 1990

HM *Is there any particular number associated with the occurrence of death?*

NURSE A It's true, they only come in threes.

NURSE B What I heard was that people died in threes, and its surprising how often it actually happens, in say the space of a week or even less than that.

NURSE C That, funnily enough, tended to happen fairly regularly. I think the thing about that is it gets distorted by the time factor. I mean when we were up in the Hospital East they used to say, 'Oh, who's next?' and you would get two or three . . . Like, depending on the time scale, some of them would wait maybe a month to be able to say that, you know. And the fact that there was maybe another one hot on the heels didnie count as a fourth. It counted as the first one towards the next three.

HM *Does death usually occur at any particular time?*

NURSE D Another thing I used to notice. In the hours between 12 and 4 [a.m.] they were more likely to go. Life seems to be at its lowest ebb.

NURSE B I think most deaths occur during the night though, do you not think that yourself? I can remember being on night shift in both medical and surgical, and feeling that there was quite a lot. And also being on the day shift and walking in in the morning and you'd see one or two empty beds. I think that death occurs more during the night.

NURSE E Either late evening to early night. Commonly after visiting times, say about half seven or something like that. From that to maybe midnight, or early in the morning, like four o'clock, five o'clock, something like that. They were the periods. But they were the periods when you tended to get the bulk of your non-expected ones anyway.

NURSE F When I worked in the hospital, inevitably death happened at the weekend and they were shoved along to the waiting room until the Monday.

HM *When there's a death on the ward is there a particular way the nurses remove the body without causing distress to the other patients?*

NURSE B You always . . . they'd stop at the end of the ward, and whoever had noticed them, you'd curtain off as many beds as possible, so that nobody would see. Everybody knew what was happening obviously. It was one of the rituals, therefore, if you knew that someone was going to die, you'd move them up nearer the exit of the ward . . . But in the hospital that we work in, the trolley itself is covered by a blanket and a pillow and a pillow is put on top of it, but it's the bread bin type, but it's got a blanket over the top so that it looks just like a normal trolley.

NURSE G The trolley that they brought in for the bodies, it was like a breid bin. But it had a casket on the top, an aluminium casket, and you put the body on the trolley and the casket went on the top. But it was the same kind of rattling sound as the porter coming round with the breid in the morning. And at breakfast time, the kitchen hadnie sent up any breid this morning, but we had a death through the night . . . and I had said to the boys . . . again it was a night shift situation, you put out the breakfast before you went off duty. And they says what about the breid? And I says, well the porters couldnie get the trolley cos they were taking that boy's body down, and you had to be blunt about it. You couldnie say, oh there wasnie a death, for as soon as there was a death in the ward, they removed the body, and all the screens were shut. You know you made a corridor of screens so that the patients that were in bed didnie see the body, but they knew that there was a body being wheeled out. Anyway as soon as we drew all the screens and they heard the rattling of the trolley, they knew somebody had died and the body was . . . [wheeled out]. And of course in the morning the empty bed's there and they knew so-and-so had died. So there was no point in messing about and saying, 'No, nobody died, he ran away or whatever, he was discharged through the night!' So I says, 'No, they never brought the breid up – the porters were using the trolley to take the body down.' See when the breid did come up . . . nobody wanted it! And the unfortunate thing about it was, it was the time of the breid strike, you couldnie get breid. So there were four loaves that nobody would eat. But I could only get one up my jaiket!

Nurses readily point out that the distress caused by death is an aspect of nursing which every member of the profession has to face. Each death will bring to the hospital staff as wide a range of reactions as can be expected in any section of society; if, for example, a lively, young person dies, it is reasonable to expect hearts to be heavier than when a very elderly and infirm person passes away. Nurses constantly remind themselves that life must go on, care of the living must not be affected by attention to the dead, even if it means lifting spirits by making light of serious matters. And just as every section of society has its anecdotes about unconventional behaviour at funerals (such as accounts which tell of abandoning the coffin because the funeral party was too drunk to carry on!) so every hospital has its stories of hilarity connected with death.

Usually, young trainee nurses are the brunt of the so-called hilarity. There are universal told-as-true stories at every hospital of some 'poor little nurse' who gets sent to the mortuary by her superiors only to 'die of fright' when the corpse (one of her 'friends' lying under a sheet) sits up and groans. The story is generally told about a 'friend of a nurse who was training with a friend of mine' and thus the victim is seldom interviewed. There are, however, a few prank-players who relate incidents such as this:

NURSE G I was in Hospital East. The Staff Nurse was telling us, 'Right, we'll have a bit of fun!' There was an old guy that was ready to die. And the drill in these days was that if you got a death in Hospital East, you did the body, and you wheeled it up to Hospital West. They had the keys of the mortuary, and they always had an extra nurse on, so they took the body down to the mortuary. The story was that that night the old boy had died, but he hadnie! I was going to be the body . . . The drill was you did the body up, tied the big toes ragether,[96] wrapped up in a sheet . . . so what they did was, I got on the trolley, shoes and socks off, trousers rolled up, and the feet sticking out with the ribbon of bandage round the two big toes tying them together with the white label with the black edges, the mortuary ticket. It was big Andy was the Staff Nurse. Well, Andy wheels me down as the body – down to these wee nurses on night shift. They'd phoned up to say he was dead of course, and says, 'We'll be bringing the body across – you get organised.' Aye fine.

So I'm on the trolley, as I say, I've got the trousers rolled up, toes tied together, mortuary card. And the thing was, that I'm supposed to frighten these nurses when they take me across to the mortuary . . . So big Andy, he wheels me up. 'There we are!' [He says] 'That's him! All done up! Just wheel him across and leave him on the trolley, they'll get him in the morning and put him into the fridge.'

So on the way out of the side door of the hospital, it's on the flat, and then it takes a dip down, and then you've got to shove it up the hill. So I timed it all wrong. I didnie know at the time I'd timed it all wrong, but anyway, I waits till they were turning the corner with me on the thing, and it's middle of the night and they're wheeling me up to the mortuary. And I sits up with the sheet over me and goes 'Aaaaarrrrggghhhhh!' Well, these two nurses let this fuckin trolley go, and me on it, with my feet tied thegither! And it starts careering down the road. 'Course the wee wobbly wheels, one of them hits the kerb and the trolley goes up in the air and I goes over it. Well see the sore ankles I had, all skint to buggery on the road! And see the state thae nurses were in! Thae lasses were shot up, you know![97]

---

[96] The practice of tying the big toes together does not pertain only to hospital procedure; it was part of the laying out custom in various domestic situations also. D.A. MacDonald recorded Angus MacKenzie in North Uist describing (in Gaelic) the standard procedure of tying the toes together. SA1977/58.
[97] Recordings and transcriptions were made by Howard Mitchell in 1990. Connecting text by MB.

Prof. Edward Duvall
Edinburgh, 1999

I have made some discreet enquiries apropos the observation (mentioned during the discussion after your talk to the Morningside Heritage Association) that undertakers left behind a small sum of money when taking away a body from a hospital. Unfortunately the explanation is a very prosaic one . . . The small sum they leave is a 'measurement fee'. In order to save themselves the bother of coming to measure the body so that they know what size of coffin to bring when they come to collect the body, they ask someone on the ward or in the mortuary to measure the body and telephone them with the results. The 'measurement fee' is a payment for this.[98]

'Pet Cemeteries'

James Allan Rennie
Strathspey, 1956

[In the area of the Cairngorms, beyond Glenmore and Loch-an-Uaine], when the trees are left behind . . . a slight divergence will bring one to what is surely one of the strangest cemeteries in Britain. Here cairns mark the last resting place of favourite horses, and miniature tombstones those of equally loved dogs. The dogs are all coffined, I understand, and many of them have been brought great distances so that, like their masters [the Grants] they could be interred in the land of their fathers . . .[99]

The occurrence of 'resting places' for 'man's best friend', and memorials for animals (usually dogs and horses) is not as uncommon in Scotland as Mr Rennie suggests. There is one at Edinburgh Castle. The tradition is widespread and goes back several centuries, with the oldest among such cemeteries generally connected to a particular family, such as the MacLeods of Raasay, the Campbells of Cawdor Castle or Sir Walter Scott's family at Abbotsford. All have their dedicated pet cemeteries, marking the graves of beloved animals while recording their owners' love and devotion.

In the twenty-first century, the idea of pet cemeteries has been adopted by enterprising businesses to capture a lucrative market. Evelyn Waugh's classic novel, *The Loved One* (1948), that scathing satire on the Hollywood attitude

---

[98] E-mail from Prof. E. Duvall, Edinburgh, Department of Pathology, University of Edinburgh Medical School, 11 March 1999.
[99] *Ibid*, p. 73.

to death, was hugely successful among Scottish readers entertained by scenarios that seemed utterly beyond reality – the doggie funerals set near the 'Wee Kirk o Auld Lang Syne', the tartan carpets, heather, and the Robbie Burns and Harry Lauder souvenirs on sale nearby. Laugh no more, for they are now springing up in Scotland. Unlike the family pet cemeteries of bygone days, however, the owners operate a sliding scale of fees (from a hamster to a horse) and employ snappy marketing devices aimed at attracting business. The 'Peternal Glen', for example, offers comfort to bereaved pet-lovers invited to spare no expense for the funeral, interment, memorial stones with set-in photos, religious symbols, Celtic knots or whatever they might wish. Meanwhile, Scotland has now entered an era when people are opting for non-religious ceremonies for their human funerals.

Indelible Memories

Revd Donald Sage
Wick, 1889

My mother died in childbed, of her sixth child. Of the circumstances connected with her illness I have no recollection; but I have been told that, about an hour before her death, we were all solemnly summoned before her, and ranged round her dying bed, to take our last farewell of her and to receive her blessing. She took particular notice of me, appeared deeply affected, and, in broken accents, prayed that I might yet be useful in the vineyard of Christ. Of this solemn scene I have no recollection, but of that which very soon followed my memory has, at this moment, a most distinct hold. On the evening of the 27th of November, 1792, when I was three years and a month old, I recollect entering in at the door of the room where my mother, but a few hours before, had breathed her last. It was the low easter-room of the manse. A bed stood at the north-east corner of the room, with dark curtains folded up in front. On the bed lay extended, with a motionless stillness which both surprised and terrified me, one whom I at once knew to be my mother. I was sure it was she, although she lay so still and silent. She appeared to me to be covered with a white sheet or robe; white leather gloves were on her hands, which lay crossed over her body. At the opposite corner of the room sat my father. He had, previous to my coming in, been indulging his grief in silence, and giving vent to the 'bitterness of the heart' in half-audible sighs. My sudden and heedless entrance seemed to open up the flood-gates of his grief. I was the favourite child of her who now lay stretched in death – the last surviving pledge of their affection. It was too much for him. He sobbed aloud, the tears rolled down his face, his frame shook, and he clasped me in his large embrace in all the agony of a great sorrow. That sobbing still rings in my ears, although then my only feeling was that of childish wonder. I gazed, now at my mother's body, especially at her gloved and motionless hands, then at my father, as I could not conceive that any but children could weep at all, or at least weep aloud. My mother died in the forty-second year of her age. Of the subsequent events – the freshness of my father's sorrow, the solemnities of my mother's funeral, the necessary arrangements in the household consequent upon her death – of these, with many other circumstances, I have not the slightest remembrance. But the scene I have just described retains its place like a framed picture in my memory.[100]

Margaret Bennett
Diary entry, 4 May 1989

Today I bought my son a black tie. Fred offered to lend him one but I said 'No, Martyn's eighteen, and there comes a time in every young lad's life when he has to have his own black tie.'

'Aye,' Fred said, 'true enough, and the more time goes by the more he'll need it.'

It's Willie Scott's funeral, and the family have asked Martyn to play 'The Floo'ers o the Forest' for the auld man. The place was absolutely packed, and though there was a great sadness in gathering there was no hint of that bitter anguish that death sometimes brings. Willie saw the best part of ninety years, and when the congregation sang 'The Lord's My Shepherd' the singing filled the chapel in a way that did the old Border shepherd proud – he'd have probably told us, 'it's reachin richt till the rafters.' Alison sang Willie's mother's favourite song, 'Time Wears Awa', and though the hankies were out dabbing more than a few eyes, everyone raised the most magnificent chorus. We filtered out of the chapel into bright sunshine as the pipes played 'The Floo'ers o the Forest', followed by 'a few more that Willie would have liked.' Afterwards we all went to the hotel where the family had laid on a spread of sandwiches, preceded by a dram, of course. For the first time we met Willie's older brother, aged 98; he was up from the Borders for the day. They'd had a church service for the family in Hawick, he said, and then they all came up for the cremation in Edinburgh. His hankie was still on his lap, having dabbed a few tears from his eyes, and he told us, 'Ah min when Wull an me gaed tae

---

[100] Revd Donald Sage, *Memorabilia Domestica*, pp. 102–3.

the schule thegither, him oan the back o the pony an me wi the reins.' There were countless memories of Willie, amusing anecdotes by the dozen, and plenty of drams going around. Before long the songs started, and song after song filled the afternoon – just like one of the best ever singing sessions at a folk festival, and Willie would have loved every minute of it. Folk sang 'Callieburn', 'Bonnie Wee Trampin Lass' and many more of Willie's songs, but nobody could sing the 'Keilder Hunt' or recite 'MacAlister Before the King'. Some of his grandsons who were there seemed quite amazed that so many folk had turned out to pay respect to the old Border shepherd, the singer of so many fine songs. But for the fact that hired cars were waiting to take relatives back to the Borders and some folk had trains and buses to catch to Glasgow, Fife, and other areas, we'd have stayed on and on. Those of us living in Edinburgh were about the last to leave, and we did so with a feeling of contentment. We had said our goodbyes to an old friend, and as Hamish remarked, this was no mournful occasion; it was a fitting celebration of a great life.[101]

Margaret Bennett
Diary entry, 11 December 2003

Joe phoned to tell me his Dad died this morning. 'Just slipped away, he was 91 . . . he'd a good innings . . . I'm glad for him, really. The real sadness is Mum – they were always that close.'

'How is she?'

'Amazing, really. It's a shock, but she accepts – it's inevitable. Tears ran down her cheeks, but she composed herself. She always does. She's having a wee rest just now and we'll see her tonight to talk about the arrangements . . . I'll phone and let you know.'

And phone he did: 'Margaret, you're not going to believe this – Mum died this evening . . . I know . . . it's an awful shock . . . The girls were over, she told them the hymns she'd chosen and everything. She seemed just fine, tired, though. Said she was going to sleep . . . It's probably what they both would have wanted. John said she likely heard Joe saying, 'Come on, honey, put your coat on, wir gaun hame.' Mind he always called her 'Honey'? And he always said that when they were out visiting!'

---

[101] Personal diary.

Evening Times, **Glasgow**
20 December 2003

'Nothing could separate Joe and Agnes in 68 years of marriage. When he died, her heart gave up on the same day.'

A devoted couple who had never been apart during 68 years of marriage died on the same day as each other. Heartbroken Agnes McAtamney, 89, passed away hours after being told her 92-year-old husband Joe had died . . . The couple were being treated in the same hospital, one floor apart – and they insisted on seeing each other as much as possible. Mrs McAtamney had already planned her husband's funeral before she died 14 hours later . . . [They] leave behind five sons, two daughters, 11 grandchildren and 10 great-grandchildren . . .

Joe and Anges McAtamney were buried together at Linn Cemetery after a joint funeral at St Joseph's Church, Clarkston, on December 17.

May Anderson
Ibrox, Glasgow, 2004

MA I once had a wonderful experience – it was some time after I found my mother dead. A terrible shock. An' I put my son up to live with his Grandpa. And my husband Davie and I were goin' to collect him, an we were comin' along the road, it was in Shawlands . . . we turned into Barrhead Road – Davie always used to slow down in case anybody was at a bus-stop he knew, an' there wasn't a soul in the street. Now, this is the truth, Margaret: As we drove past, the car stopped [of its own accord, no explanation], and Davie went, 'Oh?' An' there was a minister standin' right at that spot. Where he came from I don't know.

An' Davie says out the window, 'Do you want something?' An' he says, 'Do you know where Corkerhill Church is?' An Davie says, 'Yes, I'll take ye.' OK, we drove along, an' he says to me, 'You're troubled, daughter.' An' I went, 'Uh-huh, 'an I started telling him the story [about finding my mother dead]. An' we were driving up Barrhead Road an it's a' railings there, you know, that big, big street. An' he says to Davie, 'Just stop here.' An' Davie says, 'But this isnae near Corkerhill Church.' He says, 'My work's done.' He stepped oot the car, we turned roon, an' nobody was there. Not a soul. We went to wave to him an' he wasn't there. An my husband went, 'Oh Jesus Christ!' An' he couldnae drive! But we both saw and heard him . . . He prayed, aye.

And I never told anybody that for years. Till in the church one night, we'd two ministers, one was Scots and one was American. An' he says something, an' I says, 'Oh, I mind that experience I had.'

'What is it, May? Come on into the vestry, tell us aboot it.' I told them, an' he went, 'And do you believe it?'

'Oh, aye, I do believe it.' Well, seeing is believing, wi' anything like that! You couldnae go through railings! I mean, how could he go through railings? I'll never forget that. I mean it is weird – you know that street. It's broad. If he'd even crossed the road, but he didn't. He got oot the car, an' Davie went, 'You're no' near Corkerhill.'

An' he said, 'My work's done.' An' I went like that to wave to him, an' I said, 'Where did he go?'

An' Davie went, 'I don't know. Where did he go?'

We looked up an' down the street. That was a funny feeling. And I mind Davie saying, 'You know, May, that car stopped itself. I didn't stop that car, that car stopped itself, to pick him up. Yet when we turned in the street there was nobody there.'

So the minister I told, he said when Davie died (in the 1971 Ibrox disaster), 'You know, he might come to you again, May.' But he never did, you know. But I always think somebody's watching over you anyway. Oh, I believe that.[102]

Grave-markers, Cairns and Memorials

Traditions of tombstones, gravestones and memorial stones go back to time immemorial and could fill volumes on their own.[103] Scotland has a vast number of ancient markers commemorating death. Many were ceremoniously built as cairns, frequently in wild places, such as mountain-tops or river banks, though also on battlefields, in city centres, town market places, village squares and even sports grounds. Perpetual reminders of those who have gone before, all have a story to tell. Organisations such as The National Trust for Scotland and Historic Scotland, along with a range of tourist guidebooks, disseminate information such as:

Glenfinnan Monument, set amid superb Highland scenery at the head of Loch Shiel, was erected in 1815 by Alexander Macdonald of Glenaladale in tribute to the clansmen who fought and died in the cause of Prince Charles.

High on *Creag-an-Lurachain* is Prince Albert's memorial cairn, the largest of a number of cairns erected by Queen Victoria on the Balmoral Estate. Beyond the cairn is the majestic peak of Lochnagar, snow topped even as late as June on occasion.

[102] May was recorded in her home in Ibrox by MB, February 2004.
[103] For example, Donaldson (1991) and Mitchell (1981 and 1987)

A cairn to the memory of R. B. Cunninghame Graham of Ardoch, distinguished Scottish author, politician and traveller, was erected in 1937, one year after his death, at Castlehill, Dumbarton. It was moved to Gartmore, Stirling, in 1981.

Annual gatherings are held beside some, such as Culloden (16 April 1746) and Bannockburn (24 June 1314), while hundreds of war memorials are the focus of ceremonies every November 11, Remembrance Day, when the nation remembers the fallen of two world wars (1914–18 and 1939–45).

The fireside stories of shepherds, gamekeepers, estate workers, and fishermen help to keep alive local traditions about cairns. Many have become landmarks to hill walkers, mountaineers and natural historians.

J.J. Dixon
Gairloch, 1886

Two miles beyond Loch Clair the march or boundary between Gairloch and Applecross parishes is reached. To the right of the road, on the Gairloch side, is a pile of very large stones – evidently artificial – heaped up on a flat space. It is called 'Carn Anthony', or 'Anthony's cairn', and is said to have been erected long ago in memory of a son, named Anthony, of one of the MacKenzie proprietors of Torridon.[104]

Seton Gordon
Outer Hebrides, 1923

One day of early summer I crossed the island [North Uist] to the eastern coast, making my way by the pass that rises from peat-stained Loch Spotal, and heather-clad Coire na h' Eitich to the watershed. Here a large cairn of stones marks the little-used track, for many funerals must have passed here, and it was the custom, wherever the coffin was rested, for each of the mourners to put a stone on that place.

James Allan Rennie
Strathspey, 1956

Archie's Cairn at *Glaic Bothan* below Eagle's Cliff on Cairngorm . . . commemorates a tragedy that took place towards the beginning of the nineteenth century . . . William (nicknamed 'Foxie') Fraser and Archie Fyfe of Sleighich went out in a moonlight to shoot a fox . . . Fyfe dropped his gun

---

[104] John H. Dixon, *Gairloch*, pp. 322–3.

on a slope and, when trying to retrieve it, it went off, mortally wounding him . . .

[N]ear the junction of the Glasalt and the Uisge-dubh-pullchoin . . . a memorial to one of the soldiers who perished in a storm in 1804 when trying to negotiate the Larig Ghru . . .[105]

Memorial cairns have become increasingly significant to many groups who identify with the Scottish custom of paying respect in this way. Visit any group of American, Canadian, Australian or New Zealand Scots and you will discover that, even several generations removed from the 'Old Country', descendents of emigrants observe the tradition. For some, the memorial cairn has become an annual rallying point: in North Carolina over 40,000 tartan-clad Americans attend the annual clan gathering of emigrants and their descendants at Grandfather Mountain; in Nova Scotia, huge crowds of folk make a pilgrimage to Pictou, Cape Breton, to remember the emigrants who sailed on the *Hector*; and in Quebec the last stalwarts of the Gaels stand at the cairn with their French-speaking grandchildren to pay homage to 'les premiers arrivants Ecossais'.[106] Each occasion is deeply moving, to the onlooker as well as the participants.

At home in Scotland the Clan Memorial Cairn on Culloden Moor ranks as one of the most frequently visited sites in Britain. Countless tourists and passers-by regularly stop to pay respects at the imposing Commando Memorial near Glensheil. There, wreaths of scarlet poppies for fallen heroes are renewed every year on Remembrance Day – they defy wind, rain and snow from one November to the next.

Arguably the most visible memorial 'cairn' in Scotland is one that is made of bricks, rectangular in shape, rather than circular and of natural stones. It stands just outside Rangers' Football Stadium in Ibrox (Glasgow), where it was erected on the thirtieth anniversary of the tragic 'Stairway Thirteen' disaster of 1971.

The Herald

Glasgow, 3 January 2001

'Thousands join in silent homage'
Thousands of people gathered at Ibrox stadium in Glasgow yesterday on the 30th anniversary of Scotland's worst footballing tragedy to pay tribute to the 66 victims. About 470 relatives of the Rangers supporters who died on

---

[105] J.A. Rennie, *Romantic Strathspey: Its Lands, Clans and Legends*, pp. 70–72.
[106] M. Bennett, *Oatmeal and the Catechism*, 2nd edn.

January 2, 1971, watched David Murray, the club chairman, unveil a statue of John Greig, who captained he team against Celtic on the day.

The memorial statue [reminiscent of a brick-built cairn or war-memorial, with figure on top] lists the names of the dead and those killed in other tragedies at the ground in 1902 and 1961. Many of the families touched their loved ones' names. Just yards away, on the spot where the 66 died on the then stairway 13, Rangers and Celtic fans created their own tribute by laying dozens of wreaths, scarves and shirts . . . on the site of the long-gone Stairway 13.

A service attended by the relatives outside the stadium was related to 5000 people inside . . . A minute's silence was held before a prayer of dedication was read . . . Former Ranger's captain, John Greig, who laid a wreath during the service, said he had never been able to get over the tragedy . . . 'you still feel it even after all these years.'[107]

The Bible
Isaiah 61:20

Thy sun shall no more go down; neither shall thy moon withdraw itself: for the Lord shall be thine everlasting light, and the days of thy mourning shall be ended.

Rest in peace

Sìth do d' anam, is clach air do chàirn
Peace to your soul, and a store on your cairn

---

[107] Excerpted and rearranged from the front-page article and inside news feature, p. 3. [my square brackets]

Glossary

Abbreviations

colloq.	colloquial
F.	French
G.	Gaelic
lit.	literally
n.	noun
O.N.	Old Norse
v.	verb

aa	all
lumber	boyfriend or girlfriend, usually a one night stand or 'pick-up'
aboon	above
adee	to do (*whit's adee* = what's to do. . .)
ane	one
apartment	room
athegeether	all together
ba siller	lit. ball silver, money thrown after a wedding
banns	public announcement of marriage
barm	yeast
beadle	church officer
bean ghlùine	(G.) midwife
beddan	bedding (after marriage)
bere	a type of barley once very common in Scotland, now less so
besom	broom, sweeping brush
beukin nicht	the evening when names are registered for proclamation of marriage
bide	abide, live, stay
bit	but
blinkin fell cantie	shining quite pleasantly (as in weather)

brace, braize, brooze, running the braize	race at a country wedding, usually from the church or the bride's home to the bridegroom's home.
braize, *see* brace	
bread-bin trolley	(hospital slang), mortuary trolley
breid	bread
bridder	brother
bride-steel	bride's stool or pew
broose, *see* brace	
brooze, *see* brace	
bunbed	box-bed
but ein	but end, part of house
by	over, past
bye-path	short-cut
caff	chaff
canny	careful
cap	wooden bowl
carvey	sugar coated caraway seed
chanty	chamber pot, usually of china
cheeny	china
claes	clothes (deid claes, weddin claes)
clister, clyster	enema
clout, clouted	cloth, clothed
cog, coggie	small, staved wooden vessel
corn	oats (in Scotland)
corp	corpse
cosey-belly	stove
cottar-folk	folk (usually farm labourers) who live in farm cottages
craa	crow
craiturs	creatures
creel	basket
crook	fireside, pot-hook
crowdie	a home-made soft cheese, similar to cottage cheese
curtch	closs cap, close cap (worn by older or married women)
da	the
dan	then

dat	that
deals	planks of wood
dee	die
deid-can'le	(lit.) dead candle; sometimes ref. to as 'corpse light'
deiseil	sunwise, in the direction of the sun, clockwise
dirll	(v.) vibrate with noise
dog-hole	hole in the wall to allow passage of dog
draigie	see dredgy
dredgy, dredgie, dirgy	food and drink served after a funeral
dressing-down	(n.) scolding, rebuke
drudgy, *see* dredgy	
duine uasal	important person, nobleman
dwine	failed, declined in health and strength
'e	the
e'en	even
enceinte	(F.) pregnant
fae	(usually) from; (sometimes) when
faey	(O.N. feigr) fated to die
faht	what
fainfu'	glad, affectionate
faured, weel faured	good looking
fess	fetch, go for
fey-crop	fey (supernatural) crop; an unexpectedly good harvest
fi	for
filk	which
firlot	measure containing a fourth part of a boll
first fit	first foot, first person to enter the house (usually after a wedding or New Year)
fite	white
flett	flat, floor (of mill or factory)
forespeak, forespoken	praise or admire a child or baby, usually considered excessive
forespyke, *see* forespeak	
forrit	forward
fou' o the moon	full moon
freen	friend
fye	why
gaffer	overseer of work

gehn	if
girn	whine, moan, complain (usually persistently)
girnal	storage chest for meal
gloomin	overcast
greeance	agreement
greetin	weeping, crying
growing in a knot	growing into confusion
gruel	oatmeal boiled with water, like a thin porridge
gueede	good
hansel	gift
herd(s)	shepherd(s)
hippen	baby's nappy, diaper
hit	it
hooch(ed)	whoop(ed), as in the sudden noise made by dancers
hotched	jumped, danced
hunner	hundred
ill e'e	evil eye
infare	feast given at a bride's reception
ingle-mids	hot coals in the middle of the fire
ir	her
it	that
jaiket	jacket
jinks	nimble movements, frolics
jizzen-bed	child-bed, the bed of confinement
kaibbers	rafters
kail, win the	(win the) race at a wedding, the prize being a kiss from the bride
kebback	cheese
ken	know
kirkin	churching
kirsnin	christening
kist	chest, usually for blankets or meal
kistan	putting the body in the coffin
laan	land lane, its lane = itself
lappits	flaps (on a bonnet) that covered the ears
lichter	lighter
lum	chimney
mack	make
maister	master

mehl-bowie	barrel for storing oatmeal
meht, merry meht	food served at a feast in celebration of the birth of a child
mibbie	maybe
midden	dung-heap
mould	earth
muckle	much
muir	moor
mutch	frilled bonnet worn by married women
myne	mind, remember
mynt	remembered
neist	next
oncost men	labourers working under a contractor
oose	house (*Come our in fess a' yir oose wi ye* = Come over and fetch/bring all your family with you.)
pay-off	pre-marriage night out; celebration
pieces	sandwiches
pieces	silver
pinny	apron
pit it over	(lit.) put it over/on (colloq.); arrange
plinisan	(lit.) plenishing; providing, usually for a wedding
pluck	growth
poke	paper bag
poor, poor oot	pour, pour out (usually money, at a wedding)
providan	providing, a bride's stock of household linen for her future home
queentry	country
ragether	together
rantry	rowan tree, mountain ash
reef	roof
rick	stack, such as the large hay stacks in the stack yard
rin	run
ristin stehn	resting stone (for laying down the coffin during funeral)
sain	purify
sair	sore
sark	shirt
saut	salt
saw	sow (as in *lint seed I saw ye* . . .)

scarting	flirting in a boistrous, physical manner, such as nudging, slapping, etc.
scull	a shallow scoop-shaped basket (or wooden container) for holding fish or baited lines
seelfu	firm, binding, solemn, as if ratified by a seal, as of a vow or oath; severe, emphatic.
sehr	sore
sens	groomsmen (at a wedding)
shaimit (reel)	first dance at a wedding, danced by the bride and groom and best man and bridesmaid
shaim-spring	tune played for the shaimit reel
sheelin-coug	sharp, knife-like utensil used for shelling mussels in preparation for bait
shifters	mill workers whose job is to change the bobbins on a spinning frame
shoor	shower
sic	such
siller	silver
skaith	damage, hurt, injury, harm
skilly	skilled, knowledgeable
snell	sharp, cold (as a breeze from the sea)
sough(ing)	sighing (of the wind)
sowans	oatmeal boiled in water, of a fairly thin consistency
sowels	lit. souls; individuals
speert	asked
speirs	asks
steer, in a s.	in a stir, commotion.
streikin	stretching
strykin/streiking beuird	stretching board (for dead body)
strykit	stretched
swyl'd	swaddled
syne	then
tack	take
tatties	potatoes
te	to
teind	tithe, tenth part of one's income
thegither	together
thestreen	yestreen, yesterday evening
they	those, these

thigging	(O.N. lit.) begging; Scots usage: contributions to set up the household of newly-weds
thir	their
thirsel	themselves
thraw	train, bend
thump	knock, beat (as in beating the breast in grief)
tother	the other
trollopy	tramp-like; having clothes that are too long and untidy
tut'ry	care and protection devoted to a child
twal	twelve
umman	woman
unco	extremely, very
ur	are
usquabae	(G.) whisky
VAD	(member of the) Voluntary Aid Detachment, an organization of British volunteer nurses who served during the two World Wars
vitriol	sulphuric acid
vivers	food, provisions, victuals
waddin	wedding
waicht	sieve
wan	one
wanted	lacked
wardle	world
waulan	wake, lyke wake
wean, weeane	small child
wether	castrated male sheep
windae	window
wint	want
wir	were; our (as in *wir hoose*)
wis	was
woodie	young green sapling
wot	know
wud	would
wur	our
yammered	wailed or whined in an irritating and incessant manner
yince	once
yir	your

Further Reading

Although the subjects discussed in this anthology are relevant to all of Scotland, yet the book cannot pretend to cover even a fraction of the variants that occur from area to area. In studying any aspect of Scottish custom, (e.g. calendar festivities) it will be apparent almost immediately that there are an enormous number of regional differences. Despite the fact that there is a wide geographic sampling of customs in this collection, I have no doubt that many readers will look for a particular custom from their own locality, naturally expecting it to be included, then if they cannot find it may be quite disappointed. Initially I attempted to cover Scotland by county or (to be more up-to-date) by region, but that idea had to be abandoned, as it was instantly fraught with difficulties. While today's official regions are virtually useless as terms of reference for this subject (consider Strathclyde, for example: if you live on the Isle of Mull your regional headquarters are in Glasgow), the old counties are only marginally more specific. In reality it is not simply a matter of defining geographic district, for within one very small area (less than a mile in some cases) can be found variations in the practice or custom, and wherever you are you will be likely to encounter individuals who will tell you that their own local way 'is the *correct* way'. These brief notes are merely a guideline for further study and comparisons.

At this point I need say very little about the books I have chosen to quote in the text, except that most are over fifty years old, many are out of print, and copyright laws have been carefully observed. I hope these writers have spoken for themselves and that the reader will already have the flavour of them, and rather than discount them as 'further reading' may be inspired to read the originals. There are many that I did not include, but still regard them as worthwhile sources on the subject; they are listed in the bibliography that follows. To answer the question 'Where do I begin?' I will offer some general remarks on just a few which might help readers to 'make a start' on further reading:

Covering a wide geographic area is E.T. Guthrie's *Old Scottish Customs, Local and General*, London, 1885, and reprinted Edinburgh, 1985, which gives numerous lively accounts of aspects of the cycle of life. Despite its chaotic arrangement (and no index, even in the new edition) and the fact that primary sources for the material are only noted in a general introduction, it has a wealth of information. Also ranging over an extensive area is J.M. McPherson's *Primitive Beliefs in the North-East of Scotland*, London, New York, Toronto, 1929, which in no way confines itself to the suggested geographic area or even to the subject of the title. The complete cycle of life is discussed, details are given on such topics as cures for infertility, the treatment of ailments in infancy, with an especially informative section on old-time wakes and death customs. McPherson has also included an excellent bibliography not only for the folklore of Scotland but for world-wide comparisons.

For the Highlands and Islands there is a wide range, dating back to Martin Martin's *Description of the Western Isles, circa 1695*, which is invaluable for basic details about the way of life as he, a native of the Isle of Skye, observed it. Other early accounts from which fragments are quoted are Captain Edward Burt's *Letters from a Gentleman in the North of Scotland*, and Thomas Pennant's *Tour*. I have not, however, included Boswell and Johnson's journals since their writings are peppered with inaccuracies and value judgments that I would not encourage in any of my students of folklore fieldwork and research techniques. By way of contrast, I have included the seldom-acknowledged Revd John Lane Buchanan. His candid book, *Travels in the Western Hebrides: from 1782–1790*, is from roughly the same era as Johnson, yet it has been virtually neglected for two centuries. Instead, general readers have been taken in by the reputation of the world-famous lexicographer, Dr Johnson and his Scottish travelling companion who, if I may say so, ought to have known better. Buchanan's observations were made over a period of ten years while he was living and working among the Hebridean people, and, as he noted in his own introduction, he spoke the same language as the people whose culture he observed. His fieldwork techniques were far in advance of his better-known contemporaries.

Also invaluable for Gaelic Scotland are John Gregorson Campbell's books, *Superstitions of the Highlands and Islands of Scotland* (1900) and *Witchcraft and Second Sight in the Highlands and Islands of Scotland* (1902). Despite the slightly misleading title of *Witchcraft*, there is much relevant material, especially on the subject of death and death warnings in particular.

For the Northern Isles there are several titles, including G.F. Black's *Examples of Printed Folk-Lore Concerning the Orkney and Shetland Islands*, published by the Folk-Lore Society in 1903, which has a good bibliography, quotes many earlier writers on the cycle of life, and is unique in the fact that it deals with the subject of divorce. More recent writers of note are John Firth, Jessie Saxby and E.W. Marwick, to mention but a few.

For the Kingdom of Fife, there are also several worthwhile collections. Notable is John E. Simpkin's *Examples of Printed Folk-Lore Concerning Fife with some notes on Clackmannan and Kinross-shire*, published for the Folk-Lore Society in 1914, which has a reliable bibliography.

Dumfries and Galloway Region also has several works which are based on the old counties. One of the finest is by J. Maxwell Wood, a former editor of the journal *The Gallovidian* (a publication in itself well worth looking at). His book *Witchcraft and Superstitions Record in the South-Western District of Scotland*, Dumfries, 1911, (yet another misleading title) has a superb section on the subject of death, which I have quoted extensively, and also chapters on other aspects of the cycle of life.

On the Borders there is William Henderson's *Notes on the Folk-Lore of the Northern Counties*, published for the Folk-Lore Society in 1879, which has a title that suggests only England, but in fact is an absorbing collection of comparative accounts of customs dealing with almost every aspect of life on both sides of the Border. Other relevant books are easier to identify, as their titles bear the name of counties, towns and villages. I have included only one book by the most famous Border writer, Sir Walter Scott – his *Letters on Demonology and Witchcraft*. I decided not to include any of his novels, despite the fact that they are full of customs which Scott himself observed or heard of during his lifetime. (He also left profuse notes on such matters, as did Robert Chambers in his *Notes* on the Waverley novels.)

Enthusiasts for the Scottish novel may be disappointed that not a single one of their favourites has been included in this book, despite the fact that Scottish writers such as Robert Louis Stevenson, Lewis Grassic Gibbon, Neil Gunn, Gavin Maxwell, George Mackay Brown, Muriel Spark and many others base much of their descriptive writing on Scottish traditions. Nevertheless, for this collection (initially created for students) I have decided for the following reasons not to include any novels (though I give a brief reference to one): regardless of how often or how well novelists draw upon material from tradition, they may use the information in any manner they choose; they are at liberty to alter slightly, or drastically, or to blend together aspects of many different traditions (not only within the nation but from much further afield), just as long as the recreation serves the purpose of the novel and fits the plot. Whereas the novelist is under no obligation to remain faithful to tradition, the folklorist is compelled to do so. As a folklorist, I make no exception for a book intended to acquaint readers with primary sources for Scottish customs and beliefs. I would hope, however, that booklovers will extend their interest and read many Scottish novels with a more critical eye, and be able to decide for themselves which elements are true to tradition. What follows is by no means a comprehensive bibliography (despite the updated second edition) but merely a guide for those who wish to pursue the subject in further detail.

Bibliography

Abbreviations

Co FL   County Folk Lore
PFLS   Publication of the Folk-Lore Society
TGSI   *Transactions of the Gaelic Society of Inverness*

Alexander, William. *Notes and Sketches of Northern Rural Life*, Edinburgh, 1877.

Anton, A.E. 'Handfasting in Scotland', *Scottish Historical Review*, vol. 37, no. 124, 1958, pp. 91–102.

Bainton, R.H. *Here I Stand; a Life of Martin Luther*, New York, 1950.

Barker, Mary. 'The Bride's Cog', *Scots Magazine*, March 1984, pp. 618–620.

Barry, Rev. George. *History of the Orkney Islands, including a view of the Manners, and Customs of their Ancient and Modern Inhabitants, etc.*, 2nd ed. with corrections and additions by Rev. James Headrick, London, 1808 and Kirkwall, 1867.

Bennett, Gillian. *Traditions of Belief: Women and the Supernatural*, Penguin, 1987.

Bennett, Margaret. 'Childbirth and Infancy in Scotland' and 'Courtship and Marriage in Scotland' pp. 74–76, 107–110 in *The Oxford Companion to Scottish History* (ed. M. Lynch), Oxford, 2001.

Bennett, Margaret. 'Hebridean Childhood' in *Hebridean Odyssey* (ed. M. Sinclair), Edinburgh, 1996.

Bennett, Margaret. 'Local Dimensions in Oral Tradition', *Scottish Culture: the Local Dimension*, Proceedings of SCOTLOC Conference, ed. Don Martin, Motherwell, 1991.

Bennett, Margaret. 'Now This is True' in *The Brahan Seer Celebratory Booklet* (ed. L. MacDougall), Dingwall, 2001.

Bennett, Margaret. 'Stories of the Supernatural: From Local Memorate to Scottish Legend' in *Fantasticall Ymaginatiounis The Supernatural in Scottish Culture*, ed. Lizanne Henderson, forthcoming.

Bennett, Margaret. '1690–1990: Balquhidder Revisited', in *The Good People: New Fairylore Essays* (ed. Peter Narváez), Garland Publishing, New York, 1991.

Bennett, Margaret. *Oatmeal and the Catechism: Scottish Gaelic Settlers in Quebec*, Edinburgh and Montreal, 1998; new edition, 2003.

Bennett, Margaret. 'Plant Lore in Gaelic Scotland', pp. 56–60 in *Flora of the Outer Hebrides*, ed. R. Pankhurst, British Museum of Natural History, London, l991.

Bennett, Margaret. 'The Folklore of Plants in Scotland', in *Plants and People: Economic Botany in Northern Europe, 800–1800*, ed. J.H. Dickson and R.R. Mill, Edinburgh,1994.

Bennett, Margaret. *The Last Stronghold: The Scottish Gaelic Traditions of Newfoundland*, Edinburgh and St John's, Newfoundland, 1989.

Bennett, Margaret and Doris Rougvie. *Then Another Thing . . . Remembered in Perthshire*, Perth & Kinross Council (Museums Dept.), Perth, 2000.

Bennett, Martyn. Notes to *Glen Lyon*, a song-cycle representing five generations of Gaelic Tradition. (Songs sung by Margaret Bennett, arranged, accompanied and produced by Martyn Bennett.) Footstompin Records, Edinburgh, 2002.

Beveridge, Erskine, *North Uist: Its Archaeology and Topography with notes upon the early history of the Outer Hebrides*, Edinburgh, 1911.

Bible, The King James Version,

Black, G.F., and Thomas, Northcote W. *Examples of Printed Folk-Lore Concerning the Orkney & Shetland Islands*, Co FL, vol. III; PFLS 49, London, 1903.

Bonsor, Wilfrid. *A Bibliography of Folklore*, PFLS 121, London, 1961.

Boyd, Kenneth M. *Scottish Church Attitudes to Sex, Marriage, and the family, 1850–1914*, Edinburgh, 1980.

Brand, J. *Popular Antiquities of Great Britain*, London, 1882–83.

Brand, Rev. John. *Brief Description of Orkney, Zetland, Pightland Firth, and Caithness, with an account of the journey, people habits, etc.*, Edinburgh, 1701.

Buchanan, Donald. *Reflections of the Isle of Barra*. publ. Catholic Book Club, 1943.

Buchanan, John Lane. *Travels in the Western Hebrides: from 1782–1790*, London, 1793.

Budge, Donald. *Jura An Island of Argyll: its History, People and Story*, Glasgow, l960.

Burt, Capt. Edward. *Letters from a Gentleman in the North of Scotland to his Friend in London . . . begun in 1726*, 2 vols., London, 1754 and 1815.

Campbell, John L. (ed). *A Collection of Highland Rites and Customs Copied by Edward Lluyd from the Manuscript of the Rev. James Kirkwood (1650–1709 and Annotated by him with the Aid of the Rev. John Beaton*, Cambridge, 1975.

Campbell, John L. (ed). *Tales from Barra: Told by the Coddy*, Edinburgh, 1975.

Campbell, Revd Duncan M. *The Campbell Collection of Gaelic Proverbs and Proverbial Sayings*, ed. Donald Meek, Inverness, 1978.

Campbell, Revd John Gregorson. *Superstitions of the Highlands and Islands of Scotland*, Glasgow, 1900.

Campbell, Revd John Gregorson. *Witchcraft and Second Sight in the Highlands and Islands of Scotland*, Glasgow, 1902.

Carmichael, Alexander. *Carmina Gadelica*, 6 vols. Edinburgh, 1900, 1928, 1940, 1941, 1954 and 1971.

Chambers, Robert. *Domestic Annals of Scotland*, 3 vols., Edinburgh, 1858; abridged edition, 1885.

Chambers, Robert. *Popular Rhymes of Scotland*, Edinburgh, 1841, new edition, 1870.

Chambers, Robert. *Domestic Annals of Scotland*, 3 vols., Edinburgh, 1858 and abridged edition, 1885.

Chambers, Robert. *Traditions of Edinburgh*, Edinburgh, 1847.

Cheviot, Andrew. *Proverbs, Proverbial Expressions and Popular Rhymes of Scotland*, Paisley and London, 1896.

Christiansen, Reidar Th. 'The Dead and the Living', *Studia Norvegica*, no. 2, Oslo, 1946.

Clark, Helen, and Elizabeth Carnegie. *She Was Aye Workin': Memories of Tenement Women in Edinburgh and Glasgow*, Oxford, Edinburgh, Glasgow, 2003.

Clark, W. Fordyce. *The Shetland Sketch Book*, Edinburgh and London, 1930.

Cramond, William. *Extracts from the Records of the Kirk Session of Elgin*, Elgin, 1897.

Cumming, C.F. Gordon. *In the Hebrides*, London, 1886.

Dickson, John. *Chased in Gold, or the Islands of the Forth: Their Story, Ancient and Modern*, Edinburgh, 1899.

Dingwall, Helen. *A History of Scottish Medicine*, Edinburgh, 2002.

Dixon, John H. *Gairloch in North-West Ross-shire: its Records, Traditions, Inhabitants, and Natural History . . .*, Edinburgh, 1886.

Donaldson, Islay. *East Lothian Gravestones*, East Lothian District Library, 1991.

Edmonston, Arthur. *A View of the Ancient and Present State of the Zetland Islands; Including their Civil, Political, Natural History, Antiquities, etc.*, 2 vols., Edinburgh, 1809.

Evening Times, Glasgow, 20 December 2003

Fergusson, R. Menzies. *Rambles in the Far North*, 2nd edn, Paisley and London, 1884.

Fergusson, R. Menzies. *Reminiscences of Auld Ayr*, Ayr, 1907.

Fergusson, R. Menzies. *Scottish Social Sketches of the Seventeenth Century*, Stirling, 1907.

Fielding, William J. *Strange Customs of Courtship and Marriage*, New York, 1942.

Firth, John. *Reminiscences of an Orkney Parish together with Old Orkney Words, Riddles and Proverbs*, Stromness, 1920, reprinted Stromness, 1974.

Folk-Lore Journal, The Folklore Society, London, 1883–89 and *Folk-lore*, 1890–present.

Frazer, Sir J.G. *The Golden Bough: A Study of Comparative Religions*, 2 vols., London, 1890.

Gennep, Arnold van. *Les Rites de Passage*, Paris, 1909, and *The Rites of Passage* (translation), Chicago, 1960.

Gennep, Arnold van. 'Du Berceau à la Tombe', ed. from his article of 1916 by M. Buelpa, *La Savoie*, pp. 11–178, France, 1991.

Gibson, William. *Reminiscences of Dollar and Tillicoutry and other Districts adjoining the Ochils*, Edinburgh, 1883.

Gillies, H. Cameron. *The Gaelic Concepts of Life and of Death*, The Dundee Highland Society, Dundee and Glasgow, n.d. (*c.* 1912).

Goffman, Erving. *Presentation of Self in Everyday Life*, New York, 1959.

Goodrich-Freer, A. *Outer Isles*, Westminster, 1902.

Gordon, Anna. *Death is For the Living*, Edinburgh, 1984.

Gordon, Seton. *Hebridean Memories*, Glasgow, 1923; Edinburgh, 1995.

Gourlay, George. *Fisher Life, or the Memorials of Cellardyke and the Fife Coast*, Cupar, 1879.

Grant, Anne (ed. J.P. Grant). *Letters from the Mountains; Being the Correspondance with her Friends Between the Years 1773 and 1803, of Mrs Grant of Laggan*, 2 vols, London 1809.

Grant, Elizabeth. *Memoirs of a Highland Lady: Elizabeth Grant of Rothiemurchus*, Edinburgh, 1898 and reprinted in 2 vols, 1988.

Grant, I. F. *Highland Folkways*, London, 1961, 1975, 1977 and 1980.

Grant, James Shaw. *Discovering Lewis and Harris*, Edinburgh, 1987.

Gregor, Rev. Walter. *An Echo of the Olden Time*, Edinburgh & Glasgow, 1874, and reprinted E.P. Publ. Ltd., Wakefield, 1973.

Gregor, Rev. Walter. *Notes on the Folk-Lore of the North-East*, PFLS 7, London, 1881.

Guthrie, E.J. *Old Scottish Customs, Local and General*, London, 1885.

Henderson, Andrew. *Scottish Proverbs*, Glasgow, 1832; new edition with explanatory notes and glossary by James Donald, Glasgow, 1881.

Henderson, John. *Caithness Family History*, Edinburgh, 1884.

Henderson, William. *Notes on the Folk-Lore of the Northern Counties of England and the Borders*, PFLS 11, London, 1879.

Herald, The. 3 January 2001; 30 March 2204.

Hibbert, Samuel. *A Description of the Shetland Islands, Comprising an Account of their Geology, Scenery, Antiquities, and Superstitions*, Edinburgh, 1822, repr. Lerwick 1891.

Horne, John (ed). *The County of Caithness*, Wick, 1907.

Horne, John. *A Canny Countryside*, Edinburgh, 1896.

Hume Brown, P. (ed). *Early Travellers in Scotland (Richard Frank, 1659)*, Edinburgh, 1891.

Hyslop, John. *Echoes from the Border Hills*, Langholm and Glasgow, 1912.

Innes, Bill (ed. and transl.). *Chì Mi: The Poetry of Donald John MacDonald*, Edinburgh, 1998.

Ireland, Marylin. 'Will Ye Gang Wi' Me Lassie?' in *The Complete Odyssey: Voices from Scotland's Recent Past*, ed. Billy Kay, Edinburgh, 1996.

Ireland, Ronald. 'Husband and Wife: Divorce, Nullity of Marriage and Separation', *An Introduction to Scottish Legal History*, ed. Lord Normand, Stair Society, 1958, pp. 90–8.

Jack, John. *The Key of the Forth, or Historical Sketches of the Island of May*, Edinburgh, 1858.

Jervise, Andrew. *Epitaphs and Inscriptions*, 2 vols., Edinburgh, 1875–79.

Kirk, William. *Stories of Second Sight in a Highland Regiment*, Stirling, 1933.

Laing, Alexander. *Lindores Abbey and its Burgh of Newburgh: Their History and Annals*, Edinburgh, 1867.

Laing, Jeannie M. *Notes on Superstitions and Folklore*, Brechin, 1885, repr. by Norwood Editions, Pennsylvania, USA, 1973.

Lawson, J. P. (Trans). *The Autobiography of Martin Luther*, Edinburgh, 1836.

Logan, J. *The Scottish Gael*, 2 vols, Inverness, 1876.

Low, Revd George. *A Tour Through the Islands of Orkney and Shetland in 1774*, Kirkwall, 1879.

Luther, Martin. *The Life of Luther*, written by himself, collected and arranged by M. Michelet, translated by W. Hazlitt, London, 1846.

Lynch, Michael (ed). *The Oxford Companion to Scottish History*, 2001.

MacBain, Alexander & Revd John Kennedy (eds). *Reliquiae Celticae: Texts, Papers, and Studies in Gaelic Literature and Philology left by the late Revd Alexander Cameron, LLD*, 2 vols., Inverness, 1892.

MacCulloch, John. *Highlands and Western Isles of Scotland*, London, 1824.

MacDonald, Alexander. *Story and Song from Loch Ness-Side*, Inverness, 1914.

MacDonald, Alexander. 'Social Customs of the Gaels' in *TGSI*, vol. XXXII, pp. 272–301.

MacDonald, Donald. *The Tolsta Townships*, Stornoway, 1984.

MacDonald, Rachael. 'When I Think of Scarp', *Scots Magazine*, April 1965.

MacDonald, T.D. *Gaelic Proverbs and Proverbial Sayings with English Translations*, Stirling, 1926.

MacGregor, A. & W. Jolly. *The Life of Flora Macdonald and Flora Macdonald in Uist*, Stirling, 5th edn 1932.

MacGregor, Alexander. *Highland Superstitions*, Stirling, 1922.

MacKay, William. 'Life in the Highlands in the Olden Times . . .' in *TGSI*, vol. XXIX, 1914–19, pp. 1–18.

MacKay, William. *Records of the Presbyteries of Inverness and Dingwall*, Edinburgh, 1896.

MacKenzie, William. *Gaelic Incantations, Charms, and Blessings of the Hebrides*, Inverness, 1895.

MacKenzie, William. *Skye: Iochdar-Trotternish and District*, Glasgow, 1930.

Mackintosh, W.R. *Around the Orkney Peat-Fires*, Kirkwall, 189–, 2nd edition, 1905.

MacLagan, Robert Craig. *Evil Eye in the Western Highlands*, London, 1902.

MacLagan, Robert Craig. *Games and Diversions of Argyllshire*, PFLS 47, London, 1901.

MacLean, Calum I. 'Death Divination in Scottish Folk Tradition', *TGSI*, vol. XLII, 1965, pp. 56–58.

MacLean, Calum I. *The Highlands*, London 1959.

MacLeod, Norman. *Reminiscences of a Highland Parish*, London, n.d. (*c.* 1900)

MacLeod, R.C. MacLeod of (ed). *The Book of Dunvegan; being Documents from the Muniment Room of the MacLeods of MacLeod at Dunvegan Castle, Isle of Skye*, 2 vols., Third Spalding Club, Aberdeen, 1938–39.

Mactaggart, John. *The Scottish Galovidian Encyclopaedia*, Galloway, 1824, repr. Strath Tay, Perthshire, 1981.

Marriage in Scotland. (Leaflet RM1), The General Register Office, Edinburgh.

Marshall, Rosalind K. *Virgins and Viragos: a History of Women in Scotland from 1080-1980*, London, 1983.

Marshall, Rosalind K. 'The Wearing of Wedding Rings in Scotland', *Review of Scottish Culture*, Edinburgh, no. 2, 1986, pp. 1–12.

Martin, Martin. *A Description of the Western Isles of Scotland circa 1695*, Edinburgh, 1716; Glasgow, 1884; Stirling, 1934.

Marwick, E.W. *The Folklore of Orkney and Shetland*, London, 1975.

McPherson, J.M. *Primitive Beliefs in the Northeast of Scotland*, London, New York, etc., 1929.

Menefee, Samuel Pyeatt. *Wives for Sale: An Ethnographic Study of British Popular Divorce*, Oxford, 1981.

Miller, Hugh. *My Schools and Schoolmasters*, Edinburgh, 1889.

Miller, Hugh. *Scenes and Legends*, Edinburgh, 1855.

Miller, Hugh. *Tales and Sketches*, Edinburgh, 1869.

Milne, John. *Myths and Superstitions of Buchan District*, Aberdeen, 1881.

Mitchell, Alison. *Pre-1855 Gravestone Inscriptions in Angus: Arbroath and Seacoast*, Scottish Genealogy Society, 1981.

Mitchell, Angus et al. *Pre-1855 Gravestone Inscriptions in Bute and Arran*, Scottish Genealogy Society, 1987.

Mitchell, Arthur. *Past in the Present*, Edinburgh, 1880.

Monro, Sir Donald, High Dean of the Isles. *Description of the Western Isles of Scotland called Hybrides (1594)*, Glasgow, 1774 and 1884. Reprinted in 1934 edn. of Martin Martin's *Description*.

Montgomerie, Norah and William (ed). *Sandy Candy and Other Scottish Nursery Rhymes*, London, 1948.

Murray, Andrew. *Peterhead a Century Ago*, Peterhead, 1910.

Napier, Revd James. *Folk Lore: or, Superstitious Beliefs in the West of Scotland within this Century*, Paisley, 1879.

Narváez, Peter (ed.). *The Good People: New Fairylore Essays*, New York and London, 1991.

Neat, Timothy. *The Summer Walkers*, Edinburgh, 1999.

Neat, Timothy. *When I Was Young: Voices from Lost Communities in Scotland*, Edinburgh, 2000.

Necker de Saussure, Louis A. *A Voyage to the Hebrides, or Western Isles of Scotland; with observations on the manners and customs of the Highlanders*, London, 1822.

New Statistical Account of Scotland, Edinburgh, 1834–45.

Nicholson, E.W.B. *Golspie: Contributions to its Folklore*, London, 1897.

Nicolson, Sheriff Alexander. *Gaelic Proverbs*, reprinted with index and biographical note by Malcolm MacInnes, Glasgow, Glasgow, 1951.

Pennant, Thomas. *A Tour in Scotland and Voyage to the Hebrides*, 2 vols., Chester, 1774.

Penny, George. *Traditions of Perth, containing sketches of the Manners and Customs of the Inhabitants . . . during the Last Centruy*, Perth, 1836.

Phillips, J.G. *Wanderings in the Highlands of Banff-shire and Aberdeenshire*, Banff, 1881.

Polson, Alexander. 'The Folklore of Caithness' in *The County of Caithness* edited by John Horne, Wick, 1907.

Polson, Alexander. *Our Highland Folklore Heritage*, Dingwall and Inverness, 1926.

Polson, Alexander. *The Book of Gairloch*, Dingwall, 1920.

Ramsay, Dean E.B. *Reminiscences of Scottish Life and Character*, New York, 1873 (many editions).

Ramsay, John. *Scotland and Scotsmen in the Eighteenth Century*, 2 vols., London, 1888.

Rankin, Joyce. *At My Mother's Door*, Sydney, Nova Scotia, 2002.

Rea, E.G. *A School in South Uist: Reminiscences of a Hebridean Schoolmaster, 1890–1913*, Edinburgh, repr. 1998.

Reid, Hugh G. *Past and Present*, Edinburgh, 1870.

Reid, John T. *Art Rambles in Shetland*, Edinburgh, 1869.

Rennie, James Alan. *Romantic Strathspey: Its Lands, Clans and Legends*, London, 1956.

Robertson, J. Logie (ed). *The Poetical Works of Sir Walter Scott, with the Author's Introductions and Notes*, Oxford, 1917.

Robertson, Joseph. *Book of Bon-Accord*, Aberdeen, 1839.

Rogers, Charles. *Social Life in Scotland*, 3 vols., Edinburgh, 1884–86.

Rogers, Charles. *Traits and Stories of the Scottish People*, London, 1867.

Ross, Anne. 'Birds of Life and Birds of Death', *Scottish Studies*, vol. 3, 1963, pp. 215–223.

Rubinstein, Helen (Ed). *The Oxford Book of Marriage*, Oxford, 1990.

Sage, Revd Donald. *Memorabilia Domestica*; or, *Parish Life in the North of Scotland*, Wick, 1889.

Saxby, Jessie M.E. *Shetland Traditional Lore*, Edinburgh, 1932.

Scotland on Sunday, 17 August 2003

The Scots Magazine, Edinburgh and Dundee, 1740–.

Scott, Sir Walter. *Letters on Demonology and Witchcraft*, London, 1831. Reprints, 1868 and others.

Scottish Women's Rural Institute (Meigle Branch). *Our Meigle Book*, Dundee, 1932.

Sellar, E.M. *Recollections and Impressions*, Edinburgh, 1907.

Shaw, Margaret Fay. *Folksongs and Folklore of South Uist*, London, 1955 repr. Edinburgh, 1999.

Simkins, John Ewart. *Examples of Printed Folk-Lore Concerning Fife, with some notes on Clackmannan and Kinross-shire*, Co FL, vol. VII, PFLS 71, London, 1914.

Simpson, Evelyn Blantyre. *Folk-Lore in Lowland Scotland*, London, 1908.

Simson, James. *Reminiscences of Childhood at Inverkeithing, or Life in a Lazaretto*, Edinburgh, 1882.

Sinclair, Marion (ed.) & M. Newton, *Hebridean Odyssey*, Polygon, Edinburgh, 1996.

Sinclair, Sir John (ed.). *The Statistical Account of Scotland*, vols. I–XXI, London, 1791–99.

Sinton, Revd Thomas. *By Loch and River: being Memories of Loch Laggan and Upper Spey*, Inverness, 1910.

Smith, Preserved. *The Life and Letters of Martin Luther*, London, 1911.

Smout, T.C. *A Century of the Scottish People 1830–1950*, London, 1986.

Smout, T.C. 'Aspects of Sexual Behaviour in Nineteenth Century Scotland', *Social Class in Scotland: Past and Present*, ed. A. Allan MacLaren, Edinburgh, 1976.

Stevenson, David. *Scotland's Last Royal Wedding: The Marriage of James VI and Anne of Denmark*, Edinburgh, 1997.

Stewart, Alexander (of Egremont). *Reminiscences of Dunfermline and Neighbourhood . . .*, Edinburgh, 1886.

Stewart, Alexander. *Nether Lochaber: The Natural History, Legends and Folk-Lore of the West Highlands*, Edinburgh, 1883.

Stewart, Alexander. *'Twixt Ben Nevis and Glencoe: The Natural History, Legends and Folk-Lore of the West Highlands*, Edinburgh, 1885.

Stewart, Maj. Gen. David of Garth. *Sketches of the Character and Custom of the Highlanders of Scotland*, Inverness and Edinburgh, 1885.

Stewart, W. Grant. *The Popular Superstitions and Festive Amusements of the Highlanders of Scotland*, Edinburgh, 1823; London, 1851.

Stirton, John. *Crathie and Braemar*, Aberdeen, 1925.

Sunday Herald, 15 February 2004; 28 March 2004.

Tappert, Theodore G. (ed and transl.). *Luther: Letters of Spiritual Counsel*, The Library of Christian Classics, vol. xviii, London, 1955.

Taylor, Harry Pearson. *A Shetland Parish Doctor: Some Recollections of a Shetland Parish Doctor during the Past Half Centruy*, Lerwick, 1948.

Thistleton-Dyer, T.F. *British Popular Customs, Present and Past*, London, 1876.

Thomson, James. *Recollections of a Speyside Parish Fifty Years Ago*, Elgin, 1887, 2nd edn, 1902.

Thorpe, Benjamin. *Northern Mythology, Comprising the Principal Popular Traditions and Superstitions of Scandinavia, North Germany, and the Netherlands*, 3 vols., London, 1851–52.

Tocher, School of Scottish Studies, Edinburgh, 1971–.

Tudor, John R. *The Orkneys and Shetland; Their Past and Present State*, London, 1883.

Vernon, J.J. and J. McNairn. *Pictures from the Past of Auld Hawick*, Hawick, 1911.

Victoria, Queen of Great Britain. *More Leaves from the Journal of A Life in The Highlands from 1862 to 1882*, London, 1885.

Watson, R.M.F. *Closeburn (Dumfriesshire): Reminiscent, Historic and Traditional*, Glasgow, 1901.

Waugh, Joseph Laing. *Thornhill and its Worthies*, Dumfries, n.d. [?1905], 2nd edn., 1913.

Wilson, William. *Folk Lore and Genealogies of Uppermost Nithsdale*, Dumfries and Sanquhar, 1904.

Wood, J. Maxwell. *Witchcraft and Superstitious Record in the South-Western District of Scotland*, Dumfries, 1911.

Wood, Revd Walter. *The East Neuk of Fife. Its History and Antiquities*, Edinburgh, 2nd edn, 1887.

Index

BIRLINN LTD (incorporating John Donald and Polygon) is one of Scotland's leading publishers with over four hundred titles in print. Should you wish to be put on our catalogue mailing list **contact**:

Catalogue Request
Birlinn Ltd
West Newington House
10 Newington Road
Edinburgh EH9 1QS
Scotland, UK

Tel: + 44 (0) 131 668 4371
Fax: + 44 (0) 131 668 4466
e-mail: info@birlinn.co.uk

Postage and packing is free within the UK. For overseas orders, postage and packing (airmail) will be charged at 30% of the total order value.

For more information, or to order online, visit our website at **www.birlinn.co.uk**